THE IDENTITIES
OF PERSONS

TOPICS IN PHILOSOPHY

THE IDENTITIES
OF PERSONS

Edited by

AMÉLIE OKSENBERG RORTY

UNIVERSITY OF CALIFORNIA PRESS
Berkeley   Los Angeles   London

Frontispiece drawing by Franciszka Themerson from
Traces of Living, Gaberbocchus Press, London, 1969.

University of California Press
Berkeley and Los Angeles, California

University of California Press, Ltd.
London, England

ISBN: 0-520-03030-3
Library of Congress Catalog Card Number: 75-13156
Printed in the United States of America

3 4 5 6 7 8 9

CONTENTS

INTRODUCTION

Disagreements about the criteria for personal identity have been persistently unresolved, the battle lines repetitively drawn over the same terrain, along familiar geographical strongholds. Although they disagree among themselves about its analysis, defenders of a physical or a spatio-temporal criterion are ranged against defenders of a psychological criterion, themselves uneasily allied. Peacemakers who argue that neither the psychological nor the physical criterion can be applied without implicitly reintroducing the other have been drawn into the battle—as peacemakers often are—as third or fourth parties. Although the controversy has a long history, and although many arguments have been refined by repeated firings, there is little reason to expect a resolution that will not in time lead to renewed hostilities. What is required is not more ingenuity for more elaborate strategies, but an understanding of the conflicting interpretations of what has been at issue.

I

Controversies about personal identity have been magnified by the fact that there are a number of distinct questions at issue, questions that have not always been clearly distinguished from one another. Parties to the dispute have differed, often without arguing the case, about which questions are centrally interesting: (1) Some have concentrated on analyses of class differentiation: What distinguishes the class of persons from their nearest neighbors, from baboons, robots, human corpses, corporations? (2) Others have been primarily interested in individual differentiation: What are the criteria for the numerical distinctness of persons who have the same general description? This is sometimes called "the problem of individuation." (3) Still others have been interested in individual reidentification: What are the criteria for reidentifying the same individual in different contexts, under different descriptions, or at different times? Most philosophers who have been concerned with individual reidentification analyze conditions for temporal reidentification, trying to define conditions for distinguishing successive stages of *a* continuing person from stages of a successor or descendant person. (4) Yet others have been primarily interested in individual identification: What sorts of characteristics identify a person as *essentially* the person she is, such that if those characteristics were changed, she would be a significantly different person, though she might still be differentiated and reidentified as the same? Defining the conditions for individual identification does not reduce to specifying conditions for reidentification because the characteristics that distinguish or reidentify persons (e.g., fingerprints, DNA codes, or memories) may not be thought by the individual herself or by her society to determine her *real* identity. For instance, it might be possible that an individual be considered reidentifiable by the memory criterion, but not be considered identifiable as the same person because all that she considered essential had changed: her principles and preference rankings were different, her tastes, plans, hopes, and fears. She remembered her old principles of choice well enough and so, by the memory criterion, might consider herself the same old person; but by grace or reeducation she could be counted on to choose and act in a new way. Though all these questions are distinguishable, and though a philosopher may legitimately be interested in one without being forced to treat them all, a particular sort of solution to one problem will certainly influence, though probably not dictate a solution to the others.

Behind these differences in emphases and interests, there are differences about whether we should concentrate on conditions for strict identity (with the consequence that a biological individual may not remain the same person throughout a lifetime), or on conditions of loose typic identity (with the consequence that conditions for identity and conditions for individuation become distinct), or on conditions assuring continuity or survival (with the consequence that the conditions for *significant* continuity or survival still require to be specified).

Also at issue are methodological disagreements about what is involved in giving a criterial analysis. Some of the debates have only incidentally been about personal identity; they have been primarily about whether an adequate account should provide necessary and sufficient conditions, prepared to meet and resist any possible counterexamples. If we look for necessary and sufficient conditions, puzzle and problem cases loom large in the discussion, as possible counterexamples to the analyses. Consider the problems that arise from Shoemaker's Lockean transplant case: Brown's brain is put in Robinson's head, with the results that Brownson, the fellow with Brown's brain in (the rest of) Robinson's body remembers Brown's experience, identifies Brown's body as "his," expresses Brown's tastes and preferences. To give the question "Who is who?" some force, we might ask who goes home to which wife ("Do you love me for myself alone, or for my beautiful body?"). And if one of them committed a crime, who goes to jail?

Those who are skeptical about the utility of giving analyses of logically necessary conditions see the Brownson case as presenting an interesting curiosity, a fringe case of personal identity. They hold that the strategic conclusions to which we are forced in extremities should not be taken to reveal the workings of these concepts in their standard uses. For them, the real point of such thought-experiments is to untangle the various strands in our conceptions, to show that although they normally support one another, they are independent, and can sometimes pull apart.

Thought experiments of this kind are always underdescribed: suppose that Robinson limps painfully. Won't Brown's passion for dancing the flamenco be affected by the discomfort of expressing it in Robinson's hulking, lumbering body? Suppose Robinson's body suffers from an overproduction of adrenalin: will Brownson's memories take on an irascible tone? How can we establish the identity of tastes and memories under different emotional tonalities? In forcing decisions about such cases for the sake of assuring criterial accounts, we move subtly from analyses of concepts in their standard use to constructions whose application to standard cases become legislative and normative, no longer straightforwardly analytically descriptive. This may indeed be a useful and important enterprise: but legislation should take place openly, so that the many factors that affect the accounts of personal identification—moral and political factors, as well as coherence of accounting—can be brought into play. If we are going to tidy up a concept whose various strands have been pulled apart, we had best be clear about the consequences that our tidying will have on our social practices. The most important of these will affect the redistribution of liability and responsibility, of praise, blame, and punishment.

Perhaps the most significant source of the controversy about criteria for personal identity springs from disagreements about the function that the concept of a person plays in social life as the unit of intentional, responsible agency. Locke distinguished the identity of an individual substance, the identity of a human being, and the identity of a person, remarking that as the concept of a person is primarily a forensic, legal notion, the criterion for personal identity must reflect the conditions for an individual's being a responsible agent. Because he focused on legal liability, rather than social responsibility, he was interested in identifying the past actions of persons. He thus took the condition for forensic identity to be continuity of reflective consciousness, established primarily by memory. Those who are concerned with responsibility for future actions might stress the continuity of preference rankings, character traits, and intellectual capacities that affect rational choice and action. In any case, controversies about conditions for personal identity reflect differences about the conditions that establish an individual as a responsible agent.

II

Why are we interested in someone being the same person, and not merely the same human being or physical object? One reason is primarily retrospective: we need to know whom to reward and whom to punish for actions performed when "they" were acknowledgedly different in some respects from the present population. But we have more forward-looking reasons as well: we want to know what traits remain constant so that we can know what we can expect from the persons around us. We assign crucial responsibilities to individuals, assume important continuing relations to them in the belief that certain of their traits are relatively constant or predictible. And for ourselves, we are interested in our own identity because we make choices that will affect our futures: we set in motion a train of actions whose consequences involve "our" well-being, without knowing whether we shall have, in the future, the desires and beliefs that now direct our planning.

There is, historians and anthropologists assure us, considerable variation in the conditions that societies have regarded as significant to establish liability and responsibility. In societies where responsibility is located in families or clans, the biological individual is treated as a member of the larger unit, which is regarded as the proper agent, the real person. Criteria for identification are given by genealogies, which are not merely narrations of descent: they define essential attributes. They determine an individual's life-history, his occupation, his preoccupations. (Reformers in such societies often therefore introduce rites of rebirth, a baptism that endows an individual with a new father and a new fate. The baptized are regarded as new persons, with new desires and motives.) In societies where biological individuals are regarded as hospitable to demonic possession, capable of initiating distinct and even opposing lines of agency, the biological individual may be regarded as host to distinct persons, each with its own life span and identificatory marks. A society that focuses primarily on the sorts of actions that are thought to follow from rational choice will locate criteria for identification in the continuity of psychological traits believed to assure rational choice. If these capacities are sharply changed, the individual may be thought a different person. If they are thought to be permanently damaged, the individual may no longer be thought a person, even though she is still regarded and treated as the same human individual. Questions about the legal rights of such damaged individuals can be raised: the wills and contracts made by the senile, the insane, or the permanently infantile can be invalidated.

A society's conception of agency is closely linked to the sorts of actions that are taken as central because they preserve or enhance that society's conception of its proper survival and development. In a society of hunters, cripples are thought incapable of action; but in a society of religious ascetics, cripples may be thought most capable of the sort of action that defines the true person. The range of traits and criteria for identification are open to negotia-

tion by the moral and political reformer. Descriptive analyses of
personal identity affect the allocation of obligations and rights;
but the analysis of persons is itself affected by the allocation of
obligations and rights. When paradigm cases of action are set, the
traits that conduce to responsible agency for those sorts of actions
are fixed, and the range of agents—corporations, human beings,
demon possessors, Martians or dolphins—is also set. But in times
of social and political change, primary activities are relocated
(from hunting, to religious meditation, to symbolic communication); reformers recommend an expansion or contraction of the
class of persons. Changes in practice go hand in hand with conceptual reconstruction and reform, though it may take several genera-
tions for the hands to catch up. New conceptions of actions and
agency sometimes relocate the conditions for responsibility and
liability. That reformers can negotiate the extension of the class of
persons certainly does not make the concept of a person *merely*
conventional, if anything ever is. Both changes in practice and in
conceptual analysis are argued by demonstrating the capacities of
previously extended classes. The attribution of personhood plays
an honorific as well as a descriptive function. Certainly the
honorific and the descriptive uses play upon one another: an
attempt to extend the class of those qualified to receive the honorific attribution ("Now that's a *real* person!") is generally
defended by a descriptive analysis.

It might be objected that cultural history and anthropology at
best provide the first step in the analysis of the concept of personal
identity. Even the most subtle analysis of the interplay between the
honorific and descriptive accounts of the conditions for intentional agency do not define the class of persons, let alone determine the conditions for differentiation, reidentification, and identification. Not only do the major problems of defining the unity
and continued identity of persons remain unanswered by cultural
excursions but it might be charged that criteria for personal identity are presupposed by the historical map of transformations in
the conceptions of agency and persons. What defines the unit of
the cultural historian's analysis? Why is this the history of the concept of *persons*? If we simply give a *catalogue raisonné* of the
notion, then we would only give the provenance of various conceptions, showing how distinctive strands emerge as dominant
under some conditions, recessive in others.

There is another, even stronger objection: by concentrating on what is thought, we may fail to come to terms with the fact of the matter. This is sometimes an issue of considerable moral and political importance. It is not only the moral reformer whose normative principles can become constitutive of the concept of persons: philosophical analysis plays its part too. After all, some social beliefs and practices may be confused, perhaps plainly mistaken. The analysis of personal identity should not be tailored to cover incoherence or error.

These objections are partially, but not wholly answered by a retreat to biology and to psychology. Establishing that members of the class of human beings standardly meet the requirements for responsible agency sets the ground for extending the class of persons to the class of human beings. We require empirical as well as conceptual investigations to determine whether Martians, Superwoman, robots, and dolphins meet the minimum conditions for personhood despite their nonhumanity because they too are the sorts of entitites that are capable of intentional agency. Defenders of person-rights for women, slaves, and cripples argue that their exclusion from the rights and obligations for personhood was mistaken because all these in fact have relevant biological and psychological similarities: the crucial faculties for liability and responsibility. (As the differences between Aristotle and Rousseau attest, this issue is more difficult to resolve than one might suppose, since it is sometimes arguable that an individual's capacities for responsible agency are developed only in conditions that allow their active exercise.) Those who claim that person-rights should not be extended to corporations or to the left hemisphere of the brain must defend their case by showing that neither of these have the relevant capacities. An empirical investigation is essential, but we cannot simply settle the matter by looking (e.g.) to see whether they have a central nervous system, a memory, preference rankings, capacities for rational evaluation. It also takes a conceptual analysis to determine whether corporations and robots are persons only by metaphorical courtesy while dolphins and Martians qualify as full members by an appropriate extension of the class. (When is a batch of wires a central nervous system and when is it only an analogue? When is an analogue good enough? When is a flow chart for decision-making good enough? When is it all too good? When does behaviorial similarity suffice for literal cross-class attribution? How do we establish criteria for identifying behaviorial similarity? How can one tell whether a Martian is really thinking and conversing?) Because such determinations have important social and political consequences, we should not be surprised to discover that conceptual analyses are strongly, though often only implicitly guided by moral intuitions, ideology, and taste. Resolving these matters requires a heady blend of detailed empirical study (neuro-anatomy, endocrinology, genetics, social psychology, animal ethology), supplemented by conceptual analyses (What are the conditions for identifying different instantiations of a general formal model?) and ideological, moral, and aesthetic considerations (Is it irrational not to want one for a son-in-law?).

In meeting our philosophical obligations, we get a little bittersweet help not only from biology and psychology but also from the continuity of personal pronouns, which have all along played a subtle fugue in the background of our questions. When we raise puzzles about the psychological continuity or identity, we refer to some entity, asking whether the changes in it are significant enough to warrant our saying of *it*, that it is no longer the same person. Bodily continuity stands behind the assurance of personal pronouns. It is therefore sometimes tempting to treat bodily continuity as the basis for personal identity. But we have more bodily continuity than we can properly use. We are after all, bodily continous with our corpses, and indeed with their decay or desiccation. If we were to treat bodily continuity bold and bare, our life histories would continue behind the horizon and beyond the grave. The reidentification of entities is always an identification of an entity of a certain sort. When we come across puzzles and conflicting judgments about identifying and differentiating persons, we retreat to accounts of organic identification; coming upon difficulties there, we may move farther back to the logical and metaphysical accounts of identification *simpliciter*. But the lower level, the "foundation" does not necessarily give us the ground plan of the upper levels of the structure. However much it may genuinely support us, the place to which we retreat is not always home.

It is against the background of our beliefs about the unity and the continuity of a human being, with a standard life span, differentiated from its surroundings and from other individuals of its kind, that our judgments about the unity and continuity of persons are made. These views are themselves interwoven: beliefs about what differentiates one human being from another (the fetus from its mother, fused lovers from each other) are interdependent on beliefs about what is essential to the continuing survival of one organism (a head, but not a head-of-hair).

So now where are we, and is that an awful place to be? We have at least thrown a sop to philosophical conscience by assuring ourselves that our sallies into cultural history and anthropology will not be left uncriticized; the presuppositions of the various conceptions can be examined, their inconsistencies and factual errors exposed, and the conflict between theory and practice unmasked. Neither convention nor the reformer's fiat can determine the qualifications for being a person; and to ascertain whether an individual is the same person, we must establish whether the capacities for intentional agency—whatever they may be—remain unchanged.

But we have come full circle: determining whether an individual is the same, a continuing surviving one, or merely a successor, depends on actually establishing that they have the same (or continuing) capacities and traits. How is this to be done? Moreover, if the conditions for intentional agency shift with changes in the sorts of actions that are taken to be socially and politically crucial, we have compounded our difficulties. Not only must we establish conditions for the identity of traits and capacities but we must determine what conceptions of action and agency should regulate our analysis of conditions for responsibility. Not only will we have to settle disputes about when an individual is the same person but also have to determine when the conditions for responsible agency have been, or should be changed.

For instance, current discussions of responsible personhood concentrate on the capacities for deliberation, on memory and critical evaluation. Because we take the model of rational choice to involve an individual's selection of one among determinate alternatives, we do not stress the capacities for imaginative construction and formulation of indeterminate futures. We may consider that someone who is no longer able to weigh probabilities may not be the same person; but we do not think that a person whose imaginative faculties are damaged is a different person. And because our paradigms of action are those performed by individuals rather than by groups-of-individuals, we do not stress the capacities for mutual sensitivity and adaptibility. A social and conceptual reformer might begin by arguing that imagination and empathy are as significant for responsible agency as the capacities for rational evaluation. But this implicitly involves a modification in the conception of action and agency, with corresponding changes in the qualifications for personhood. The determination of whether someone is the same person will then involve decisions about whether these capacities are significantly changed.

Philosophical analyses—philosophical decisions—of such cases will have both normative presuppositions and normative consequences. This does not mean that we must find a new method, abandon the complicated combination of conceptual analysis and empirical investigation that we now use, and plunge into a wholly distinct ethical investigation. By making explicit the conceptions of rights and obligations that have implicitly guided our analyses of persons, we shall be able to weigh the consequences of various conceptual revisions more clearly. For example, although there is no logical connection between our analyses of personal identity and our views of corporate responsibility and corporate punishment, it is idle to pretend that they will not influence one another. The actual social consequences of their mutual relevance might well be explored: they are likely to affect the accounts we give of persons and of responsibility, even though we would shy of admitting that they logically determine those analyses. This means that besides continuing the task of tracing the shifts in the mutually supportive relations between persons, agents, human beings and individuals, we must also come out of the closet and reveal ourselves to be the moralists that we really are.

III

From a different direction, the voice of philosophical conscience strikes again: as we have described them, the various perspectives of persons as intentional agents neglect the crucial force of the problem of personal identity. Even if—*per impossible*—we came to think of responsible agency as an illusion, the problem of the identity of the self, the "I" would remain. What are the conditions for the identity of the reflective, conscious subject of experience, a subject that is not identical with any set of its experiences, memories or traits, but is that which *has* all of them, and can choose either to identify with them or to reject them as alien? Of course from a large world-historical perspective, this version of the problem of personal identity is one that could only appear under very special social and intellectual conditions. Nevertheless, it is a view whose presuppositions and consequences remain to be understood even if they are exposed as either a curious regional epicycle in the history of the concept of personal identity or as yet another normative recommendation in disguise.

First, let us sketch the historical conditions that gave rise to the view of the person as the "I" of reflective consciousness, owner and disowner of its experiences, memories, attributes, attitudes. The philosophic conditions: the movement from Descartes's reflective "I" to Locke's substantial center of conscious experience, to Hume's theater of the sequence of impressions and ideas, to Kant's transcendental unity of apperception and the metaphysical postulate of a simple soul, to Sartre's and Heidegger's analyses of consciousness as the quest for its own definition in the face of its non-Being. The social conditions: the movement from the Reformation to radical individualism. The cultural conditions: Romanticism and the novel of first person sensibility.

There are at least two construals of the "I" as reflective consciousness which the proponents of that view regard as an unacceptable "reduction" of their claim. The first argues that the *sense* of the special character of the "I" as subject can be treated as a physiological and/or psychological condition, to which some individuals are more sensitive than others. On this view, the sense of the "I" and its concerns for its identity will one day be discovered to be an extension of the proprioceptive sense, a monitoring or scanning of the organism to determine whether the systems are "go." It would require an empirical investigation to identify the conditions under which the sense of the self—and anxieties about its nonexistence—becomes strongly developed. Some of the conditions may be psychological, the result of early experiences of loss and anxiety. It will of course be a matter of contention whether it is the absence or the presence of this state that is abnormal or deviant: whether its absence is a pathological denial of contingency or its presence a special case of anxiety induced by hormonal imbalance or insufficient mothering at a crucial stage of ego development. Since the proponents of the view claim that even the most subtle and empirically sound versions of the psychological or physical concern for the special identity of the "I" fail to capture the force and meaning of that concern, we must examine their account of the identity of the "I," whatever the empirical explanation of its genesis may be.

Another construal of the special condition of the "I" that strict constructionists of consciousness identity find unacceptable makes the "I" simply a place holder forced upon us by the structure of declarative sentences. The subject is not the reflective subject of consciousness, but simply the subject of attribution, the indexical personal pronoun that is not replaceable by names or descriptions, because all of these are predicated of it. But defenders of strict consciousness identity remain unconvinced: the same sort of grammatical constraint obtains for any subject of predication; typewriters, toothbrushes, and tenterhooks also require an "it" as the ultimate subject. The problem is to give an account of the difference between the "I" and the "she," "he," and "it." It is just the difference between a person referring to herself as "I" rather than as "she" that requires explication.

Perhaps it might be helpful to list some of the candidates for the "I," indicating something of the range of contrasts—none of which entirely maps on to each other—in which it has served. It has been identified with the interior or internal perspective in contrast with the external; with the subjective in contrast with the objective; with the subject-of-experience in contrast with its experiences; with rationality and will in contrast with causality and desire; with spontaneity and creativity in contrast with the conditioned; with the decider and agent in contrast with the predictor and observer; with the knower or interpreter in contrast with the known or interpreted with reflective consciousness in contrast with the content reflected; with mind in contrast with body.

Although each of these marks quite a different opposition, strict constructionists for the identity of the "I" follow the same argument, despite important details of the differences in the ways they formulate the contrast between the "I" and the "non-I." Since strict constructionists of reflective consciousness identity resist identifying the "I" with any set of its attributes, they postulate a subject, an experiencer not itself experienced, that remains unchanged in the course of a life. The logic of this position sometimes forces its adherents to a place that is quite different from where they began. The original intuition is that the "I" bears a relation to itself that is quite unlike its relation to other objects. There are, it is claimed, a set of experiences—ego-oriented attitudes of anxiety, remorse, pride, guilt—which are quite distinctive, and which originally give rise to the idea of the self. But the reflective "I" can reject or identify with *these* ego-oriented attitudes as easily as it can with its body or its habits. It is no more identical with any set of "existential attitudes" than it is with any of its more externally defined attributes. The *act* of reflecting on an attribute or attitude, asking "Is that *me*?" ("putting the self in question"), is always different from the attitude or attribute itself, even if the attitude reveals—as anxiety is said to do—the precarious position of the "I" as the act of self-constituting reflection. Being anxious is one thing; being the act that identifies with its anxiety is another. So strict constructionists find themselves forced to postulate a something-perhaps-a-nothing-I-know-not-what, or a simple soul beyond experience, or a pure act of reflection that constitutes itself. All these—different as they are from one another—are far from the original starting point of the "I" as a being that is distinctively experienced.

The view that the "I" is postulated outside the realm of experience and understanding is but a shadow's step away from regarding the "I" as illusory. A necessary illusion is no less an illusion for being necessary. When the "I" is not an object of experience, it is not an entity either. As things go, it is not one of them. The next move is to transform the no-thing into nothing; and the move after that, is to transform "it" into Nothing trying to objectify itself.

With this, we are full circle to the Moralist again. However they differ from one another in important detail, strict constructionists of the identity of reflective consciousness come to one of two apparently quite opposed positions. One view postulates the existence of a simple subject, which remains identical at least through an individual's biological lifetime; the conditions of its identity and existence are quite different from the conditions of the identity and existence of the empirical self. Christians identify it with the soul. The other position takes the postulation of the soul to be yet another attempt to turn the *pour-soi* into an *en-soi*, another attempt of Nothingness to allay its anxiety by objectifying itself. Both adherents of ego-as-soul and adherents of reflective-consciousness-as-non-being tell us that the failure to accept their respective accounts of the real character of the "I" are the natural fallen condition, the bad faith of unrealized life. Each regards the other as prey to self-deception. Both begin with a disarmingly Olympian attempt to give a neutral, purely philosophical descriptive analysis of the conditions of the identity of a person. Both end with an exhortation to authenticity: whoever fails to identify with the soul (or non-being) remains only in the fallen condition, in self-deception. Of course the proper act of identification with the real "I" does not assure either salvation or freedom from self deception; and it cannot even be done properly unless one is in some sense already there.

What makes further discussion difficult is that we are forbidden to ask whether one or another or both of these positions are *right*. According to the proponents of this view, the bandying and evaluation of arguments, evidence and reasons all takes place in the objective or empirical realm, and it is precisely the nonempirical or subjective realm that is in question. Even if we construe both positions as constructing a transcendental argument that it is necessary to postulate reflective consciousness or subjectivity or soul because "it" is presupposed by the possibility of objective experience, still we are exhorted to acknowledge and to identify with that postulate, to reinterpret the world and our lives through the light of that acknowledgment, despite the fact that we are told that we cannot experience it in the usual sense. We are told that though the question the "I" asks itself about the conditions for its identity cannot be answered, that question must continuously be asked.

The voice of philosophical conscience that led us to this scandalously sketchy exploration of persons as centers of reflective consciousness has certainly not been stilled. But perhaps we have shown that, by its own admission, no philosophical analysis *could* satisfy it. And we, on the other hand, have satisfied ourselves that the problem of determining the conditions for personal identity is, in an extended sense, a moral one. For the proponents of strict consciousness identity, accepting the proper account of the "I" reveals the attitude one ought to take to the world and to oneself-as-a-being-in-and-out-of-the-world. One cannot reach this attitude by examining anything in experience, including the experience of the empirical self. On the contrary, it is by taking this perspective that one's relation to experience is changed. The authentic and the inauthentic live in different worlds. With this, the voice of the evangelist in philosophic clothing speaks openly: *crede ut intellegas*. But we are assured that while identifying with the "I" as soul or as reflective consciousness changes everything, it also leaves everything as it was: all decisions of social life, all allocation of responsibility are still to be made, and made in the same terms even by those who regard persons in a wholly different light. And so we are thrown back to our original investigation of persons as intentional agents, whatever else they may also be. That investigation proceeds most fruitfully when its historical antecedents and social consequences are acknowledged and explored.

SURVIVAL AND IDENTITY

DAVID LEWIS

What is it that matters in survival? Suppose I wonder whether I will survive the coming battle, brainwashing, brain transplant, journey by matter-transmitter, purported reincarnation or resurrection, fission into twins, fusion with someone else, or what not. What do I really care about? If it can happen that some features of ordinary, everyday survival are present but others are missing, then what would it take to make the difference between something practically as good as commonplace survival and something practically as bad as commonplace death?

I answer, along with many others: *what matters in survival is mental continuity and connectedness*. When I consider various cases in between commonplace survival and commonplace death, I find that what I mostly want in wanting survival is that my mental life should flow on. My present experiences, thoughts, beliefs, desires, and traits of character should have appropriate future successors. My total present mental state should be but one momentary stage in a continuing succession of mental states. These successive states should be interconnected in two ways. First, by bonds of similarity. Change should be gradual rather than sudden, and (at least in some respects) there should not be too much change overall. Second, by bonds of lawful causal dependence. Such change as there is should conform, for the most part, to lawful regularities concerning the succession of mental states—regularities, moreover, that are exemplified in everyday cases of survival. And this should be so not by accident (and also not, for instance, because some demon has set out to create a succession of mental states patterned to counterfeit our ordinary mental life) but rather because each succeeding mental state causally depends for its character on the states immediately before it.

I refrain from settling certain questions of detail. Perhaps my emphasis should be on *connectedness*: direct relations of similarity and causal dependence between my present mental state and each of its successors; or perhaps I should rather emphasize *continuity*: the existence of step-by-step paths from here to there, with extremely strong local connectedness from each step to the next. Perhaps a special place should be given to the special kind of continuity and connectedness that constitute memory;[1] or perhaps not. Perhaps the "mental" should be construed narrowly, perhaps broadly. Perhaps nonmental continuity and connectedness—in my appearance and voice, for instance—also should have at least some weight. It does not matter, for the present, just which version I would prefer of the thesis that what matters is mental continuity and connectedness. I am sure that I would endorse some version, and in this paper I want to deal with a seeming problem for any version.

The problem begins with a well-deserved complaint that all this about mental connectedness and continuity is too clever by half. I have forgotten to say what should have been said first of all. What matters in survival is survival. If I wonder whether I will survive, what I mostly care about is quite simple. When it's all over, will I myself—the very same person now thinking these thoughts and writing these words—still exist? Will any one of those who do exist afterward be me? In other words, *what matters in survival is identity*—identity between the I who exists now and the surviving I who will, I hope, still exist then.

One question, two answers! An interesting answer, plausible to me on reflection but far from obvious: that what matters is mental connectedness and continuity between my present mental state and other mental states that will succeed it in the future. And a compelling commonsense answer, an unhelpful platitude that cannot credibly be denied: what matters is identity between myself, existing now, and myself, still existing in the future.

If the two answers disagreed and we had to choose one, I suppose we would have to prefer the platitude of common sense to the interesting philosophical thesis. Else it would be difficult to believe one's own philosophy! The only hope for the first answer, then, is to show that we need not choose: the answers are compatible, and both are right. That is the claim I wish to defend. I say that it cannot happen that what matters in survival according to one answer is present while what matters in survival according to the other answer is lacking.

PARFIT'S ARGUMENT

Derek Parfit has argued that the two answers cannot both be right, and we must therefore choose.[2] (He chooses the first.) His argument is as follows:

(a) Identity is a relation with a certain formal character. It is one-one and it does not admit of degree.

(b) A relation of mental continuity and connectedness need not have that formal character. We can imagine problem cases in which any such relation is one-many or many-one, or in which it is present to a degree so slight that survival is questionable.

Therefore, since Parfit believes as I do that what matters in survival is some sort of mental continuity or connectedness,

(c) What matters in survival is not identity. At most, what matters is a relation that coincides with identity to the extent that the problem cases do not actually arise.

Parfit thinks that if the problem cases did arise, or if we wished to solve them hypothetically, questions of personal identity would have no compelling answers. They would have to be answered arbitrarily, and in view of the discrepancy stated in (a) and (b), there is no answer that could make personal identity coincide perfectly with the relation of mental continuity and connectedness that matters in survival.

Someone else could just as well run the argument in reverse. Of course what matters in survival is personal identity Therefore what matters cannot be mental continuity or connectedness, in view of the discrepancy stated in premises (a) and (b). It must be some better-behaved relation.

My task is to disarm both directions of the argument and show that the opposition between what matters and identity is false. We can agree with Parfit (and I think we should) that what matters in questions of personal identity is mental continuity or connectedness, and that this might be one-many or many-one, and admits of degree. At the same time we can consistently agree with common sense (and I think we should) that what matters in questions of personal identity—even in the problem cases—is identity.

I do not attack premises (a) and (b). We could, of course, say "identity" and just mean mental continuity and connectedness. Then we would deny that "identity" must have the formal character stated in (a). But this verbal maneuver would not meet the needs of those who think, as I do, that what matters in survival is literally *identity*: that relation that everything bears to itself and to no other thing. As for (b), the problem cases clearly are possible under Parfit's conception of the sort of mental continuity or connectedness that matters in survival; or under any conception I might wish to adopt. The questions about continuity and connectedness which I left open are not relevant, since no way of settling them will produce a relation with the formal character of identity. So we do indeed have a discrepancy of formal character between identity and any suitable relation of mental continuity and connectedness.

But what does that show? Only that the two relations are different. And we should have known that from the start, since they have different *relata*. He who says that what matters in survival is a relation of mental continuity and connectedness is speaking of a relation among more or less momentary person-stages, or time-slices of continuant persons, or persons-at-times. He who says that what matters in survival is identity, on the other hand, must be speaking of identity among temporally extended continuant persons with stages at various times. What matters is that one and the same continuant person should have stages both now and later. Identity among stages has nothing to do with it, since stages are momentary. Even if you survive, your present stage is not identical to any future stage.[3] You know that your present stage will not survive the battle—that is not disconcerting—but will *you* survive?

THE R-RELATION AND THE I-RELATION

Pretend that the open questions have been settled, so that we have some definite relation of mental continuity and connectedness among person-stages in mind as the relation that matters in survival. Call it the *R-relation*, for short. If you wonder whether you will survive the coming battle or what-not, you are wondering whether any of the stages that will exist afterward is R-related to you-now, the stage that is doing the wondering. Similarly for other "questions of personal identity." If you wonder whether this is your long-lost son, you mostly wonder whether the stage before you now is R-related to certain past stages. If you also wonder whether he is a reincarnation of Nero, you wonder whether this stage is R-related to other stages farther in the past. If you wonder whether it is in your self-interest to save for your old age, you wonder whether the stages of that tiresome old gaffer you will become are R-related to you-now to a significantly greater degree than are all the other person-stages at this time or other times. If you wonder as you step into the duplicator whether you will leave by the left door, the right door, both, or neither, you are again wondering which future stages, if any, are R-related to you-now.

Or so say I. Common sense says something that sounds different: in wondering whether you will survive the battle, you wonder whether you—a continuant person consisting of your present stage along with many other stages—will continue beyond the battle. Will you be identical with anyone alive then? Likewise for other questions of personal identity.

Put this way, the two answers seem incomparable. It is pointless to compare the formal character of identity itself with the formal character of the relation R that matters in survival. Of course the R-relation among stages is not the same as identity either among stages or among continuants. But identity among continuant persons induces a relation among stages: the relation that holds between the several stages of a single continuant person. Call this the *I-relation*. It is the I-relation, not identity itself, that we must compare with the R-relation. In wondering whether you will survive the battle, we said, you wonder whether the continuant person that includes your present stage is identical with any of the continuant persons that continue beyond the battle. In other words: whether it is identical with any of the continuant persons that include stages after the battle. In other words: you wonder whether any of the stages that will exist afterward is I-related to— belongs to the same person as—your present stage. If questions of survival, or personal identity generally, are questions of identity among continuant persons, then they are also questions of I-relatedness among person-stages; and conversely. More precisely: *if common sense is right that what matters in survival is identity*

*among continuant persons, then you have what matters in survival
if and only if your present stage is I-related to future stages.* I shall
not distinguish henceforth between the thesis that what matters in
survival is identity and the thesis that what matters in survival is
the I-relation. Either way, it is a compelling platitude of common
sense.

If ever a stage is R-related to some future stage but I-related to
none, or if ever a stage is I-related to some future stage but R-
related to none, then the platitude that what matters is the I-relation will disagree with the interesting thesis that what matters is the
R-relation. But no such thing can happen, I claim; so there can be
no such disagreement. In fact, I claim that *any stage is I-related
and R-related to exactly the same stages.* And I claim this not only
for the cases that arise in real life, but for all possible problem
cases as well. Let us individuate relations, as is usual, by necessary
coextensiveness. Then I claim that *the I-relation is the R-relation.*

A continuant person is an aggregate[4] of person-stages, each one
I-related to all the rest (and to itself). For short: a person is an
I-*inter*related aggregate. Moreover, a person is not part of any
larger I-interrelated aggregate; for if we left out any stages that
were I-related to one another and to all the stages we included,
then what we would have would not be a whole continuant person
but only part of one. For short: a person is a maximal I-interrelated aggregate. And conversely, any maximal I-interrelated
aggregate of person-stages is a continuant person. At least, I cannot think of any that clearly is not.[5] So far we have only a small
circle, from personhood to I-interrelatedness and back again. That
is unhelpful; but if the I-relation is the R-relation, we have something more interesting: a noncircular definition of personhood. I
claim that *something is a continuant person if and only if it is a
maximal R-interrelated aggregate of person-stages.* That is: if and
only if it is an aggregate of person-stages, each of which is R-
related to all the rest (and to itself), and it is a proper part of no
other such aggregate.

I cannot tolerate any discrepancy in formal character between
the I-relation and the R-relation, for I have claimed that these relations are one and the same. Now although the admitted discrepancy between identity and the R-relation is harmless in itself, and
although the I-relation is not identity, still it may seem that the I-

relation inherits enough of the formal character of identity to lead to trouble. For suppose that S_1, S_2, . . . are person-stages; and suppose that C_1 is the continuant person of whom S_1 is a stage, C_2 is the continuant person of whom S_2 is a stage, and so on. Then any two of these stages S_i and S_j are I-related if and only if the corresponding continuant persons C_i and C_j are identical. The I-relations among the stages mirror the structure of the identity relations among the continuants.

I reply that the foregoing argument wrongly takes it for granted that every person-stage is a stage of one and only one continuant person. That is so ordinarily; and when that is so, the I-relation does inherit much of the formal character of identity. But ordinarily the R-relation also is well behaved. In the problem cases, however, it may happen that a single stage S is a stage of two or more different continuant persons. Worse, some or all of these may be persons to a diminished degree, so that it is questionable which of them should count as persons at all. If so, there would not be any such thing (in any straightforward way) as *the* person of whom S is a stage. So the supposition of the argument would not apply. It has not been shown that the I-relation inherits the formal character of identity in the problem cases. Rather it might be just as ill behaved as the R-relation. We shall examine the problem cases and see how that can happen.[6]

It would be wrong to read my definition of the I-relation as saying that person-stages S_1 and S_2 are I-related if and only if the continuant person of whom S_1 is a stage and the continuant person of whom S_2 is a stage are identical. The definite articles require the presupposition that I have just questioned. We should substitute the indefinite article: S_1 and S_2 are I-related if and only if a continuant person of whom S_1 is a stage and a continuant person of whom S_2 is a stage are identical. More simply: if and only if there is some one continuant person of whom both S_1 and S_2 are stages.

One seeming discrepancy between the I-relation and the R-relation need not disturb us. The I-relation must be symmetrical, whereas the R-relation has a direction. If a stage S_2 is mentally connected to a previous stage S_1, S_1 is available in memory to S_2 and S_2 is under the intentional control of S_1 to some extent—not the other way around.[7] We can say that S_1 is R-related *forward* to S_2, whereas S_2 is R-related *backward* to S_1. The forward and back-

ward R-relations are converses of one another. Both are
(normally) antisymmetrical. But although we can distinguish the
forward and backward R-relations, we can also merge them into a
symmetrical relation. That is the R-relation I have in mind: S_1 and
S_2 are R-related *simpliciter* if and only if S_1 is R-related either
forward or backward to S_2.

While we are at it, let us also stipulate that every stage is R-
related—forward, backward, and simpliciter—to itself. The R-
relation, like the I-relation, is reflexive.

Parfit mentions two ways for a discrepancy to arise in the problem cases. First, the R-relation might be one-many or many-one.
Second, the R-relation admits in principle of degree, and might be
present to a degree that is markedly subnormal and yet not negligible. Both possibilities arise in connection with fission and fusion
of continuant persons, and also in connection with immortality or
longevity.

FISSION AND FUSION

Identity is one-one, in the sense that nothing is ever identical to
two different things. Obviously neither the I-relation nor the R-
relation is one-one in that sense. You-now are a stage of the same
continuant as many other stages, and are R-related to them all.
Many other stages are stages of the same continuant as you-now,
and are R-related to you-now. But when Parfit says that the R-
relation might be one-many or many-one, he does not just mean
that. Rather, he means that one stage might be R-related to many
stages that are not R-related to one another, and that many stages
that are not R-related to one another might all be R-related to one
single stage. (These possibilities do not differ once we specify that
the R-relation is to be taken as symmetrical.) In short, the R-relation might fail to be transitive.

In a case of fission, for instance, we have a prefission stage that
is R-related forward to two different, simultaneous postfission
stages that are not R-related either forward or backward to each
other. The forward R-relation is one-many, the backward R-relation is many-one, and the R-relation simpliciter is intransitive.

In a case of fusion we have two prefusion stages, not R-related
either forward or backward to each other, that are R-related for-

ward to a single postfusion stage. The forward R-relation is many-one, the backward R-relation is one-many, and the R-relation simpliciter is again intransitive.

Identity must be transitive, but the I-relation is not identity. The I-relation will fail to be transitive if and only if there is partial overlap among continuant persons. More precisely: if and only if two continuant persons C_1 and C_2 have at least one common stage, but each one also has stages that are not included in the other. If S is a stage of both, S_1 is a stage of C_1 but not C_2, and S_2 is a stage of C_2 but not C_1, then transitivity of the I-relation fails. Although S_1 is I-related to S, which in turn is I-related to S_2, yet S_1 is not I-related to S_2. In order to argue that the I-relation, unlike the R-relation, must be transitive, it is not enough to appeal to the uncontroversial transitivity of identity. The further premise is needed that partial overlap of continuant persons is impossible.

Figure 1.1 shows how to represent fission and fusion as cases of partial overlap. The continuant persons involved, C_1 and C_2, are the two maximal R-interrelated aggregates of stages marked by the two sorts of cross-hatching. In the case of fission, the prefission stages are shared by both continuants. In the case of fusion, the postfusion stages are likewise shared. In each case, we have a shared stage S that is I-related to two stages S_1 and S_2 that are not I-related to each other. Also S is R-related to S_1 and S_2 (forward in the case of fission, backward in the case of fusion) but S_1 and S_2 are not R-related to each other. More generally, the I-relation and the R-relation coincide for all stages involved in the affair.

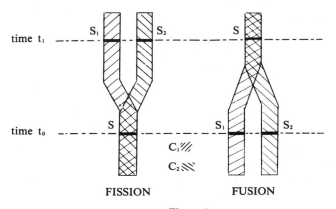

Figure 1

There is, however, a strong reason for denying that continuant persons can overlap in this way. From this denial it would indeed follow (as it does not follow from the transitivity of identity alone) that the I-relation cannot share the possible intransitivities of the R-relation.

The trouble with overlap is that it leads to overpopulation. To count the population at a given time, we can count the continuant persons who have stages at that time; or we can count the stages. If there is overlap, there will be more continuants than stages. (I disregard the possibility that one of the continuants is a time traveler with distinct simultaneous stages.) The count of stages is the count we accept; yet we think we are counting persons, and we think of persons as continuants rather than stages. How, then, can we tolerate overlap?

For instance, we say that in a case of fission *one* person becomes *two*. By describing fission as initial stage-sharing we provide for the two, but not for the one. There are two all along. It is all very well to say from an eternal or postfission standpoint that two persons (with a common initial segment) are involved, but we also demand to say that on the day before the fission only *one* person entered the duplication center; that his mother did not bear twins; that until he fissions he should only have one vote; and so on. Counting at a time, we insist on counting a person who will fission as one. We insist on a method of counting persons that agrees with the result of counting stages, though we do not think that counting persons just *is* counting (simultaneous) stages.

It is not so clear that we insist on counting a product of fusion as one (or a time traveler meeting himself as two). We are not sure what to say. But suppose we were fully devoted to the doctrine that the number of different persons in existence at a time is the number of different person-stages at that time. Even so, we would not be forced to deny that continuant persons could overlap. We would therefore not be driven to conclude that the I-relation cannot share the possible intransitivities of the R-relation.

The way out is to deny that we must invariably count two non-identical continuants as two. We might count not by identity but by a weaker relation. Let us say that continuants C_1 and C_2 are *identical-at-time-t* if and only if they both exist at t and their stages at t are identical. (More precisely: C_1 and C_2 both have stages at t, and all and only stages of C_1 at t are stages of C_2 at t.) I shall speak of such relations of identity-at-a-time as relations of *tensed identity*. Tensed identity is not a kind of identity. It is not identity among stages, but rather a derivative relation among continuants which is induced by identity among stages. It is not identity among continuants, but rather a relation that is weaker than identity whenever different continuants have stages in common. If we count continuants by tensed identity rather than by identity, we will get the right answer—the answer that agrees with the answer we get by counting stages—even if there is overlap. How many persons entered the duplication center yesterday? We may reply: C_1 entered and C_2 entered, and no one else; although C_1 and C_2 are not identical today, and are not identical simpliciter, they were identical yesterday. So counting by identity-yesterday, there was only one. Counting by identity-today, there were two; but it is inappropriate to count by identity-today when we are talking solely about the events of yesterday. Counting by identity simpliciter there were two; but in talking about the events of yesterday it is as unnatural to count by identity as it is to count by identity-today. There is a way of counting on which there are two all along; but there is another way on which there are first one and then two. The latter has obvious practical advantages. It should be no surprise if it is the way we prefer.

It may seem far-fetched to claim that we ever count persons otherwise than by identity simpliciter. But we sometimes *do* count otherwise. If an infirm man wishes to know how many roads he must cross to reach his destination, I will count by identity-along-his-path rather than by identity. By crossing the Chester A. Arthur Parkway and Route 137 at the brief stretch where they have merged, he can cross both by crossing only one road. Yet these two roads are certainly not identical.

You may feel certain that you count persons by identity, not by tensed identity. But how can you be sure? Normal cases provide no evidence. When no stages are shared, both ways of counting agree. They differ only in the problem cases: fission, fusion, and another that we shall soon consider. The problem cases provide no very solid evidence either. They are problem cases just because we cannot consistently say quite all the things we feel inclined to. We must strike the best compromise among our conflicting initial opinions. Something must give way; and why not the opinion that of course we count by identity, if that is what can be sacrificed with least total damage?

A relation to count by does not have to be identity, as the example of the roads shows. But perhaps it should share the key properties of identity. It should at least be an *equivalence* relation: reflexive, symmetrical, and transitive. Relations of tensed identity are equivalence relations. Further, it should be an *indiscernibility* relation; not for all properties whatever, as identity is, but at least for some significant class of properties. That is, it ought to be that two related things have exactly the same properties in that class. Identity-at-time-t is an indiscernibility relation for a significant class of properties of continuant persons: those properties of a person which are logically determined by the properties of his stage at t. The class includes the properties of walking, being tall, being in a certain room, being thirsty, and believing in God at time t; but not the properties of being forty-three years old, gaining weight, being an ex-Communist, or remembering one's childhood at t. The class is sizable enough, at any rate, to make clear that a relation of tensed identity is more of an indiscernibility relation than is identity-along-a-path among roads.

If we are prepared to count a product of fusion as two, while still demanding to count a person who will fission as one, we can count at t by the relation of identity-at-all-times-up-to-t. This is the relation that holds between continuants C_1 and C_2 if and only if (1) they both exist at some time no later than t, (2) at any time no later than t, either both exist or neither does, and (3) at any time no later than t when both exist, they have exactly the same stages. Again, this is a relation among continuants that is weaker than identity to the extent that continuants share stages. Although derived from identity (among stages) it is of course not itself identity. It is even more of an indiscernibility relation than identity-at-t, since it confers indiscernibility with respect to such properties as being forty-three years old, gaining weight (in one sense), being an ex-Communist, and remembering one's childhood at t; though still not with respect to such properties as being, at t, the next winner of the State Lottery.

It may be disconcerting that we can have a single name for one person (counting by tensed identity) who is really two nonidentical persons because he will later fission. Isn't the name ambiguous? Yes; but so long as its two bearers are indiscernible in the respects we want to talk about, the ambiguity is harmless. If C_1 and C_2 are identical-at-all-times-up-to-now and share the name "Ned" it is idle to disambiguate such remarks as "Ned is tall," "Ned is waiting to be duplicated," "Ned is frightened," "Ned only decided yesterday to do it," and the like. These will be true on both disambiguations of "Ned," or false on both. Before the fission, only predictions need disambiguating. After the fission, on the other hand, the ambiguity of "Ned" will be much more bother. It can be expected that the ambiguous name "Ned" will then fall into disuse, except when we wish to speak of the shared life of C_1 and C_2 before the fission.

But what if we don't know whether Ned will fission? In that case, we don't know whether the one person Ned (counting by identity-now) is one person, or two, or many (counting by identity). Then we don't know whether "Ned" is ambiguous or not. But if the ambiguity is not a practical nuisance, we don't need to know. We can wait and see whether or not we have been living with a harmless ambiguity.

This completes my discussion of fission and fusion. To summarize: if the R-relation is the I-relation, and in particular if continuant persons are maximal R-interrelated aggregates of person-stages, then cases of fission and fusion must be treated as cases of stage-sharing between different, partially overlapping continuant persons. If so, the R-relation and the I-relation are alike intransitive, so there is no discrepancy on that score. If it is granted that we may count continuant persons by tensed identity, then this treatment does not conflict with our opinion that in fission one person becomes two; nor with our opinion (if it really is our opinion) that in fusion two persons become one.

LONGEVITY

I turn now to a different problem case. Parfit has noted that mental connectedness will fade away eventually. If the R-relation is a matter of direct connectedness as well as continuity, then intransitivities of the R-relation will appear in the case of a person (if it is a person!) who lives too long.

Consider Methuselah. At the age of 100 he still remembers his childhood. But new memories crowd out the old. At the age of 150 he has hardly any memories that go back before his twentieth year. At the age of 200 he has hardly any memories that go back before his seventieth year; and so on. When he dies at the age of 969, he has hardly any memories that go beyond his 839th year. As he grows older he grows wiser; his callow opinions and character at age 90 have vanished almost without a trace by age 220, but his opinions and character at age 220 also have vanished almost without a trace by age 350. He soon learns that it is futile to set goals for himself too far ahead. At age 120, he is still somewhat interested in fulfilling the ambitions he held at age 40; but at age 170 he cares nothing for those ambitions, and it is beginning to take an effort of will to summon up an interest in fulfilling his aspirations at age 80. And so it goes.

We sometimes say: in later life I will be a different person. For us short-lived creatures, such remarks are an extravagance. A philosophical study of personal identity can ignore them. For Methusaleh, however, the fading-out of personal identity looms large as a fact of life. It is incumbent on us to make it literally true that he will be a different person after one and one-half centuries or so.

I should imagine that this is so just in virtue of normal aging over 969 years. If you disagree, imagine that Methuselah lives much longer than a bare millennium (Parfit imagines the case of immortals who change mentally at the same rate as we do). Or imagine that his life is punctuated by frequent amnesias, brainwashings, psychoanalyses, conversions, and what not, each one of which is almost (but not quite) enough to turn him into a different person.

Suppose, for simplicity, that any two stages of Methuselah that are separated by no more than 137 years are R-related; and any two of his stages that are separated by more than 137 years are not R-related. (For the time being, we may pretend that R-relatedness is all-or-nothing, with a sharp cutoff.)

If the R-relation and the I-relation are the same, this means that two of Methuselah's stages belong to a single continuant person if and only if they are no more than 137 years apart. (Therefore the whole of Methuselah is not a single person.) That is the case, in particular, if continuant persons are maximal R-interrelated aggregates. For if so, then segments of Methuselah are R-interrelated if and only if they are no more than 137 years long; whence it follows that all and only the segments that are exactly 137 years long are maximal R-interrelated aggregates; so all and only the 137-year segments are continuant persons.

If so, we have intransitivity both of the R-relation and of the I-relation. Let S_1 be a stage of Methuselah at the age of 400; let S_2 be a stage of Methuselah at the age of 500; let S_3 be a stage of Methuselah at the age of 600. By hypothesis S_1 is R-related to S_2 and S_2 is R-related to S_3, but S_1 and S_3 are not R-related. Being separated by 200 years, they have no direct mental connections. Since S_1 and S_2 are linked by a 137-year segment (in fact, by infinitely many) they are I-related; likewise S_2 and S_3 are I-related. But S_1 and S_3 are not linked by any 137-year segment, so they are not I-related. The R-relation and the I-relation are alike intransitive.

The problem of overpopulation is infinitely worse in the case of Methuselah than in the cases of fission or fusion considered hitherto. Methuselah spends his 300th birthday alone in his room. How many persons are in that room? There are infinitely many different 137-year segments that include all of Methuselah's stages on his 300th birthday. One begins at the end of Methuselah's 163rd birthday and ends at the end of his 300th birthday; another begins at the beginning of his 300th and ends at the beginning of his 437th. Between these two are a continuum of other 137-year segments. No two of them are identical. Every one of them puts in an appearance (has a stage) in Methuselah's room on Methuselah's 300th birthday. Every one of them is a continuant person, given our supposition that Methuselah's stages are R-related if and only if they are no more than 137 years apart, and given that continuant persons are all and only maximal R-interrelated aggregates of person-stages. It begins to seem crowded in Methuselah's room!

Tensed identity to the rescue once more. True, there are continuum many nonidentical continuant persons in the room. But, counting by the appropriate relation of tensed identity, there is only one. All the continuum many nonidentical continuant persons are identical-at-the-time-in-question, since they all share the single stage at that time. Granted that we may count by tensed identity, there is no overcrowding.

DEGREE

We turn now to the question of degree. Identity certainly cannot be a matter of degree. But the I-relation is not defined in terms of identity alone. It derives also from personhood: the property of being a continuant person. Thus personal identity may be a matter of degree because personhood is a matter of degree, even though identity is not. Suppose two person-stages S_1 and S_2 are stages of some one continuant that is a person to a low, but not negligible, degree. Suppose further that they are not stages of anything else that is a person to any higher degree. Then they are I-related to a low degree. So if personhood admits of degree, we have no discrepancy in formal character between the I-relation and the R-relation.

Parfit suggests, for instance, that if you fuse with someone very different, yielding a fusion product mentally halfway between you and your partner, then it is questionable whether you have survived. Not that there is a definite, unknown answer. Rather, what matters in survival—the R-relation—is present in reduced degree. There is less of it than in clear cases of survival, more than in clear cases of nonsurvival.[8] If we want the I-relation and the R-relation to coincide, we may take it that C_1 and C_2 (see fig. 1.1 for cases of fusion) are persons to reduced degree because they are broken by abrupt mental discontinuities. If persons are maximal R-interrelated aggregates, as I claim, that is what we should expect; the R-relations across the fusion point are reduced in degree, hence the R-interrelatedness of C_1 and C_2 is reduced in degree, and hence the personhood of C_1 and C_2 is reduced in degree. C_1 and C_2 have less personhood than clear cases of persons, more personhood than continuant aggregates of stages that are clearly not persons. Then S and S_1, or S and S_2, are I-related to reduced degree just as they are R-related to reduced degree.

Personal identity to reduced degrees is found also in the case of Methuselah. We supposed before that stages no more than 137 years apart were R-related while states more than 137 years apart were not. But if the R-relation fades away at all—if it is a relation partly of connectedness as well as continuity—it would be more realistic to suppose that it fades away gradually. We can suppose that stages within 100 years of each other are R-related to a high enough degree so that survival is not in doubt; and that stages 200 or more years apart are R-related to such a low degree that what matters in survival is clearly absent. There is no significant connectedness over long spans of time, only continuity. Then if we want the R-relation and the I-relation to coincide, we could say roughly this: 100-year segments of Methuselah are persons to a high degree, whereas 200-year segments are persons only to a low degree. Then two stages that are strongly R-related also are strongly I-related, whereas stages that are weakly R-related are also weakly I-related. Likewise for all the intermediate degrees of R-relatedness of stages, of personhood of segments of Methuselah, and hence of I-relatedness of stages.

It is a familiar idea that personhood might admit of degrees. Most of the usual examples, however, are not quite what I have in mind. They concern continuants that are said to be persons to a reduced degree because their stages are thought to be person-stages to a reduced degree. If anyone thinks that the wolf-child, the "dehumanized" proletarian, or the human vegetable is not fully a person, that is more because he regards the stages themselves as deficient than because the stages are not strongly enough R-interrelated. If anyone thinks that personhood is partly a matter of species membership, so that a creature of sorcery or a freak offspring of hippopotami could not be fully a person no matter how much he resembled the rest of us, that also would be a case in which the stages themselves are thought to be deficient. In this case the stages are thought to be deficient not in their intrinsic character but in their causal ancestry; there is, however, nothing wrong with their R-interrelatedness. A severe case of split personality, on the other hand, does consist of perfectly good person-stages that are not very well R-related. If he is said not to be fully a person, this *is* an example of the kind of reduced personhood that permits us to claim that the R-relation and the I-relation alike admit of degrees.

Let us ignore the complications introduced by deficient person-stages. Let us assume that all the stages under consideration are person-stages to more or less the highest possible degree. (More generally, we could perhaps say that the degree of I-relatedness of two stages depends not on the absolute degree of personhood of the continuant, if any, that links them; but rather on the relative degree of personhood of that continuant compared to the greatest degree of personhood that the degree of person-stage-hood of the stages could permit. If two wolf-child-stages are person-stages only to degree 0.8, but they are stages of a continuant that is a person to degree 0.8, we can say that the stages are thereby I-related to degree 1.)

If we say that a continuant person is an aggregate of R-interrelated person-stages, it is clear that personhood admits of degree to the extent that the R-relation does. We can say something like this: the degree of R-interrelatedness of an aggregate is the minimum degree of R-relatedness between any two stages in the aggregate. (Better: the greatest lower bound on the degrees of R-relatedness between any two stages.) But when we recall that a person should be a maximal such aggregate, confusion sets in. Suppose we have an aggregate that is R-interrelated to degree 0.9, and it is not included in any larger aggregate that is R-interrelated to degree 0.9 or greater. Suppose, however, that it *is* included in a much larger aggregate that is R-interrelated to degree 0.88. We know the degree to which it qualifies as an R-interrelated aggregate, but to what degree does it qualify as a maximal one? That is, to what degree does it qualify as a person, if persons are maximal R-interrelated aggregates? I am inclined to say: it passes the R-interrelatedness test for personhood to degree 0.9, but at the same time it flunks the maximality test to degree 0.88. Therefore it is a person only to degree 0.02!

This conclusion leads to trouble. Take the case of Methuselah. Assuming that R-relatedness fades out gradually, every segment that passes the R-interrelatedness test to a significant degree also flunks the maximality test to almost the same degree. (If the fade-out is continuous, delete "almost.") So *no* segment of Methuselah passes both tests for personhood to any significant degree. No two stages, no matter how close, are stages of some *one* continuant that is a person to high degree. Rather, nearby stages are strongly I-related by being common to many continuants, each one of which is strongly R-interrelated, is almost as strongly non-maximal, and therefore is a person only to a low degree.

We might sum the degrees of personhood of all the continuants that link two stages, taking the sum to be the degree of I-relatedness of the stages.

But there is a better way. Assume that R-relatedness can come in all degrees ranging from 0 to 1 on some scale. Then every number in the interval from 0 to 1 is a possible location for an arbitrary boundary between pairs of stages that are R-related and pairs that are not. Call every such number a *delineation* of this boundary. Every delineation yields a decision as to which stages are R-related. It thereby yields a decision as to which continuants are R-interrelated; a decision as to which continuants are included in larger R-interrelated aggregates; a decision as to which continuants are persons, given that persons are maximal R-interrelated aggregates; and thence a decision as to which stages are I-related. We can say that a certain continuant is a person, or that a certain pair of stages are I-related, *relative to* a given delineation. We can also say whether something is the case relative to a set of delineations, provided that all the delineations in the set agree on whether it is the case. Then we can take the degree to which it is the case as the size (more precisely: Lebesgue measure) of that set. Suppose, for instance, that two stages count as I-related when we set the cut-off for R-relatedness anywhere from 0 to 0.9, but not when we set the cut-off more stringently between 0.9 and 1. Then those two stages are I-related relative to delineations from 0 to 0.9, but not relative to delineations from 0.9 to 1. They are I-related to degree 0.9—the size of the delineation interval on which they are I-related. Yet there may not be any continuant linking those stages that is a person to degree more than 0. It may be that any continuant that links those stages is both R-interrelated and maximal only at a single delineation. At any more stringent delineation, it is no longer R-interrelated; while at any less stringent delineation it is still R-interrelated but not maximal.

The strategy followed here combines two ideas. (1) When something is a matter of degree, we can introduce a cutoff point. However, the choice of this cutoff point is more or less arbitrary. (2) When confronted with an arbitrary choice, the thing to do is not to make the choice. Rather, we should see what is common to all or most ways (or all or most reasonable ways) of making the choice, caring little what happens on any particular way of making it. The second idea is van Fraassen's method of supervaluations.[9]

On this proposal the I-relation admits of degree; and further, we get perfect agreement between degrees of I-relatedness and degrees of R-relatedness, regardless of the degrees of personhood of continuants. For at any one delineation, two stages are R-related if and only if they belong to some one maximal R-interrelated aggregate; hence if and only if they belong to some one continuant person; hence if and only if they are I-related. Any two stages are R-related and I-related relative to exactly the same set of delineations. Now if two stages are R-related to a degree x, it follows (given our choice of scale and measure) that they are R-related at all and only the delineations in a certain set of size x. Therefore they are I-related at all and only the delineations in a certain set of size x; which means that they are I-related to degree x. The degree of I-relatedness equals the degree of R-relatedness. In this way personal identity can be just as much a matter of degree as the mental continuity or connectedness that matters in survival.

PERRY'S TREATMENT OF FISSION

It is instructive to contrast my way and John Perry's way[10] of overcoming the seeming discrepancies in character between personal identity and mental continuity or connectedness. Perry and I have the same goals, but our priorities differ. Perry does not need to resort to tensed identity to rescue the common opinion that in fission there is only one person beforehand. However, Perry's way does not permit identification of the R-relation and the I-relation themselves, but only of certain time-dependent subrelations thereof. Further, he must introduce an unintuitive discrimination among the persons who exist at (have stages at) any given time. Some of them (all, except in the problem cases) are classified as *determinable* at that time. These are the ones who count. There may be others, not determinable at that time, who are left out of consideration for certain purposes.

Say that stage S_1 is *R-related at time* t—for short, R_t-*related*—to stage S_2 if and only if stages S_1 and S_2 are R-related simpliciter, and also S_2 is located at time t. The R_t-relation, then, is the R-relation between stages at t and stages at other times (or at t).

Say that stage S_1 is *I-related at time* t—for short, I_t-*related*—to stage S_2 if and only if both S_1 and S_2 are stages of some one continuant person who is determinable at time t, and S_2 is located at time t. The I_t-relation, then, is the I-relation between stages at t and stages at other times (or at t), if we leave out any continuant persons who are not determinable at t.

Perry proposes that something C is a continuant person determinable at t if and only if, for some person-stage S located at t, C is the aggregate comprising all and only the stages R_t-related to S. A continuant person, in general, is a continuant person determinable at some time. (No one is doomed to permanent indeterminability.) If something is a continuant person according to this proposal, Perry calls it a *lifetime*. If something is a continuant person according to my proposal—that is, if it is a maximal R-interrelated aggregate of person-stages—Perry calls it a *branch*. In normal cases, all and only lifetimes are branches.

In a case of fission, however, some lifetimes are not branches (see fig. 1.1 for cases of fission). Branch C_1 is a lifetime determinable at t_1, since it comprises all and only the stages R_{t_1}-related to S_1. Likewise branch C_2 is a lifetime determinable at t_1. But C—the whole thing—though not a branch, is a lifetime determinable at t_0, since it comprises all and only the stages R_{t_0}-related to S. Note that C_1 and C_2 are not yet determinable at t_0, whereas C is no longer determinable at t_1.

On Perry's proposal, the R-relation is not the same as the I-relation in this case. Since C is a lifetime, and hence according to Perry a continuant person, S_1 and S_2 are I-related. However, they are not R-related.

What does follow from Perry's proposal is that, for any time t, the R_t-relation is the same as the I_t-relation. Perhaps that is good enough. Any particular question of survival, or of personal identity in general, arises at some definite time. If the question arises at time t, it is the R_t-relation and the I_t-relation that are relevant. We want them to give the same answer. The rest of the R-relation and the I-relation are not involved. In particular, it is harmless that S_1 and S_2 are I-related, since they are neither I_{t_0}-related nor I_{t_1}-related, nor indeed I_t-related for any time t whatever.

On Perry's proposal, any person-stage existing at any time must belong to exactly one continuant person who is determinable at that time. Persons can share stages, to be sure. More so on Perry's proposal than on mine, in fact: stage S in the fission case belongs to three lifetimes (C, C_1, and C_2) but only two branches (C_1 and

C_2). Stage S_1 belongs to two lifetimes (C and C_1) but only one branch (C_1). But Perry's persons share stages only when all but one of the sharers is not determinable. Therefore we can count by identity, counting only the persons determinable at the time, and we will get the right answer. One determinable person (counting by identity) exists before the fission, but two exist afterward. There are three all along, counting by identity but including the non-determinables; but at the fission one loses determinability and the other two gain it.

I grant that counting by tensed identity is somewhat counter-intuitive; but isn't excluding the nondeterminable persons just as bad? They *are* (timelessly speaking) persons; they *do* exist at (have stages at) the time; they are *not* identical to persons we are counting. If we want to count the persons at the time, is it not gratuitous to exclude them? Perry can say: Yes, but we just do. Or: we do it for excellent practical reasons. I will say the same about counting by tensed identity without any exclusions. Both are counterintuitive; neither is unbearably so; either is better than not having any way to count that gives the correct answer; either is better than permitting the possibility of fission to create a discrepancy between personal identity and what matters in survival.

Perry considers only fission and fusion, but his proposal can apply also to the case of Methuselah. I do not know whether Perry would wish so to apply it. He might prefer to let mental continuity predominate over connectedness in the R-relation, so that the whole of Methuselah is both a branch and a lifetime, and thus an unproblematic person.

Suppose as before, however, that the R-relation fades out with an (arbitrary) cutoff at 137 years. For me, the 137-year segments (the branches) are the continuant persons; for Perry, the 274-year segments (the lifetimes) are the continuant persons. For instance, a segment that begins on Methuselah's 420th birthday and ends at the same time on his 694th comprises all and only the stages R_t-related to a certain stage S on his 557th, t being the time of that stage. The lifetimes are not branches and the branches are not life-times. (With a trivial exception: the initial and final 137-year segments are both branches and lifetimes. More generally: the initial and final lifetimes are shorter than the others, being cut off by birth or death.) Any stage at any time belongs to exactly one person determinable at that time, and to infinitely many nondeterminable persons. Counting by identity gives the right answer, provided the nondeterminable hordes are left out. The R_t-relation and the I_t-relation are the same for any time t, but the R-relation and the I-relation disagree for any two stages separated by more than 137 years but no more than 274.

Perry says nothing about degrees of personal identity. However, there is nothing to prevent him from taking over all I have said. If the R-relation admits of degree, then so does personhood, no matter whether continuant persons are branches or lifetimes. Then the I_t-relations also admit of degree, and there is no obstacle here to identifying them with the corresponding R_t-relations.

I have one serious misgiving about Perry's treatment of the problem. Perry has concentrated on making things come out as they should from the standpoint of any particular time, provided that persons not then determinable are not counted among the persons existing at that time. But what shall we do when we wish to generalize over persons existing at various times? Exclusion of the nondeterminables requires a definite point of reference, which is lacking. Overpopulation sets in again. Of course my cure for overpopulation—counting by tensed identity—also requires a definite point of reference. But let us count by identity, if we count from the standpoint of no definite time. How many persons were involved in an episode of fission long ago? I say: two. Perry says: three. Or else he says: none now determinable. Isn't two the correct answer?

NOTES

1. Better, *quasi-memory*: that process which is memory when it occurs within one single person, but might not be properly so-called if it occurred in a succession of mental states that did not all belong to a single person.
2. Derek Parfit, "Personal Identity," *Philosophical Review* 80 (1971), 3-27.
3. Unless time is circular, so that it is in its own future in the same way that places are to the west of themselves. But that possibility also has nothing to do with survival.
4. It does not matter what sort of "aggregate." I prefer a mereological sum, so that the stages are literally parts of the continuant. But a class of stages would do as well, or a sequence or ordering of stages, or a suitable function from moments or stretches of time to stages.
5. The least clear-cut cases are those in which the stages cannot be given any "personal time" ordering with respect to which they vary in the way that the

stages of an ordinary person vary with respect to time. But it is so indeterminate what we want to say about such bizarre cases that they cannot serve as counter-examples to any of my claims.

6. The argument also takes it for granted that every person-stage is a stage of at least one person. I do not object to that. If there is no way to unite a stage in a continuant with other stages, let it be a very short-lived continuant person all by itself.

7. As before, it would be better to speak here of quasi-memory; and likewise of quasi-intentional control.

8. No similar problem arises in cases of fission. We imagine the immediate postfission stages to be pretty much alike, wherefore they can all be strongly R-related to the immediate prefission stages.

9. See Bas van Fraassen, "Singular Terms, Truth-Value Gaps, and Free Logic," *Journal of Philosophy* 63 (1966), 481-495. See also the discussion of vagueness in my "General Semantics," *Synthese* 22 (1970), 18-67.

10. John Perry, "Can the Self Divide?," *Journal of Philosophy* 69 (1972), 463-488.

SURVIVAL

Georges Rey

I

The philosophical problem of personal identity can seem a matter of life and death. For what matters to us in our personal survival seems to involve, partly because in our experience it always has involved, the preservation of at least our bodily identity over time.

The supposition that it does, however, the supposition that what matters is some form of identity, is susceptible to certain intractable logical difficulties arising from some recent results in neurophysiology. The Sperry experiments[1] on epileptics whose *Corpora Collosa* have been cut present fairly persuasive evidence that the human brain exists as a pair of very similar hemispheres, each one of which could in principle exist and (with a little tampering) function fully independently of the other. Only technological (and perhaps some moral) difficulties prevent a brain being divided into two, one hemisphere being transplanted to one new skull, the other to another. In such a case, our usual criteria of personal identity—bodily[2] or psychological continuity—would break down. For they would present us with two (over time) equally eligible, but (at a given time) bodily and psychologically quite distinct candidates for the continued identity of the original person. And that would involve a violation of the transitivity of that relation: the original person could not be identical with both of the resulting persons without both of the resulting persons being, as they fairly clearly are not,[3] identical with each other. On the other hand, whatever it is that matters to us in our personal survival would seem to be preserved between the original and each of the resulting persons. There is no reason to suppose there to be at any time even a break in the (diverging) streams of consciousness. Such duplication couldn't be as bad as death:[4] it might arguably be preferable to the usual uniqueness. Rather, then, than have what matters to us in survival be contravened by logical law, it seems more reasonable to suppose, as Derek Parfit has recently done us the service of supposing, that what matters to us is not identity over time:[5]

> The relation of the original person to each of the resulting ones contains all that interests us—all that matters—in any ordinary case of survival.... Identity is a one-one relation. [This] case serves to show that what matters in survival need not be one-one.

Indeed, not only may what matters be one-many, as in the envisaged case of fission, but, considering fissions of two brains followed by fusions of the odd halves, what matters may also be many-one.

This would, to be sure, involve a travesty of ordinary talk. A person, on this account, may *survive* yet not continue to *exist*, since she may survive as two different persons. For example: a candidate for fission would survive but not continue to *exist* as (would not be identical with) either of the resulting persons. Where it will be important to avoid equivocation between this and ordinary use, I shall speak instead of a relation xt_1Syt_2 (or simply "S") which is satisfied by persons x and y at times t_1 and t_2 ($t_1 \le t_2$)[6] when y at t_2 preserves what matters in x's survival from t_1 to t_2 (and which in the usual case is satisfied just when x = y). Similarly, I shall use 'death' to refer not to the end point of a single personal existence, but, rather, to the furthest temporal point(s) of the longest stretch of any given S-related chain.[7] It may well have been the obvious awkwardness of this manner of speaking that obscured for so long this way of dealing with Sperry's results.

Such a modification of our suppositions and our talk has the further advantage of relieving philosophy of something of a red herring, or, in the figure of a recent and right complaint,[8] of a dog-wagging tail of a problem. It has always felt, obscurely, that puzzles about the logic of "=" were somehow remote from matters of life and death; and it should always have been clear that mere matters of life and death could not, themselves, admit of the generality of the considerations that appropriately bear upon the logic of " = ". We are simply too special, small, and few. Identity, I submit, should never have been the primary source of our concern with survival; it is, rather, survival, and our belief that our survival depended upon our continuing identity, which was the significant source of our concern with that identity. In assigning responsibility, for example, according praise or blame, it is not identity that would always interest us: "We should hardly allow a malefactor to evade responsibility or punishment by contriving his own fission!"[9] Similarly, I think, for the rest of our interests in justice, in the morality of the above and related medical practices, for the rationality of our hopes and expectations, for the sensicality of many people's religious beliefs.

But if it is not identity, what is it that matters so much to us in our personal survival? It would be odd if matters of life and death, the matters to which all else that also matters is so frequently compared, were no matters whatsoever. Yet, for all their centrality to, for example, the above interests, it can seem vexatiously difficult to say precisely what they are matters of. In this paper I hope to say something in the way of at least a simplification of the problem, reducing, perhaps, the highly to the slightly less problematic.

I shall not, however, be concerned, as many people might well be concerned, to assess or criticize our concerns. Matters of life and death may or may not be matters of great importance. Perhaps they are felt to be so more by the young than by the old. Perhaps, too, what importance they do possess has a great deal to do with what projects a person has undertaken, and the morality and importance of those projects.[10] But whatever their moral or prudential worth, it will surely depend in part upon determining just what it is, what conditions of the world, they are matters of. It is this issue, this sense of "what matters," that I shall be at pains to explicate: what conditions underwrite our usual personal concern; what conditions must obtain for a person properly to be said to survive in the *outré* examples envisaged, in (some of) the traditional problem cases, no less what does in fact obtain, coinciding so neatly with identity, in the actual cases with which we are every day acquainted.

Still, a certain factlessness can be felt to linger here, as with the more blatantly normative issues. While it seems fairly clearly not "up to us" in determining (on the whole) what counts as, say, kidney malfunction—kidneys function or fail to function quite independently of what any of us think on the matter—what counts as survival cannot be similarly isolated from what people are in fact willing to regard as survival, what as death. It is a lot like humiliation or honor: it is in the end what people regard as humiliating or honorable which determines what is ultimately to count as humiliating or honorable. If people began being humiliated or honored by very different sorts of things than those by which they presently are, we at least are not in a position to say, a priori if ever, that they are mistaken, or that they would be using those words differently than we do, that they ought to be differently translated. There might even be irresolvable disagreements. Similarly, if people were concerned with themselves and the future differently from the way they seem to be (or perhaps if there were good reasons why they should be), then survival might not be whatever I shall presently argue it is, and we might have to decide problem cases, and even clear ones, differently than I will. This can tend to make the issue look like one that might call for opinion, decision, persuasion: "Our notion of two things having the same color, say, is only as secure as our ability to muster an overwhelming majority who see them as having the same color."[11] Of course, there's usually a considerable amount of system involved in such secondary ascription, having to do *inter alia* with our *explanation* of people's concurrence, and of whatever divergences. But even ignoring the systematicity ignored in such a view, such dependence upon people does not render the issue arbitrary: not all decisions are arbitrary. And at least with respect to the kinds of concerns with which we shall be dealing in explicating S, we can rely on the very important fact that we are all, after all, only human: many of our concerns, and the distinctions we make on their behalf, are simply given to us, either by nature, or by significantly unalterable ways in which we live (cf., indeed, our agreements about colors, sounds, humiliation, or, in an even more problematic vein, about the immorality of gratuitously imposed pain). Beyond such facts we can only ask that our concerns and their application be not capricious: that there be some fairly well defined or definable basis, rooted in some general view, upon which we may systematically apply or withhold our concern. It is in view of such facts and by appeal for such a basis that we may straightaway disregard such otherwise perfectly possible candidates for S as "has the same number of eyelashes as"; indeed, it is in virtue of such facts and by appeal for such a basis that we rejected, as I presume we were right in rejecting, identity.[12]

II

In rejecting identity, however, it might seem that we risk losing what language we have for even beginning to talk about what matters in survival. For most of our talk of survival is suffused with, indeed, it is often taken to presuppose, identity.

But this is really no cause for alarm. The situation surely arises in any scientific inquiry that what may, even at the time of selection, appear to be an accidental, even nonuniversal, property of some kind of object, may, because it is in fact *a* property of some of the conveniently placed objects of that kind, serve as a temporary criterion of the kind. In determining, for example, what it is about roses that provides a basis for distinguishing them from rhododendrons, someone might simply go for a while by a difference in, say, color, until, and thereby that, a more universal and theoretically satisfying criterion be found. Similarly, in attempting to characterize S, we may very well go by the obvious fact that, in the overwhelming abundance of cases, people survive as themselves: identity, and the kind of concern each person ordinarily displays for her syn- and diachronic identity, ordinarily coincides with, and is thereby sufficient for S. That Sperry has provided us reason to abstract from that specific condition is no reason not to use it in seeking a more general one. It is in this way (and, unless we are lucky, perhaps only in this way) that we may proceed with discovering that more general condition without already knowing it. All the while, of course, we reserve the right to dismiss the specific condition as ultimately accidental: we may kick away our ladders after climbing up them.[13] (And if this involves changing the meanings of some of our terms, so much the worse for those meanings.)[14]

Thus may we take seriously the kind of concern each person normally exhibits about all and only the person with whom she is identical. That there is such a distinct kind of concern I shall not pause here to doubt. It very probably arises from our biology.

And, at least *synchronically*, it seems to be intimately bound up with what I take to be the very general, let us call it the "experiential" relation that obtains between a person and usually only her own present experiences:[15] however much a person may regret the fact of other people's present pains, or be gladdened by the news of their present pleasures, only each of those other people can (normally) suffer or languish in only each of their own, only that person in only hers. Let us call this kind of concern to which this relation gives rise "personal concern," and assume that it is a species of the same kind of concern, even if it may be based upon a slightly different relation, which persons usually exhibit about only themselves *across* time: however much a person may regret the fact of other people's impending pains, or be gladdened by the prospect of their coming joys, only each of those other people can (normally) dread or anticipate and so be personally concerned about only each of their own, only that person about only hers. (Similar feelings, if not a similarly sensitive vocabulary, are available with regard to a person's relation to just her own past.)[16] I shall take this kind of concern to be just the kind of concern that is involved in our concern with our survival, for which we are seeking a basis in seeking a basis for S. And so we might adopt the following strategy: by examining what underlies our personal concern, first synchronically—namely, the experiential relation, in the remainder of this section—and then diachronically—section III—we may discover some common conditions that may be abstracted from their association with identity. These conditions may be regarded as the most general conditions underlying our personal concern, and so then be identified with S.

We begin, then, with our present tense personal concern. As obvious as its intimacy with the experiential relation may be, it is not equally obvious just wherein that experiential relation consists. Many philosophers have thought it arises from and is delineable by reference to the unique, what has been called "privileged" epistemological position a person enjoys in regard to only some of her present tense psychological states, experiences, events. Paradigmatically, those states comprise most of a person's present sensations, seeming perceptions, seeming memories, and conscious intentions: let us refer to them, as I hope we innocently may, as a person's own "present conscious states." The privileged epistemological position with regard to such states has often been said to consist in the fact that a person's belief or knowledge about her own present conscious states is somehow more direct, automatic, and less susceptible to error and doubt than her beliefs and knowledge about anyone else's present conscious states. And it is true that we would *ordinarily* appeal to such an epistemological fact in the event someone were to claim to be experiencing someone else's present conscious states, or not to be experiencing her own. If, for example, a husband were to claim to be suffering from his wife's present labor pains, or if the wife were to claim that her ("seeming") labor pains were not hers but her husband's, we would surely want to inquire about the basis of their claims, about whether they would consider it possible (whether indeed it had ever occurred) that the wife really (seem to) be having or originating those pains without her husband believing that she is, or whether the husband could believe that she is without her actually being so, without her in fact being in labor at all. And the reason we would press such questions is that these latter possibilities arise, normally and some would say conceivably, only with regard to *other* people's present pains, that they cannot in regard to one's own; and that this is so regardless of whether a person might feel his own *empathetic* pains, or whether a person might wish further to distinguish among her pains those that she would "disown" or toward which she might adopt some special attitude.

But such epistemological claims, as correct as the intuitions that enliven them may be, are notoriously difficult to set out, at least in epistemological terms alone. Extravagances, "logical" and ontological, are too often committed on their behalf. And, even if they were unexceptionably articulated, in terms such as the above, we would, I think, tend to find them unilluminating. For the question would still arise about how it came to be that we each enjoy such a personally privileged epistemological stance, what natural conditions an entity must satisfy to enjoy it, what place that stance has in the general nature of things. In marking distinctions, that is, whether between roses and rhodendrons, S and not-S, or between different epistemological stances, we should like our marks to be in the terms of whatever *explanation* we have or might ultimately provide for those distinctions and the further differences to which they might give rise. Thus, for the roses and rhododendrons we favor those marks that bear upon origins, reproduction, genetic structure; and, for epistemological stances, as recent writings amply testify, we turn to facts about the causal origins of beliefs. The germinal example seems to have been Grice's analysis of perception: a person may rightly be said to perceive an object or event if and only if her seeming perception of it is caused by it in some specific, appropriate manner.[17]

This gets us some way up our ladder. For surely a similar sort of condition must play a role in explaining and so marking whatever distinct epistemological position we are justified in claiming for a person toward her own present conscious states. We would not, for instance, claim that a person enjoyed any such privileged position with regard to one of her own particular present intentions if the cause of her belief that she had that intention were, say, merely her perception of her behavior in a mirror. For that kind of cause is presumably indistinguishable from the kind of cause that is typically involved in the production in a person of beliefs about others; and it would be open thereby to the same sorts of mishaps and mistakes to which any instance of that kind of causal chain is typically open. Eyes and ears, if eyes and ears were the way one learned of one's present conscious states, could go as wrong in one's own case as in anyone else's: there would be no special epistemological position to mark. It is only because we have good reason to believe that it is not by our eyes and ears that we learn of our own conscious states—that they are significant causal links only in the cases of our beliefs about others, and that therefore our learning about ourselves and our learning about others are not subject to the same sort of mishap and mistake—that we have reason to believe that the distinction between the first- and other-person epistemological position is not arbitrary or unfounded. We could, I think, go wrong about even our own pains, but the mistake would be of a different kind than that about one another's.

Of course, a significant limitation on any such analysis is the shy specification of the specific, appropriate causal chains. Eyebrows well might raise at such generous wavings of the hand. Grice himself flinched, but then made this appropriate reply:[18]

I suggest that the best procedure for the causal theorist is to indicate the mode of causal connection by examples: to say that, for an object to be perceived by X, it is sufficient that it should be causally involved in the generation of some sense-impression in X in the kind of way in which, for example, when I look at my hand in a good light, my hand is causally responsible for its looking to me as if there were a hand before me...(and so on) *whatever that kind of way may be*: and to be enlightened on that question one must have recourse to the specialist.

In rather the way that we are using normal cases of identity to provide us with paradigm cases of survival, so may we use seemingly normal cases of perception as rungs toward discovering the specific kind of causal chain constitutive of perception; and so might we proceed toward marking the privileged epistemological stance. (Which is not to suggest that all such ladders must be afterward kicked away.)

It cannot be overemphasized, however, that such analyses in terms of causal chains do commit us to the existence, within the resources of the specialist's presumably general theory, of some definite means of delineating the specific, appropriate *kind* of causal chain peculiar to just the analysandum. Perception and privileged belief, that is to say, must be the products of particular *kinds* of processes; and those kinds must be (natural) kinds of the theory.[19] If this condition fails, if the chains are theoretically motley, it becomes difficult to imagine how the claim might be sustained that perception or the privileged stance could be (on this analysis) genuine phenomena, that there are any facts whatsoever of either of the matters.[20] Of course, possibly there are no such facts. Maybe we don't perceive, or enjoy any privileged stances. The predicates involved might be entirely gratuitous, arbitrary, like the "natural" versus the "violent" motion of Aristotelian physics. But *that* fact would be immensely perplexing: how would we begin to explain the (rough) convergence of widely independent judges, or the regularities they each claim to observe, or the immense utility of these distinctions in our ordinary experience? —But in any case I have already presented *some* evidence for the difference in stance: for example, eyes and ears are typically links in the chains for the one but not the other.

Well defined though the privileged epistemological stance may ultimately be, it does not quite perfectly capture what I have called the experiential relation. There could be complete cognitive breakdowns, with still perhaps some vestige of conscious experience. Moreover, there could well be telepathy, at least *some* forms of which might be naturally describable as a person enjoying the privileged stance to conscious states not her own, states that perhaps she herself doesn't even experience.[21] Such cases are possible simply because the nature of the experiential relation is so complex, its functional relations so multifarious. This is reflected in the diversity of the phenomena we take as evidence of the relation: the behavior typical of the particular conscious state; the person's ability to relate and compare different states; the person's own opinions on the matter. This evidence, too, needs explaining. We should want to know causes. Conceivably, the explanations could go divergent ways: the husband might stand, amazingly, in the privileged stance toward his wife's present pains, and so could relate and compare them, but the causes of his complaining and attendant writhings might not be ("directly") her pains, but rather a culturally inculcated response to his own special knowledge. Or, still more bizarre, his own pains might be the ("direct") cause of his writhings, but not of his claims and comparings, which might not even be available, or which might be tentative, confused, partially "inferential."

If we are inclined to balk at such possibilities, protesting that in cases like these our usual talk of *experience* would begin to break down, perhaps it is because, in identifying these other phenomena as evidence of the experiential relation, as with demarcating the privileged position, we are inclined to appeal to the right ("direct") sorts of causal chains. Certain behavior is pain behavior because it is typically caused in a specific way by a person's experiences of pains, which are also, typically, the causes of her abilities to relate and compare them, as of her privileged beliefs. Typically, that is to say, the evidence converges. Indeed, I do not think it would be far wrong to conceive of the network formed by these typical and appropriate kinds of causal chains, or mechanisms, as largely *constitutive* of the experiential relation: without any of the chains—without the appropriate causes for the (dispositions toward) privileged reports, the abilities to compare, the behavior typical of the particular states—it would seem extravagant to suppose that there was, nonetheless, some full conscious experience.[22] At least, one would expect, the "experience" would be diminished. It is phenomena such as these, and especially their interrelations, that are the material, insofar as there be any material, of conscious life. Given, then, that this experiential relation is the object of our present tense personal concern, it would seem that the basis for that concern, at least at any particular time, consists in the normal functioning of that causal network: it is what must obtain if, for any particular t, xtSyt.

Are those cases where x = y? Does the functioning of that network at a particular time entail personal identity at that time? There are powerful reasons to think so: the individuation of experience would seem to be intimately bound up with the individuation of persons. But the identity of persons at a given time is also inescapably bound up with the identity of those persons *across* time. And so we would be forced, in answering these questions, to grapple again with Sperry's results. Indeed, as Thomas Nagel has vividly detailed, we should have to grapple not with mere science fiction, but with the disturbing facts about the actual people Sperry tested. How are we to relate their experimental to their everyday behavior? Are they one person per skin or two? There does not seem to be any conclusive argument against treating them as two persons that ordinarily function as one (this one person would be *constituted* of two people): the apparent "integration" and "unity of consciousness" is hardly the compelling fact Nagel takes it to be, especially if one bears in mind relatively more commonplace difficulties about persons: ambivilence, *akrasia*, schizophrenia. Regarding them as two, however, might well encourage similarly dividing their personal concern, right hemisphere from left. In which case we would seem to have to worry about the rights and feelings of *three* people, where before we considered those of only one. And why stop at division into two? Why even treat these particular epileptics as particularly special? The solution to these and related problems would depend, I think, in part upon the relation of both the hemispheres, normally and experimentally, to the above mentioned experiential network (which perhaps provides some reason to be less pessimistic and dismissive than Nagel urges over the relevance of neurophysiology to the philosophy of mind).[23] But these problems do not demand resolution here. The present concern is with survival, not identity. Let us simply allow that it may well be possible, even if it is not altogether imaginable, that S even at a particular time not coincide with identity: a person could be (in our sense) personally concerned at a given time about someone other than herself.

But however much the experiential network is the basis for survival at any particular time, it would seem to be of little avail *across* time. For, so far as we know, a person does not stand consistently in any special experiential relation—there is no privileged stance, nor any specially caused behavior—with regard to her own or anyone else's *future* conscious states. Her position with regard to any future event is, in general, no better or worse than anyone else's. So we must look elsewhere for what matters across time.

Traditional views about personal *identity* across time were, of course, concerned with a similar issue, and so bear examining.

III

Traditional discussions of personal diachronic *identity* focused upon two main criteria, bodily and psychological continuity. As appropriate as some suitably mutilated versions of these criteria will prove to be for *survival*, no little care must be exercised in their presentation in the slightly altered role.

Care is particularly required in entertaining the psychological candidate. It has generally been presented in terms of the persistence of a person's personality, character, beliefs and, especially, (personal)[24] memory. If this last condition has loomed rather large, it has also been the most problematic, because the most seemingly presuppositious. Butler, for instance, begat a long and respected tradition which claimed it presupposed identity.[25] Perhaps our fission cases alone, but in any case some conclusive independent argument,[26] give the lie to that claim. Still, it might be felt to presuppose S. Lest there linger the suspicion of a question being begged, and since the proposal is itself not without its lure, it is worth considering memory of an entirely unpresuppositious sort. Let us call it "seeming memory." It could be what Locke had in mind when he was prepared to consider himself, if he were to (seem to) remember the experiences of Noah, to be thereby Noah's survivor.[27]

There are, however, an alarmingly diverse number of ways in which one person might come to share the seeming memories of another: vivid stories, hallucinations, brain stimulations, mere accidents. All my and my grandfather's hopes to the contrary, he does not survive as me, no matter how much I seem to recollect (and even take as my own) the experiences of his life from having heard of them at his knee. This is partly because we were both alive when I heard and identified with them; and, for all our not inconsiderable mutual concern, none of it was (strictly) personal. I didn't thereafter enjoy any privileged access to his feelings and thoughts. I did not tremble at the prospect of his worsening rheumatic aches, as I certainly would have had they been my own; nor did he look forward to my sunny days at camp. These attitudes would seem to have won their rationality from the point of part two: at the particular time of my "identification" (supposing there was some one particular time), his knee and voice and the expressions of his face were not links in the right sort of causal chain. His experiential network was, at that time, and remained, at each particular subsequent time, entirely distinct from my own.

Yet someone might reply that, while indeed, per the point of part two, as a result of merely hearing him I didn't become S-related to him *at that particular time*, still, his imparting to me his memories, if sufficiently detailed, could well be a way that his earlier self—the stretch from his earliest recollection to the particular recollecting—succeeded in surviving as me from the time of that hearing on. Communicating one's thoughts and experiences was often felt by romantics to offer the promise of immortality. And perhaps there is not (and ought not to be) any conclusive argument against such a hope. But there is the following difficulty.

For all any of us know, there are at the present moment in remote hospitals or on faraway planets, or in some still more horrendous museum of Madame Tussaud, persons who are hallucinating or otherwise seeming to have precisely our own conscious experiences: as a result of neurosurgical pokings or accidental similarities of environment, one of these persons, call her K_1, seems to recollect all and only the experiences that my good friend K recollects, and is seeming to experience all and only those she is presently experiencing. By our earlier discussion, we would not want to say that K_1 is S-related *at any particular time* to K at that particular time: for all their similarity, the causal network is not (*ex hypothesi*) interpersonally the least appropriate. But, by the present suggestion, we would be committed to saying that K_1 is, at each particular time, S-related to both the past and future stretches of K's life, just as K, whether she liked it or not, would be to the same stretches of K_1's. And this would be so even if their respective futures would, at some later time, happen qualitatively to diverge.[28] Consequently, come what may after such coincidence, K should dread (and not merely regret) not only her own but also K_1's impending pains—or at least she should if she is prepared to look forward to any of K_1's coming happiness— and vice versa. They are each, on this account, in precisely the position in which we left our candidates for hemispherical fission; but they are each in that position at each and every moment of their psychological coincidence! The topology of the position is most bizarre, and would become even more so in the surely not much more unlikely event of an indefinite number of such psychological duplicates, $K_1, \ldots, K_n$, drifting about intergalactically, or miming her movements in some museum: at every point of their psychological coincidence each $K_1, \ldots, K_n$, are S-related and thus personally concerned about the futures and pasts of K and each other (as K is about each of theirs), yet none are ever so related or concerned about K's or any of the others' *present* selves. It would *seem* (although of course it would not on this view strictly be the case) that each of those persons should fear, and later be relieved about, fates they would in fact never endure. In any case, surely such a suggestion is extravagant with people's personal concern: both with each of these persons', and, were such a circumstance to obtain for each of us, with each of our own. (Indeed, wouldn't we be inclined to be vaguely jealous of our duplicates, the way one often is of one's approximates, that, for instance, fortunes and distinctions might be to them that would otherwise come to oneself? On the present account this would be like being jealous of one's right hand being caressed rather than one's left.) If such oddities and prodigality are not enough to deter the determined romantic, it is not irrelevant to point out that, the romances we spin notwithstanding, few of us *really are* quite so romantic. We are not and would not be personally concerned about such psychological duplicates; and I know of no forceful arguments why we should be. Moreover, it would seem to be a fundamental intuition about either personal identity or survival that it is a matter, first and foremost, of *tokens*, particulars; not *types*. Our survival is at least as some particular thing(s) through space and time. If we branch as we have envisioned, it is surely from some common spatial-temporal points. "Has the same seeming memories as" may be satisfied by any number of individuals, quite irrespective of their continuity through space and time. Reasons enough not to pursue seeming memory any longer, but to turn instead to memory of a more plausible, if presuppositious sort.

A recent discussion of memory[29] has perhaps helpfully narrowed its presuppositions down. And it is nicely tailored to the Gricean model we have already entertained: a person can properly be said to remember an event if and only if her seeming memory of that event was caused in some specific, appropriate way. That way may or may not involve "some sort of trace, or structured analogue of what was experienced";[30] as in the case of perception and the privileged stance, those details may be left to the specialist's examination and extrapolation from paradigm cases. But one thing we may reasonably expect it will not involve is the *identity* of the person remembering the event with the person who experienced it. At any rate, it would certainly be surprising if the appropriate kind of causal chain could not stretch between persons whom, for independent reasons, we might want to distinguish. Indeed, it is with precisely such a circumstance that we are presented in speculating over Sperry: the seeming memories of each of the persons resulting from fission at least seem to be caused in the standard way by the experiences of the original person, despite the evident failure of identity.[31]

It is just such a criterion that can, I think, begin to save us from the above "seeming" difficulties. My grandfather does not survive as me, nor any of $K, K_1, \ldots, K_n$ as any of each other, nor any one of us as any of our accidental duplicates, because things like knees, voices, neurosurgical polings, and whatever *accidents* are simply not links in normal mnemonic chains. What concerns us about our memory experiences, particularly in their bearing upon survival, is not merely the quality of that experience; but, additionally, *that* the experience has been produced in a very particular sort of way. (Similar arguments can be made, perhaps even more obviously, for other psychological relations: e.g., between intentions and their execution.) Indeed, isn't it precisely considerations of this sort that we would enlist in settling some of the traditional problem cases of survival: for example, whether, as Norbert Wiener once envisioned, a person might travel to Mars via radio wave rather than rocketship;[32] or, as Bernard Williams once proposed, a person might submit to rejuvenation by aid of an "information parking device"?[33]

Before acquiescing too blithely, however to a (genuine) mnemonic and psychological criterion, it is worth bearing in mind some of the traditional sorts of objections that have been lodged against it. It is not only personal amnesia that ought at least to give us pause. Even more commonly, there are dreams, drugs, love affairs,[34] meditations, religious conversions: such changes are sometimes dreaded, more often eagerly anticipated, depending upon many things, but not only if the resulting persons are mnemonically and psychologically identical to the original. Quite the contrary, these changes are feared or sought often just because the person a person dreams herself to be, or becomes as a result of drugs or conversion, may be a very different sort of person, with perhaps none of the distinguishing beliefs, character, or memory of the person she is awake or beforehand. (N.B., our [strictly] personal concern over whether our sleep be filled with nightmares or pleasant dreams, when we know full well we invariably will forget who we are during the dream, as well as all the details of the dream after we awake. And believers in reincarnation are surely in an identical position with regard to their future lives.) To be sure, such changes might (but probably don't) affect personal *identity*; but however much or little they affect that issue, how much less do they affect *survival*. Surely they are not all as bad as death: not all those hopes and fears are pointless? Proust regarded some such changes to be a form of "resurrection."[35] And, in any event, we ordinarily suppose and talk quite as if, for all their psychological changes and loss of memory, at least some infants survive to adulthood, some adults to old age. I know of no compelling reason not to so suppose and talk.[36] Thus, while a causally grounded psychological criterion may promise sufficiency for S, we have no reason to think it necessary, some reason to think it not.

Of course, through all such changes we normally and happily rely upon bodily continuity and identity. Such reliance is, I think, not far wrong. Suitably amended, it can be seen to provide not only an elegant order to our diverse intuitions, but also a way of bringing together the seemingly antagonistic bodily and psychological criteria, and a way, then, of dealing with the above qualms. For if the central psychological criterion, namely memory, requires a causal chain, then it also requires some kind of stuff to serve as links. Causation (at least for the purposes at hand) seems to require substance. And it is of some kind of substance that our bodies are always composed.

IV

We are led, then, both by the presuppositions and by the failure of a purely psychological criterion, to our bodies. We were really led there already by considerations of the causal basis of our survival at a given time; and, in a different way, by reflections on our tokenhood over time. We might have been led there independently by even a casual inspection of the notion of a person: whatever the details, such creatures consist at least of a complex of capacities, abilities, dispositions; and, as such, as many writers have rightly insisted,[37] they cannot float about somehow unanchored in space and time. Dispositions require some underlying, continuous matter to be so disposed; persons, their capacities, need embodiment. Let us call the matter underlying a person's personal capacities (intellect, character, personal memory, etc.) her "personal embodiment."

Now there has been, historically, no meager dispute over just what sort of stuff it is that comprises our personal embodiment. The bulk of that dispute may, I trust, be left to physiologists—or to the champions of rare ectoplasms distilled in the laboratories at Duke or in the jungles of Brazil. Suffice it to say that it is of some such stuff that dreams of "disembodiment" must be made if those dreams are to be at all intelligible. The possibility of an *entirely* disembodied, yet still somehow *personal, existence* seems simply capricious: idle "image mongery".[38] *Where* would such persons exist? What possibly could be the explanation of their seeming experiences, perceptions of physical objects, memory, intentional action? What would justify us in taking physical disturbances as evidence of their "presence"?

Of course, we all the time imagine ourselves imagining ourselves "disembodied." At any rate, we do sometimes imagine ourselves disembodied of our *physical body*, outside it, looking in. And it is tempting to infer from such imaginings that it is therefore *possible* for us to be disembodied *tout court*. Now, as Kripke has reminded us,[39] the inference is invalid: to be imaginable is one thing, to be (metaphysically) possible, quite another. But, even allowing the inference: are we characterizing our imagining correctly? Most pictures of souls and ghosts are pictures of familiar physical bodies, just paler.[40] I submit that what we imagine when we imagine ourselves disembodied is not our disembodiment tout court, but rather our embodiment in a fashion other than that in which science tells us we are in fact embodied: that it is not these frail bones and frighteningly delicate organs, much less the color- less, convoluted pulp of our brains, that embodies us, but some- thing else, a little clearer, simpler, hardier; certainly a little longer lasting. Somehow we find the findings of science in this area par- ticularly discomfiting and difficult to believe (which may have to do not only with wishful thinking, but with the very different man- ners in which we learn physical and psychological predicates). My point is not that we must be made of the stuff science has so far found; but that we must be made of *something*, some continuous, sufficiently complicated stuff. For otherwise we would not be able to be "outside, looking in," understanding, remembering, being moved by what we see. Either we find some bona fide soul stuff, or we accept what the bulk of the scientific evidence endows us with, namely, a brain (and nervous system).

Notice that it is our brains and nervous systems, not our flesh and bones. It is easy to imagine oneself "disembodied" if what "disembodied" comes to (as it does on a surprising number of views)[41] is having one's brain removed from one's skull. We know too much about ourselves to be equally concerned about just any part of our bodies. What brings the bodily and psychological cri- teria together is the fact that there are *certain* parts of our bodies that are crucial to important parts of our minds. The network of appropriate causal relationships underlying our character, memo- ries, and especially our ability to have conscious experiences, is far more important than, as it were, the wires that hold it in place. Not all our embodiment is, that is, strictly personal. So it is that (metaphors notwithstanding) our brains are more crucial to us than our hearts (and why it is that it is Sperry's, not Christiaan Barnard's, experiments that arouse philosophical worry).

Which is not to say that we are *identical* with even the crucial stuff of our bodies, that what matters to us is merely our matter. Memories et al. don't abide in just any stuff, no matter how arranged. Indeed, as Wiggins has emphasized, echoing Aristotle, even the identification of bodily parts (*qua* parts) depends heavily upon their characteristic functioning.[42] Failure in the functioning of the mechanisms of our personal embodiment is failure of ourselves to be embodied: we die, even if the matter of which we are composed endures.

Nor is it to say that our survival depends upon the *continuing identity* of that brain. That particular ladder, so useful to our investigation, may now be kicked away. The relevant causal network, the categorical states underlying our dispositions, do not seem to require, if our speculations from Sperry's results are correct, the identity of that brain over time, or perhaps even at a given time. What matters is only that brain's *continuity*, that the causal networks may be picked out, the mechanisms underlying the various capacities be so traced. So it is that a brain may divide, lose its identity, but S still obtain: each part is continuous, but is of course not identical, with the original whole.

In sum, S, or the basis of what matters to us in our personal survival, seems to consist in the *not necessarily identical continuity of our functioning personal embodiment*. This is what seems to be preserved, even if nothing else, through dreams, drugs, and conversions, fissions, fusions, and in our normal, day to day oblivion, infancy through old age. It underwrites and explains our syn- and diachronic personal concern, and our toleration of such a wide variety of physical and psychological changes. Such a view is, again, rather like looking to genetic material to distinguish roses from rhododendrons: it is that material (whatever the geneticist finally discovers its particular nature to be) that determines the kind of plant a particular plant is, that underlies and explains the wide diversity in colors and shapes. Moreover, just as the color and shape of an individual rose may change over time, while the kind of plant it is remains the same, so may a person mature, undergo profound psychological change, forget the experiences of her infancy—maybe even lose her *identity*—and yet still survive.

(Indeed, just as certain changes in a plant may be determined by its genetic structure, so may certain psychological changes be a natural part of a person's survival.)

Even old hopes on this view have a chance. At any rate, they are not unintelligible. Reincarnation awaits the discovery of that substance that inheres in our brains in the way that science suggests our brains inhere in our heads: perhaps then it could pass on to the brain of a cockroach, or a cow, or, more plausibly, to that of another human being. Resurrection, at least Catholicly conceived, is perhaps more likely, if less attractive: the revitalization of our moribund bodies would seem to involve only technological (although hopefully some moral) difficulties.

I do not claim to have established this view conclusively. Indeed, I have fairly leaped at it, as one does to those elegant principles that promise to accommodate the greater number of our intuitions with the least conceptual disruption. On this score, this view seems to be at least not as badly off as others that have been proposed. In any case, if this account is correct, it shows that something very close to what many people regard as personal survival is not arbitrary or unfounded. But, even if it is wrong, its defense has brought to bear some considerations that, so far as I have read, have not received the attention they deserve, and so has ruled out what some philosophers may have too incautiously regarded as genuine (metaphysical) possibilities.

But it has not ruled out all. There are deep problems about what constitutes the proper functioning of our bodies (we needn't remember *all* our experiences whatever that would be like; but there must be some retention, or at least continuities therein). And there is all that uncertainty about the particular kinds of causal chains, what they really look like, whether they are theoretically delineable at all (one's view of Wiener's and Williams's proposals ought to await just such empirical research). Even then, there remain the usual problems with "cause" and "continuity," notions that, moreover, may in their application admit of degree (physical continuity seems to withstand replacement of parts only so long as that replacement is gradual over time). And over all of this there hovers the possible evanescence, or simply differences, in our concerns and accompanying differences in the distinctions we find useful to draw: perhaps Parfit's recommended indifference to one's own, as opposed to anyone else's, personal fate will one day seem quite natural, and the distinction that I have drawn quite odd. But to reduce the highly to the slightly less problematic is perhaps the most one can expect by way of progress in this difficult and peculiar topic.[43]

NOTES

1. These were experiments, of which there were and continue to be a great many, begun in the 1950s and first published by M. S. Gazzinaga, J. E. Bogen, and R. W. Sperry in their "Some Functional Effects of Sectioning the Cerebral Commisures in Man," in *Proceedings of the National Academy of Sciences* 48 (1962), pt. 2, p. 1765. Very briefly, the experiments consisted in the following. For relief of some particularly severe cases of epilepsy, the fibers connecting the right and left hemispheres of the epileptics' brains (roughly, the *Corpus Collosum*) were severed. The original operations had been performed in the 1940s, and the patients had all reported living quite normally thereafter. What Sperry et al. did was meticulously to segregate, by means of an elaborate set of screens, the stimulation affecting one hemisphere from that affecting the other. For example, an object causing tactile stimulation in the left hand, and consequently associated neural activity in the right hemisphere, was prevented by a screen from causing retinal stimulation in the left halves of either retina, and consequently from causing any associated activity in the left hemisphere. The result was that, for the duration of the experiment, the original person seemed to be divided into two: most (although not all) personal cognitive capacities—thinking, identifying, comparing, retrieving objects—were sharply divided between the two hemispheres in such a way that, while each hemisphere seemed to embody fairly whole and adept persons, neither was able to integrate its functioning with that of the other. The right hand literally couldn't know what the left hand was doing. (There were some asymmetries, chiefly having to do with all but rudimentary *production* of language. Since they did not seem also to involve problems in the *reception* and *processing* of linguistic material—both sides seemed to respond equally well to verbal instructions—I shall assume for the philosophical purposes at hand that such asysmmetries may be ignored.) Much discussion has ensued over how to interpret the results. See especially R. W. Sperry, "Brain Bisection and Mechanisms of Consciousness," in J. C. Eccles, *Brain and Conscious Experience* (Berlin: Springer-Verlag, 1966), and, for an engaging, if despairing, philosophical treatment, Thomas Nagel, "Brain Bisection and the Unity of Consciousness," in *Synthese* (May 1971).

2. For reasons advanced in D. Wiggins, *Identity and Spatio-temporal Continuity* (Oxford: Blackwell, 1971), p. 51 and footnotes thereunder, and discussed in this paper, I shall regard the brain and nervous system as the relevant portion of the body intended by a "bodily" criterion.

3. N.B., they may be (after the fission) in different places at the same time, having very different, and unintegratable experiences, becoming very different sorts of characters. Indeed, all they might share are some personal memories of the original person's experiences, and perhaps not even those for very long. By most criteria of individuation of persons at a given time, they would seem to be (or, without enormous effort, would eventually become) as different as any two

different people might be. For further difficulties in treating them nevertheless as one discontinuous person, see D. Parfit, "Personal Identity," *Philosophical Review* (January 1971), p. 8, particularly the footnote.

4. There do seem to be *some* people who, nevertheless, would regard such fission as death. For them, what matters just *is* identity. Providing they can present a consistent and coherent account of their concern, there is perhaps nothing we can say to them.

5. Parfit, op. cit., p. 10. The possibility of distinguishing the issue of survival from that of identity was perhaps anticipated in a way by Kant when, attempting to block the move from the transcendental unity of apperception to the identity of the person, he imagined that consciousness might pass through different persons as momentum does between contiguous elastic balls, see "Third Paralogism," *Critique of Pure Reason*, trans. N. K. Smith (New York: St. Martin's Press, 1968), especially A364, footnote a. Another anticipation is perhaps implicit in Proust, see nn. 34 and 35 below.

6. '$\leq$', since I take the sort of concern we exhibit, normally, for only ourselves *at a given time* to be of a kind with the sort of concern we exhibit normally for only ourselves *across time*. Since the assumption of identity has been abandoned in the latter case, surely it may have to be in the former as well. That is, what matters to us in survival may, rather unidiomatically, not only exceed our identity over time, but even *our* (identical) *existence* at a given time.

7. Where length is only temporal, and the chains are measured only from earlier points to later ones.

8. S. Shoemaker, "Wiggins on Identity," in *Identity and Individuation*, ed. K. Munitz (New York: New York University Press, 1971). See also Quine's further argumentation in his review of that collection, *Journal of Philosophy* (September 7, 1972).

9. D. Wiggins, "Locke, Butler and the Stream of Consciousness," Chap. VI in this collection.

10. Cf. J. Perry, "The Importance of Being Identical," Chap. III in this collection.

11. J. Bennett, *Locke, Berkeley, Hume*, (Oxford: Oxford University Press, 1972), p. 96.

12. As I mentioned in n. 4 above, there do seem to be some people who would not (perhaps in any circumstance) reject identity. I find such a view, for many of the reasons advanced in various places in this paper, quite surprising. But it, or some form of it (perhaps *bodily* identity), is surely *coherent* and meets the demands laid out in this paragraph. Indeed, it would diverge from the view I propose (in section IV) perhaps only in the bizarre, as yet counterfactual cases of fission and fusion. It is precisely the point of this paragraph that such alternatives are possible and that, at some point, rational selection would be quite futile.

13. For a similar pattern of argument see e.g., Quine's replacement of a semantic by a syntactic criterion of logical truth, in his "Reply" to Strawson, in *Synthese* (1970), pp. 296-297. The ploy with the ladders is, of course, Wittgenstein's.

14. That is, pending some way of rendering an appeal to meaning stronger than an appeal to mere conservativism of theory, my argument will not be affected by extra-theoretic (e.g., more usage) considerations of the meaning of e.g. "survival."

15. We need not pursue here any specious present. Let us assume that there is some shortest temporal stretch of a person, than which no shorter is possible (can

still satisfy "is a person"); and let all references to a person's present experiences be to experiences within such a stretch.

16. "Remorse," I believe, is distinguishable in this way from "regret."

17. H. P. Grice, "The Causal Theory of Perception," in *Perceiving, Sensing, and Knowing*, ed. R. J. Swartz (New York: Doubleday, 1965), especially section V.

18. Ibid., p. 463.

19. Which is not to say that the general theory must be one restricted to the *terms* of e.g., neurophysiology. There can (and probably must) be nonneurophysiological—e.g., functional, intentional—descriptions of, still, neurophysiological phenomena. And those descriptions might figure importantly in a good (macro-) theory.

Nor do I mean to suggest that there must be just *one* natural kind explicating our ordinary descriptions: our rough, but ready, ordinary types might divide into several natural ones, as "fishes" did into "fishes" and "mammals."

20. And I do not mean that the situation would then be merely as bad as that we encountered with "survive," as with secondary predicates in general. The kind of failure of typification I am imagining is one in which there would presumably be no "relational" typifications either.

21. E.g., suppose that in a certain pair of Siamese twins there is a causal chain (of the appropriate kind) between the "pain center" of one and the "belief center" of the other. This may not be a genuine (meta-)physical possibility; it suffices for the present point that it be an epistemological one.

22. The specific capacities and causal networks are doubtless more numerous and complex than could possibly be indicated here. I am relying only upon the general form of such an analysis being correct. I am sympathetic, for example, to the trend, although not to all of the details, of D. C. Dennett's discussion of "consciousness" in his *Content and Consciousness* (London: Routledge and Kegan Paul, 1969), Chapter VI.

23. Nagel, op. cit., pp. 396-397.

24. A distinction may and ought to be drawn between what might be called "capacity" (how to . . .), "factual" (that . . .), and "personal" (. . .ing there then), memory; see C. B. Martin and Max Deutscher, "Remembering," in *Philosophical Review* (April 1966), p. 161. It is with only this last sort, I take it, that any defender of the memory criterion has been seriously concerned.

25. J. Butler, "Of Personal Identity," in e.g., *Body, Mind, and Death*, ed. A. Flew (New York: Macmillan, 1964). An influential, contemporary representative of that tradition is the editor of this collection, as is indicated, for example, in his introduction to it.

26. D. Wiggins, Chap. VI in this collection, and see this paper.

27. John Locke, *Essay on Human Understanding* (New York: Dutton, 1961), II-27-xv.

28. By way, that is, of *content* of those coming experiences, not necessarily, of course, by way of memory of past ones. Those future stretches of both K and K_1 will both, we may assume, share identical seeming memories of experiences in the coincident stretch (as well as of the seeming memories they enjoyed *during* that stretch), just as we may assume each of the persons resulting from fission would.

29. Martin and Deutscher, op. cit., pp. 189-190.

30. Ibid., p. 189. Neurophysiologists, I am told, do not share the optimism over "traces" as the mechanism of memory: much memory seems to be less

"storage" than "reconstruction" of information (see also F. C. Bartlett, *Remembering* [London: Cambridge University Press, 1932]). And, in any case, there are more than merely neurophysiological difficulties with the notion, uncritically accepted by Martin and Deutscher, of "what was experienced."

On the other hand, "leaving the details to the specialist" should not be taken to invite the kind of vagary involved in many accounts of "q(uasi)-memory," in which it is not enough (although it is not wrong) to appeal to "direct connections, whatever they are" between e.g., an action and a memory of its performance as a plausible criterion of survival, see Parfit, op. cit., p. 12. One must also be prepared to accept the general characterizations those connections must ultimately receive from some general theory if they are to ground any distinctions whatsoever. Evidence that Parfit is *not* so prepared comes in his later article, "On 'The Importance of Self-Identity,'" *Journal of Philosophy* (1971), pp. 683-690. There he entertains the possibilities of someone being psychologically continuous with Guy Fawkes, or being so resurrected, adding: "Nor does it matter in the slightest that the psychological continuity will lack its normal cause. All that is needed is some reliable cause" (p. 698). Not only does this "reliable" beg the question—reliable for what?—but it blatantly disregards the need for some bases for the distinctions we draw, whether between memory and seeming memory, or survival and death.

31. It might be argued that the meaning of "memory" commits us to the identity condition. Could there be a clearer example of the indistinguishability of meanings and merely conservative beliefs (cf. n. 12 above)? Indeed, in this case it is not surprising that identity is felt to be part of the meaning: ordinary experience is everywhere presented with cases in which there's not the slightest reason to think identity and memory might diverge. Ordinary language is (or may be) fine for ordinary experience. But we should not be restricted to it in considering e.g., the extraordinary results of Sperry.

32. Norbert Wiener, *The Human Use of Human Beings* (Garden City: Doubleday, 1954), p. 98 ff.

33. Bernard Williams, "The Self and the Future," in his *Problems of the Self* (London: Cambridge University Press, 1973), p. 47; cf. also the role Grice sees his causal theory of perception playing in determining whether some peculiar creature may correctly be said to *see* or not, in Grice, op. cit., p. 463.

34. Cf. M. Proust, *Within a Budding Grove*, in his *Remembrance of Things Past*, trans. C. K. Scott Moncrieff (New York: Random House, 1934), p. 446: "we are incapable while we are in love as acting as fit predecessors of the next persons who, when we are in love no longer, we shall presently have become. . . ." I owe both this and the quotation in the footnote that follows, and their slightly altered translations, to Derek Parfit. It should be emphasized, however, that such welcome passages from Proust argue *not* for the slightest change in our attitudes toward personal *survival*, as Parfit sometimes seems to suggest (see "Personal Identity," pp. 25-27), but only toward our *identity*, providing yet another reason for distinguishing those issues as we have (see the second and third pages of this article and n. 5). This is not to denigrate the proposed changes. Indeed, I think Parfit is quite right, as was Hume before him, to undermine the illusion of a certain psychological constancy we are inclined to impose upon the really quite psychologically diverse different portions of our lives. And we would very likely impose it as much upon our surviving, as upon our identical selves. Perhaps this illusion is part of the source of our personal concern. But, for the

reasons I have been adducing in this paper, it need not be regarded as the whole of that source.

35. Contemplating the eventual loss of his feelings for the loss of his friends, Proust writes: "If that should occur...it would be in a real sense the death of oneself, a death followed, it is true, by a resurrection, but in a different self, the loves of which are beyond the reach of those elements of the existing self that are doomed to die," in Proust, op. cit., pp. 509-510, quoted in Parfit, "On 'The Importance of Being Identical,' " p. 686.

36. Parfit seems to believe that memory and other such "direct psychological connections" (e.g., between intentions and their executions) are the most important elements in survival ("Personal Identity," p. 21). Leaving aside the unacceptable vagary of "direct," deplored enough in n. 26, it should be emphasized that, as he himself admits, he has provided no argument for such a claim. (In recent conversation, he has expressed doubts that any such argument could possibly be given.) The preceding discussion, it seems to me, is *some*, albeit not conclusive, argument *against* it. And so we may resist the suggestion, to which he nevertheless proceeds (p. 21), that "it seems clearly true" that, for beings periodically undergoing fission, the relation between one such being and another four times divided would be "as distant" as that between a normal person and her great-great grandchild. The "direct psychological connections" may be as lacking in the one case as the other; but, as Parfit's own discussion ought to have led him to notice, the relevant psychological (not to say bodily) continuities would amply suffice to distinguish them. Indeed, aside from the bewildering flock of duplications, the relation between one such being and another four times divided should be exactly "as close" as that between a normal person at one stage of her life and herself four stages later!

37. See e.g., D. M. Armstrong, *A Materialist Theory of the Mind* (London: Routledge and Kegan Paul, 1968), pp. 85-88. Also, more generally, W. V. O. Quine, "Natural Kinds," in his *Ontological Relativity and Other Essays* (New York: Columbia University Press, 1969).

38. L. Wittgenstein, *Philosophical Investigations* (New York: Macmillan, 1953), section 390. I should add that, in making these dismissive claims about "disembodiment," I am not depending upon any dubious, *semantic* notion of "intelligibility." I am simply taking for granted the greater, coherent lot of our beliefs about the world, and emphasizing the immense difficulty that would be involved in fitting the idly imagined possibility of total disembodiment into that lot. Perhaps it is, after all, possible; but only, I submit, at the cost of a massive revision of what we presently take to be true.

39. S. Kripke, "Identity and Necessity," in Munitz, op. cit., pp. 149-151.

40. Cf. Wittgenstein, op. cit., sect. II, pt. iv: "The human body is the best picture of the human soul."

41. E.g., S. Shoemaker, *Self-Knowledge and Self-Identity* (Ithaca: Cornell University Press, 1963), chap. 1.

42. Wiggins, *Identity and Spatio-Temporal Continuity*, fn. 61, pp. 77-78.

43. Derek Parfit provided the stimulation to the earliest version of this paper. Raymond Barglow, Eunice Belgum, Ned Block, Jerry Fodor, and David Israel commented helpfully on that or subsequent versions. My debt to the published and yet to be published writings of David Wiggins exceeds footnote: indeed, if I have understood him correctly, I suspect that what I have written here diverges from what he might say (or may already have said) only in points of approach,

emphasis, and detail. I am particularly grateful to Amélie Oksenberg Rorty for pleasurable discussions, encouragement, and impatience with lesser and glibber arguments than those that may yet remain.

THE IMPORTANCE OF BEING IDENTICAL

JOHN PERRY

I

Most of us have a special and intense interest in what will happen to us. You learn that someone will be run over by a truck tomorrow; you are saddened, feel pity, and think reflectively about the frailty of life; one bit of information is added, that the someone is you, and a whole new set of emotions rise in your breast.

An analysis of this additional bit of information, that the person to be run over is you, is offered by theories of personal identity, for to say it is you that will be hit is just to say that you and the person who will be hit are one and the same. And so it seems that those theories should shed some light on the difference this bit of information makes to us. If it gives us more reason to take steps to assure that the person is not run over, our theory should help explain why that is so. And if this bit of information gives us reasons of a different kind than we could have if it were not us to be hit, our theory should help explain this too.

The most famous theory of personal identity, Locke's analysis in terms of memory, was criticized on just these grounds.[1] Butler's most serious charge against Locke was that his account "rendered the inquiry concerning a future life of no consequence."[2] And Butler did not just have in mind an inability to explain our interest in an afterlife, but an inability even to explain why we care about what happens to us in this life, tomorrow. From a natural extension of Locke's "hasty observations," Butler draws the conclusion "that it is a fallacy upon ourselves to charge our present selves with anything we did, or to imagine our present selves interested in anything which befell us yesterday, or *that our present self will be interested in what will befall us tomorrow.*"[3]

Butler's arguments for this conclusion are confused,[4] but the point remains that there is nothing in Locke's account of personal identity to explain *why* I care what happens to me tomorrow. That I will be run over by a truck means, says Locke, that the person who is run over by a truck will remember thinking and doing what I am thinking and doing now. But why would I care especially about that? Why should a person who is having such memories be of any more concern to me than anyone else? One is inclined to respond, "because to have such memories is just to be you"; but now the explanation goes wrong way round; isn't it fair to demand that the *analysans* shed light on why the *analysandum* has the implications for us that it does?

Some of the difficulties here can be brought out by noting that Locke's account (and any account which analyzes personal identity in terms of an empirical relation between person-stages or phases) will allow *indeterminate* cases. For our concepts of empirical relations, such as *having a memory of an experience of*, are inevitably vague. This means I could conceivably be presented with facts that could only be interpreted as neither a clear-cut case of my own death, nor a clear-cut case of my survival. But how should I *feel* about such a case? "There seems to be an obstinate bafflement to mirroring in my expectation a situation in which it is conceptually undecidable whether I occur."[5]

Take for example, what I have elsewhere called a "brain rejuvenation" case.[6] Smith's brain is diseased; a healthy duplicate of it is made, and put into Smith's head. On the assumptions about the role of the brain usually made in these discussisons, the survivor of this process will be just like a healthy Smith. But will he be Smith? It seems that people of good faith can differ over the answer to this question (and, if this case is not one that is truly indeterminate, it points in the direction in which such a case could be constructed). How is Smith to react to this? Is he to look forward to the painful convalescence of the survivor with terror, or merely sympathy?

Is the need here for further conventions, which will clear up the area left vague by our concept of personal identity? We can imagine the French Academy, or the American Philosophical Association, or the Supreme Court, passing resolutions or handing down decisions which have this effect. (Perhaps the Court decides the survivor can cash checks on Smith's account.) And from one point of view, this seems perfectly reasonable. But from Smith's point of view, it seems insane. Whether he should think of the survivor's pain as something he himself is to endure, and so can without impropriety fear, or should think of it in some other way, is not something to be decided by adopting a convention.

Perhaps any treatment of personal identity which admits of this sort of case must contain a fundamental mistake. But I do not think Locke's analysis is *fundamentally* mistaken. I wish in this paper, to put forward a theory of personal identity which is a descendant of the memory theories of Locke, Grice, and Quinton, and to show what kind of account *can* be built upon it, of the intense and special interest we have in our own futures. And then, in the light of this account, I shall remark on the case just described, as well as others.

II

The theory of personal identity I advocate is a descendant of the memory theories of Locke, Quinton,[7] Grice,[8] and others. A sophisticated version of such a theory might maintain that a sufficient and necessary condition of my having participated in a past event is that I am able to remember it, or that there be come event I am able to remember such that, at the time it occurred, the person to whom it happened could remember the event in question, or there be two events, such that at the time the first occurred, the person to whom it happened could remember the second, and the person to whom the second occurred could remember the event in question, or there be three events. . . .[9] I have argued elsewhere[10] that by adopting a causal theory of memory the advocate of such an account of personal identity can reply to the famous charge of circularity which Butler leveled against memory theories, but that he does so at the cost of making "the self" an inferred entity, a result contrary to the intentions of some of the memory theorists. That my present apparent memory of a past event stands at the end of a causal chain of a certain kind leading from that event is not something I can directly perceive, but something believed because it fits into the simplest theory of the world as a whole which is available to me. Moreover, once one has moved this far, it becomes attractive to simply adopt a *causal* theory. In such a theory, all the ways in which a person's past normally affects his future are built into the account and not simply the peculiarly discursive form of memory which preoccupied memory-theorists. Such a theory I now proceed to sketch.

By "human being" I shall mean merely "live human body." It is a purely biological notion. Thus, in a "brain transplant" operation, the *same human* being acquires a new set of memories and personality, whatever we say about the *persons* involved. We are all in possession of a great deal of information about how human beings may be expected to behave—to move, to think, to feel—in various circumstances. We know that if we ask a human being if he would like his toe stepped on, he will probably say "no"; that when deprived of food for a long time he will seek it; that shortly after observing something with care he will be able to recall what he observed, and so forth. Some of the things we know about human beings we also know about rocks: if either is dropped from a cliff, they will fall. But there are a large number of principles, which I shall call the "human-theory," which have no application to rocks, or any of the lower forms of life, and a great many of which seem to have application only to humans. The principles of the human-theory are not iron-clad rules; they are sprinkled with "probablys," and the theory as a whole is applied confidently only in relatively normal circumstances; there are many cases in which we have no idea what to expect from humans. It is, I shall say, "approximately valid."

Particular cases of human thought and action are explained by reference to the human-theory; but it is only human nature to suspect that what we may call the "approximate validity" of the human-theory itself has an explanation; that something about human beings, some relationship that a human's past states have to his present states, explain why the principles of human behavior to which we subscribe are as reliable as they are. In this inclination to have an explanation for the human-theory lies, I believe, the origin of our concept of a person.

Let us say that stages of a single human being are H-related. We can think of the human-theory as a theory about the effects earlier members of an H-related sequence have on the later members. But their being H-related does not explain the approximate validity of our principles concerning the effects earlier H-related stages have on the later. The human-theory tells us *how* humans may be expected to think and act; it does not tell us *why* humans do think and act that way. Our speculation is that there is an explanation; that H-related stages are, at least for the most part, related by some other relation (or at least by a relation that, for all we know, may not be the H-relation), and their being related by that other relation explains the effect of the earlier stages on the later. This new relation, under the description, the relation that explains (or, if known, would explain) the approximate validity of the principles about humans that we subscribe to, is my candidate for the analysis of personal identity. That is, it is the *unity relation* for persons, that relation which obtains between two stages if and only if there is a person of which both are stages.

I shall call this relation the P-relation. The entities that stand in the P-relation are stages of human-bodies, the very same entities that stand in the H-relation. (Although it might turn out that the P-relation, unlike the H-relation, can relate a human body stage to something other than another human body stage.) But there is nothing about the way we introduce the P-relation which makes it necessary that human-stages which stand in the P-relation invariably stand in the H-relation, or vice versa.

How would we identify the P-relation? It should satisfy the following conditions: (i) in normal circumstances, human-stages are P-related if and only if they are H-related; (ii) in abnormal circumstances, when we have H-related stages that are not P-related, the human-theory breaks down; (iii) in unusual cases, when we have P-related stages that are not H-related, the P-related stages exemplify relationships that human-theory leads us to expect normal circumstances of H-related stages. We might summarize these points by saying that the Person-theory—the set of principles we obtain by substituting "the P-relation" for "the H-relation" in the human theory—should be more accurate than the human theory. Finally (iv), the nature of the entities or processes involved in the relation should explain the kinds of events involved in the human theory.

A philosophical theory about the mind (that, for example, it is an immaterial substance, operating not by efficient, but by some other species of causality) will generate views about what the

P-relation turns out to be; but all, or at least many, such views would be compatible with the analysis of personal identity I have given. But if the assumptions about the role of the brain made by recent philosophers who discuss personal identity are correct, the relation of *having the same brain* is at least a promising candidate for the P-relation. For in normal circumstances, human-stages are H-related (are stages of the same body) just when they have the same brain. In abnormal cases, when we have H-related stages that do not have the same brain (e.g., Shoemaker's Robinson and Brownson), the human-theory breaks down (Brownson doesn't remember what Robinson carefully observed).[11] And in abnormal cases when we have stages with the same brain that are not H-related (Shoemaker's Brown and Brownson), relations are exhibited which are usually found in H-related stages (Brownson remembers what Brown carefully observed). And the nature of the human brain may account for the special kinds of events that humans participate in.

The advantages of this view are as follows:

1. As just pointed out it allows for the possibility that two human-body stages, which are not stages of the same human body may be, nevertheless, stages of the same person. This is the puzzling feature of the puzzle cases (Locke's cobbler and prince; Shoemaker's Brownson) which have played such an important role in philosophizing about personal identity. For all that our account requires is that there be a general correspondence between the H-relation and the P-relation; there is no reason that it might not turn out that stages could be related by P, which are not related by H. What we count as a case of this, will depend on what we take the relation P to be; if for example, we think that the nature of the human brain explains that which is characteristically human about human behavior, we will be likely to suppose that in the case of a brain-transplant, the relation P will obtain between the non-H-related stages that share a brain.

2. The account explains the importance of bodily identity. Bodily identity is neither a necessary nor a sufficient condition for a personal identity; but bodily identity is nevertheless importantly involved in our concept of personal identity. We know the P-relation only as the relation that explains the validity of the theory we have about how earlier and later stages of a single human body are related. The stable relation between persons and bodies is, in this

sense, not an accident although purely contingent; if the P-relation was not generally accompanied by, and causally related to, the H-relation, we would not have the concept of a person we do have.

3. This account explains the plausibility, and the limits, of attempts to analyze personal identity in terms of memory. The problems with memory-theories are, briefly, these: any theory which requires a continuous path of overlapping memories is too stringent; for personal identity is preserved in amnesia, and, for that matter, in sleep. This can be avoided by reference to possible memories—the memories the amnesiac person would have if he hadn't been conked on the head or the sleeper would have were he awake, etc. (as the theory mentioned previously did, in virtue of the phrase "is able to remember"). But to do so is to covertly bring in a causal requirement; for it is only in terms of causal counterfactuals that possible memories can be understood. But once we have introduced a causal relation as the principle of personal identity, there is no reason not to widen the kind of causal relationship required. The memory theory is plausible, because memory is one of the most important effects that the past of a human body has on its future.

4. Finally, this account puts the vagueness in our concept of a person in the right place. I believe there are conceivable cases in which we do not know what to say, or in which people of good will differ over what to say, even though they pretty much agree about the way human beings work. Many philosophers, who are perfectly willing to accept that the brain donor and the survivor in a "brain-*transplant*" operation (of the Shoemaker sort) are the same person, are not willing to say, in the brain rejuvenation case described in section I, that personal identity is preserved. This, I think, reflects the vagueness of "the relation which explains. . . ." There are a number of relations at different levels of abstraction, which fit the description of the P-relation: having the same brain; having brains with certain relationships (i.e., the relationships stages of the same brain usually have with one another), and so forth. The more abstract we take the relation to be, the more bizarre will be the circumstances in which we are able to say it holds. There may be several equally acceptable candidates, given the concept we actually have. If indeterminate cases become common, linguistic decisions will have to be made.

III

It may seem that whatever virtues this account may have in sorting out various real and imagined cases the way we more or less feel they should be, it shares with Locke's the defect noted by Butler. For why do I *care* so particularly and intensely about that future self that has the P-relation to my present self? And how could the appropriateness of the feelings in indeterminate cases be decided by linguistic decisions?

But I believe there is an explanation for its peculiar importance to us. I shall reconstruct the question of the interest we have in our own futures in this way: what reasons would we have for present action which would ensure future benefits for ourselves? Thus I shall phrase the question in terms of having a reason to act so as to promote or prevent my having a certain property in the future. To keep as many things constant as possible, I shall take the future time to be tomorrow, the property, *being in great pain*, and the present act that will prevent it, *pushing a button*. If I am told that by pushing a button I will prevent someone from being in great pain tomorrow, I will have a reason to push it. But intuitively, if the person is *me*, I will have more reason, or perhaps special reasons, for pushing it. What basis can the theory of personal identity sketched provide for this feeling?

A person has a reason for an act, if he wants some event to occur, and believes his performance of that act will promote the occurrence of that event. I shall call any events a person at a given moment wants to occur in the future his projects (at that moment). (I mean to use the words "events" quite broadly, to include processes, states, etc. And so my use of the word "project" is much wider than its ordinary use.) Assume I will be in pain unless I push the button. If I am not in pain tomorrow, I will contribute to the "success" of many of my projects: I will work on this article, help feed my children, and so forth. If I am in great pain, I will not do some of these things. Thus I have what I shall call "project-related" reasons for pushing the button.

It is a principle of the human-theory, that personality, values, character, and so forth change only gradually along sequences of H-related human-stages in normal conditions. And since the P-relation is that which explains the approximate validity of the human-theory, we expect the same of sequences of P-related human-stages, that is, persons. Our concept of a person does not require that no one, in any circumstances, undergo dramatic changes in personality and character. But the theory, in terms of which the concept of a person is introduced, maintains that this will be exceptional. That persons usually do not undergo such dramatic changes, is a straightforwardly contingent fact. But the statement, that they usually do not, is importantly connected with our concept of a person, for it is a condition of our having the concept of a person employed in the statement that the contingent fact it reports be a fact. The facts collected by the human-theory, and explained by the person-theory, need not have been so. But if they had not been so, we would not have the concept of a person we do.

In this sense, then, it is part of our concept of ourselves, as persons, that we are reliable. I expect to have tomorrow much the same desires, goals, loves, hates—in a word, projects—as I have today. There is, in the normal case, no one as likely to work on my article, love my children, vote for my candidates, pay my bills, and honor my promises, as me.

Thus, it is a consequence of the theory of personal identity that I have offered, that we probably have more reasons to push the button, when it is us who will be in pain, then when it is any other arbitrarily chosen person. (I say "arbitrarily chosen" because there may, of course, be *some* persons who are more essential to certain of our important projects than we ourselves.)

This goes, I think, some way to responding to Butler's demand.

IV

But, one feels, the sorts of reasons just adumbrated certainly do not exhaust the sorts of reasons I might have; indeed, they are not the crucial ones at all. I can imagine being told that someone a lot like me, perhaps even with delusions of being me, will want to do just what I want to do tomorrow, will make as much or more of a contribution to my projects as I will, and will be hit by a truck. I would feel sympathy, but not terror; I would not think of the event as happening to me. And surely, this is what is crucial.

Discussion of this requires introduction of the concept of *identification*. I shall say a person *identifies* with the participant in a past, future, or imaginary event, when he imagines perceiving the event from the perspective of the participant; that is, when he imagines seeing, hearing, smelling, tasting, feeling, thinking, remembering, and so on, what the person to whom the event happened did (or will or might) see, hear, smell, taste, feel, think, remember, and the like, as the event occurs. Identification is a matter of degree. I imagine seeing what Napoleon saw, and hearing what he heard while losing the battle of Waterloo; but I'm not up to imagining the smells, tastes, feelings, and memories. Perhaps I imagine having my own feelings and memories, or perhaps my imagining doesn't concern itself with feelings and memories.

When we remember events in our past, we do not always identify with the participant in those events; when we expect things to happen to us, we do not always identify with the participant in those future events. When we do so identify, the memory or expectation has more "impact" on us. As long as I think of tomorrow's pain as something that's going to happen to me, but refrain from imagining being in pain, I keep my equilibrium; but when I begin to imagine being in pain, I become fearful or terrified. Similarly, certain attitudes toward our own past, such as guilt, seem to arise with identification with the doer of the past misdeed.

If I am identifying with myself, feeling pain tomorrow, I am more likely to push the button, than if I am not. It is not, I suggest, that so identifying gives me additional *reasons* for pushing the button. Rather, it is a condition that makes it more likely that I will be motivated by the reasons I have. (Just as, although I am more likely to be motivated by my reasons for pushing the button if I am awake than if I am asleep, my being awake does not provide me with additional reasons for pushing the button.)

What is the relation between identification and personal identity?

Identity is not a necessary condition of identification. I can identify with the participant in events I did not do, will not do, and would not do, even if they were to be done. I can imagine losing the battle of Waterloo; I can imagine giving the 1978 inaugural address; I can imagine being hung in 1850 for stealing a horse. Nor is it necessary even to *believe*, or *imagine*, myself identical with the participant with whom I identify. Imagining myself to have won the battle of Waterloo does not involve the difficult feat of imagining the course of world history to be such that Napoleon and I are one. I cannot easily imagine a possible world in which one person is both Napoleon and John Perry. But it is quite easy to imagine winning the battle of Waterloo, that is, imagining having certain perceptions, thoughts, and so forth.[12]

Neither identity, nor the belief in identity, nor even the imagining of identity, is necessary for identification. What limits are there, on our ability to identify with participants in past and future events? Virtually none at all, insofar as the logic of the situation dictates.

Thus, the relation between identity and identification is not so intimate as one might have thought. But there are important relationships, which my theory of personal identity goes at least some way toward explaining.

I wish to consider two important questions. First, why are we so much more likely to identify with ourselves than with others? We are more likely, of course; that is why it is natural to borrow the cognate "identify" for the phenomenon in question. We might have expected this to be explained by logical constraints on identification, but I have denied that there are any. What then is the explanation? Second, why is our identification with our own "future selves" so likely to motivate us to act to prevent or promote the real occurrence of the imagined events, while our identification with others does not?

Let us suppose that there were beings, more or less like us, except that the above facts were not true of them. An individual of this species is no more likely to identify with, or be motivated to present action by identification with, his own future discomforts and pleasures, than those of others. In the first place, note these beings would be *significantly* different from us; that is, it is a part of the human-theory, and so the person-theory, that most of us are not like that. Thus, in this sense, these truths are connected with our concept of a person. Second, note that in a world anything like ours, such beings would have difficulties surviving. We are, by and large, in a *better* position to watch out for ourselves than others. If I am not motivated to feed this body by thoughts of future hunger, I may starve. In that sense, then, it is not an accident that we are as we are—that the human theory contains the principles about identification that it does. And this, again, is connected without concept of a person. For that I will in the future probably have *this* body, is a part of the person-theory.

These explanations may seem to be inappropriate to what is explained. One wants, perhaps, a necessary truth, a transcendental argument, a reflection of the innermost structure of reality, to get to the bottom of our intimate relation to our future self; I have offered only an empirical truth (which is, nevertheless, woven into our very concept of a person) and an evolutionary derivation of the facts explained. Butler would not have felt his demand met, I am sure. But I believe he would be wrong. My explanations explain and by theory of personal identity allows the explanation of why we are more or less assured to have a preponderance of reasons for acting in our own behalf, and strong motivation for acting on them. There is nothing left to explain.

V

But still, one may feel, what is essential in the matter has somehow been missed, been passed over. The discomfort may take the following form: that I will make a contribution to some project of mine if I am not in pain tomorrow, is perhaps a reason I might have for pushing the button. But it's the same sort of reason I might have for pushing the button to spare someone else pain. And, on the explanation given of identification, I might, without incoherence or conceptual impropriety, be motivated to spare another pain by identifying with him, in pain. So neither my reasons for my act, nor my motivation, are special and unique in the case where my act is selfish, where it is *me* who will feel the pain if I do not act. But surely, my reasons for acting in such a case are special. They are not the sort of reasons I can have for sparing someone else pain.

I believe that the claim that there are such special reasons can be expressed within the framework of projects, as consisting of either one or both of the following claims. (i) That there are some projects I might have, to which I will (or may) make a contribution that no one else could make; if so, my project-related reason for pushing the button to spare myself pain will be one I could not have for pushing it to spare someone else pain; (ii) further, that some of these projects are such that I will be in a position to make my special contribution, no matter what I am like tomorrow; my reason for pushing the button to spare myself pain will be one I will have, whatever I think I will be like tomorrow.

Now, to satisfy the first condition, the description of the project would simply have to include *my being in a certain state*, for there is a contribution to any such project only I can make—namely, existing, and being in that state. Such projects I shall call "private projects." And, to satisfy the second condition, the project merely needs to require my existence. We might call this "the ego-project" —I may want tomorrow's world to find me alive, whatever I may be like, whatever I may remember, whatever desires I may then have. It seems clear that many of us have the ego-project, and most of us dozens of other projects that satisfy the first condition. For example, I want not merely that this article be completed, but that it be completed by me.

What sorts of challenge do these "special reasons" pose for the account I am trying to construct? On the one hand, we might want an explanation of why we have such special reasons. On the other, we might want a justification. We feel that the desires that are a part of these special reasons are rational for us to have, and irrational for us not to have.

With regard to projects meeting the first condition, the responses to each of these demands are, for a way at least, coordinate. In the normal case, it will be reasonable to want not merely that my article be completed but that I complete it. For if I do not do so, but someone else does, that could only be because of a variety of catastrophes, which will leave other projects uncompleted, and this one, perhaps, ill completed. We may say, in this case, that I am *derivatively* justified in having the private project (that I finish the article) because I have the relevant nonprivate project (that the article be completed) and beliefs that if the nonprivate project is not contributed to by me, other of my nonprivate projects will fail. And that such desires are reasonable, is an explanation of why they occur. But as we move from the ordinary case to the metaphysical, what we can explain, and what we can justify, begin to diverge. Suppose I believe that not just my article, but everything I will do tomorrow, and for the rest of my life, will be done, and done as well, and done in just the same way, by someone else. Still, I want that I complete it, and not this benign imposter. The retention, in the metaphysical case, of the same sorts of desires, which are reasonable in the ordinary case, can be explained as habit; usually surviving is the only way to achieve a good part of what we want done, and it is natural that the desire, fostered in the real world, is not extinguished when we enter the fairyland of contemporary discussions of personal identity. And to this habit, we can add another; we identify usually with our own doings, and not those of others, however similar to us they may be. This habit too, ingrained in us as it is by the demands of evolution, and its utility for achieving our purposes in ordinary circumstances, stays with us even when contemplating the metaphysical example.

This will, I realize, leave many unsatisfied. They will maintain that, in contemplating the case of the benign imposter, it is not only to be expected, and natural, and only human that I should not feel I have just the reasons for pushing the button for him as I would for myself, but also that these reactions are completely justified. As long as it is not *me* who will do all of these things, I not only will not, in all probability, have the reasons, and the motivation, for sparing him pain I would have for myself, but should not; my desire, that it be I who finish the article, is not justified only in the normal circumstances, but even in the metaphysical.

I deny this.

The only justification for a private project that seems at all compelling to me is a derivative one: I have the relevant nonprivate project, and others as well, and believe that if it is not I who survives and contributes to the project in question, the others will not succeed.

Do I maintain that such unsupported private projects—those which remain, even as we move to the metaphysical case—are *irrational*? Not in the sense of being incoherent or self-contradictory. I am inclined to think they are irrational, in that sense analyzed by Brandt: they "would *not* survive...in the vivid awareness of knowable propositions."[13] But I do not wish to argue that here. My claim is simply that our having such private projects can be explained by what I take to be the correct theory of personal identity, as the result of habit, and the demands of evolution. But there is no justification for these projects, in the way one might have felt there clearly must be. It is not, I think at all irrational *not* to have them. The importance of identity is *derivative*. Apart from those other relationships it normally guarantees, it need be of no interest to us.

The position I advocate strikes many as quite implausible. Its plausibility may be enhanced by noticing how extreme a metaphysical case has to be, for the sort of derivative importance that I claim is all that personal identity has, to be completely absent. And two lines of argument are particularly important here.

First, in order for there to be no justification for private projects, it has not merely to be the case that there *will* be a benign imposter, ready, willing, and able to do what I will do if I survive, but also that I believe it, and that my belief be justified. That X will finish my article tomorrow gives me a reason for pushing the button to spare him pain, only if I believe that he will. And I will not have as strong a reason to spare my benign duplicate pain, as I do myself, unless I believe it is as likely that he will do what I want done as it is that I would, were I to survive. And my reason, for pushing the button for him, will only be as reasonable as my reason for pushing it for myself would be, if my belief about what he will do, is as justified as my beliefs about what I will do usually are. But if he is to be created by accident, or supernatural chicanery, it is difficult to see how these conditions could be met.

A second consideration requires some preliminary remarks. The properties that a person has at a given time can be divided into those he has just in virtue of events occurring at that time, and those which he has in part in virtue of events occurring at other times. For example, I could not now have the property of sitting in a forty-year-old house, unless some houses had been built forty years ago. If they had not been built, nothing I or anyone else could do now could make it true that I now have this property. And, for some such properties, the past events must have happened to *me*. I could not now have the property of having been born a certain number of years ago, unless, that many years ago, I had been born. And, finally, some of the properties that are now mine are so in virtue of my having a relation to past events no one else has. Since these events are in the past, no one else can ever be so related to them. Tomorrow, anyone could have the property of believing he worked on this article today. But only I can have the property of truly believing that I worked on this article today.

There are certain properties, which, given the history of the world until today, no one but me can have tomorrow. These are properties, that, if a person has them tomorrow, he has them partly in virtue of having the P-relation to one of my person-stages. But then he is me.

Suppose I am writing an autobiography. Tomorrow I plan to write the sentence, "And Fido died." I desire not just that the sentence be written, but that I write it. And I desire that I write it, in part because I want the event in question reported by someone who remembers it, and, given that I am the only one who observed the event, no one else but me can do that. This is a property, then, which I wish the contributor to this particular project to have. Having this property does not, in and of itself, require being me; anyone could have watched Fido die. But given the contingent fact that only I did, no one but me can have this property.

This possibility might be used to argue that the theory of personal identity in question can, after all, justify private projects. For surely, one's devotion to accuracy, to honesty, to truth-telling, to freedom from illusion, and the like, themselves constitute projects, and these might impose constraints on who is to say the things I want said, write the things I want written, and so forth, which only I could satisfy. My duplicate, however benign, will be deluded, claiming to be who he is not, saying he did things he did not do.

But this will not quite do. For the question of the importance of personal identity must simply emerge as a question about the importance of the properties that require it. Why is it important, for example, that people say they did only what they did? Perhaps because of the unfortunate nature of the ordinary consequences and causes of saying one did what one did not do. But in the case of the benign imposter these ordinary implications may be absent: he may be honest, and what he says, may never mislead anyone. Perhaps because the act of saying one did what he did not do has some other property. But then we need to be assured that this property attaches to just the act in question, and not any of the other sorts of acts that a person would normally be performing when he says he did what he did not do, but which the benign imposter would not be performing (such as lying, being intentionally misleading, and so forth).

But, in terms of showing the conditions a case of the benign duplicate must meet, in order to cancel all the special but derivative reasons I might have for preferring my own survival, this line of argument does get us somewhere.

These consideratons, I think, suggest that such a case will have to be one in which the explanation of the benign duplicate's being like me, is that he was produced "from me," by a process I know to be reliable. By saying "from me," I mean that my being in the states I am in, is a part of the explanation of his being in the states he will be in. And by a reliable process, I mean one which, as reliably as the natural processes involved in aging another minute or another day, preserve accurate information. In short, the duplicate's initial stages will have to be related to mine by a reliable causal relation—and this means the relation will be not the same as, but will be of the same "species" as, the P-relation.

So my theory can justify the difference we feel between surviving and being replaced, where the replacement is incomplete or accidental or unsure. And it can explain the difference we feel, in any case.

But suppose the following. A team of scientists develop a procedure whereby, given about a month's worth of interviews and tests, the use of a huge computer, a few selected particles of tissue, and a little time, they can produce a human being as like any given human as desired. I am a member of the team, have complete (and justified) confidence in the process and the discretion of my colleagues, and I have an incurable disease. It is proposed that I be interviewed, tested, and painlessly disposed of; that a duplicate be created, in secret, and simply take over my life. Everyone, except my colleagues, will think he is me (the duplicate himself will not know; he is made unlike I would be, only in not remembering the planning of this project), and my colleagues, who have all studied and been convinced by this article, will treat him as me, feeling that the fact that he is not is, in this case, quite unimportant.

He would not be me. The relation between my terminal and his initial states is too unlike the P-relation to be counted, even given the vagueness of the concept of a person, as an instance of it. But on my account, I would have the very same legitimate reasons to act now so as to secure for him future benefits as I would if he were me.

I believe that this is not a defect to be charged to my account, but an insight to be gained from it.

VI

What then, of the *ego-project*? Suppose I believe that tomorrow I will be struck by amnesia incurable in fact, though not in principle; that my character and personality will suddenly change, so I will hate what I now love, and work against what I now hope for. If the person I am to be were not me, I would have no reason at all to push the button and spare him pain, except those that derive merely from his being a sentient being. What additional reasons am I given, by the fact that it is me?

The common feeling that we do have an additional reason seems to me clearly not accounted for my my analysis in any direct way. That is, the fact that I do especially care about this fellow, is not made clear when I see that his being me consists in his stages having the P-relation to mine. It's quite the other way around; believing that his stages had the P-relation to mine produces concern only when and because I realize that if *that's* so, then he is me.

But, as before, it can be explained, in terms of habit. We take identity always to be a good reason for care and concern, because usually it is.

At this point, one may be inclined to speak of the "ineffable me-ness" of the fellow which would survive any change, and which is the real object of our concern. But this ineffable me-ness, when it is not the remnant of a bad theory of personal identity, is simply the shadow of the enormous contribution that we are in the habit of expecting ourselves to make to the projects we have.

VII

My central claim is that the importance of identity is *derivative*. In ordinary cases, identity will guarantee innumerable special relationships. Particularly important, I will in all probability be assured that the person who is me will be a major contributor to my projects, and I will find it difficult to avoid identifying (in my technical sense) with him. Any of these relationships I could have to someone else. But it is incredibly unlikely that I should have all of them I will have to myself, to anyone else. And all of this is, in a sense, no accident, for it is a part of the human-theory that H-related stages have these special relationships in ordinary circumstances, and the P-relation is that relation which explains this. That these special relationships will probably obtain, is part of our concept of a person.

It should now be clear what to say to Smith, whom we left, unsure of his feelings in section I. Smith is about to undergo a brain rejuvenation, with his survival uncertain, not for medical but for conceptual reasons.

Smith should go ahead and be fearful of the painful convalescence, whether or not he is to survive. His survival is a question for linguistic decision or linguistic evolution to take care of. We may think of our concept of personal identity as designed to meet many conditions. In cases like Smith's various of these considerations pull us in different ways. By saying that Smith survives, we keep the intimate connection between identity and that complex of special relationships it guarantees in the normal case. But the more abstract relation we would thereby be choosing for our unity relation for persons does not have the empirical guarantee of transitivity that normal maturation does, and such consideration as this may pull in the other direction.[14]

But for Smith, such subtleties are irrelevant. He can expect to have as tight of a web of special relationships to the survivor of the operation as personal identity in its purest form could provide. And this, I think, is all that need matter to him.

I believe my account may also shed some light on an example discussed by two recent writers on personal identity: Methuselah.

David Lewis[15] and Derek Parfit[16] have recently claimed that "what matters" in survival is not present in the case of Methuselah; since (as they assume) Methuselah at 930 will have no memories of Methuselah at 27, Methuselah at 27 should not consider his living to 930 to be survival. Parfit takes this to show that there can be *identity without survival*; Lewis wants to say that each 137-year stretch of Methuselah is a separate person (137 years, Lewis imagines, is the time it takes memory to completely fade). According to Lewis, when Methuselah celebrates his 300th birthday in his room alone, there are really "continuum-many" persons in the room.

Lewis's view, and perhaps Parfit's too, result from confusing two senses of "what matters in survival." The insight is that *what is of importance* in survival, need not occur in every case of survival, or of identity. Thus, identity is not "what matters" in survival. But by "what matters in survival" we might also mean "what makes a case of survival a case of survival." I think the view that Methuselah is a case of identity without survival, or that (in order to insure the common-sense equivalence of identity and survival) we must reckon there to be "continuum-many" Methuselahs, result from confusing these two senses.

It seems to me that my analysis illuminates all of this. When I said that the human-theory tells us the stages of the same body are likely to have the "special relations" to one another, and likely to identify with one another, I oversimplified. For it will tell us (or would, if what Lewis imagines about memory were true) that under certain circumstances this is not to be expected at all, and one such circumstance is that of human-body stages that, though stages of the same body, are separated by 900 years. That is to say, our concept of the P-relation is not just of a relation that explains why various special relations, such as sharing of projects and identification, are likely to obtain among H-related human-body stages, but also why, in certain circumstances, they cannot be expected to obtain.

We expect then, that Methuselah at 27 will not find it easy to identify with Methuselah at 930. He won't expect Methuselah at 930 to have much in common with him. He won't have many special reasons to care about the old man he is to be, as much motivation to act on them. Does he have any special reason, say, to refrain from smoking, knowing that if he does, it's quite likely that by 930, he will have lung cancer? Perhaps, for he alone, by refraining now, can help the old man's health. But this is more like the obligation I have to an office-mate, with whom I have little in common, not to blow smoke in his face than the special and intimate concern I have for myself. There are a lot of reasons we ordinarily have for concern for our future that Methuselah at 27 doesn't have in thinking about life at 930. Enough, I think, to vindicate the opinion that it's quite possible that "what matters" in survival does not occur in the case of Methuselah's survival to 930.

I agree with some of Parfit's central claims in "Personal

Identity." But I think one of the claims, or suggestions, which Parfit makes, has little merit. Having recognized the importance of the various special relationships, and the only derivative importance of identity, should we adopt, as Parfit proposes, a "new way of thinking," which (as I reconstruct it) involves taking the special relations *themselves* to replace the P-relation as our unity relation for persons?

This would guarantee that "what matters in survival" in the first sense mentioned previously, is just what matters in the second. I mentioned one problem with this early in this section, with regard to Smith's brain rejuvenation. Further objections are as follows:

Although Parfit describes this as giving up the language of identity, it really amounts to trading talk of one kind of object, persons (P-related sums of human body-stages, perhaps), for another, lets call them "Parfit-persons," which are S-related sums of human-body stages, where S is the complex of special relationships which "matter" in the second sense, in personal identity. There will be identity among the new objects as much as among the old. As long as one has predication, one will have identity; one merely needs to look and see under what conditions sentences ascribing past or future states to a presently existing Parfit-person are reckoned as true, to find out what kind of objects these are.

Parfit does not tell us enough about the rules of predication involved in his "way of thinking" for us to determine exactly what Parfit-persons will be. They are not to be, I think, just Lewis-persons—the objects Lewis found continuum-many of at Methuselah's birthday party. But of both Lewis-persons and Parfit-persons, I think it is clear that it's much easier and simpler to talk about persons. The reasons for dropping talk about persons for talk about Lewis-persons or Parfit-persons will have to be enormously strong.

Notice, for example, that certain simplifying assumptions Lewis makes are pretty dubious. There are going to be no general truths about how long it takes memory to fade out, or personality structure to undergo basic changes; this will vary from person to person and situation to situation. So rather than counting 137-year stretches as Lewis-persons, we will have to make a separate determination in every case. Many of us undergo quite dramatic changes without taking 930 years to do it; others of us, I suspect, might actually make it through 930 years without many dramatic changes occurring.

Moreover, there is no reason to assume Lewis-persons or Parfit-persons will be composed of temporally continuous stages. In the amnesia case, with later recovery, they would have to be reckoned as ceasing to exist for a time (for there is no one around during the period of amnesia with special relations to the pre-amnesiac), and then coming back into existence with his recovery.

Perhaps such numerous and ill-behaved entities would be worth talking about, if our ordinary concept of a person locks us into various misconceptions. Parfit thinks it does. He maintains, I think insightfully, that the principle of self-interest is not especially compelling: "there is no special problem in the fact that what we ought to do can be against our interests. There is only the general problem that it may not be what we want to do." And he thinks that the compellingness of the principle of self-interest, and other misconceptions, is rooted in our concept of personal identity.

I think there is a point here. As I observed, identity comes by habit to be regarded as in and of itself a reason for special care and concern, even when it does not, or is not likely to, support the various special relationships which naturally give rise to this special concern. This habit has social importance, and is reinforced: we teach prudence, and saving for old age, even among those who don't particularly like old people. Philosophers do their part here. Thus we find even the admirable Sidgwick saying, "my feelings a year hence should be just as important to me as my feelings next minute, if only I could make an equally sure forecast of them. Indeed this equal and impartial concern for all parts of one's conscious life is perhaps the most prominent element in the common notion of the *rational*—as opposed to the merely *impulsive*—pursuits of pleasure."[17]

But dropping the concept of a person would be neither necessary nor sufficient for removing these misconceptions. Not necessary, because we can explain the true importance of identity, and the true rationale of self-interest, without jettisoning the concept of a person. Not sufficient, for the P-relation, as our only reasonable guarantee of the S-relation, is too important to be ignored; the concept of a person forces itself upon us.

Moreover, the habit of taking identity in itself, without consideration of whether the special relations will or won't obtain, has good effects as well as bad. There are characteristically human projects, such as settling on a long-range plan, or dedicating one's life to a goal, or making a promise, that depend on it. Let us say that a person's life is integrated, to the extent that his various stages are S-related. The habit of taking identity itself as a reason for special concern, promotes as well as reflects integration, for the sorts of long-range commitments and projects this habit makes possible, are themselves the source of the continuity of character and personality and values that constitute integration.

And, finally, a remark that perhaps applies as much to what I have said so far as to Parfit. It would be wrong, however tempting, to take one's concern for his present self as a given, capable of shedding light on his concern for his earlier and later selves, but not requiring and not capable of the same sorts of explanation itself. "My present self," that is, the currently existing person-stage belonging to me, far from being the immediate object of my concern, is an object that may answer only to a rather abstract conception we have when doing philosophy (but no less an object for that). It is an object, moreover, which if taken to exist "instantaneously," or even over a very short interval, cannot, for conceptual reasons, suggested in the remarks in section V, have many of the properties that make persons interesting. In a well-developed account of the concept of a person, of which the present essay is but a sketch of a part, concern for oneself generally would, I think, be explained in terms of the concepts of a project and of identification, and there would be room for a version of the claim that our concept of a person enjoys one sort of primacy, which excessive concentration on person-stages may, and no doubt in this essay does, obscure.[18]

NOTES

1. John Locke, *An Essay Concerning Human Understanding*, Book II, chap. 27, sect. 11 ff.

2. Joseph Butler, "Of Personal Identity," a dissertation attached to *The Analogy of Religion*. The quote is from the Everyman edition (London; Dent, 1906), p. 257.

3. Ibid., pp. 260 ff. Italics added.

4. Butler thought that because Locke did not require identity of substance for personal identity, and took the inquiry into the identity of vegetables to be rele-

vant to the discussion of personal identity, it was clear that Locke was not using "same" in a "strict and philosophical manner of speech" (p. 259). Thus, on Locke's theory, we are not, in this strict sense, identical with ourselves tomorrow, not to mention ourselves in the hereafter.

5. Bernard Williams, "The Self and the Future," *Philosophical Review*, LXXIX, 2 (April 1970), 178. Williams mounts a subtle and ingenious attack on memory theories of personal identity, whose theme is reminiscent of Butler's.

6. John Perry, "Can the Self Divide?" *Journal of Philosophy*, LXIX, 16 (September 7, 1972), 463-488.

7. Anthony Quinton, "The Soul," *Journal of Philosophy*, LIX, 15 (July 19, 1962), 393-409.

8. H. P. Grice, "Personal Identity," *Mind*, L, 200 (October 1941), 330-350.

9. This approximates one of Grice's preliminary versions, and is less flexible than his final proposal.

10. John Perry, "Personal Identity, Memory, and the Problem of Circularity," in John Perry, ed., *Personal Identity* (Berkeley, Los Angeles, London: University of California Press, 1975).

11. See Sydney Shoemaker, *Self-Knowledge and Self-Identity* (Ithaca: Cornell University Press, 1963), p. 23: "Two men, a Mr. Brown and a Mr. Robinson, had been operated on for brain tumors, and brain extractions had been performed on both of them. At the end of the operations, however, the assistant inadvertently put Brown's brain in Robinson's head, and Robinson's brain in Brown's head. One of the men immediately died, but the other, the one with Robinson's body and Brown's brain, eventually regained consciousness. Let us call the latter 'Brownson.'"

12. See Bernard Williams, "Imagination and the Self," (London: British Academy, 1966), particularly pp. 118 ff.

13. Richard Brandt, "Rational Desires," *Proceedings and Addresses of the American Philosophical Association*, XLII (1969-70), 46.

14. See "Can the Self Divide?" Section VII.

15. David Lewis, "Survival and Identity," chap. I in this volume.

16. Derek Parfit, "Personal Identity," *Philosophical Review*, LXXX, 1 (January 1971), 3-27. Parfit actually discusses beings that *never* die.

17. Sidgwick, *Methods of Ethics* (London, 1907), p. 124.

18. Versions of this paper were read at the University of California, Los Angeles; the North Carolina Colloquium; California State University at Northridge, and the University of Minnesota. In each case, the version emerged scathed and the paper improved. I am especially grateful to Marilyn Adams, Robert Merrihew Adams, Tyler Burge, Keith Donnellan, Sharon Hill, Tom Hill, Greg Kavka, and Peter McAllen for detailed comments on the penultimate draft, and to John Bennett, Terence Leichti, Derek Parfit, and Michael Tooley for fruitful discussions on this topic.

LEWIS, PERRY, AND WHAT MATTERS

DEREK PARFIT

'We can agree with Parfit', Lewis writes, '. . . that what matters in questions of personal identity is mental continuity or connectedness. . . . At the same time we can consistently agree with common sense. . . that what matters in questions of personal identity is identity' (p. 19).[1] Despite the great resourcefulness of Lewis's paper, I still believe that this cannot be done. I shall first explain why, then suggest what this might show, and end with some remarks about Perry's paper.

I

Though the case of Methuselah is more important, it will be easier to discuss the case of division. This case seems to involve three people: the original person, and two resulting people. If we decide that the resulting people are indeed, as they seem to be, two people, we cannot claim that each of them *is* the original person. But we may conclude that 'the relation of the original person to each of the resulting people. . .contains. . .all that matters. . .in any ordinary case of survival.'[2] If this is so—if this relation does contain all that matters, but is not identity—then what matters cannot be identity.

Lewis redescribes the case. He suggests that it involves two partially overlapping continuant persons who share their initial stages (p. 25).[3] The shared stage before the division Lewis calls 'S'; the two later stages 'S_1' and 'S_2'. The 'two. . .continuant persons' are 'C_1', who consists of S and S_1, and 'C_2', who consists of S and S_2. Lewis also calls mental continuity and connectedness 'the R-relation'.

Suppose we are discussing this case *before* the division. Let us first ask, 'Is C_1's present stage R-related to the future stage of C_2?'

It might be objected that, before the division, we should not refer to 'C_1'. Lewis claims that, when we are discussing people before a certain time, we should count them by the relation of identity-up-to-that-time. If we count in this way, we shall not now distinguish C_1 and C_2; we shall instead say that there is only one person who is going to divide. But this 'one person... is really two non-identical persons' (p. 28). While it may be 'harmless' to talk of the two people *as* one when they 'are indiscernible in the respects we want to talk about', Lewis admits that even 'before the fission... predictions need disambiguating' (p. 29). And if we can guess, now, that it is C_1 and not C_2 who is 'the next winner of the State Lottery', we can surely ask, 'Is C_1's present stage R-related to the future stage of C_2?'[4]

The answer must be, 'Yes'. C_1's present stage is the stage S; C_2's future stage is S_2; and, as Lewis writes, S is R-related to S_2 (p. 25).

We can now question the thesis of Lewis's paper. Can it be true, as he claims, *both* that 'what matters to survival' is identity, *and* that what matters to survival is the R-relation? We have just seen that C_1's present stage stands to C_2's future stage in the R-relation. On the thesis, this relation is what matters. But if C_1 now stands in the relation that matters to *someone else* in the future, how can this relation be identity?

Lewis has an ingenious reply. The R-relation holds between stages, so of course it cannot *be* the relation of identity. But it may *correspond* to identity—it may be the relation between stages which corresponds to the fact that they are stages of the same person. If it were, the R-relation would in this way coincide with identity: all and only stages which are R-interrelated would be stages of the same person. This coincidence, Lewis thinks, would preserve the view that the R-relation and identity are *both* 'what matters to survival.'

Lewis puts this point in another way. The relation which corresponds to identity—'the relation that holds between the several stages of a single continuant person'—he calls 'the I-relation' (p. 21). He then claims that the R-relation *is* the I-relation.

Turning to the case of division, Lewis would say: 'C_1's present stage is, as you point out, R-related to C_2's future stage. S, that is, is R-related to S_2. But S is also *I*-related to S_2; these are both stages of the same person. So the R-relation and identity still coincide.'

Will this do? C_1's present stage and the future stage S_2 are indeed stages of the same person; they are both stages of C_2. But isn't this the *wrong* person?

According to one half of Lewis's thesis, the R-relation is what matters in survival. So if there are future stages R-related to *my* present stage, they stand to my present stage in the relation that matters in survival. *Whose* survival? Obviously, *mine*. (When Lewis writes, 'what matters is mental. . .continuity between *my* present mental state and other mental states', he must mean 'what matters in *my* survival. . .' [p. 18, my italics].) The first half of the thesis must, then, involve the following claim: if there are future stages R-related to any person's present stage, this is what matters in *this* person's survival.

This half of the thesis is what Lewis calls the 'interesting philosophical. . .answer' to the question of what matters. The other half is the 'unhelpful. . .common-sense answer'. This runs: 'what matters. . .is identity—identity between the I who exists now and the surviving I who will. . .exist then' (p. 18). Just as obviously, this involves the following claim: future stages stand to any person's present stage in the relation that matters in *this* person's survival if, and only if, they are future stages of *this* person.

Let us apply this to the case of division. S_2 is R-related to C_1's present stage; so, by the first half of the thesis, S_2 stands to C_1 now in the relation that matters in C_1's survival. To reconcile this with his second claim, that what matters is identity, Lewis need not show that S_2 and C_1's present stage are themselves identical. But he must show that they are both stages of C_1. It is not enough to show that they are both stages of *someone else*. This is not enough even if this someone else—C_2—shares his present stage with C_1. 'Sharing a present stage with' is of course a peculiarly close relation; but it is not identity—and to Lewis 'what matters. . .is literally *identity*: that relation that everything bears to itself and to no other thing.' (p. 20).

More briefly: By the first half of Lewis's thesis, S_2 stands to C_1's present stage in the relation that matters in C_1's survival. The second half of the thesis therefore requires that S_2 be a stage of C_1. It is not. So the case of division seems a counter-example to the thesis.

Why does Lewis think otherwise? The crucial passage runs:

It is pointless to compare the formal character of identity itself with the formal character of the relation R that matters in survival. Of course the R-relation among stages is not the same as identity either among stages or among continuants. But identity among continuant persons induces a relation among stages: the relation that holds between the several stages of a single continuant person. Call this the *I-relation*. It is the I-relation, not identity itself, that we must compare with the R-relation. In wondering whether you will survive the battle, we said, you wonder whether the continuant person that includes your present stage is identical with any of the continuant persons that continue beyond the battle. In other words: whether it is identical with any of the continuant persons that include stages after the battle. In other words: you wonder whether any of the stages that will exist afterwards is I-related to—belongs to the same person as—your present stage (p. 21).

In this passage Lewis treats the question, 'Will a certain person have a certain future stage?', as equivalent to the question, 'Is that future stage I-related to this person's present stage?' Let us call this 'the First Equivalence'.

If we accept this Equivalence, the account of division collapses. Both the later stages are I-related to the first stage of both the continuant people, so on the Equivalence they are both stages of both people. Lewis, then, must reject this Equivalence. In effect, he later does so. It is only after the quoted passage that he introduces the possibility that people might share stages. If we wish to allow for this possibility, much of the quoted passage needs to be revised, as does the assumed Equivalence.[5]

We can now return to the thesis of Lewis's paper—to the claim that the relation which matters in survival is both the R-relation and identity. This claim obviously requires that these two relations coincide. (If the two relations could diverge, they could not each be 'what matters'; each could at most be 'part of what matters'.) But there are two ways in which they could coincide. It may be true

(1) that all and only stages which are R-interrelated are stages of the same person—are, that is, I-related,
or it may be true

(2) that, for any stage of any person, all and only stages R-related to this stage are stages of this same person.

What I argued earlier was this. Lewis's thesis requires the truth of (2). The claim that the R-relation is what matters in survival must involve the claim that what matters in *my* survival is that future stages be R-related to *my* present stage. Only if these future stages are stages of *me*, as (2) requires, can we also claim that it is identity which is what matters. Lewis's account of division does not satisfy requirement (2). S_2 is R-related to C_1's first stage, but is not a stage of C_1. So his thesis cannot be maintained.

Lewis thinks it can. He believes that his thesis only requires the truth of (1). ('It is the I-relation', he writes, 'not identity itself, that we must compare with the R-relation.') And his account of division satisfies requirement (1); on the account, as he remarks, 'the I-relation and the R-relation coincide' (p. 25).

We can now suggest why Lewis only sets himself requirement (1). In the passage where he does so (quoted above) he assumes the First Equivalence. He assumes, that is, that all and only stages I-related to any stage of any person are stages of this same person. Naturally, on this assumption, it will seem enough to require (1), for on this assumption (1) and (2) are the *same* requirement, in different words. To require (1) is to require that all and only stages R-related to any stage of any person are I-related to this stage; and all such stages are, on the First Equivalence, stages of this same person, as required by (2).

In sum: if we accept the First Equivalence, Lewis only needs to show, as he can, that his account of division satisfies requirement (1); but on the First Equivalence the account collapses. The account is coherent only if we reject this Equivalence; but if we do, Lewis needs to show that the account satisfies requirement (2), which he cannot do.[6]

Could a different account satisfy the requirement? The main feature of Lewis's account is the suggestion that what seemed, before the division, to be one person, 'is really two non-identical persons.' In the paper he discusses, I had made—but rejected—a similar suggestion. This ran: 'We might say, "What we have called 'the two resulting people' are not two people. They are one person" '.[7] Lewis's two people start with a single body and a single mind; my one person ends with two bodies and a divided mind.

Both suggestions make us count people in a strange way. But there is a difference. My rejected suggestion treats what appear to be two people as one, but at least these two people are not just like any ordinary pair of different people. They seem to remember living the same past life, they have the same character, and so on. Lewis's suggestion treats what appears to be one person as two, and in contrast this one person is just like any ordinary single person. We are to claim that he is really two people, not because of what he is like now, but only because of what will happen later. (Here is a parallel. We might claim that East and West Germany are not two different nations, but one nation with two territories and two governments. This is like my suggestion. We might instead claim that East and West Germany were different nations even before 1945. This is like Lewis's suggestion.)

Apart from this difference, the two suggestions are analogous. So we should expect that if Lewis's account does not satisfy requirement (2), nor would mine. This is so—for S_1 and S_2 are on my (rejected) account stages of the same person without being R-related, which violates (2).

I had also sketched—and rejected—a third account. According to this, we claim that the two resulting people *are* the original person—not that each of them is this person, but that they together are this person. They compose the original person, just as the Pope's crown is composed of three crowns.[8] If we adopted this account, we should have to decide whether stages of the component people are also stages of the composite person. If they are, then S_1 and S_2 are again stages of the same (composite) person without being R-related, which violates (2); if they are not, then S and S_1 are R-related, but are not stages of the same person, again violating (2).

Our accounts so far take division to involve: a single person, a duo, and a trio. We could doubtless conjure up a quartet. But it would be tedious to consider more accounts—it seems safe to assume that none could satisfy (2). If so, the case of division remains a counter-example to Lewis's thesis. However we describe the case, the R-relation and identity fail to coincide—so they cannot *each* be 'what matters in survival'.

II

What conclusion should we draw? The immediate conclusion is that 'the interesting philosophical thesis'—that what matters is the

R-relation—and 'the platitude of common sense'—that what matters is identity—cannot both be right. We must choose between them.

Lewis has no doubt which we ought to choose. 'If the two... disagreed', he writes, 'we would have to prefer the platitude of common sense.... Else it would be difficult to believe one's own philosophy!' (p. 18). I am equally sure that we both can and ought to prefer the philosophical thesis. But this requires a great deal of argument, none of which I can give here.

What I shall do is assume the argument, and sketch two of the further conclusions that we might draw. One of these is that common sense has a false view about the nature of personal identity. But it will be simpler to start with a more direct conclusion.

We have seen that identity and the R-relation cannot *each* be 'what matters in survival'. Suppose we are convinced, by the argument assumed above, that what matters is the R-relation. Then, says Lewis, our conclusion would be this: 'What matters in survival is not identity. At most what matters is a relation that coincides with identity to the extent that the problem cases do not actually arise' (p. 19).

This seems to me misleading. Very few of the problem cases do arise. In almost every actual case, questions about personal identity have definite answers. But even in actual cases it is still not true that what matters *fully* coincides with identity. We have been considering one difference between identity and the R-relation— that, while identity is one-one, we can imagine cases where the R-relation takes a branching form. There is a more important difference. 'Identity', as Lewis writes, '... cannot be a matter of degree' (p. 32),[9] but the R-relation, even in actual cases, holds to different degrees.

Lewis understates this second difference. He suggests that it is only 'in principle' that 'the R-relation admits... of degree' (p. 24). The reason that he writes 'in principle' is that he is thinking only about 'problem cases'—cases where, in his words, the R-relation holds 'to a degree so slight that survival is questionable' (p. 19). In actual lives the weakening of the R-relation very seldom goes so far. That is why Lewis invokes Methuselah. But it is still true that between the parts of actual lives the R-relation holds to different degrees.[10]

We must remember here that the R-relation has two components: continuity and connectedness. To distinguish these, we first need the notion of a 'direct' psychological relation. Such relations hold between: the memory of an experience and this experience, the intention to perform some later action and this action, and different expressions of some lasting character-trait. We can now define 'connectedness' as the holding, over time, of particular 'direct' relations, and 'continuity' as the holding of an overlapping chain of such relations. For 'continuity', each 'link' in the chain must have a certain strength—must include enough direct relations. With the help of this requirement, we can define 'continuity' so that it has no degrees: if there is a chain of the required strength, it holds, if there is not, it does not. 'Connectedness', in contrast, has degrees. Between the different parts of a person's life the various direct relations—of memory, character, intention, and the like—are (in strength and number) more and less.

We can now return to the R-relation. Since one of its components holds, in actual lives, to different degrees, so too does the R-relation. This is why it makes a difference if it is the R-relation, not identity, which is what matters. For this will mean that even in actual lives there is this discrepancy: identity is all-or-nothing, what matters has degrees.

This discrepancy has various implications. One of these is hinted at in a remark of Lewis's. 'If you wonder', he writes, 'whether it is in your self-interest to save for your old age, you wonder whether the stages of that tiresome old gaffer you will become are R-related to you-now to a significantly greater degree than are the other person-stages at this time or other times' (p. 21). To this particular question the answer is always 'Yes'. The R-relation between you now and yourself in old age is always significantly stronger than the R-relation between you now and other people—for, as things are, there is *no* R-relation in this latter case. But it is also true that the R-relation between you now and yourself in old age is significantly *weaker* than the R-relation between you now and yourself in the nearer future. This is the fact which bears upon the question of self-interest.

The bearing is oblique. This fact cannot support the claim that it is any *less* in your self-interest to save for your old age. The notion of self-interest requires that equal weight be granted to all the parts of a person's life—that the interests of his distant future count for as much as those of his near future. Nor can we criticise this feature of the notion by appealing to the fact that the R-relation has degrees. The R-relation holds between a person *at one time* and himself *at another time*, but the notion of self-interest is only relative to a person, not to a person at a time. When we ask if it is in *my* self-interest to save for my old age, we can ignore the R-relatedness of my old age to me now, for we are not asking about the interests of *me now*.

Though the notion of self-interest cannot be challenged by an appeal to the weakening of the R-relation, its importance can be. Many accounts of what it is rational to do give a central place to what is in the agent's interest. If what matters in survival is the R-relation, these accounts need to be revised. Since the R-relation holds between person-stages, we need a substitute for the notion of self-interest which is relative not only to a person but also to a time. It would be barbarous to speak of the interests of *me now*. But just as we speak of what is best from my point of view as opposed to other people's, so we could speak of what is best from my present point of view as opposed to my point of view at other times. This notion can be developed in various ways, and there are various grounds for giving it a central place in accounts of rationality.[11] But the fact we are discussing here, the weakening of the R-relation, seems to have at least the following significance. Most of us care less about our own more distant future simply because it is more distant; we have a 'discount rate' with respect to time itself. Some of us, though, have a discount rate with respect to the weakening of the R-relation. We care less about our further future, not because it is further, but because we know that less of what we are now—less, say, of our present hopes or plans, loves or ideals—will survive into the further future. We may, because of this, act knowingly against our own long-term self-interest. To act in this way, on these grounds, would be widely thought irrational. We should be told, 'Your further future is as much a part of your future.'[12] We could now reply: 'True—but since what matters is the R-relation, not personal identity, this fact is irrelevant. Where what matters holds to a lesser degree, it cannot be irrational to care less. My further future is less strongly R-related to me now; so it cannot be irrational for me now to grant it less weight.'[13]

This reply rests on the claim that what matters has degrees. This claim has, I think, various other implications, both for morality, and for the justification of certain attitudes and emotions.[14] If we are convinced by the argument assumed above, we may come to accept a second claim, which in turn seems to have further implications. We may decide that what matters is 'less deep'—or 'involves less'—than common sense believes. We may decide that common sense thinks there is more to personal identity than, in fact, there is. We are back to the conclusion mentioned earlier: that common sense has a false view about the nature of personal identity.

This conclusion seems to be supported by our reactions to the 'problem' cases. For example: suppose we are persuaded that Lewis's thesis cannot be maintained—that the R-relation and identity cannot each be what matters. Suppose we are then presented with the argument assumed above, the argument to show that what matters is the R-relation. We may now reject this argument. We may say: 'Of course what matters in survival is personal identity! Therefore what matters cannot be mental continuity or connectedness' (p. 19).

This reaction—that identity must be what matters—'cannot', Lewis thinks, 'credibly be denied' (p. 18). I think that it ought to be denied; but it is certainly 'compelling'. Return to the case of division—on the account which involves three people: the original person, and two resulting people. If the R-relation is what matters, the original person should not be troubled by the thought that he will be neither of the resulting people, for his relation to each of them is as good as survival. But when we imagine ourselves as about to divide, we may well say: 'This cannot be right. If there will be no one alive who will be me, this is what matters. How can *ceasing to exist* be as good as surviving'?[15]

Before I sketch what this reaction shows, I must define a certain phrase. Suppose that the truth of a certain statement just consists in the truth of certain other statements. If this is so, we might say that the fact reported by the first statement is not a 'further fact', apart from the facts reported by the other statements. It is not a further fact because it just involves these other facts.[16]

We might now claim, as a first approximation, that the truth of statements about personal identity just consists in the truth of certain statements about psychological and (perhaps) physical continuity. The fact of personal identity is not a further fact, apart from certain facts about these continuities.[17]

Most of us seem inclined, at some level, to reject this kind of view. This is what is shown by our reactions to the 'problem' cases. We are inclined to think that even when, in these cases, we know all the facts about psychological and physical continuity, there must still *be* an answer to the question about personal identity. If we do think this, we seem to be assuming that the fact of personal identity is a further fact.[18]

A similar reaction is the one mentioned earlier—that identity must be what matters. Suppose that I am the original person, and am about to divide. If we took the kind of view that I have just sketched, we might reason as follows. The relation between me and each resulting person is the R-relation with its normal cause, the persistence of a sufficient part of my brain. If this same relation held between me and only one resulting person, he would be me.[19] So the fact that, in this case, no resulting person will be identical with me just consists in the fact that I stand in this same relation to *more* than one resulting person. If we viewed the case in this way, it would be quite mysterious if we also claimed that this non-identity would, here, matter. If we do insist on this, we seem to be assuming that identity would be a further fact—that, in the relation between me and each resulting person, *something is missing*.[20]

III

I shall end with a few remarks about Perry's paper. These will be brief, for as he says our views are very similar.

We agree upon the main point: that 'the importance of identity is *derivative*' (p. 81)—that what matters in the continued existence of a person are various 'special relationships' (p. 84).

Our views about the criteria of identity are also very close. Perry's view is that a person at one time and a person at another time are the same person if they stand in the relation which normally causes psychological continuity (p. 71). My view was that they are the same person if they stand in the relation of psychological continuity, my account of which required a normal cause.[21] So we agree that there is personal identity when there is both psychological continuity and its normal cause.

There are two special cases. There might, first, be psychological continuity without its normal cause. We both assume that the normal cause is the continuity of the brain, and both discuss a case where psychological continuity is instead produced by the creation of a replica.[22] Perry thinks that in this case the replica would not be the original person. I thought that, if we wished, we could say that he was. But the difference here is trivial, for we agree that, whichever we say, being replicated in this way is as good as surviving.[23]

In the second special case, there is the normal cause—the continuity of the brain—without psychological continuity. Perry thinks that in this case there would be personal identity (p. 84), as (more guardedly) did I.[24] But there would not be, we agree, what matters.[25]

NOTES

1. David Lewis, 'Survival and Identity', chap. I in this volume. (All my simple page numbers refer to this volume.)

2. 'Personal Identity' (hereafter cited as PI), *Philosophical Review,* lxxx (January 1971), 10.

3. A 'person-stage' is just a person during a period. (Lewis writes both, 'You are wondering' and 'Your present stage that is doing the wondering.' Since you and your present stage are not identical, this implies that the same mental act has two different 'subjects'. This suggestion may seem absurd. (Criticising Locke and Russell, Shoemaker wrote, 'I am confident that nobody would want to hold this' (*Self-Knowledge and Self-Identity*, Cornell, [Ithaca: University Press, 1963], p. 54). But there are respectable precedents. The very same act can be the act both of a country and of its present government. So it is not absurd to introduce a way of talking according to which every act is done both by a person and by his present stage—or by his 'present self'.)

4. A different objection might be that, before the division, we have no descriptions which differentiate C_1 and C_2. But we could easily give the name 'C_1' to 'the person who, after the division, will regain consciousness first' (or 'in the left-hand bed'). Besides, the argument in the text could be recast in terms of the following question: 'Is the present stage of each of the two continuant people R-related to the future stage of the other'?

5. Take the remark, 'In wondering whether you will survive the battle. . . you wonder whether the continuant person that includes your present stage is [one of the] persons that continue beyond the battle.' As Lewis later says, if your present stage is shared with another person, 'there would not be any such thing. . . as *the* person' who includes your present stage (p. 23). Nor can we just substitute the indefinite article; it is not enough to ensure *your* survival that *a* person who includes your present stage should survive, for that person may not be you. Nor

can the question 'whether you will survive the battle' be equivalent to the question 'whether any of the stages that will exist afterwards is I-related to...your present stage', for as we saw it is essential to Lewis's account of division that S_2, though I-related to C_1's first stage, not be a stage of C_1. (If the First Equivalence must go, what should take its place? Something is needed, for as Lewis writes, 'questions of identity among continuant persons...are also questions of I-relatedness among person-stages' (p. 21). The natural suggestion would be this: 'Is that stage a stage of this person'? cannot be equivalent to 'Is it I-related to this person's present stage?', but it could be equivalent to 'Is it I-related to *all* of this person's stages'? This may seem, as Lewis writes, 'unhelpful; but if the I-relation is the R-relation, we have something more interesting' (p. 22). That this is the right equivalence is suggested by the remark: 'something is a continuant person ...if and only if it is an aggregate of person-stages, each of which is...R-related to all the rest' (p. 22). This new Equivalence does not undermine the account of division. Though S_2 is R-related and hence I-related to C_1's first stage, it is not R-related, nor hence I-related, to C_1's second stage—to S_1. So, on the new Equivalence, S_2 is not a stage of C_1.

6. One remark of Lewis's calls for further discussion. This is: '*More precisely: if common sense is right that what matters in survival is identity among continuant persons, then you have what matters in survival if and only if your present stage is I-related to future stages*' (p. 21-22). The 'future stages' referred to here must be intended to be stages of *you*. (If they were not, the remark would not express the view that 'what matters...is identity.' It would allow that you might 'have what matters in survival' even though there will be no one alive in the future who will be you.) But only on the First Equivalence must the 'future stages' to which 'your present stage is I-related' be stages of you. Without this Equivalence, they might be stages of someone else (someone who shares your present stage). We are back with the dilemma presented in the text.

7. PI, p. 5.

8. Ibid., pp. 7-8. (On this account, the existence of the resulting people dates from the division.)

9. I should rather say, 'has no degrees', for identity may be said to be a 'matter' of degree in the sense that 'what it involves' has degrees.

10. There is perhaps a second reason why Lewis understates this second fact. He writes: 'We sometimes say: in later life I will be a different person. For us short-lived creatures, such remarks are an extravagance. A philosophical study of personal identity can ignore them. For Methuselah, however, the fading out of personal identity looms large as a fact of life. It is incumbent on us to make it literally true that he will be a different person after one and a half centuries or so' (p. 30). But we must distinguish (1) 'He will be a different person' from (2) 'It will not be him any longer, but a different person.' Only in (2) does the phrase 'a different person' mean 'numerically different'. In (1) it means 'changed'; what (1) says is that he, numerically the same person, will be qualitatively a different person. Consequently claims like (1) are not, as Lewis calls them, 'an extravagance'. Nor are they irrelevant to a study of personal identity. For the claim, 'He's become a different person', may report the kind of weakening in the R-relation which, if it took a more extreme (imaginary) form, would support the claim, 'It's no longer him; it's a different person'. (But, to anticipate, I would agree with Perry [p. 86] that this requires a break in continuity, not just in connectedness.)

11. The central feature of this notion, that it is relative to a person *at a time,*

can be supported by an argument which makes no reference to the nature or importance of personal identity. This argument attempts to show that 'self-interested' theories of rationality occupy an untenable mid-way position between the theories which do and the theories which do not make reasons for acting relative to a point of view. (If we allow force to the question, 'Why should *I* grant weight to desires which aren't *mine*?', why not to the question, 'Why should *I now* grant weight to desires which aren't *mine now*?'? (Cf. Sidgwick, *Methods of Ethics* [London, 1907], p. 418. This is just the opening move in the argument; much more needs to be said.) The resulting notion of rationality, relativised to the agent at the time of acting, is of course central to decision theory and to much of economics, but is there defended on different grounds.

12. Cf. John Rawls: 'In the case of the individual, pure time preference is irrational: it means that he is not viewing all moments as equally parts of one life' (*A Theory of Justice* [Cambridge, Mass.: Harvard University Press, 1971], p. 295). This criticism is directed at a discount rate with respect to time itself—Rawls may not intend it to apply to a discount rate with respect to the weakening of the R-relation, and only if it were so applied could we directly give the answer in the text. (Someone who discounted with respect to time might answer Rawls by appealing to the weakening of the R-relation over time—but this would be a rationalisation.) (In Thomas Nagel's *The Possibility of Altruism* [London: Oxford University Press, 1970]), it looks at first as if he intends to argue for the irrationality of imprudent actions with a similar appeal to the importance of personal identity—see, for example, the remark at the foot of page 42. However, Nagel does not defend a self-interested theory of rationality; on the contrary, prudence for him is justified in the same way as altruism. Both justifications rest on his denial that reasons are relative to a point of view. Nagel's argument for prudence therefore appeals, not to personal identity, but to the claim that all of a person's life is 'equally real'—that 'the present is just a time among others' (p. 88).

13. Perhaps, though, we should start to consider it morally questionable. Later selves would otherwise be disenfranchised. (Cf. Rawls, op. cit., pp. 422-423, and Nagel, op. cit., *passim*.)

14. Some of these I discuss, briefly, in 'Later Selves and Moral Principles', in *Philosophy and Personal Relations*, ed. Alan Montefiore (London: Routledge & Kegan Paul, 1973) (hereafter cited as LSMP)—and in 'On "The Importance of Self-Identity"', *Journal of Philosophy* (21 October 1971) (hereafter cited as OIS).

15. Compare the chapter 'Resurrection' in T. Penelhum's *Survival and Disembodied Existence* (London: Routledge & Kegan Paul, 1970).

16. There might be said to be one sense in which it *is* a 'further fact'—viz., that a report of this fact has a different meaning from a report of the other facts. In LSMP I contrasted these two senses by saying that the fact of personal identity was only 'in its logic', not 'in its nature', a further fact; but I have now been persuaded (by P. Benacerraf and C. Peacocke) that these phrases are unfortunate. (C. Peacocke and J. De Witt have also helped me throughout the writing of this paper.)

17. It is a view of this kind which I seem to share with both Perry and Lewis. Compare IOS, footnote 11 with Perry's claim, 'his being me consists in his stages having the P-relation to mine' (p. 84). Lewis's equation of questions about identity and about R-relatedness suggests a similar view. (This equation seems to go too far. Lewis says that if you wonder about identity you *are* wondering about

the R-relation; I should rather say, 'You ought, instead, to be...'. He continues: 'If you are entering the duplicator, and wonder whether you will leave by the left door, or the right door, or both, or neither, you are... wondering which future stages, if any, are R-related to you-now' [p. 21]. This cannot be right; for you already know [since the machine is a *duplicator*] that both of the resulting people are R-related to you-now.)

18. Quine writes: 'The method of science fiction has its uses in philosphy, but... I wonder whether the limits of the method are properly heeded. To seek what is "logically required" for sameness of person under unprecedented circumstances is to suggest that words have some logical force beyond what our past needs have invested them with' (*Journal of Philosophy* [7 September 1972], p. 490, reviewing Milton K. Munitz, ed., *Identity and Individuation*). True; but the science fiction cases may serve a different purpose. Our reactions to these cases may show that we have beliefs about the nature of personal identity which go beyond, and even conflict with, the 'logical force' of our words. Thus the reaction I have mentioned—that, in these cases, questions about personal identity must have answers—suggests that we take a non-reductionist, realist view about personal identity; (cf. Dummett, 'The Reality of the Past', *Proceedings of the Aristotelian Society*, 69 [1968-69], 240-243). This reaction is particularly clearly expressed by R. Chisholm in his 'Reply to Strawson's Comments', in *Language, Belief, and Metaphysics*, ed. H. E. Kiefer and Milton K. Munitz (Albany: State University of New York Press, 1970), pp. 188-189. Reviewing the case of division, Chisholm writes: 'When I contemplate these questions, I see the following things clearly and distinctly to be true... the questions "Will I be Lefty?" and "Will I be Righty?" have entirely definite answers. The answers will be simply "Yes" or "No."... What I want to insist upon... is that this will be the case even if all our normal criteria for personal identity should break down.' In 'The Self and the Future (*Philosophical Review*, lxxix [1970], reprinted in *Problems of the Self* [London: Cambridge University Press, 1973]), Williams shows how natural this reaction is; in 'Imagination and the Self' (reprinted in *Problems of the Self*) he diagnoses one of the illusions on which it rests.

19. Cf., PI, p. 5. It might be denied that in this case the resulting person would be me. One argument for this denial is suggested by Williams in 'Are Persons Bodies?', reprinted in *Problems of the Self*, p. 78. If we accept such an argument, the reasoning in the text should be re-applied. We should ask ourselves: granted that in this case there is no identity, is there still what matters? If we insist that there is not, on the ground that identity is what matters, we seem to be assuming that identity is a further fact—we seem to be rejecting the kind of view advanced in the text. According to such a view, the fact that there is not here identity (if it is a fact) just consists in the fact that there is not, here, continuity of the whole body. Why should this matter, if there is still psychological continuity (caused, moreover, in the normal way)?

20. We seem to believe, as I said, that there is *more to* personal identity than psychological and physical continuity. It is of course hard to imagine, or to suggest coherently, what this 'more' might be. But there are other areas (Free Will?) where common sense reveals, under pressure, beliefs which are either quite opaque or incoherent. (Here is a different reaction to the prospect of division. I might think that the relation between me and the two resulting people does not preserve what matters, not because, without identity, 'something is missing', but because multiplication brings *too much*. Multiplication, I may feel, threatens my integrity.) This reaction (suggested to me by Michael Woods) may not rest on any

false belief. But it only seems defensible if the reaction is that multiplication isn't *quite* as good as ordinary survival. (We might claim that being married twice can't be quite as good as being married only once; but it would be absurd to claim that it amounts to remaining single.)

21. The claim that (non-branching) psychological continuity is a sufficient condition of identity came in PI, p. 13. The requirement of a normal cause came in the definition of 'q-memory' (p. 15), which provided the model for the other components of continuity.

22. Cf. Perry, p. 83, and OIS, pp. 689-690.

23. Perry's two objections to speaking of identity here seem inconclusive. The first is that the psychological continuity has a cause which is 'too unlike' its normal cause (p. 83). But there seem to be grounds in such cases for allowing any reliable cause; (see, for instance, Williams, 'Are Persons Bodies?', p. 79, and Strawson's remarks in 'Causation and Perception', in *Freedom and Resentment* (London: Methuen, 1974). Perry gives a different objection when he discusses the case of 'brain-rejuvenation' (p. 85). Against saying that the resulting person would here be the original person, Perry writes: 'The more abstract relation we would thereby be choosing for our unity relation for persons does not have the empirical guarantee of transitivity that normal maturation does'. But the obvious version of this more abstract relation would be (roughly): any relation which is a reliable cause of psychological continuity—and this relation seems to be, like continuity itself, logically transitive. (We can easily specify that it provides the 'unity relation' for persons only when it takes a one-one form. [Though against this see again Williams, 'Are Persons Bodies?', p. 78.] If we accepted Williams's point, the remainder of n. 19 [above] would apply.)

24. PI, n. 17.

25. Even on the few points where Perry thinks that we disagree, we don't. Commenting, for instance, on my version of the case of Methuselah, Perry writes, 'Parfit takes this to show that there can be identity without survival' (p. 85). What I in fact took the case to show was that there could be continuity without connectedness (PI, p. 24). Perry next criticises my proposed 'way of thinking'. The proposal that I meant, as opposed to the one he takes me to mean, seems to me to avoid his criticisms. But in PI I hardly explained myself (in OIS I tried to make amends). Briefly: Perry thinks that on my proposal we should take the 'special relations'—i.e., a sufficient degree of connectedness—as 'our unity relation for persons' (p. 87). But the descriptive equivalent of the concept of a person was on my proposal the concept, not of a single self, but of a series of successive selves; and for this series the unity relation is—as it is for persons—psychological *continuity*. (This was implied in PI, p. 24 [last sentence], and asserted in OIS p. 687.) *Connectedness,* if sufficiently strong, provides the unity relation not for the whole series but for each successive self (PI, pp. 24-25). Perry also says that when we know 'the rules of predication' for successive selves, we can find out 'what kind of objects these are' (p. 88). But 'successive selves' were not intended to be thought of as a new *kind of object,* any more than (say) 'Medieval England' is a kind of object. That was one reason why the rules of predication were so loose—why the distinction between selves was 'left to the choice of the speaker' and 'allowed to vary from context to context' (PI, p. 25). (Cf. 'The point of these remarks is to assign to some event, like a change in character, particular importance. So the remarks can only be more or less defensible. They cannot be [literally] false', OIS, p. 686.) In LSMP I have sketched a case where this

way of talking seems better than our normal way; but—as I should have said—I did not intend 'dropping talk about persons'. Finally, Perry says that in my view 'various misconceptions' are 'rooted in our concept of personal identity' (p. 86). The direct cause of the misconceptions I took to be, not the *concept*, but our beliefs about the *nature* of personal identity (PI, p. 3). These beliefs I did take to be partly caused by the concept ('This use of language. . . can lead us astray', PI, p. 11); but I added that, to undermine these beliefs, we should need to discuss their various other causes—such as 'the projection of our emotions' (PI, p. 4 and p. 7, n. 11). Much of this (and much else) seems to me excellently done in Perry's paper.

V

EMBODIMENT AND BEHAVIOR

SYDNEY SHOEMAKER

A prominent question in recent philosophy of mind is whether some of the connections between mental states and behavior are (in some interesting sense) "logical," "necessary," "internal," or "conceptual," as opposed to being "purely contingent." Another prominent question, a much older one, is whether subjects of mental states, in particular persons, can exist in "disembodied form," that is, whether it is possible (logically possible) for there to be something (or someone) that has mental states without having (or being) a body and so without having any physical states whatever.[2] While both of these questions concern the relationships that hold between the realm of the mental and the realm of the physical, they are on the face of it very different questions, and they are often discussed as if their answers were independent of one another.

But suppose that it could be made out that it is a necessary truth that *if* a person is embodied (has a body) *then* certain of his mental states will *(ceteris paribus)* manifest themselves in certain ways in the behavior of whatever body is his. By itself this would not conflict with the view that all psychophysical connections (lawlike connections between mental and physical states) are basically contingent. A Cartesian dualist, who thinks that disembodied existence of persons or minds is at least a logical possibility, need not dispute the claim that this conditional proposition is necessarily (logically, conceptually) true; but he would claim that if it is necessarily true, it is so merely because it spells out part of what it means to say that a person is embodied in a particular body, and that this leaves it a purely contingent fact that the causal connections between minds and bodies are such that the minds count as being embodied in the bodies.[3] (Analogously, we could introduce a notion of "automotive embodiment" which is so defined that an engine counts as being automotively embodied in a particular automobile body just in case it is so related to it that certain movements in the engine result in locomotion of the automobile body, thus making it a logical truth that if an automotively embodied engine is operating in a certain way the associated automobile body will move in a certain way. We would hardly take this as showing that there is [in any interesting sense] a conceptual or logical connection between the operation of an internal combustion engine and automotive locomotion.) But if we conjoin the claim that this conditional proposition is necessarily true with the radically anti-Cartesian claim that disembodiment is logically impossible (that being a subject of mental states necessarily involves being embodied), we get the conclusion that it is a necessary truth that certain mental states lead *(ceteris paribus)* to certain sorts of behavior; and this certainly does conflict with the view that all psychophysical connections are basically contingent.

So far I have been simply supposing that it could be made out that some conditional proposition linking embodiment with the existence of certain psychophysical connections is necessarily true. I have not given any reason to suppose that any such proposition has this status, and have not produced any proposition that is a plausible candidate for having it. I have hinted, however, that some such proposition may be necessarily true in virtue of what it means to say that a particular body is the body of a particular person.[4] If this is so, we should not expect the consequent of that proposition to assert the existence of *all* of the psychophysical connections that we believe to hold in the case of normal human beings, for it seems plain that many of these connections could fail to hold, in the case of someone or in the case of everyone, without this affecting anyone's embodiment. If embodiment consists in the holding of certain psychophysical connections, these must be a proper subset of all the psychophysical connections we believe to hold in normal cases. What subset might this be?

In what follows I shall assume an account of action, or at least of central cases of action, according to which the connection between wants and beliefs, on the one hand, and the overt behavior to which they give rise, on the other, is always mediated by a mental event which can be characterized as an attempt or effort on the part of the person to do a certain thing, as the person's trying to do a certain thing, or, in philosophical jargon, as a "volition" to do a certain thing. I realize that this account is controversial, but I have not the space to defend it here.[5] I shall also assume an account of perception according to which veridical perception, as well as sensory illusion and hallucination, always involves the occurrence of mental states or events that can be characterized as sense-impressions or sense-experiences, and which a person is sometimes reporting when he says how things look, feel, sound, and so forth, to him.[6]

Many connections between mental states and behavior are not mediated by volitions. Fear sometimes gives rise to perspiration and trembling, but not because the fearful person *tries* to perspire or to tremble. Likewise, embarrassment sometimes leads to blushing, but not by leading someone to try to blush. In cases like these there is, I think, very little plausibility in the view that the mental states and their associated bodily manifestations are logically or conceptually connected; it is not difficult to imagine that a change in human physiology might result in its no longer being the case that fear leads to perspiration or trembling, and it is quite implausible to suppose that it is only in an altered sense of the word "fear" that it would apply to people after such a change. And in such cases it is likewise implausible to say that the holding of the psychophysical connections is partially constitutive of the relationship of embodiment—for example, it is surely implausible to hold that part of what it *means* to say that a body is my body is that fear on my part tends to produce perspiration and trembling in that body, that embarrassment on my part tends to produce blushing in that body, and so on.[7] This suggests that any connections between mental states and behavior that are "conceptual," and any that are constitutive of embodiment, are ones involving volitions.

The connection between fear and "avoidance behavior," unlike that between fear and perspiration, is one that many philosophers have found it plausible to regard as a conceptual or logical connection. But this connection seems to resolve into more elementary connections; roughly speaking, my fear of the snake before me leads to a desire to be elsewhere, which leads to an attempt to run (a "volition"), which leads to the bodily movements constitutive of running. Some of the links in this chain, for example the connection between the fear of snakes and the desire to be elsewhere, are connections between different mental states rather than between mental states and behavior (they are "psycho-psycho" rather than psychophysical), and can hardly be expected to be constitutive of the psychophysical relationship of embodiment. The one link that is itself psychophysical is that between the volition and the movements constitutive of the action one is trying to perform—in this case, the movements constitutive of running. The existence of this sort of causal connection does seem to me a central aspect of embodiment, and I will say that a person is "volitionally embodied" in a certain body to the extent that volitions of the person produce in that body movements that conform to them or fulfill them, that is, movements that the person is trying to produce or which are constitutive of actions he is trying to perform. (Henceforth I shall abbreviate this by saying that the volitions produce movements "appropriate to them.")

In somewhat the way in which volitions mediate the connection between desires, and so forth, and behavior, sense experiences mediate the connections between a person's bodily circumstances and his beliefs. This points to another central aspect of embodiment; I will say that a person is "sensorily embodied" in a certain body to the extent that the interactions of that body with its surroundings produce in the person sense-experiences corresponding to, and constituting veridical perceptions of, aspects of those surroundings. And I suggest that volitional embodiment and sensory embodiment are together the primary criteria of, or constitutive factors in, embodiment *simpliciter*.[8]

Most people would be prepared to allow that it is at least logically possible for someone to have mental states while being not only completely paralysed but also blind, deaf, and otherwise cut off from sensory contact with the world. And such a person would certainly have a body. This may seem to conflict with what I have claimed about volitional and sensory embodiment; but I shall try to show, by means of a "Gedankenexperiment," that it does not.

Let us suppose that at some time in the future, when biological science and technology are much more highly developed than now, a new disease strikes mankind; those afflicted by the disease can be kept alive for indefinitely long periods of time by intravenous feeding and the like, but they are completely paralysed, and are totally blind, deaf, and otherwise cut off from ordinary sensory stimuli. I shall assume that it is possible that we should discover correlations between mental states and brain states that would enable us to "read off" a good deal of information about someone's mental states from the states of his brain, and that there could be devised a brain state recording device—a "cerebroscope" —which would inform us of the relevant brain states. We will suppose that while it is impossible to communicate with victims of this disease, except perhaps by direct brain stimulation, cerebroscopes reveal that they have intervals of consciousness. Although the brain itself remains healthy in these cases, the deterioration of the rest of the body is irreversible. It seems at first that the only solution is to transplant the healthy brains into other bodies, and for this purpose duplicates of bodies are grown (by an accelerated process) from cells taken from them prior to the onset of the disease. But alas, in this possible world, unlike others that have been imagined, brain transplantation proves to be impossible. Finally, however, a solution, or at least what some regard as a solution, is found. Highly sensitive cerebroscopes are developed which are capable of recording the brain states of afflicted persons and transmitting information about them to receivers planted in the skulls of duplicate bodies, and the receivers in turn are connected with the nervous and muscular systems of the duplicate bodies. And transmitters placed in the skulls of the duplicate bodies are fed information from their nervous systems and sense organs, and transmit this information to receivers planted in the brains of the afflicted persons, which in turn provide sensory input into those brains. The effect of this is that the afflicted person has just the sense-impressions he would have if his brain were in the duplicate body and connected up with it in the ordinary way, and he has voluntary control over the movements of that body—so if his duplicate body's eyes are open and directed toward a tree, he has sense-impressions as of a tree, and if he tries to raise his arm, then, in the absence of "countervailing factors," the arm of his duplicate body goes up.

Let us grant that there is a criterion of embodiment—I will call it the "biological criterion"—which assigns a body to a person if his brain is inside the skull of that body and stands to it in certain biological relationships that do not exclude paralysis, blindness, deafness, and so forth, that is, do not guarantee any degree of volitional or sensory embodiment. In the actual world, I will assume, anyone who is embodied in a body according to the volitional and sensory criteria is also embodied in it according to the biological criterion—although because of the existence of paralytics, the converse does not hold. The world I have imagined is one in which it is possible for a person to be, at one and the same time, embodied in one body according to the biological criterion and in a different body according to the volitional and sensory criteria. If this happened, which body should we say is *really* the person's body? Perhaps this question can be bypassed. If cases of this sort actually occurred, people would probably distinguish different senses of expressions like "my body"; much as we now speak of natural parents and adopted parents, they might speak of a person's "biological body" and his "volitional-sensory body." But I think that it is clear that most of the work now done by the notion of a person's body would be done by the notion of a person's volitional-sensory body rather than by the notion of a person's biological body; for example, when a person uses expressions like "my arm," "my leg," and so forth, he would mostly be taken to be referring to parts of his volitional-sensory body, and when someone locates something by its relation to himself—for example, when he says "It is right in front of me"—he would usually be taken to be locating it in relation to his volitional-sensory body. This gives support to the claim that the volitional and sensory criteria are primary, and that biological embodiment derives its status as a criterion from the fact that in normal circumstances it is a causally necessary condition of volitional and sensory embodiment.

It should also be noted that it makes sense to speak of a biological criterion of embodiment only on the assumption that we have already identified some kind of bodily organ, for example the brain, as the primary physiological seat of consciousness and mental functioning, or as what we might call the physiological core of a person; only so can we identify a person by reference to an organ of this sort and ask how a larger biological entity must be related to that organ in order to be the body of the person so identified. But of course a biological criterion for answering this question does not tell us what it is that makes an organ of that sort the physiological core of a person—and so it falls far short of giving us a full account of embodiment. It seems obvious that what does single out the brain as the physiological core of a person is mainly its role in bringing about or controlling on the physiological level the behavior that on the psychological (or mentalistic) level we take to be brought about or controlled by mental states of persons; and this is a role it can play only in cases in which there is a significant degree of sensory and volitional embodiment. This points up again the primacy of the volitional and sensory criteria of embodiment.

Let us say that normal, healthy human beings are "paradigmatically embodied" in their bodies in virtue of the significant extent to which they are volitionally and sensorily embodied in them. While I can thus indicate the intended extension of the notion of paradigmatic embodiment, I cannot define it to my satisfaction; for I am unable to specify, in general terms, the "significant extent" of volitional and sensory embodiment which it involves. But one obvious requirement for paradigmatic embodiment is that the extent of sensory embodiment (and also the rationality and learning capacity of the person) be sufficient to enable the person to determine the extent of his volitional embodiment. Let us say that a person is volitionally embodied relative to volition-type V and body B if his having a volition of type V results, *ceteris paribus*, in movements appropriate to V occurring in B. Then this requirement for paradigmatic embodiment can be put by saying that the extent of sensory embodiment (and of rationality and learning capacity) must be such that the person will not as a rule be mistaken in thinking that he is volitionally embodied relative to a particular volition-type. And whatever definition we give of paradigmatic embodiment, it ought to be such as to make it a definitional tautology that if a person is paradigmatically embodied in a body, then (a) for some volition-types he is volitionally embodied relative to those volition-types and that body, and (b) if he believes that he is volitionally embodied relative to a volition-type and that body, then as a rule he is volitionally embodied relative to them. And given the centrality of volitional and sensory embodiment as criteria of embodiment *simpliciter*, it seems reasonable to characterize paradigmatic embodiment as normal embodiment (where "normal" implies a conceptually central and paradigmatic status rather than statistical predominance), and to say that it is a conceptual truth that if a person is embodied then his volitions, or at least those volitions that are of types relative to which he believes himself to be volitionally embodied, normally issue in movements of his body which are appropriate to them.

The conceptual truth we have uncovered (supposing we have uncovered one) is of the form "If someone has a body, such and such of his mental states manifest themselves in such and such ways in the behavior of that body." As I noted at the beginning of this paper, the claim that some propositions of this form are necessarily or conceptually true is perfectly compatible with Cartesian dualism and with the view that all connections between mental states and behavior are at bottom purely contingent. We must consider whether this conceptual claim can be supplemented in such a way as to warrant a philosophically interesting version of the claim that there are conceptual connections between mental states and behavior. What obviously has to be considered is whether disembodied existence of persons is possible, or, what is the same thing, whether persons are necessarily embodied. But before I do this I want to look again at the notion of volitional embodiment.

My most recent definition of "volitionally embodied" makes it a necessary truth that if a person is volitionally embodied relative to his body and the volition to raise his right arm, then, *ceteris paribus*, his trying to raise his right arm results in the right arm of his body going up. But we could introduce a notion of X-embodiment (or, if you like, X-misembodiment) which is so defined as to make it a necessary truth that if a person is X-embodied relative to a certain body and the volition to raise his right arm, then, *ceteris paribus*, his trying to raise his right arm results in the *left leg* of that body moving in a certain way—and this certainly would not establish any interesting conceptual connection between trying to raise one's arm and some leg's moving. So what is it, if anything, that gives conceptual importance to the necessary truths generated by the notion of volitional embodiment but not to those generated by the notion of X-embodiment (and by other notions of volitional misembodiment we might devise)? It is a partial answer to this, but I think only a partial answer, that volitional embodiment is, while X-embodiment most definitely is not, partially constitutive of embodiment *simpliciter*.

One fact worth noting is that the notion of X-embodiment could not play any significant role in the explanation of observed behavior. To be sure, it might be true of a paralytic that he is X-embodied relative to his body and the volition to raise his arm, and if we knew this we might explain his leg movements by reference to his attempts to move his arm. But it would be essential to the intelligibility of such an explanation that we suppose that the man is ignorant of the effects of his volitions, that is, does not know or believe that he is X-embodied relative to those volitions. For if he knew that what formerly constituted trying to move his arm now results (as a matter of course) in leg movements rather than arm movements, it could no longer constitute trying to move his arm; it would have come to constitute trying to move his leg. And it seems clear that the hypothesis that someone having certain mental states is *systematically mis*embodied (e.g., X-embodied) in a certain body relative to certain sorts of volitions could not, except in very special circumstances, constitute the best explanation of any substantial stretch of behavior of that body. Since volitional misembodiment would have to involve mistaken beliefs about the effects of one's volitions, it would have to be accompanied by sensory misembodiment in order to persist for any period of time— otherwise (assuming a minimal degree of rationality) the mistaken beliefs would be corrected on the basis of the person's sense-experiences. And certainly the hypothesis that someone is volitionally *and* sensorily misembodied in a certain body would provide no ready explanation of the fact that the movements of that body are such as to keep it nourished and out of danger, to say nothing of the fact that some of its movements and interactions with its environment are of the complex and intricate sorts which in a paradigmatically animated body would constitute threading a needle, repairing a radio, or painting a portrait. So if the behavior of a body is anything like normal human behavior, the misembodiment hypothesis would not provide much competition to the hypothesis that the body is paradigmatically animated, that is, is the body of someone who is volitionally and sensorily embodied in it to a significant degree. On the other hand, if the movements of a body are not such as to call for an explanation in terms of its being paradigmatically animated—that is, do not seem to constitute "appropriate" responses to its circumstances, and do not appear to show intelligence and purpose—then there will normally be no reason to invoke mental states in their explanation at all; such "behavior" will be most economically explained in nonmentalistic terms. To be sure, if an outlandish hypothesis is suitably supplemented with other outlandish hypotheses, it can be made to explain virtually anything. If we suppose that the connections between mental states and states of a body are mediated by the machinations of a Cartesian evil genius or a malicious remote-controlling physiologist, we can suppose any series of mental states to lead to any series of bodily states, and vice versa. But presumably we have more than ample grounds for rejecting such outlandish hypotheses, despite the logical possibility (if it be such) of their being true. So unless we have evidence for believing in the existence of certain volitions which is independent of the occurrence of the behavior to which they give rise, the existence of these volitions cannot enter into a plausible explanation of that behavior except on the supposition that the person having the volitions is paradigmatically embodied in the body exhibiting the behavior.

What this last argument shows, if correct, is that volitional embodiment, and more generally paradigmatic embodiment, has a kind of epistemological necessity; it is a necessary condition of our knowing about the mental states (especially volitional states) of other persons in the way we normally do that they be volitionally embodied to a significant degree (indeed, that they be paradigmatically embodied), and we could not know them in any other way if we could not sometimes know them in this way. But of course, to show that something must be true of persons and their volitions if they are to be known is not the same as showing that something must be true of them if they are to exist; the epistemological necessity of volitional embodiment does not establish its ontological necessity.

There is, however, another difference between the notion of volitional embodiment and such notions as that of X-embodiment. The notion of volitional embodiment and that of X-embodiment are of course alike in involving the notion of a volition. In the case of X-embodiment this "involvement" goes in only one direction; the notion of a volition does not in any natural or interesting sense involve the notion of X-embodiment. There is a fairly clear sense, however, in which the notion of a volition involves, as well as being involved by, the notion of volitional embodiment. A volition is always a volition to perform some bodily action. And the notion of bodily action involves the notion of volitional embodiment; for in order for the movements of a body to constitute the performance of a certain action by a certain person, it must be the case that the person is volitionally embodied relative to that body and the volition to perform that action. For example, my arm's going up constitutes my raising my arm only if I am volitionally embodied relative to my body and the volition to raise my arm, that is, am such that my trying to raise my arm results, *ceteris paribus*, in my arm's going up. Thus it can be said that the connection between the having of volitions and volitional embodiment is an internal one, the notion of each of these involving the notion of the other. This being so, the necessary truth linking volitions and behavior which is generated by the definition of volitional embodiment can be said to be explicative of the notion of a volition as well as of the notion of volitional embodiment. And this constitutes a difference between this necessary truth and that generated by the notion of X-(mis)embodiment, and also between it and the necessary truth generated by the notion of automotive embodiment mentioned at the beginning of this paper. For there is no such internal connection between the having of volitions and X-embodiment, or between the existence of a certain sort of engine and automotive embodiment.

But if this is all there is to the "conceptual connection" between mental states and behavior, it is not what it has been cracked up to be. The existence of this "internal connection" between volitions and volitional embodiment does not entail that volitional embodiment, or anything approaching volitional embodiment, is required for the *existence* of volitions; and so it does not entail that it is a conceptual truth that volitions typically or normally occur in people who are volitionally embodied relative to them and so typically or normally give rise to bodily movements that are appropriate to them. To see whether the latter is so we shall have to consider what sort or degree of embodiment, if any, is required for the existence of a person (or, more generally, subject of mental states). It is to the latter question that I now turn.

We know, of course, that it is not necessary for a person to be *paradigmatically* embodied in order to exist and be a subject of mental states. Paralysis actually occurs, and complete paralysis coupled with blindness, deafness, and the like, seems to be at least possible. And both states seem compatible with the possession of mental states and incompatible with paradigmatic embodiment.

It is natural to feel that the case of complete paralysis coupled with blindness, and so forth, is not significantly different, with respect to its possibility and its compatibility with the possession of mental states, from the hypothetical case of a "brain in a vat," that is, a detached brain kept alive *in vitro*. If information about the brain states of the blind, deaf, paralytic could justify ascribing mental states to him, it would seem that the same information about the states of a detached brain could justify us in regarding it as the brain of a still existing and still conscious person having those mental states. And such a person would be, in one sense, without a body.

I shall not dispute the claim that a brain in a vat can be a subject of mental states—or, better, that such a brain can be the brain of (and all that physically remains of) a still existing person having mental states. But I am concerned to draw the teeth of this claim, insofar as it is thought to show that there is no essential connection between the having of mental states and embodiment (and the potential for behavior it involves). The view I wish to defend is that what I have called "paradigmatic embodiment" is paradigmatic not only of the *embodiment* of persons but of their very *existence*. While we can give sense to the idea of a person existing without being paradigmatically embodied, this is essentially the idea of a person having a damaged, defective, or truncated body. In general we can know what it is for something to be a damaged or defective so-and-so only by knowing what it is for something to be an undamaged and nondefective so-and-so. It is also true, I think, that in order to be able to characterize something as damaged or defective we must have *some* notion of what it would be for the damage to be repaired or the defect remedied; in still other terms, we must have a notion of what it would be for the thing to be restored or brought to a condition in which each of its parts, if it has parts, performs its proper function. And so it seems to me to be with persons. The body of a person can be thought of as having among its parts various mechanisms each of which has the function of contributing in a determinate way to the person's paradigmatic embodiment. These include sense organs, limbs, muscles, nerves, and so on—and of course the brain, which can be said to function as the "control mechanism" for the entire organism. If enough of these perform their functions satisfactorily, the person is paradigmatically embodied. If something has some of these parts, including the brain, but lacks others whose proper functioning is required for paradigmatic embodiment, or if it has all these parts but some (not including the brain) are misfunctioning, we will regard it as significantly similar to a paradigmatically animated body and will be willing, under some circumstances, to regard it as the body of a conscious person. Thus we have the cases of the multiple amputee and the blind and deaf paralytic. And whether or not it is medically possible for such a person to be restored or brought to a condition of paradigmatic embodiment, we have a notion of what it would be like for this to be done. It is perhaps because the case of the detached brain can be thought of as a limiting case of amputation—the amputation of everything except the brain—that many philosophers are prepared to allow that such a brain could be the brain of a still existing and still conscious person; and it goes with this that we have at least a crude idea of what it would be like for such a person to be restored to a state of paradigmatic embodiment. And here I should reiterate a point made earlier: it is because of the causal role played by the brain in cases of paradigmatic embodiment—roughly, its role in mediating connections between sensory stimuli and behavioral responses—that we are prepared to think of it as the physiological core of a person.

But now what are we to make of the idea that a person might exist in a *totally* disembodied state? We have some notion of what it would be for an amputee, a paralytic, or even the owner of a detached brain to be restored to a state of paradigmatic embodiment; but do we have any comparable idea of what it would be for a totally disembodied person to be so restored? It is clear that the paradigmatic reembodiment of a human brain would require one sort of body, that of a chimpanzee brain would require a different sort of body, that of a robot brain made of transistors and the like would require a still different sort of body, while that of a Martian brain (supposing there to be intelligent life on Mars) would very likely require a sort of body radically different from any of these. Crudely speaking, the structure and causal powers of the body in each case would have to be such as to "mesh" with the structure and causal powers of the brain, in such a way as to bring about the causal connections between volitions and bodily movements, and between sensory stimulation and sense experiences, that are constitutive of volitional and sensory embodiment. But what sort of body would be required for the paradigmatic reembodiment of a completely disembodied mind? If someone says that no particular sort of body is required, and that such a mind would be capable of animating any body that could be the body of a subject of mental states—human bodies, Martian bodies, robot bodies of various constructions, and so on—this seems tantamount to the admission that he has no notion of what it would be for such a mind to be reembodied. Suppose, then, that it is said that a mind requires for its embodiment a particular sort of body, and that an embodied mind is related to its body, including especially its brain (presumably the point of contact between mind and body on any plausible dualistic theory), in a way analogous to that in which the brain is related to the rest of the body. This requires that the mind be thought of as having a structure, or at any rate a set of causal powers, which must "mesh" in a certain way with the structure and causal powers of a physical body if it is to be paradigmatically embodied in that body. I shall try to show in what follows that conceiving the mind in this way (as it must be conceived, I think, if the dualistic theory is to be at all intelligible) is incompatible with conceiving it as something whose states *are* mental states (which a Cartesian mind is supposed to be); on the former conception a "mind" turns out to be a sort of ghostly brain, and mental states will be related to it in whatever way a physicalist ought to think of mental states as related to brain states (not all of which are mental states, even on the "identity theory"). I assume that there is no good reason to think that there are "minds" on this conception of them (the ghostly brain conception). And the possibility (if it is one) of there being such entities, and of their existing in "disembodied form," turns out to be of no more philosophical interest, from the point of view of our current investigation, than the possibility of an ordinary human brain existing in "disembodied form," that is, being detached from its body and kept alive *in vitro.*

I shall assume in the ensuing discussion that it makes good sense to suppose that creatures whose physical-chemical makeup is very different from ours might be capable of having the same mental states as we have, and that we could be justified in ascribing these states to such creatures on the basis of their behavior despite the differences between their physiology and ours. There are neither empirical nor conceptual reasons for thinking that if a creature having certain mental states has a certain physical-chemical makeup, then any creature having those mental states must have that physical-chemical makeup. In the debate over the mind-body "identity theory" this point has been urged, by philosophers like Fodor and Putnam, as showing that mental states (or at any rate mental properties) cannot be straightforwardly identified with physical states.[9] As the point is sometimes put, since the same mental state can be physically "realized" in a variety of ways (just as, to use a favorite analogy, the "abstract" machine states of a Turing machine will be realized in different ways in different sorts of "hardware"), a mental state cannot be identical with any of the physical states that realize it on particular occasions or in particular sorts of creatures. While this point seems to refute some versions of the identity theory, there are other versions that are immune to it; and as I hope to show, it is considerably more damaging to dualism than to physicalism.[10]

If a mind requires for its embodiment a certain sort of body (one whose structure "meshes" with its own in the right way), then equally a body should require for its "animation" a certain sort of mind (again, one whose structure "meshes" with its own in the right way). And if there are different sorts of bodies all of which are equally capable of being the bodies of persons having certain mental states, and if a body is the body of a person in virtue of being animated by a mind whose structure meshes with its own in the right way, then there will be different sorts of minds, all of which are equally capable of being the minds of persons having certain mental states. On the dualist view, states of minds play a crucial role in mediating the connections between sensory input and behavioral output in cases of paradigmatic embodiment. But presumably the states of minds needed to mediate in this way between input and output will be different in the case of radically different sorts of bodies. It is implausible to suppose, for example, that the very same sort of mental happening produces the movements constitutive of arm waving even when the inner physiological antecedents of the movements are entirely different in character; for since this mental happening would have to produce the arm movements by producing certain of the inner physiological antecedents, it would have to be the case that its immediate physical effects are radically different in different cases, and yet that these effects are always events that lead, given the structure of the body as a whole, to the same gross bodily movements. In the absence of design, this seems unlikely. It seems far more likely that if two minds animate very different sorts of bodies, then what is in one of them a volition to perform a certain sort of action will be different (because of a difference in causal powers) from what in the other is a volition to perform that sort of action. And if volitions differ from one sort of mind to another, it would seem that other mental states—those that cause volitions, those that cause those that cause volitions, and so on—will differ as well. For example, if desires and beliefs cause volitions, then if a certain sort of volition (e.g., trying to wave one's arm) is something different in different sorts of minds, it will have to be the case that the desires and beliefs capable of causing that sort of volition (e.g., the desire to attract someone's attention, and the belief that waving will achieve this) also differ in nature depending on the nature of the mind in which they occur.

But what can it mean to say that the *same* mental state is something different (has a different nature) in different sorts of minds? I think that this makes no sense if we take minds to be entities whose states just are mental states, in the way bodies (or "material objects") are entities whose states just are physical states. It makes *prima facie* sense to say, as some physicalists would, that states of different *brains* can be the same *qua* mental states and different *qua* physical states (perhaps this will mean that the states are different physical "realizations" of the same "functional state," this being the mental state; or perhaps it will mean that the states are different disjuncts of a disjunctive state that is identical with the mental state; or perhaps it will mean just that it is a lawlike truth that the mental state is realized if any of the physical states is realized). But if states of different *minds* are the same *qua* mental states, *qua* what can they be different? They cannot be different *qua* physical states, for minds (on the dualist conception of them) do not have physical states.

Let us introduce the terms "immaterial substance" and the "immaterial state"; an immaterial substance will be a substance not possessing any physical properties, and an immaterial state will be a state that can belong only to immaterial substances, that is, cannot belong to anything having physical states. Now we might say that on the conception of minds under consideration (a conception on which minds are immaterial substances), states of different minds (or perhaps even of the same mind on different occasions) can be the same *qua* mental states and different *qua* immaterial states. But this involves abandoning an assumption that I think is commonly made in discussions of the philosophy of mind, namely that *if* there are immaterial states, then mental states just are immaterial states and immaterial states just are mental states (in such a way that being the same mental state necessarily goes with being the same immaterial state, and vice versa). And surely this assumption ought to be abandoned. It is hardly plausible to hold that it is analytic that all mental states are immaterial states (if it were analytic, opponents of dualism would hold a self-contradictory position unless they deny the existence of mental states), and it is hard to see why it should be thought to be analytic that all immaterial states are mental states.[11] And if the hypothesis that there are immaterial substances were introduced and adopted as an empirical hypothesis, one needed to explain human behavior, then questions would arise about the relationship between immaterial states and mental states that are precisely analogous to the currently discussed questions about the relationship between brain states and mental states. Perhaps mental states could be held to be "functional states" that are "realized in" immaterial states. Perhaps they could be held to be disjunctions of immaterial states, or disjunctions of immaterial states and physical states. Conceivably particular mental events could be held to be identical with particular immaterial events in a way analogous to that in which Donald Davidson holds particular mental events to be identical with particular neurophysiological events, that is, in a way that does not require the existence of generic identities between kinds of mental events and kinds of immaterial events.[12] But if, as I have argued, the causal role played by mental states in the production of behavior would have to be played by different immaterial states in the case of different sorts of "minds" (i.e., minds that "mesh" with different sorts of bodies), then it is as much out of the question that anger, for example, should just be, in all possible circumstances, a certain immaterial state as that such a mental state should just be, in all possible circumstances, a certain neurophysiological state of the brain.[13]

But now for a qualification. I suggested earlier that the volition to wave one's arm would have different causal powers, and so would be "something different," in minds animating radically different sorts of bodies, because its immediate physical effects (on the brain, or whatever) would have to be different. More generally, I have suggested that if there were immaterial substances, different sorts of bodies would be animated by different sorts of immaterial substances. But this would not necessarily be the case, and I think that we can make sense of the notion of a mind (immaterial substance) that is capable of animating a variety of different sorts of bodies (assuming that we can make sense of the notion of an immaterial substance to begin with).

One way of making sense of this is to suppose, in effect, that the mind has a part—call it the "adaptor"—which mediates the causal connections between the remainder of it and the body it animates, and does so in a different way depending on the nature of the body. When the mind comes into "contact" with a body (what "contact" can mean here is of course totally unclear, since immaterial substances have traditionally been conceived as not having spatial location in their own right), the adaptor "scans" the body in order to determine of what sort it is, and then, depending on the outcome of this scanning, goes into an appropriate "mediating state"; and when the adaptor is in a mediating state appropriate to the body with which it is in "contact," the sensory input from the body is translated into a form suitable for the production of appropriate sense-impressions in the mind, and the volitional output from the mind is translated into a form suitable for the production of appropriate movements in the body, the total effect being that the mind is paradigmatically embodied in the body (unless the body is defective in some way). If minds were like this, it might seem, there would be no need to distinguish mental states from immaterial states, since the same mental state would always be "realized in" the same immaterial state, no matter what sort of body the mind is embodied in.

If we can make sense of the notion of an immaterial substance at all, I think we can make sense of the notion of an immaterial substance of the sort just described, that is, one having an "adaptor" as a part. But if anything this makes matters worse for the view that mental states just are immaterial states. To begin with, if there can be adaptor-equipped minds (immaterial substances) which are capable of animating any of a variety of sorts of physical bodies, there would seem to be no reason why there cannot *also* be simpler minds (immaterial substances) not having adaptors, each of these being capable of animating only one sort of body. Also, there would seem to be no reason why there should not be more than one sort of adaptor-equipped mind. Suppose that A-type minds are capable of animating only Alpha-type bodies, while B-type minds are capable of animating only Beta-type bodies. If we can imagine an A-type mind augmented by an adaptor that enables it to animate bodies of other sorts, including Beta-type bodies, we can equally imagine a B-type mind augmented by an adaptor (one of a different sort than is required for A-type minds) which enables it to animate bodies of other sorts, including Alpha-type bodies. This introduces a new possibility, namely that two bodies of the same sort might be animated by minds of different sorts, the persons having the same mental states and the same physical states but their minds having different immaterial states. Thus, for example, one of the bodies might be animated by an adaptor-equipped A-type mind while the other is animated by an adaptor-equipped B-type mind, the total structure of each mind (including its adaptor) being such that when in "contact" with a body of that sort they both mediate in the same way between sensory input and behavioral output.

But there is another, and perhaps simpler, way of making sense of the notion of a mind that is capable of animating (paradigmatically) more than one sort of body. Since the immediate causal effects of any event or state depend on what other events or states occur or exist at the same time, why shouldn't the very same mental (or immaterial) state or event act differently on different sorts of bodies, its immediate physical effect depending on the antecedent physical state of the body affected?[14] Supposing that Alpha-type bodies, Beta-type bodies, Gamma-type bodies, and so forth, are different sorts of bodies, all of which are capable of being bodies of persons having the same repertory of mental states, it might be that the causal powers of a particular immaterial state I could be expressed in a set of conditionals stating how I affects these various sorts of bodies when a mind in which it occurs is in "contact" with them; thus we might have "If I occurs in a mind which is in 'contact' with an Alpha-type body, it produces physical state P_1 in that body," "If I occurs in a mind which is in 'contact' with a Beta-type body, it produces physical state P_2 in that body," and so on. And it might be, compatibly with this, that the effect of I on overt behavior is (*ceteris paribus*) the same in these various sorts of bodies, despite the fact that it produces this effect sometimes by producing inner physical state P_1, sometimes by producing state P_2, and so on. If in all cases the contribution of I to the causation of overt behavior is the same (despite the differences in the way in which it makes this contribution), and is that which is appropriate to a particular mental state (in other words, if I is, in D. M. Armstrong's terminology, "apt for bringing about" behavior manifesting a certain mental state,[15] no matter what sort of body is involved), let us say that I "universally realizes" that mental state; and if the immaterial states of an immaterial substance universally realize a complete repertory of mental states, let us say that it is a "universal mind."

I do not wish to deny the possibility of there being universal minds and immaterial states that universally realize mental states. But it seems at least equally possible that there should be immaterial states whose causal powers are more limited, each of these states being such that only in the case of one sort of body would the state contribute to the causation of overt behavior in the way appropriate to a particular mental state; these would be states that are "apt for bringing about" behavior manifesting a certain mental state only when the mind in which they occur is in "contact" with a body of a particular sort. So instead of, or in addition to, state I, which universally realizes (let us suppose) the state of trying to wave one's arm, we might have state I_a, which has the same effect as I on Alpha bodies (i.e., produces arm waving by producing physiological state P_1) but has no effect, or no relevant effect, on bodies of other sorts; state I_b, which has the same effect as I on Beta-type bodies (i.e., produces arm waving by producing physiological state P_2) but has no relevant effect on bodies of other sorts; and so on. Thus we seem to have the possibility of the same mental state (the volition to wave one's arm) being "something different" in different minds, that is, of immaterial states (I, I_a, I_b, etc.) being the same *qua* mental states and different *qua* immaterial states. And this is all that my argument requires, since it is enough to preclude a straightforward identification of mental states and immaterial states.

Against all this someone might try to take the heroic line of holding that for any mental state there is exactly one immaterial state that essentially is that mental state and which that state essentially is. This might mean that every mental state is identical with some immaterial state that universally realizes it. This has the absurd consequence that none of us is entitled to think that he himself has a mind or mental states; for none of us has any reason to think that his own body is animated by a universal mind, or that his behavior is brought about by immaterial states that universally realize mental states. Alternatively, the claim might be that for each mental state M there is exactly one immaterial state I which is such that instances of I will necessarily be instances of M quite independently of their causal role in the structures in which they occur, and that instances of states other than I can never be instances of M, no matter what their causal role is in the structures in which they occur. One consequence of this is to make the problem of knowledge of other minds unsolvable. For consider the case mentioned above in which there are two physically identical bodies one of which is animated by an adaptor-equipped A-type mind and the other of which is animated by an adaptor-equipped B-type mind, both of them having exactly the same behavioral dispositions (as well as the same inner physiology). On the view now under consideration, if the behavior of these bodies were such that we would naturally take them to be bodies of someone having certain mental states, at most one of them could be the body of someone having those mental states—and it would be impossible to discover on the basis of any physical or behavioral evidence which, if either, this was. If this is so, it would seem that in no case could behavioral or other physical evidence entitle us to believe that we were confronted with a subject of mental states. Nor could other evidence entitle us to believe this. Even if we could somehow discover the nature of the immaterial substance animating a body (and how might we do this?), this would not tell us anything about what mental states (if any) that substance had, unless we already knew which immaterial states are identical with which mental states. And how could we know this? It is no good saying that each person can discover "from his own case" that certain mental states are certain immaterial states; introspection no more reveals identities between mental states and immaterial states than it reveals identities between mental states and neurophysiological states of the brain, and it is quite unclear what could be meant by the suggestion that it might reveal identities of either sort. I conclude that the view under consideration renders other minds totally unknowable; and I hope I can hold this against it without being accused of "verificationism."

My argument has rested, of course, on the claim that if it is possible for there to be "immaterial substances" at all then it is possible that there should be different sorts of immaterial substances (as different from each other as human bodies are from the robot and Martian bodies of science fiction), which are capable of "animating" different sorts of bodies (or even, if augmented with "adaptors," the same sorts of bodies) in such a way as to yield the same potential for behavior. An opponent might deny this claim. But I do not see on what grounds he could deny it.

I shall not consider here the question of whether the notion of an immaterial state (and that of an immaterial substance) is a coherent one, and for the purposes of this discussion I am assuming (or pretending) that it is—I am assuming (or pretending) that the notion of a "physical state" can be given an intuitively satisfactory analysis which leaves it logically possible that there should be entities that are capable of interacting causally with entities having physical states but do not themselves have physical states. I shall not consider whether such entities could be assigned spatial location and, if not, how they might be individuated. One of the main points I have been concerned to make is that if there are such entities, their states have no more claim to *be* mental states than brain states do. Once this point is seen, it should be clear that there is no *conceptual* reason for supposing that the existence of mental states involves the existence of immaterial substances and immaterial states, and it should be clear, in particular, that the conceptual falsity of particular forms of the mind-body identity theory provides no such reason.[16] Any reasons for adopting the hypothesis that there are immaterial substances would have to be empirical. I assume that if there is any empirical evidence for the existence of such substances (perhaps in phenomena reported by spiritualists and parapsychologists), it is not overwhelming. But even if there are such substances, and even if they do sometimes exist in "disembodied form" (i.e., without being related to bodies in such a way as to be capable of interacting causally with them in the ways constitutive of paradigmatic embodiment), this turns out, I think, to be compatible with my contention that paradigmatic embodiment is paradigmatic of the very existence of persons. The causal role played by such immaterial substances in the determination of behavior would be, at best, that which nowadays is generally ascribed to the brain; they would be, at best, ghostly brains. And the (perhaps) logically possible case of the disembodied immaterial substance seems in essential respects like the logically possible case of the detached brain kept alive *in vitro*; in both cases, I think, it is only the causal role that the states of the brain or quasi-brain would play if it were paradigmatically embodied which would justify regarding them as realizing, or in some sense being, mental states.[17]

I began this paper by pointing out that if we can establish both (1) that it is a necessary truth that if a person is embodied then certain of his mental states will typically manifest themselves in certain ways in the behavior of his body, and (2) that it is a necessary truth that the existence of persons requires their embodiment, we will have established (3) that it is a necessary truth that certain of the mental states of persons typically manifest themselves in certain ways in bodily behavior. But only as a very rough approximation could one describe my strategy in this paper as that of arguing for a version of (3) by arguing for versions of (1) and (2). I summed up the first part of the paper by saying that what I have called "paradigmatic embodiment" is genuinely paradigmatic of the embodiment of persons, and hence that it is a conceptual truth that if a person is embodied then his volitions, or at least those volitions that are of types relative to which he believes himself to be embodied, normally issue in movements of his body that are "appropriate" to them. This, call it (1'), seems to qualify well enough as a version of (1). In the remainder of the paper I defended the view, call it (2'), that paradigmatic embodiment is paradigmatic of the very existence, and not just the embodiment, of persons. But (2'), while in the spirit of (2), is not really a version of it, and there is no version of (3) that follows from (1') and (2') in the way (3) follows from (1) and (2). Still, if the claim that paradigmatic embodiment is paradigmatic of the embodiment of persons warrants a conceptual claim about the normal or typical effects of volitions in cases of *embodied* persons, the claim that paradigmatic embodiment is paradigmatic of the very existence of persons would seem to warrant a corresponding claim about the normal or typical effects of volitions in the case of persons *simpliciter*. And the latter claim, that it is conceptually true that the volitions of a person (or at least those relative to which the person believes himself to be embodied) normally give rise to bodily movements appropriate to them, would seem to qualify as a version of (3).

Early in my discussion I put on one side, as being "psycho-psycho" rather than psychophysical, such connections as that between wanting to do something and trying to do it, that between fearing something and wanting to avoid it, and so on. But I have not really been able to keep such connections out of my discussion; for in order to get the result that a paradigmatically embodied person will have generally correct beliefs about the extent of his volitional embodiment, I had to stipulate that paradigmatic embodiment involves a significant degree of rationality and learning capacity, and this is to say that it involves the existence of psycho-psycho connections as well as psychophysical ones. To complete my examination of the logical status (i.e., the contingency or otherwise) of psychophysical connections I would have to consider the status of these psycho-psycho connections. Indeed, I think that it has often been connections of the latter sort (e.g., between wanting X, believing that doing Y is the most efficient way of getting X, and trying to do Y) that philosophers have had in mind in asserting that there are "conceptual connections" between mental states and behavior. I believe that in a consideration of the logical status of these psycho-psycho connections the notion of rationality can play much the same role that the notion of embodiment has played in my discussion here. Roughly, we can argue that it is necessarily or conceptually true that *if* a person is rational then certain lawlike connections will hold among his mental states (or, better, that such connections hold to the extent that the person is rational), and can then proceed to consider to what extent, if any, the very existence of the mental states requires rationality and hence the existence of these connections. While I cannot undertake this investigation here, my hunch is that its outcome would be, if combined with the conclusions of the present paper, a version of the "causal theory of mind" in which the various sorts of mental states are characterized as having, essentially, such causal powers as tend to yield lawlike connections constitutive of rationality and paradigmatic embodiment.[18]

I should remark, in conclusion, that while I have attempted to defend a version of the view that there are "conceptual connections" between mental states and behavior, nothing that I have said supports, or is intended to support, the view that there are necessary truths that directly license inferences from behavioral premises to mentalistic conclusions, for example, necessary truths of the form "If a body is moving in such and such ways, then (normally, or *ceteris paribus*) it is the body of someone having thus and such mental states." It is difficult enough to come up with a proposition of this form that is true, and it is quite impossible, I now think, to come up with one that is necessarily, or conceptually, true. If there is to be truth in the view that there are behavioral "criteria" for mental states, it must not be interpeted as implying that there are necessary truths of this sort.[19]

NOTES

1. I should like to express my gratitude to the University of Oxford, for the opportunity to give the lectures on which this paper is based; to Cornell University, for a leave that made possible the completion and delivery of those lectures; to Tufts University, for an opportunity to try out an earlier version of this paper; and to The Center for Advanced Study in the Behavioral Sciences, in Stanford, California, for a fellowship that provided me with time, and a delightful setting, in which to write the present version of this paper.

2. It is important to distinguish the question of whether there could be disembodied subjects of mental states from the question of whether actually existing people are such that it is possible that they should exist in disembodied form, e.g., whether it is possible that I should exist in disembodied form. A negative answer to the first question implies a negative answer to the second, but the converse does not hold. It is arguable that if it is so much as logically possible that I should at some time exist without having a body, then even now, when I do have a body, I cannot be identical with that body and cannot be the subject of its

physical states (or of any other physical states). On this view, dualism is true of whatever creatures are capable (logically capable) of existing in disembodied form—the idea behind this being, roughly, that whatever has physical states is *essentially* something having physical states (and, what follows from this, that whatever can fail to have physical states essentially lacks physical states). But even if this is so, and even if I and other human beings have physical states and so are essentially embodied, it does not follow that it is impossible that there should be subjects of mental states which are capable of existing in disembodied form. Note that a materialist, while he must deny that he and other actually existing human beings are capable of disembodied existence (or, at least, must do so if the essentialist view just stated is correct), can consistently allow that it is logically possible that there should be disembodied subjects of mental states.

3. I do not mean to suggest that it is only Cartesian dualists who will take this line; it can equally well be taken by a materialist who happens to believe that disembodied existence is a logically possible, although in fact nonexistent, phenomenon. See n. 2.

4. For an explicit statement of this view, see Jerome Shaffer, "Persons and Their Bodies," *Philosophical Review*, LXXV (1966), especially p. 72. Shaffer defends in this paper a view he calls Cartesian, although he does not commit himself to the possibility of disembodied existence. See also C. J. Ducasse, "Mind, Matter and Bodies," in J. R. Smythies, ed., *Brain and Mind* (London, 1965), p. 96.

5. For an admirable defense of such an account, see Brian O'Shaughnessy, "Trying (as the Mental 'Pineal Gland')," *Journal of Philosophy*, LXX (July 19, 1973), 365-386. I understand that a similar view has been defended by D. M. Armstrong in a still unpublished paper, and I employed such a view in my John Locke lectures at the University of Oxford in 1972.

6. The most common objection to this view about perception—that under normal circumstances it cannot appropriately be said of someone who sees something red (for example) that it looks to him as if he were seeing something red, or that he is having a visual impression or visual experience of something red—seems to me to have been decisively answered by H. P. Grice in his paper "The Causal Theory of Perception," *Proceedings of the Aristotelian Society*, Supplementary Volume, XXXV (1961). And I think that Grice's analysis can be used to answer a parallel and equally common objection to the view that all cases of intentional action involve a mental episode of trying, or what I am calling a volition. It is true that in ordinary circumstances it would be inappropriate to say of someone who raised his arm that he tried to raise it, because saying this carries the implication that in the circumstances raising his arm was, or might have been supposed to be, difficult or impossible for the person to do. But this implication is, in Grice's terminology, "cancellable"; having said that someone tried to raise his arm one can go on to say without inconsistency that he experienced no difficulty in raising his arm and that no one had supposed that he would have difficulty. And this is because the implication is carried, not by the meaning of what is said (that the person tried to raise his arm) but by the saying of it; the speaker's calling attention to the fact that someone tried to raise his arm indicates that the case is an atypical case of arm raising, not because it is unusual for such trying to occur but because it is unusual for it to be worth commenting on.

7. After writing this I found that on this point I am apparently in disagreement with Ducasse, who writes that one of the "decisive marks" of one's own body (as contrasted with such "accidental marks of it" as that one never sees its eyes) is

that it is "the only body in which one's being ashamed causes blushing automatically" (Ducasse, op. cit.).

8. Talk of "criteria" of embodiment will strike some readers as off. For when do we have occasion to employ such criteria? Ordinarily a question of the form "Which body is S's body?" would ask for the identification of a corpse, and it would not seem that such an identification requires the use or possession of criteria of embodiment. But recent work on the problem of personal identity strongly indicates that the identity conditions for persons are different from those for bodies, in such a way as to make it possible for a person to have different bodies at different times; that persons cannot, therefore, be identical with their bodies; and that at any given time in a person's life it is a contingent fact that he has the body he has instead of some other one. This indicates that there is a relationship of "being embodied in" or "having as one's body" which persons have to bodies; and an account is needed of what this relationship consists in which explains, when combined with an account of personal identity, how we know that in fact people retain the same bodies throughout their lives and how we would detect a change of body if it occurred.

9. See J. A. Fodor, "Explanations in Psychology," in M. Black, ed., *Philosophy in America* (Ithaca, N. Y., 1965); H. Putnam, "Minds and Machines," in S. Hook, ed., *Dimensions of Mind* (New York, 1961); "The Mental Life of Some Machines," in H. N. Castaneda, ed., *Intentionality, Minds, and Perception* (Detroit, Mich., 1967); and "Psychological Predicates" in W. H. Capitan and D. D. Merrill, eds., *Art, Mind, and Religion* (Pittsburgh, 1967); and N. J. Block and J. A. Fodor, "What Mental States are Not," *Philosophical Review* LXXXI (1972), 159-181.

10. One version that seems immune to it is that of Donald Davidson in "Mental Events," in L. Foster and J. W. Swanson, eds., *Experience and Theory* (Amherst, Mass., 1970). Another is that of David Lewis in "An Argument for the Identity Theory," in D. M. Rosenthal, ed., *Materialism and the Mind-Body Problem* (Englewood Cliffs, N. J., 1971); see especially the addenda to this reprinting, and see Lewis's comments on Putnam's views in his review of *Art, Mind, and Religion*, in *Journal of Philosophy* LXVI (January 16, 1969), 23-25.

11. In "Incorrigibility as the Mark of the Mental" (*Journal of Philosophy* LXVII [June 25, 1970], 399-424), Richard Rorty says that " 'immaterial' gets its sense from its connection with 'mental' " (p. 402). The trouble with this is that "immaterial" contrasts with "physical" (or "material") in a way that "mental" doesn't. It may well be, as Rorty goes on to say, that "The notions of 'ghostly stuff' and 'immaterial substance' would never have become current if Descartes had not been able to use *cogitationes* as an illustration of what he intended" (ibid.). But Rorty surely cannot think that what he regards as the essential "mark" of the mental, namely incorrigibility, makes mental states immaterial in the sense of being states of a substance having no physical properties. "Mental" does not contrast with "physical" in a way that suffices to get this sense of "immaterial" going. It may be that this sense of "immaterial" is no sense at all, because the notion of a substance having no physical properties is not coherent (and only seems coherent because of muddles about mental states). All I am saying is that there is no reason to think it analytic, or true, that *if* the latter notion is coherent then immaterial states are mental (or, conversely, that mental states are immaterial).

12. See Davidson, op. cit.

13. I put the matter in this way so as to allow for a view parallel to David

Lewis's version of the psychophysical identity theory (see Lewis, op. cit.). As I understand him, Lewis would deny that the attribute of being angry is identical with any physical attribute, but would claim that "anger" nevertheless always names some physical state or other—perhaps a different physical state depending on the species of the creature (e.g., whether man or mollusk), and perhaps even a different physical state depending on the identity of the individual (e.g., whether Lewis or Putnam). Analogously, a dualist might deny (as I think my argument requires) that the attribute of being angry is identical with any immaterial attribute, but hold that "anger" always names some immaterial state or other, though perhaps a different one depending on the species or identity of the individual to which anger is ascribed. (But I think he would do better to take the view sketched in n. 15.)

14. Here I am indebted to Professor J. V. Canfield, who pointed out to me that I was mistaken in maintaining, in an earlier version of this paper, that this would violate the principle "Same cause, same effect."

15. See David M. Armstrong, *A Materialist Theory of Mind* (London, 1968), who suggests that "The concept of a mental state is primarily the concept of *a state of the person apt for bringing about a certain sort of behavior.*"

16. What seems to me conceptually false is the view that mental attributes or properties are identical with physical attributes or properties, where this implies that in any creature, actual or possible, that mental attribute is instantiated if and only if that physical attribute is instantiated.

17. It is worth noting that the view that our mental states are realized in the states of immaterial substances, which serve as "ghostly brains" (this being, according to me, the only version of dualism that has a chance of being coherent), is perfectly compatible with the Strawsonian conception of persons as entities which are, irreduceably, subjects of both mental and physical states (as opposed to being subjects of mental states alone, or composites of subjects of mental states ["minds" or "souls"] and subjects of physical states ["bodies"]). The acceptance of this view would no more require one to identify the person with the immaterial substance whose states realize his mental states than the acceptance of the usual views about the causal role of the brain would require one to identify the person with his brain (and we cannot make the latter identification unless we are willing to say that no person ever weighs more than a few pounds, that persons are grey in color and roughly hemispherical in shape, and so on). Although mental states will be realized in states of immaterial substances, on this view, they should not be thought of as being states of immaterial substances; instead, they will be states of persons, which, since they have physical states as well as mental states, are not immaterial substances (and do not have immaterial states). It is true that if it is possible for an immaterial substance to exist in disembodied form, it is possible for a person to exist without having physical properties. But even then the mental states of the person will not be immaterial states, since they will still be states that are capable of belonging to something having physical states. However, if this sort of disembodiment is possible, then it cannot be true, as was tentatively suggested in n. 2, that whatever has physical properties is essentially something having physical properties—although it will be true (by definition) that whatever has immaterial properties is essentially something that lacks physical properties.

18. The causal theory of mind has been championed in recent years by a number of writers. See especially David Armstrong, *A Materialist Theory of Mind* (London, 1968); David Lewis, "An Argument for the Identity Theory" and

"Psychophysical and Theoretical Identifications," *Australasian Journal of Philosophy*, 50, 3 (December 1972), 249-257; and Alvin Goldman, *A Theory of Human Action* (Englewood Cliffs, N. J., 1970).

19. I tended to interpret it in this way in my book *Self-Knowledge and Self-Identity* (Ithaca, N. Y., 1963), but I did not there distinguish adequately between this view and the view that there are necessary truths of the form "If someone knows such and such about the behavior of a body, he is *(ceteris paribus)* entitled to take this as evidence that it is the body of a person having such and such mental states." It is possible that the latter view can be upheld even though the former cannot; but I would no longer put any stock in it.

LOCKE, BUTLER AND THE STREAM OF CONSCIOUSNESS: AND MEN AS A NATURAL KIND

DAVID WIGGINS

I

John Locke on persons and one objection of Joseph Butler

Locke defined a person as 'a thinking intelligent being, that has reason and reflection, and can consider itself as itself, the same thinking thing, in different times and places' (Essay II.XXVII.II). To many who have been excited by the same thought as Locke, continuity of consciousness has seemed to be an integral part of what we mean by a person. The intuitive appeal of the idea that to secure the continuing identity of a person one experience must flow into the next experience in 'some stream of consciousness' is evidenced by the number of attempts in the so-called constructionalist tradition to explain continuity of consciousness in terms of memory, and then build or reconstruct the idea of a person with these materials. The philosophical difficulty of the idea is plain from the failure of these attempts. Hindsight suggests this was as inevitable as the failure of the attempt (if anyone ever made it) to make bricks from straw alone—and just as uninteresting. (Which is not to deny that the memory theorist might get from it a sense that some of the difficulties in his programme have arisen from his leaving flesh and bones, the stuff of persons, out of his construction.)

There is a distinction, well founded in the texts of Locke and Descartes on the one hand and Hume, James, Russell and Ayer on the other, which is sometimes put as the distinction between 'subject' and 'no-subject' theories of the self. (It is not happily put so, because no-subject theories aim not so much to reject as to reconstruct the subject, and it comes back into discourse as a complex.) But the continuity of persons is to be discussed here on a level at which this division in the traditions of speculation about the nature and persistence of selves is irrelevant. When James writes that 'the continuing identity of each personal consciousness is treated as a name for the practical fact that new experiences look back on old ones, find them warm and appropriate them as mine,' and that subsequent experiences must judge that 'these feelings are the nucleus of me,' this 'no-subject' theory is founded in the same sorts of question as Locke's theory.[1] Some of these questions are, admittedly, misconceived.[2] But it does not follow that either tradition is wholly wrong to interest itself in the idea that memory and reflection help to constitute the continuity of the persisting self.

The first aim of what follows is to examine the charges of circularity or manifest absurdity brought against the theory that some such continuity is part of the essence of persons and their identities. Of these charges the theory can be cleared. The second aim is to pursue a potentially conflicting insight suggested by the first defence itself. Even if this insight finally subverts the Lockean identity condition it cannot, I think, refute the whole Lockean conception of a person. There is something so interesting about the idea that a person is an object essentially aware of its progress and persistence through time—a self recorder so to say—and this notion is so closely related to some of the profoundest contentions of Kant,[3] that one should look very critically at any attempt to demonstrate irreducible circularity in the continuity of consciousness condition of personal identity. But one ought to examine even more sceptically the view that adequate experiential memory is no essential part of the concept of a person.

Bishop Butler wrote in criticism of Locke 'And one should really think it self-evident, that consciousness of personal identity presupposes, and cannot therefore constitute, personal identity any more than knowledge, in any other case, can constitute truth, which it presupposes' (*First Dissertation to the Analogy of Religion*). It must be allowed that if one defines a person in Locke's manner (if one means to be defining persons and not describing them merely), and if one really attaches enough importance to some self-recording capacity *d* to make *active possession of d* a definitive property of persons then, because exercise of the capacity *d* becomes a condition of the very existence and persistence of a person, *d* must indeed register upon the identity conditions for people. This only reflects a wider truth familiar from the teachings of Aristotle, Leibniz and Frege about the intimate relation holding between an account of *what a thing is* and the elucidation of the identity-conditions for members of its kind. If, as some have suggested, a difficulty is involved in stating a Lockean personal identity condition, then this difficulty can only exemplify a more general difficulty attaching to the attempt to build into the definition of any thing-kind *f* a reference to the capacity of a member of *f* to have at *t* some relation or other *to its own states before t*. There has, I suppose, to be (what I doubt there is) some systematic difficulty about this *its*.

There may be room for disagreement about what exact objection Bishop Butler's famous sentence was meant to make against Locke. It does not seem to recapitulate the point made in Butler's preceding sentence, which reads 'But though consciousness of what is past does thus ascertain our personal identity to ourselves, yet to say it makes personal identity or is necessary to our being the same persons, is to say that a person has not existed a single moment nor done one action but what he can remember; indeed none but what he reflects upon. And one should really think it self-evident....' We shall come in due course to the point Butler is making in this earlier sentence. The sentence we are concerned with at the moment, about what is self-evident, appears to relate to some point of logical hygiene which, according to Butler, Locke ought to have been able to note before he even embarked on his ill-starred project—something as manifest as 'knowledge presupposes truth.' And the point seems to be that one cannot define A's identity with B in terms of A's *being conscious of having been identical with B or remembering being B*. But why, one wonders, should a Lockean adherent not, instead of that, make the definition of A's being the same person as B in terms of *A's really or apparently remembering X-ing-at-time-t, just in case if X-ing is what B in fact did at time t?*[4] There will be obvious and extreme difficulties about this, but they are not the difficulties which the

particular sentence of Butler's seeks to exploit. For such a definition does not even mention A's consciousness of identity with B.

At this point, however, other philosophers, Flew for instance,[5]
have been willing to reinterpret, amplify or extend Butler's argument. Flew writes 'It is absurd to say that "he can remember that
he is the same person."' The absurdity is usually slightly masked
since expressions such as "I remember doing, feeling, seeing something" do not contain explicit reference to the fact that what is
remembered is that the speaker is the same person as did, felt, or
saw whatever it was.'[6] This does Locke the same injustice as Butler
did him. It also imports a new claim, that 'A remembers X-ing' is
a disguised or 'masked' version of what should be rendered explicitly as 'A remembers A's X-ing.' But so far from 'A remembers
X-ing' having 'A remembers A's X-ing' as its canonical and equivalent form (or 'A remembers B's X-ing' implying the identity of A
and B), the two locutions are (I submit) importantly different in
both construction and sense; though it may well be the idea that 'A
remembers X-ing' has as its canonical form 'A remembers A's
X-ing' which leads Flew himself into a curious oversight. He says
(page 56) that it is a necessary truth 'that x at time two is the *same
person* as y at time one if and only if x and y are both persons, and
x can (logical) remember at time two what y did etc. at time one.'
To this I object that I still remember Hitler invading Russia during
the Second World War, and still remember Field Marshal Montgomery reminiscing in some speech or other he once gave when I
was at school about how he won the battle of Alamein. If remembering these things makes me into Hitler or Montgomery, it makes
me into both. But it doesn't matter exactly why Flew says this
extraordinary thing. The important point is that the relation of
A's *remembering* X-ing to A's *remembering* A's X-ing is really
quite complicated.

If a very cool paratrooper, call him the first parachutist, forgets
that he is to jump first; if for some reason, when he does jump, he
pays no attention to the fact that he is jumping first; and does not
remember afterwards that he jumped first; then he, the first parachutist, may remember jumping without remembering the first
parachutist's jumping. (Anyway, if you ask him about it he may
say 'I don't remember the first parachutist's jumping.') And, conversely, he may remember the first parachutist's having his equip-

ment checked—he watched not realizing it was his equipment but realizing that it was the first parachutist's equipment—and may remember this without remembering having *his* equipment checked. For, whatever else he remembers, 'having my equipment checked' is not what he remembers about this event. There is much more to be said here[7] but the difficulties of equating A's remembering X-ing with A's remembering A's X-ing, or remembering his X-ing, are part of a larger phenomenon deserving of more attention than philosophers have given it. Is my imagining being Moses, or an elephant, or Paul Klee's paintbrush equivalent to my imagining (the impossible state of affairs of) me being a paintbrush or Moses or an elephant? Compare also foreseeing, visualizing, conceiving. Here, as with imagining, the inability to leave oneself out of the picture precisely disables one from achieving anything much by way of imagination.

That there can be no jumping first or having one's equipment checked, no being Moses or being an elephant or being a paintbrush, without *some* subject's doing or suffering or being these things is not the same as to say that the subject must be specified, or must if specified be the same as the subject of the psychological verbs remembering, imagining...(jumping/being...). What is more, even if one always could rewrite 'A remembers X-ing' as 'A remembers A's X-ing'—which one can't, but even if one could—it would still be right to ask why *should* one rewrite it so? One can rewrite 'C is the same tree as D' as 'C is one and the same tree as D.' Will that refute logicism? If we must rewrite everything that we can rewrite then all attempts at philosophical analysis must be either incorrect or 'circular.'

II

Another line of objection and a restatement of the requirement of continuity of consciousness

Butler remarks in the same passage of the *First Dissertation* that to say that 'memory makes personal identity, or is necessary to our being the same persons, is to say that a person has not existed a single moment, nor done one action, but what he can remember; indeed none but what he reflects upon.'

This is a charge not of circularity but of outright absurdity. We might think it a decent first attempt at adjusting Locke's development of his project to evade it, and enough to secure something like the continuity which Locke desired between person P_{tj} and person Q_{tj} that, for some *sufficiency* of things actually done, witnessed, experienced... at any time by P_{tj}, Q_{tk} should later have *sufficient* real or apparent recollection of then doing, witnessing, experiencing...them.[9] Let us call this relation (suitably tidied up, with more about 'sufficiency,' and glossed somehow to allow for sleep) the relation C of *strong co-consciousness*, and symbolize its holding as (Q_{tk}) C (P_{tj}). Then anyone bent on grasping the nerve of Locke's conception of person would see, as Leibniz saw but not all of Locke's critics have seen,[10] that the identity-condition he had to refute was one which made the persistence of a person *P* depend only upon *P*'s being related at each successive phase of his biography in this C-relation to *P* at each previous phase. C itself is a nontransitive relation but the *ancestral* *C of the C-relation, the weaker and transitive relation of x's being either C-related to *y* or C-related to some *z* which is C-related to *y* or...I shall say *co-consciousness* simply—provides us with all we need for the statement of a general neo-Lockean identity-condition:

Ip: *P* is the same person as Q if and only if (Q)*C(P).

The shortcomings of this will be quickly evident, and they are rehearsed in section III; but they are not the defects of circularity, logical impropriety or outright absurdity; nor are they symptoms of any inherent defect in the more complex conditions which *C might be used to formulate. What these shortcomings really signify is the unexpected richness and concreteness of the requirements on any satisfactory realization of Locke's original idea. As will appear, these requirements are radically inconsistent with the immaterialist conception which Locke himself arrived at. But it is not that part of his conception which this paper is to defend. The defects relate to (i) the formal adequacy of (x)*C(y) to define an equivalence relation like identity, and (ii) the need to fortify *C in order to secure what is actually intended by the continuity of consciousness requirement.

III

*The inadequacy of *C, as of any uncontaminated 'remembering'* *condition of mental continuity. The involvement of remembering with the physical*

Defining *C as we have, is there any positive reason to think that it is symmetrical and reflexive as well as transitive? Unless *C has these properties its obtaining between some *x* and some *y* is certainly insufficient for personal identity, and may be insufficient even for what was intended by continuity of consciousness.[11]

Suppose $(\exists y)\,[(x)*C(y)]$. Then does it follow that $(x)*C(x)$, that x sufficiently remembers doing a sufficiency of what x has just done? Even if we scale this down a little to require only that x has the *potentiality* to remember sufficiently at each stage a sufficiency of what x has done just before, there is already a problem. If a person is knocked down in a road accident and never recovers consciousness or memory at all, can he not remain biologically alive in hospital for years afterwards? Is he not an unconscious, or memoriless person? Some will find Locke's disqualification of this person strained or absurd, or will complain that it smacks of legislation, which it does. But it is not necessarily pointless legislation. It is not with reflexivity that the obvious or immediate difficulty lies. Symmetry and transitivity are the challenge.

Nothing in our definitions so far seems to have ruled out the following possibility: A stream of consciousness divides at some point and flows into a delta of two consciousness which are separate thereafter. Here we have, say,

$$(Q_{t_3})\ {}^*C\ (P_{t_1})$$

and also

$$(R_{t_3})\ {}^*C\ (P_{t_1})$$

One way of persuading oneself one can conceive of this is by picturing a man split from top to toe, exactly through the *corpus callosum*, artificial replacements being supplied to each half for all missing limbs and organs. Less ghoulishly, one may suppose he can conceive a Lamarckian state of affairs in which children inherit some substantial experiential memories corresponding closely to the life of the mother up to the moment of conception.[12]

If these things are truly conceivable (which for *persons* I doubt, but more of that later), then *C cannot be both transitive *and* symmetrical. If the stream of consciousness of someone who (say) planted the fig tree beside a certain wall divided in the fashion we have described, and if there were later two people who claimed to remember planting the tree (and did indeed remember planting it —all the factual and circumstantial and causal requirements of memory being satisfied in the fantasy), then the criterion Ip would force us to identify the two claimants with one each other.[13] But one may shout and the other may sulk when the dispute breaks out. They cannot be the same people.[14]

Where does this leave us? If we were interested in continuity of consciousness for its own sake without wanting to define the identity and difference of persons by its means, we might rely on the fact that remembering is done by people (constituted as they are with the physical limitations they have) in order to underwrite it as an equivalence relation. But it is the other way about. Our only reason for insisting that *C must be an equivalence relation is precisely our desire to use it to define personal identity. In the absence of any commitment to that project, we might be content for *C to be (say) reflexive, transitive and non-symmetrical.

Should we then abandon our interest in continuity of consciousness and scuttle the whole Lockean conception of a person? Not yet. If anything, Ip's insufficiency to define identity properly for the case of a delta in the stream of consciousness draws attention to the actual plausibility of the co-consciousness condition. For, in spite of the difficulty about *identity*, many people feel an almost overwhelming pressure in such thought-experiments to find a way to allow *both* the resulting splinters something like identity with the person who split. In a society where people occasionally divided, but which persevered in its interest in what Locke calls 'that consciousness which draws punishments or reward with it,'[15] a malefactor could scarcely evade responsibility by contriving his own fission. Nor, as Chisholm, Parfit and Williams in their very different ways have brought out, can reflection on the transitivity of identity be enough to make me cease to care about the future if I know that I am about to divide and there will shortly be two splinters, both co-conscious with me. Such possibilities (or possible possibilities) do not show the mutual irrelevance of co-

consciousness and personal identity. What are stirred up here are problems about survival, rationality, altruism, and prudence which are nothing if they are not problems of the self.

I announced that there were two difficulties in the *C conditions as stated. The first, just completed, related to the formal adequacy of *C. The second, to which I now come, is the need to fortify *C to play the role it was always intended to play. As it stands it comes nowhere near defining or capturing that mental continuity which animated the Lockean and constructionalist traditions. This is because it offers no plausible account of *error*.

Suppose that at t_3 I think I remember locking the back door, though the fact is that some well-disposed neighbour, slipped the latch (at t_2) after I had gone off without locking up. Then, unless we are already possessed of a criterion of identity or something else to refute the memory claim somehow, we seem to have

(Wiggins who at t_3 imagines he remembers locking the door) *C
(person who remembers slipping the latch at t_2).

This is bad enough, but suppose that later at t_4 I begin to doubt that I locked the door, remembering that at t_3 I had supposed I remembered doing so. Then undoubtedly

(Wiggins who doubts at t_4 that he locked the door) *C (Wiggins who thought at t_3 he remembered locking the door).

But then, whether I like it or not, *C must by the intended transitivity and symmetry hold between me (even as I doubt) and the man, or woman more likely, who locked the back door. But here I don't even have what Locke intended by continuity of consciousness with the person who locked it. And stiffening the subjective requirements on remembering locking the door (the vividness, stability, richness, etc., of the inner representation) will scarcely alter the position. The troublesome example itself could always be correspondingly enriched.

This is a fundamental objection. If we try to answer it by writing 'remember' instead of 'really or apparently remembers' in the definition of C and *C, then we encounter the difficulty that identity may be already involved in deciding, in some cases, whether someone really remembers planting the fig tree.[16] To avoid the difficulty satisfactorily we must say what really remembering really is, and do so in such a way as to embrace the typical (Lockean) cases of remembering *witnessing*, remembering *perceiving*, remembering *feeling*, remembering *thinking*, remembering *remembering*, remembering *suffering*, remembering *doing*. . . . Nothing less will suffice to make *C the stuff of a correct usable Lockean criterion of identity, with the range of decidable cases we actually ascribe to the relation *is the same person as*. It will not do to define *C in vacuo as we did before—as if everything else could be defined at will, and without even relating a person and his actions in such a way as to say what it is for a person to *own actions* (Locke's phrase, *Essay*, Fraser, p. 479). If we do proceed as we ought, however, then no account of memory will suffice which does not arise out of a life-like account of the *whole range* of faculties which are distinctive of persons. The objection scarcely shows that it is impossible to adjust the execution of the Lockean project while conferring a special role upon memory amongst other faculties. But it shows something about the sort of enterprise of which the analysis of memory must form part. For that reason, I shall pause here for a moment to say a word or two about the account of memory offered by Max Deutscher and C. B. Martin.[17]

Deutscher and Martin point out that even if A did (say) plant a fig tree in a certain spot at a certain time, A's thinking he remembers planting it is not enough to establish that A remembers doing so. He may have forgotten the actual planting. If someone has told him about it later, then A may have subconsciously imagined the planting; and even as he imagined it he may have forgotten that he knew about the action only from another person's account. This is a real if remote possibility. What is required then, in addition to some sufficiently vivid and plausible inner representation on A's part, is that there should be a causal relation between A's planting the tree and his subsequent memory-representation. This is a sufficiently familiar point.[18] What is original in Deutscher and Martin's contribution to the subject is to have demonstrated, as a conceptual contention, that it was impossible to define the *right sort* of causal connection between an incident and the memory representation of it without recourse to the notion of the memory trace (which might be identified by reference to the normal neurophysiological connection, whatever it is, between rememberings and the incidents of which they are rememberings).[19] They carefully explore a multiplicity of alternatives to the explicit memory-trace account of the causal connection between incident and experiential memory of incident. They show that none of these accounts can simultaneously allow for the possibility of *prompting* and define the particular sort of *operativeness* we are looking for between incident and representation.

In their physicalist tendency these arguments about memory have important parallels with what seems to hold of other faculties which are distinctive of persons. If we are to make the distinction we believe we want to make between perception and misperception, for instance, there has to be something independent of what is subjectively given in perception to fix the *position* of the perceiver. What else can fix it but the body of the perceiver? Somewhat similarly, it seems to follow from Deutscher and Martin's analysis that experiential memory is inconceivable without some matter on which a trace is imprinted by the original incident, and which may carry the trace forward to the time when the person involved recalls it. What Deutscher and Martin lighted upon when they criticized 'if...then—' analyses of the conceptually requisite causality was, I think, a completely general difficulty in pinning down by conditionals the character of any mental disposition.[20] A disposition is the sort of thing which can rest latent, be revived and refreshed, and is at the disposal of its owner to use under all sorts of different circumstances—or not to use. It is impossible to conceive of memory causality by analogy with action at a distance as a transaction over a matterless gap between the external world at one time and mind at a later time.[21]

In this sort of reasoning I think we begin to see how *C needed to be tackled. Defining it is just one part of the general exercise of describing a persisting material entity essentially endowed with the biological potentiality for the exercise of *all* the faculties and capacities conceptually constitutive of personhood—sentience, desire, belief, motion, memory, and so forth.

IV

The charge of circularity rephrased and reconsidered

That Locke and so many others have concentrated on memory to the virtual exclusion of almost all the heterogeneous other things which are characteristic of persons and which register in the stream of consciousness—the sensory and kinaesthetic aspects, the play of the practical imagination over possible outcomes, the constant surveillance of the fit of means to ends and ends to means and all the other forward and sideways looking elements—this, it may be said, is a lamentable even pathological symptom of much that is wrong with philosophy. Yes. But the charge of blindness or incompetence must not be allowed to obscure the Lockean claim that x is a person only if x has and exercises some sufficient capacity to remember or record sufficiently well from one time to the next enough of his immediately previous states or actions. That may yet prove to be true. But because this statement gives a part of the purported essence of persons it must impinge on the individuation of persons. And some will say that one circularity was manifest from the outset here. What about the *his* in 'enough of *his* immediately previous states and actions'? I reply that if there were really something illegitimate about the way in which the *his* turns up here in the Lockean condition, then there would have to be something equally illegitimate about the way in which the pronoun *it* occurs in the following definition of a black box recorder: *a machine designed to record certain aerobatical data useful in case of accident befalling the aircraft which carries it.* I shall not try to add to Geach's deadly criticisms of philosophers who have been unable to understand the occurrence of pronouns as variables.[22]

This confused objection does however lead into a better line of objection, which claims that, contrary to what I have implied, the criterion sketched above cannot operate effectively. 'Suppose P claims to remember planting the fig tree. We cannot settle the truth of his claim that he remembers planting the fig tree until we can establish by some criterion independent of memory whether P is *identical* with the person (if any) who planted it. But then memory is doomed always to bring too little too late to determine any identity question. For we must already have settled the identity question by other means,' it will be said, 'before memory is allowed onto the scene at all. If the memory condition is an extra condition applied after it is already fixed by some criterion K *what* we are to trace through space and time, then either it contradicts K, or at best it restricts (determines some subset of) the kind determined by K. Suppose K defines *animal*, then the memory-restriction may define *self-conscious animal*. But this,' the objector will say, 'is going to create a very nasty situation for you. It is going to be possible for the victim of the car crash who loses his memory to be the same animal as the patient who walks out of the hospital to start a new life, but not the same person—even though both are persons.'[23]

So runs the objection: and every difficulty it deduces from the mistaken idea that memory must be an extra condition applied *after* another criterion K has fixed an individuative kind is correctly deduced. (What is more, we shall revive something from the objection in due course, though not in the form of a charge of circularity.) But, against the objection as it stands, I have to ask what is this other precedent criterion K? Bodily continuity, it may be said. But that would make the person the same even as his skeleton and restore Jeremy Bentham (even the Pharaohs, presumably more competently preserved) to the number of persons still extant and, so to speak, knocking about the place. Bodily continuity is not enough without life.[24] And surely sufficient exercise of the capacity for memory is conceptually connected with a whole cluster of vital functions, of which Locke can consistently argue that memory is just one. Locke's definition does not oblige us to say that memory determines identity questions autonomously, only that it contributes and, in conjunction with other considerations, is *crucially relevant* to our choice of continuity principle for determining the biographies of persons. What the objection really had to confront was a thesis about memory as part and parcel with other vital functions characteristic of persons. But against that thesis it simply begs the question.

The objection says: 'We surely cannot determine whether P is remembering planting the fig tree until we have independently established whether P is indeed one and the same person who planted the fig tree.' It sounds for a moment as if there is something in that. But why not the other way round? Put the other way round the objection says: 'We surely cannot establish the identity or non-identity of P with the person who planted the fig tree until we have established whether (e.g.) this thinking he planted it counts as remembering planting it or not.' Perhaps there are cases in which this might be an equally good thing to say (or the only thing we could say). Shoemaker's brain-transfer case is the obvious example. If the back to front version has less weight than the first version, then we must remember that (on the neo-Lockean view) what is happening here is that we are ranging a *whole battery of components* of the continuity principle for persons against what is (on the neo-Lockean view) *only one component* of the continuity principle.

V

Two senses in which a person may be supposed to transcend his body, one correct, the other impossible

Let us pause here and take stock. We have neither formulated exactly—for reasons which will later become plain—nor demonstrated as sound or correct the Lockean condition of continuity of consciousness. But no argument we have examined, nor yet any obvious extension of one, shows that the Lockean notion partakes of outright absurdity or logical flaw. Nor is the revised conception of the memory condition which we have arrived at redundant in the presence of some distinct physicalistic criterion. Whether plausibly or implausibly, the memory condition informs and regulates the continuity condition of personal identity, holds it apart from mere continuity of material body, and leaves its distinctive mark on judgements founded in it.[25]

The answer to Butler also provides a way to draw together certain other 'phenomena.' I have in mind the discomfort which almost everyone feels about any straightforward equation between himself and his body; the idea to which many of us are prey that the lifeless corpse is not the person; the fact that there is something absurd—so unnatural that the upshot is simply falsity—in the proposition that people's bodies play chess, talk sense, know arithmetic, or even play games or sit down. We bring these findings to the subject before speculation begins. The advantage of a neo-Lockean theory is that we do not need to force the facts to account for them.

A person is material in the sense of being essentially enmattered; but in the strict and different sense of 'material', viz. being definable or properly describable in terms of the concepts of the sciences of matter (physics, chemistry and biology even) *person* is not necessarily a material concept.[25] The neo-Lockean functional cum psychological principle of individuation for persons shows how it is possible for *person* to fail of materiality in that sense, and shows it in a manner compatible with the strictest physicalism. For the continuity principle defines a material entity in the first 'enmattered' sense of 'material', while leaving it possible for the concept *person* to be (i) primitive relative to the concepts that pull their weight in the sciences of matter, (ii) primitive relative to the concept *human body*. If we understand what a living person or an animal is, then we may define the body of one as that which realizes or constitutes him while alive and will be left over when he dies. The instability of the argument from analogy, like the scepticism which it was meant to answer, must testify to the difficulties of reversing this definitional order.

So much for an unexciting and satisfying way in which persons transcend bodies. But the supposed logical possibility of Lamarckian memory and of delta formations in the stream of consciousness (neither of which is manifestly excluded by a good account of memory itself) inevitably suggests another way.

If lines of consciousness could really divide—if the exigent requirements for this to have happened were fully satisfied—then it may be said we should need at least a dual use of '*person*.' There would have to be (1) a new use to denote a group-person or 'clone,' whose members' consciousnesses all derived from a point in some common biography:[27] and (2) the residue of our present use, to denote individual mental continuants which act separately and communicate interpersonally. Call (2) the 'splinter' use. Splinter persons will come into being either by birth or as the outcome of a fission, and will cease to exist if and when they either die or split. Consider figure 6.1 with its 'tree' of divisions in a consciousness originating from a person S.[28]

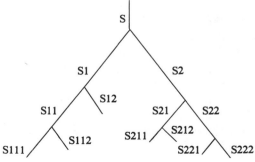

Figure 6.1

Note that in figure 6.1 the S designations denote not nodes but arcs. The proposal is that if the divisions represented by such a tree come to pass, then the *arcs* S1, S2, S11, S12...are all different splinter persons. In addition, there is the clone or subclone person constitute of S111 and S112, the distinct but related (sub)clone person constituted of that *plus* S11, the distinct but related (sub) clone person constituted of that *plus* S12...and so on, enumerating at every point of division all arcs which lie beneath it until we get the whole archetype, the clone person proper, comprehending S and everything which diverges from S. On this use Smith is flesh and bone, but he has as members both individual (i.e., arc) members, and subclone members. He is a concrete universal. Each arc or splinter person bears here the same relation to the archetype clone as all individual Cox's Orange Pippin trees (which have the ancestral of the relation 'produced from a cutting of' to an original hybrid tree) bear to the clone or concrete universal which they perpetuate and jointly constitute, namely, Cox's Orange Pippin.

One quickly comes to think there is yet a third use of 'person' we should need in order to make sense of a mental entity's having personal memory of experiences before the splitting of the consciousness. Conception (3) of a person picks out all the distinct continuous paths which can be traced back to the original arc S, that is, S $\longrightarrow$ S111, S $\longrightarrow$ S112.... Let us say these paths define life-histories. The reason why they are needed is this. Suppose a person R remembers being, say, the first to sail between Scylla and Charybdis single-handed, R did navigate so, and R was the first to do so single-handed. He was there. But a branching may have intervened since this feat was executed. S1, say, may have been the splinter agent involved, but S1 is no longer. How then does R survive? He is perpetuated by the splinters S11 and S12. They authentically remember the feat, but the actual navigator cannot be identified with the splinters S11 or S12. Neither of these splinters was there at the sailing. Nor can the clone conception help. We want to say of whoever survives the splitting of S1 something we need not want to say of splinter members which branched off before the sailing. Nor again can any subclone, for example (S111 + S112 + S11 + S12), help us. For we may wish to say that the persons whom S11 and S12 represent or perpetuate, that is, the life histories S $\longrightarrow$ S111, S $\longrightarrow$ S112, S $\longrightarrow$ S12, think and feel in importantly different ways about the feat. In these different lives the feat may represent different things. Only the life history gives us a way to say this.

Before we enter into any of the difficulties or absurdities this project involves, it may be well to note how widespread in different cultures is the idea that persons may transcend not only particular bodies but even individual lives. Clifford Geertz has described the lengths to which the Balinese push the hyostasization of social roles, and the strange fusion of role and actor which is involved in their system or naming.[29] Perhaps the concrete universal conception of person is an extant conception then. Perhaps we could even discover it was our own conception. Within our own culture, or a neighbouring compartment, J. P. Sartre has written in his book about Flaubert: "Un homme n'est jamais un individu; il vaudrait mieux l'appeler un universel singulier; totalisé et, par la même, universalisé par son époque, il la retotalise en se reproduisant en elle comme singularité.[30]

But there are serious doubts. If we want from the concrete universal conception only what the Balinese seem to get from having something of that sort—if this is really what they have—then perhaps the clone or the life history will serve to reconstruct it. For if this is all we want then there is no question of building up a coherent historical record of the individual passions, thoughts and actions of any individual person who is (say) Wayan. Nothing in Balinese culture is calculated to highlight the individual or, as it were, perspectival aspect of human experience. The whole ordering of the events of human history is reinterpreted by the Balinese so far as possible in terms of the recurrence of generic types of acting and suffering.[31] Where there scarcely is such a thing as history, the idea of an individual biography loses all purchase. It would be implausible to claim that the resultant conception of a person is utterly foreign to us. But if we take seriously as a thought experiment a world with persons liable to fission, and if we are anxious to hold fast to the very thing which made Locke's conception of a person interesting to us in the first place, then what we cannot abandon without forgetting completely the point of the exercise is our interest in constructing internally consistent, mutually consistent, indefinitely amplifiable, individual biographies. I suppose it might be claimed (implausibly I think) that we could jettison the ideas of childhood, maturity and death if people were perpetuated after the manner of plants in a hedgerow. (Reduplication by fission would be scarcely very different.) But an interest in the Lockean conception commits us to try to preserve the possibility of an account of the formation of individual character—the path which a man picks through good and bad fortune to be what he in particular is. If so, the question is: can the three uses of 'person' be deployed somehow, singly or in concert, to salvage this individual conception—even in the description of a world of fissiparous persons? I doubt it.

Consider again the claim to have been the first person to sail *single-handed* between Scylla and Charybdis. Can the claim be reinterpreted to accommodate the fact there are now three equally good claimants, $S \longrightarrow S12$, $S \longrightarrow S111$ and $S \longrightarrow S112$, with differing attitudes to that feat? I see only one way. The boast must be read as the claim that there was once an as yet undivided life history which performed the feat, a life history having the fortified *C relation to all three of the life histories just mentioned, one of them being the claimant. The as yet undivided entity must comprise life histories which *will* be separated as distinct life histories. But at the time of the feat they were unseparated. The question must now be: What sort of a thing is a person if a life history is a person? For there will prove to have been one period, before the separation, during which two or three of them were in the same place at the same time. (An idea harder to accept than that of one place being occupied by two distinct things of different category or kind.)[32] Unless our preconceptions about material objects are sadly astray, it follows that people are not only not human bodies but not even material objects. Well, there are those who thought this all along. But how is R, or any of the three life histories which now represent him, and on the importance of whose remembering such things as the sailing single-handed between Scylla and Charybdis the Lockean motivation lays such stress, to conceive (how is he to make a notion for himself) of the person that he is?

There is only one answer I can think of: as a Lesniewskian fusion or aggregate of person-moments or person-stages. The point about such Lesniewskian aggregates is that they may have common members, and that they will coincide as one person-fusion if and only if they have *all* their constituent person-

moments in common. What is more, two, three or several Lesniewskian fusions *can* be in the same place at the same time; in this
respect they are unlike material objects as we normally conceive of
them. The trouble is that they are also much too unlike people.
Look at the contrast between the predicates of ordinary material
objects and the predicates of Lesniewskian fusions. A fusion has
its relevant properties derivately from the properties of its constituent *moments.* But at least half of the things we want to say about
persons cannot be even tortuously explained in terms of the states
at an instant of person-moments. Consider for example *weak,
strong, clever, stupid, brave, cowardly, a good goalkeeper, a bad
slip fielder, resolute, opportunistic, erratic, honest, a fair weather
friend,* or (Galba's predicate) *capax imperii nisi imperasset.* We
might, I suppose, explain what one or two of these meant in terms
of person-moments if we were already possessed of their significa-
tion for persons. What seems inconceivable is the reverse
procedure.

VI

Real possibility: the limits of personhood

This is the unenviable position into which obsession with the Lockean condition apparently forces us if we accept fission and fusion
of persons as logical possibilities. Most of us are committed to
thinking that if any of our concepts are sound then *person* is. We
think that, being people, we understand what a person is. We also
have a very exact understanding of the relation of sameness.
Together these understandings should suffice to give a sound principle for *same person*—a criterion of individuation for persons.
How then can personal identity confront us with such a variegated
multitude of apparently insoluble cases? Yet the possibilities of fission and fusion which the recent literature of the subject has been
obliged to rehearse are not on the face of it marginal indetermina-
cies which, however capriciously we find we have to decide them,
leave undiminished our confidence in our comprehension of what
is at issue here. The conceptual possibility of a delta in the stream
of consciousness jogs our whole focus on the concept of personhood. So, rather than jump to the conclusion that we have no idea
at all what we are about, let us ask: is such a delta really a concep-

tual possibility? It would be easy to rule out such a thing in a lordly fashion, after the manner of the followers of a certain great philosopher, as 'undermining the whole application of the concept of person.' But what we really need is a *good pretext* to rule it out. This is to say that we need a reason arising out of a moderately well confirmed bit of semantical theory. My own attempt arises out of Hilary Putnam's 'Is Semantics Possible?'[33] and his theory of kind words. This I shall shortly apply to the sortal concept *person*.

If we look at the usual accounts of substance-words in the tradition of Locke's nominal essence they are all, as Putnam pointed out, curiously unrealistic. Such accounts invariably seek to fix the sense of *sun* or *horse* or *tree* by a description (which always fails either of necessity or of sufficiency) in terms of their properties and relations and/or appearances. Putnam's counter-proposal is that x is an f (horse, cypress tree, orange, caddis-fly) if and only if x is grouped by the most explanatory and comprehensive true scientific theory with a set of arbitrarily selected normal *exemplars* of the kind f. But if the correct articulation of natural kinds ultimately depends on good theory, and good theory is part and parcel of true statement of natural laws, then it follows from Putnam's proposal that any putative definition of a natural kind f will stand or fall with the existence of some set of laws which collect together its actual extension. Unless there are such laws, the putative kind name has no extension, nor even the sense it is required to have. If there are such laws, on the other hand, then their holding is nothing less than constitutive of the existence of fs: and these laws must define the characteristic development and typical history (or at least the limits of any possible development or history) of individual fs. It follows that, *if* person is a natural kind, then when we consider the problem of the identity of persons through change, the whole logic of the situation must exempt us from taking into account any but the class of situations which conform to the actual laws of the actual world. For these serve, and nothing but these can serve, to define the class of persons. And this seems to excuse us from allowing the spontaneous occurrences of delta formations in the consciousness of persons. The condition of persons' *existence* seems, subject to one obvious and important qualification concerning interference, to exclude this.

Before we attend to the antecedent of the conditional just asserted—'*if* persons are a natural kind. . .'—it is important to determine the ambit of Putnam's doctrine. It is not intended to cover the whole range of sortal words which we use to answer Aristotelian 'what is it?' questions. Consider artifact-words. There are virtually no natural laws about spades or clocks or tables or writing instruments *as such*. There scarcely could be. Clocks, for instance, may be made of a variety of different kinds of material and may function by radically different kinds of mechanism. Artifacts are things in nature, but they are not collected and classified together *as this or that artifact* by virtue of resemblances of any scientific or nomological import. They are collected up not à la Putnam, but under functional descriptions. A pen is a writing implement, a clock is a time keeping device and so on. The description gives what is impossible to specify in other cases, a *nominal essence*. But nominal essence is precisely not what the members of natural kinds have in common. What they have (and Putnam's account at last enables us to see how they can have this) is a scientifically palpable *real essence*. For the theory of individuation this is an important difference, and it results in a related and important difference between natural things and artifacts in respect of conditions of identity through time. I shall touch on this before homing again upon persons.

When there is any dispute concerning an object identified under a natural kind, then one can readily conceive of getting more facts. Remember the nineteenth-century discovery that the elvers *Leptocephali* were in fact the young of the species Conger Eel. Or the humble (but in some sense proto-scientific) discovery that tadpoles become frogs. This observation enlarges the understanding of the concept. On the exemplar theory we can see how these scientific discoveries relate to the semantics of 'eel' or 'frog.' They reveal something which was always fixed by the sense of the kind-word, regardless of whether anyone knew this. It follows that identity questions about members of natural kinds can be expected to find the notion of identity at its best. They are the least plausible possible candidates for conventionalist treatment. Consider by contrast the identity problems of artifacts—the disassemblage of six or seven watches say, and their eventual reassemblage with some confusion of individual parts.[34] Here we do not have natural things pursuing their natural courses—there is no such thing as the natural development of a watch, or a natural law about watches as such; and, in the last analysis, if parts get muddled there may be no point in arguing about which watch was which. (The one cast-iron indubitable sufficient condition of identity is a condition of limited utility on the lines of a criterion suggested for *quantities*, in the alien category of *stuff*, by Helen Cartwright,[35] a condition excluding any addition or subtraction of matter whatever.)

So much for artifacts and natural things. But are people a natural kind? Certainly a pure conventionalist view of the identity of people would fly in the face of the innermost convictions of almost everyone. Nobody thinks of the persons we actually encounter in nature as artifacts, or as having identities which are 'for decision' as artifact-identities are sometimes 'for decision' when there is a changing of parts. Yet *person* is not manifestly equivalent to the real essence *homo sapiens*, and the Lockean project looks much more like the analytical excogitation of a nominal essence than a piece of scientific research into the essence of a natural kind. What is more, it is a highly important fact about homo sapiens that in the way he conceives himself he does not allow his imagination to be constrained by that status. Men can readily conceive of having the faculties and powers of other animals. More concretely and practically we sometimes conceive of securing some or all of these and other powers to ourselves by means of tools. We may then start—in philosophy we have started—to abstract from our own biological condition altogether and imagine applying our technology to ourselves—as if to fashion men anew into the artifacts of men. Man as his own creature or tool. These thought-experiments may culminate in the assimilation of persons to creatures with powers conferred by magical artifacts which are themselves the product of imagination (Excalibur or Nothung or Gyges' ring) —even in the assimilation in thought of ourselves to such artifacts. We cannot assimilate artifacts to natural things, but certainly we are learning to assimilate natural things to artifacts.

What then is the present status of the sortal word *person*? Any answer to this is bound for many reasons to be controversial. One possible opinion is that its sense is still rooted in the sense of the animal species word 'man'; and that as human beings have come to the point where their powers of reason and analogy make it possible for some of them to transcend mere species loyalty, the sense of *person* has been very slightly modified. We have become open to the suggestion that other species may in varying degrees enjoy many of the attributes which we value highly in ourselves (not excluding the capacity to transcend species-loyalty, if the poet Arion is to be believed). As a result, the extension of the sortal word *person* could now be widened to accommodate members of the natural kinds who come near enough to us. To this (fitful) perception of the claims of other species to 'humane' consideration (and more) may also be added a desire to build into the concept *person* certain distinctive aspirations for the human condition; but it is characteristic of the view I have indicated that it insists on treating the essential characteristics of persons, both their capacities and their inherent limitations, as a matter of empirical investigation. (An investigation which is urgent and important but not, it is consistent to add, so important as to overwhelm all other importance, or to justify any and every method of research.)

Against certain opponents this view of the concept is, I fear, simply question begging. A second and slightly milder view would be that *person* is a *second order classificatory concept defined jointly in terms of natural kinds and a functional specification* somewhat as follows: x is a person if x is an animal falling under the extension of some natural kind whose members perceive, feel, remember, imagine, desire, make projects, move themselves at will and carry out projects, acquire a character as they age, are susceptible to concern for members of their own or like species,... conceive of themselves as perceiving, feeling, remembering, imagining, desiring, making projects, and so forth,...have, and conceive of themselves as having, a past accessible in experience-memory and a future accessible in intention,...and so on. On this account *person* is a non-biological qualification of *animal*, and a cross-classification with respect to zoological classifications, against the grain so to speak of an evolution-based taxonomy. Again it is not excluded that the extension of *person* should give hospitality to dolphins, to porpoises, or even (in exchange for suitably amazing behaviour suitably explained in neurophysiological terms) to a parrot. A person is then an animal who has or is of a kind to have the biological capacity to enjoy the attributes enumerated above.

A third view which dispenses with the *animal* component altogether will be mentioned in due course, but let me concentrate for a moment on the second view. I think it would be worthwhile to pause longer than I can and ask where, on this view, we get the functional part of the definition of *person* from. It is not presumably intended to recapitulate and simply exhaust the biologically, historically, and culturally determined typical characteristics of homo sapiens as we know him. But what else constrains the list? Are we free, conceptually speaking, to shorten or lengthen this component at will?

These doubts relate to the second part of the second definition. The more they worry us, the quicker we recoil from the implausibly total subjectivity in which they ultimately threaten to engulf questions of norm and value, the less I think we shall want to dispense with the natural kind component in the definition. And so long as that component remains, the conviction that personal identity is a bad case for conventionalism is vindicated. What is more, the theory of individuation (whether we prefer the first or the second theory of *person*) suggests the possibility of rational grounds for what has previously looked like fear or prejudice—the conviction that robots and automata do not have any title to civil or personal rights or to any of the consideration due to sentient creatures. For the substance-concept under which we individuate such things is not that of any natural kind. To have feelings or purposes or concerns a thing must, I think we still think, be (at least) an *animal*. (None of this should be confused with the claim I do *not* make—that no higher animal can be artificially synthesized. What seems certain is that this would not be an *automation*.) Finally, we understand the inherent limitations not only of speculation which goes contrary to the physical laws of the actual universe, but also of some not *physically* inconceivable thought-experiments involving the interchange of brains or their parts, the 'carbon copy' replication or reduplication[36] of skills and memories, or the implantation of artificial devices to replace, enhance, or supplement the operation of the natural organs. I am not arguing here against such practices. I am only saying that we must not be surprised if the associated thought-experiments—not to say their implementation—begin to subject us to the strain of thinking of ourselves as clones, as concrete universals, or as part of one another. Perhaps this strain is good for us.[37] What we should first understand is what makes this strain. It is the apparent inability of homo sapiens to treat the essence he defines for himself as the essence of a natural kind, as the essence of one thing in nature amongst the other things in nature. It is his inability to immunize himself from delusions of technological omnipotence. What can result from this, amongst other things which cause more immediate consternation, is at the limit a kind of thought experiment, even a kind of practical experiment, which literally denatures the subject. In place of an animal or organism with a clear principle of individuation one finds an artifact whose identity may be a matter of convention, or even caprice. Certainly we do not, at this limit, find a person, if my account of the status of the concept *person* is correct.

VII

*Amnesia reconsidered and the abandonment of the *C condition. A small amendment to Locke*

At this point it may be asked what difference it makes to any specific identity problem whether the indicated view of person is right or not; and how we shall decide whether the view is right or wrong.

The reader will have noticed that we never quite concluded the problem of the man who suffers total amnesia as a result of some appalling physical or mental shock and then begins life anew after a discontinuity which no meaningful *C condition could tolerate or let pass. The case is not impossible, still less counternomic, and there is no interference which pushes the subject towards the status of an artifact. It holds a part of the answer to the question just raised.

There are at most four ways of appraising such a case.

(1) We may hold that it voids any application of the concept of person. But in practice, when people do lose their memory, we never adopt this view.

(2) We may attempt to do honour to *C by deciding that the man who begins life anew after total amnesia is the same organism or animal as, but a different person from, the man who lost his memory. This is a tempting but incoherent decision. If y is the same animal as x then he is the person that x was. But then he is

the same person as x (see note 23).

(3) We may decide to say that y is a different person from x, *and* a different animal or homo sapiens. Here there is no outright logical obstruction, unattractive though the view appears. We may disclaim any suggested equivalence between 'animal' and 'living body'—the suggestion is wrong anyway—and we may even extend the psychologistic Lockean individuative procedure as far down the evolutionary hierarchy as there remain 'psychologically' interesting differences between different members of any single species of animal. We may hold that *animal*, of which *person* is a restriction, is not really individuative in the same way as *horse, cat, man,* or *person* are. What coincidence under the concept *animal* amounts to, we may say, differs according to the kind of animal, the genus-sortal being in this sense less fundamental than the species sortal.[38] And we may hold that *homo sapiens*, being a natural kind consisting of persons, permits of the individuation of its members in accordance with some *C requirement. What obstructs this view, however, if anything does, is the violence it does to what in real life we actually want to say about amnesic persons. In the last stages of Nijinsky's breakdown and madness, his friends and attendants tried, I believe, to reactivate his memory and recognition of the world about him by playing the music or performing the dances of the Diaghilev ballets he had formerly danced in. But by *C this was already a different person. Surely, though, the homo sapiens Nijinsky had neither died nor vanished, even in the last stages of (his) madness.

(4) The last or commonsensical view is that, *pace* the *C requirement, it is the same person and same animal throughout. It is wrong to suppose that one can decide between this and decision (3) in isolation from all other cases. The force of analogy and the weight of other cases may make tolerable the element of legislation involved by decision (3). But in truth a case by case examination will not get very far unless it is informed from the start by some overall theoretical concern with the kind of concept that *person* is. If so we need to be clearer about the theoretical rationale, if any, for decision (3) and for its being preferred to (4).

I think it would be fair to confront an upholder of decision (3) with this question: Since you allow the functional element in the notion of *person* to dominate the *animal* element, and permit a *C condition to invade and reshape the biological principle of individuation of *homo sapiens*, why stop there? What import does it have to insist that a person is an *animal* who. . .? Why not allow a mere artifact to qualify as a person provided only that it is programmed to satisfy the functional description in a substantial manner? And why not retreat to a position where the concept *person* is a nominal not a real essence? It seems to me that the champion of decision (3), like any upholder of the view that *person* is a primarily social concept, is pretty well defenceless against this suggestion. Many, in pursuit of analogies which it is not my present purpose to show how to block, will in any case embrace it and are already anxious to take physicalists, purists, and reactionaries of the identity relation to task for failing to see that the concept of person *is* a 'social' concept with identity criteria of an adaptability and pliability suited to this role.[39] But some day I think some identity purist should try his hand at drawing out the social and philosophical implications (in bourgeois, totalitarian and all other situations) of treating the concept of person otherwise than as a particular restriction of the natural kind concept *animal*. Which, I would ask, is really the philosophically more misleading or practically more dangerous conception of a man: a *pretentious imaginative tool using animal who is* ϕ or *a demiurge of animal origin and some residual animal inclinations who is* ϕ (where ϕ is in both cases some Lockean functional specification).

I am not sure that I know how to take the point further (beyond a rhetorical question that is). But it is not merely *ad hominem*. The 'social concept' theorist is perfectly right to point to the conceptual importance of the role of the notion of a person in social and moral philosophy. His principal error lies in the instant deduction he makes from this, and in his however unwitting withdrawal of human nature from that morally directed objective empirical scrutiny which is our sole mode of access to men's real capacities and to the difference between what is variable and what is naturally invariable in their make-up. If we dispense with the *animal* component, and if the functional specification captures everything that is essential to personhood,[40] then I think there is no specifically *conceptual* strain in supposing that, provided only they continue to satisfy the specification, men can be adapted by whatever means, without the slightest detriment to personhood, to no matter what (politically stable) outcome. But then the focus of any rationally argued inquiry into political science must either be purely descriptive of existing forms of society and existing behaviour; or if possibility enters then the focus of the inquiry can only be technological—the pursuit of a social engineering interest in optimizing the quantity or distribution of want satisfactions. Where the empirically given nature and potentiality of man has no essential relevance or conceptual title beyond that which registers at the level of desire—or (worse) of behaviour, interpreted in terms of some (necessarily atomistic) theory of desiring—there can be no other 'hard' data, nothing else from which an inquiry in political science can rationally proceed. The discrimination for any time t between the different possible outcomes projected by the managers of a society for time t will be with respect to the total (and distribution) of satisfactions of wants existing at t, and the temporally discounted net present value at t, of satisfactions actually or hypothetically existing at times after t. I do not deny that this view, recently celebrated by Marco Ferreri in his film *La Grande Bouffe*, is actually entertained by intelligent men; indeed I suppose that, with certain saving inconsistencies, this (reduced into mythical order by 'the' social welfare function) is more or less the utilitarian theory of public rationality. So (at least in this place) I must rest content simply to remark upon the connection, and to note the distortion which the purely functional view must (in my opinion) induce in every moral or political concept or conceptual distinction that depends upon the idea of human nature. I cite as one instance the distinction (to whose practical and theoretical neglect our ravaged landscapes and the plundered social and architectural fabric of modern cities testify) between the basic needs of human beings—what because of their nature they must have to flourish[41]—and all their other appetitive states. This distinction between what depends upon the variable and what depends upon the naturally invariable elements in human life is not foreign to ordinary men, or even to the subjectivity of their most unreflective experience. It is indispensable to practical thinking in a world of scarcity. But if the distinction is conceptually inaccessible to a utilitarian manager he can scarcely interpret the everyday human behaviour he surveys as expressive of the distinction. And when his concept of person has lost any determinate centre of gravity (can be anything at all he makes of it), his methodology scarcely even requires this additional reassurance that 'there is no such thing as human nature.'

In *Prometheus Vinctus* Prometheus reports how he found men witless, with ears to hear and eyes to see but perceiving nothing. Like shapes in dreams they passed long ignorant lives without purpose or achievement.[42] When he taught them to tame the beasts of the field and sail the sea, to heal illness, to count and write, and to foretell the future from the entrails of birds, he gave men not only fire and tools, but optimism. He relieved men of foresight of their fate, and in the place of that, he says, he put blind hope. Without hope certainly nothing much could have been done. But without some vestige of the sight which Prometheus says he took away, my theory of individuation would predict that men will face something worse than the disappearance of fossil fuels. Not only will ambiguity have aggravated the older difficulties of the ancient question *'What shall I do with myself?'* We may confront a situation where there is no firm answer to what we are or even who we are, and where the limits of the class of persons is no longer supplied from outside us. For me (judging from here and now—where else?) it is difficult to see how the bulwarks, the shallow foundations if there are indeed any, of what Strawson has called the participative attitude[43] will continue at that point to sustain that view of the world and other persons.

There is too much guesswork and too much rhetoric here. Rather than add to it, let me summarize my conclusions. Decision (3) is quite plainly the wrong decision, using 'person' in the sense in which we still employ it. By *person* we mean a sort of animal, and for purposes of morality that (I maintain) is the best thing for us to mean. There is more to be said no doubt and the concept *person* is in some way open-ended. We may (to some little extent) make of it what we will. But it is on pain of madness that we shall try to see ourselves as both *homo sapiens* and something with a different principle of individuation. Not even the cleverest *charcutier* could slice the world so to accommodate decision (2). In any case decision (4) is, I think, manifestly correct. The hospitalized amnesic, or Nijinsky even at the last stage of madness, are the same man and the same person.

What then about the *C condition? Its critics have been wrong to maintain that the *C proposal was absurd or circular. The only thing wrong with the *C condition was that for purposes of actual decision it was not quite right. Its critics have also overlooked how easily the project out of which it arose can be repaired. Let us amend Locke, and say a person is any animal the physical makeup of whose species constitutes the species' typical members thinking intelligent beings, with reason and reflection, and typically enables them to consider themselves as themselves the same thinking things, in different times and places. . . . Memory is not then irrelevant to personal identity, but the way it is relevant is simply that it is one highly important element amongst others in the account of what it is for a person to be still there, *alive*. It plays its part in determining the continuity principle for persons, as opposed to bodies or cadavers. Its bearing beyond this on individual problem cases is uncertain.[44]

NOTES

1. Like the role in which James casts 'stream of experience,' 'the transition of one experience into another,' 'consciousness,' 'conjunctive relations.' See *Essays in Radical Empiricism* (London, 1912).

2. See n. 4 and Sydney Shoemaker, *Self-Knowledge and Self-Identity* (Ithaca, N. Y.: Cornell University Press, 1963).

3. Put by Bennett (*Kant's Analytic* [Cambridge, 1963], p. 117) in this way: 'the notion of oneself is necessarily that of the possessor of a history: I can judge that this is how it is with me now, only if I can also judge that that is how it was with me then. Self-consciousness can coexist with amnesia—but there could not be a self-conscious person suffering from perpetually renewed amnesia such that he could at no time make judgements about how he was at any earlier time.'

I have argued elsewhere (*Identity and Spatio-Temporal Continuity*, 1st ed., [Oxford: Blackwell, 1967], p. 49), and in a similar fashion, that to be a person in any full sense is to be capable of believing and ceasing to believe things *on evidence*, which in its turn requires the possibility of memory of experience. One can be forgetful and enjoy the state of person. But one must at least have the biological *potentiality* for experience-memory of a sufficiently sophisticated sort. The purpose of the first part of the present article is not to repeat the arguments offered against Butler in the book referred to but to amplify and to extend with new arguments what is begun in the first edition at n. 55 and Appendix 5.6.

4. A defender of Locke might be momentarily misled into thinking that this definition came to the same thing as one which did mention that, if he failed to see that he must decline what Butler offers to him under the guise of a concession —that 'consciousness of what is past does. . . ascertain our personal identity to ourselves.' The offer is unlikely to have been disingenuous, but it must certainly be refused. What identity problem about ourselves does 'consciousness of what is past' help us to solve? We often want to know whether we earlier honoured our promise to write that letter, make that telephone call, etc. But this is hardly an

identity problem because, standardly, it is to be ignorant whether the letter was written or the call was made at all. Possession of this information is usually a prior condition of raising the identity question, 'am I the one who wrote/telephoned?' Standardly, but not I admit *always*, to know that that telephone call was made is (under such circumstances) to remember making it. Normally this leave over no identity problem for the maker. *A fortiori*, he does not need to possess a special criterion in order to answer it. On the other hand, when identity questions do arise about oneself—as unusually and non-standardly they perfectly well can—then one must have recourse to the same sort of criterion as anyone else employs in identifying and reidentifying him. Here there is only one privilege one enjoys. One may use personal memory, remembering X-ing, in applying that common criterion. But I shall leave this matter (which is complicated but not transformed by the possibility or possible possibility of fission or inherited memory). For what I am concerned with here is what it is for A to *be* identical with B, not what it is for A to know that he is identical with B, nor what it is for A to know who he, A himself, is.

5. See A. G. N. Flew's 'Locke and the Problem of Personal Identity,' *Philosophy* XXIV (1951).

6. Ibid., p. 55.

7. The argument needs to be reinforced by examples free of the complications of scope imported by definite descriptions. To go into these and the other important syntactical ambiguities latent in such examples would be diverting but irrelevant, as would the larger task of assessing the putative equivalence of *A remembers X-ing* and *A remembers his X-ing*.

8. Cp. B. A. O. Williams, 'Imagination and the Self,' *Proceedings of the British Academy* (1966).

9. 'P' (or 'Q') stands in for a definite description of a continuing person, not of a 'slice.' The subscripts t_j, t_k...index the *time at which* the definite description *applies* to the continuing person. The subscript will be omitted where this does not need to be indicated. The letters 'R,' 'S,'...may be used where it is necessary to multiply definite descriptions beyond two. The notation leaves it an open question whether 'P' and 'Q' stand in for the same or different descriptions.

10. Even though it is a possible elucidation of 'extend' in Locke's words *Essay* II, xxvii.ii, Frazer, (p. 449) 'as far as this consciousness can be extended backward to any past action or thought, so far reaches the identity of that person; it is the same self now as it was then; and it is by the same self with this present one that now reflects on it that that action was done.' Locke did not have the logical apparatus for a ready distinction between C and *C. This is no reason for holding him to C, even though it is clear from the sequel (Frazer, p. 450) that Locke himself was miles away from formulating the distinction.

11. The reader may have believed it to be an objection to I_p that *C is already an asymmetrical relation. Here we must guard against a misconception of what was meant by P_{tj} and Q_{tk}. What such descriptions stand for are not time-slices of people or 'person-moments.' They are people, persisting three-dimensional things which are born, live for some time, and then in one manner or another die. If P_{ti} and Q_{tj} are the same person then, regardless of the fact that these descriptions may pick out the person by reference to predicates which hold of the person at the different times t_i and t_j their references are one and the same. Everything true of one is true of the other and, with certain merely grammatical adjustments, the designations are everywhere intersubstitutable *salva veritate*. Suppose that a boy called Johnny Jones dislikes his name and that when he grows up he succeeds

in getting people to call him John Jones. Suppose John Jones remembers at $_{tm}$ doing some sufficient number of things X Y Z which Johnny actually did much earlier at $_{ti, tj, tk}$. Then we have (John) *C (Johnny). Now it is true that we should ascertain the truth of this by taking John's rememberings at $_{tm}$ and Johnny's actions at $_{ti, tj, tk}$. This certainly imports an asymmetry into the proposed method of verifying that John = Johnny. But all this asymmetry reflects is the fact that, as here stated, the problem has been stated in terms of identifications of John and Johnny made by predicates or descriptions relating to different times, earlier for Johnny and later for John. Nevertheless if John *is* Johnny then (contrary to John Jones's wishes) we *can* truly say that the man who was little Johnny Jones, and is in fact the same as Johnny Jones, still at $_{tm}$ remembers X-ing, Y-ing, Z-ing, which is what John Jones did in fact do way back at $_{ti, tj, tk}$. And the same will apply to the *C relation. If (John) *C(Johnny) and John = Johnny then (Johnny) *C(John). *C is not then asysmmetrical. The proper question is as in the text: is *C non-symmetrical?

There is reason to think one must, at whatever risk of tedium, labour these points. The time references we have introduced relate to the time of the remembering and to the time of the actions remembered, not to entities. There is no such object as John-Jones-at-$_{tm}$ or Johnny-Jones-at-$_{ti}$. Nor is Johnny Jones the name of an earlier slice of John Jones. If it were then it would be false that Johnny Jones = John Jones.

12. Cp. Hide Ishiguro 'The Person's Future and the Mind-Body Problem,' in *Phenomenology and Linguistic Analysis*, ed. Wolfe Mays and Stuart Brown (London, 1971).

13. Cp. Flew, op. cit., p. 67 and B. A. O. Williams, 'Personal Identity and Individuation,' *Proceedings of the Aristotelian Society*, (1956-57).

14. Nor would it be right to insist on redescribing the situation as one where a single dissociated or scattered person did X and also, with another part of him, did not-X. Such insistence might be based on an analogy with the way in which, without prejudice to his unity, a normal person can fidget with his left foot and not fidget with his right. There may be ideas of what a person is which allow this sort of redescription. But it is in the spirit of the Lockean notion and of our ordinary notion of person—the notion of a three-dimensional thing whose only genuine parts are *spatial* parts—to disallow it. When P_{ti} splits into Q_{t_3} and R_{t_3}, it splits into two *whole* persons, and T_{t_3} does not share R_{t_3}'s consciousness of doing X. Even if Q_{t_3} and R_{t_3} both do X, their consciousness of doing K may be as distinct as if they were two people with no common origins at all. And they will communicate *inter-personally*. One need not refuse to make sense of the supposition that identical twins sometimes experience a strange community of consciousness in doing things. But both logically and actually they *can* do the same thing without feeling this community. And similarly with the race of creatures who figure in this fantasy.

15. Cp. Leibniz, Gerhardt IV. 460.

16. This is to suggest that just as the functions of remembering and intending and much else play a crucial role in regulating the individuation of persons, so perhaps identity itself regulates the correct application of the predicate *remembers X-ing*. To the critic who sees in this relationship of reciprocal regulation the chance of reviving Butler's objection to Locke, I offer the following *a priori* refutation of the generally received account of how clockwork functions in a timepiece. It is said that the mainspring unwinds, and in unwinding affects the hair-

spring. But it is also said that the hairspring affects the speed and manner of unwinding of the mainspring. How can that possibly be? If the normal operation of the mainspring presupposes the normal operation of the hairspring how can the normal operation of the hairspring presuppose the normal operation of the mainspring? Well, it can and it does. Presupposition like mechanical regulation can be reciprocal.

17. 'Remembering,' *Philosophical Review* (1966).

18. Cp. H. P. Grice, 'The Causal Theory of Perception,' *Proceedings of the Aristotelian Society*, vol. 35 (1962)—an analogy to which I was already indebted in the analysis of memory at *Identity and Spatio-Temporal Continuity*, pp. 45, 55 and fn. 55.

19. This is not a circular procedure: but even if it were circular that would not matter for my purposes which relate to the *necessary* conditions of remembering.

20. For a more careful statement of this see my 'Towards a Reasonable Libertarianism,' in *Essays on Freedom and Action*, ed. T. Honderich (London: Routledge & Kegan Paul, 1973) p. 49.

21. It scarcely improves matters to think of the memory trace as an immaterial imprint on immaterial stuff. This can only help to the extent that immaterial mind is made intelligible by being modelled on the material, and distinguished from it only by the vacuous contention that it is immaterial.

22. See, e.g., *Analysis*, vol. 21, no. 3 (1961).

23. An impossibility if we subscribe to Leibniz's Law. See my *Identity and Spatio-Temporal Continuity*, p. 3. In rejecting this possibility I distance myself yet further from Locke's own development of his theme. Locke tries to overcome the standard difficulties of C (amnesia, sleep, etc.) by distinguishing questions of identity of *man* from questions of identity of *person*. This is a thoroughly unsatisfactory part of his discussion. However well one makes the distinction between the concepts *man* and *person*, this can hardly show that nothing falls under both concepts (under which is John Locke?), or that identity can be so relativized as to make the two identity questions independent of each other.

24. It may be said that we can and do distinguish between the corpse of a man freshly dead—he is still here but dead—and his mere earthly remains. When ashes (say) are all that is left then he is no longer there, it may be suggested. But the whole distinction which is relied upon by the objecter is parasitic upon the point of distinguishing between life and death. Here material continuity is not sufficient. And if life or its absence gives the *point* of these distinctions, then the *principal* distinction is between being live and being dead, and the best overall view will make existence or non-existence depend upon the principal distinction.

25. Cp. my *Identity and Spatio-Temporal Continuity*, p. 45, para. 2.

26. Nor, contrary to the purely physiological view of the question, is the seat of memory and consciousness just one part of the body: although, purely physiologically speaking, I suppose that the difficulties of replacing a brain are simply *more severe* than the difficulties of replacing a kidney or an eye. The physiological view would not be a doctor's view, but this is part of what people have in mind when they say doctors must be men of science and something else besides. Amongst the first to have thought into what thought-experiments involving change of bodily parts really involve is Stefan Themerson. See the last chapter of *Bayamus: A Semantic Novel* (London: Gaberbocchus, 1949).

27. Cp. *Identity and Spatio-Temporal Continuity*, Appendix, 5.7 and 5.6, and Part Two, 4.3, p. 54.

28. For simplicity, and because they raise special and even graver difficulties, I exclude from consideration here the *fusion* of lines of consciousness.

29. The conception of person by which our own everyday life sets such store registers only in rarely-used nonsense names. The names which matter are birth order names, kinship terms, teknonyms and status titles. Clifford Geertz, *Person, Time and Conduct in Bali*, Yale University, S.E. Asia Studies 14, 1966. I owe the pleasure of discovering this work to Amélie Rorty.

30. *L'Idiot de la famille: Gustave Flaubert de 1821 a 1857* (Paris: Gallimard, 1971).

31. See especially the vivid and extraordinary description of the Balinese practice of drama at Geertz, op. cit.

32. Cp. My 'Being in the Same Place at the Same Time,' *Philosophical Review* (January 1968).

33. *Metaphilosophy*, no. 3 (1970). See also *Language Belief and Metaphysics (Vol. 1 of the International Philosophy Year conference at Brockport)* (Albany, N. Y., 1970). Similar conclusions have been arrived at independently by Rogers Albritton and Saul Kripke, and related ones by Mr. Vernon Pratt of University College, Cardiff in 'Biological Classification,' *British Journal of the Philosophy of Science* (1972), pp. 305-27. See also W. V. Quine 'Natural Kinds,' in *Essays in Honour of C. G. Hempel*, ed. Rescher (Dordrecht: Reidel, 1969).

34. Cf. Paul Ziff, 'The Feelings of Robots,' *Analysis*, 19, 3 (January 1959), 67, and compare Hobbes's problem of Theseus's ship, cited at my *Identity and Spatio-Temporal Continuity*, 2.1, p. 37. There are some telling considerations one can use to try to resolve dispute about that ship. (Pure conventionalism is not a very good story even for artifact identity). But if doubt or dispute persists this is at least partly because one party is looking for an archaeological relic and the other for a functionally persistent continuant. Is one partly wrong and the other right? There is scarcely anything to *discover* to vindicate either conception against the other. I do not mean the decision is arbitrary—only rarely is it entirely arbitrary—but nothing, as it would in the case of a natural kind, *compels* it. The antiquarian who favours the reconstructed ship has a different interest from the priest who favours the continuously repaired continuant. But both are struck with the identification *ship*. Neither can base his view upon the natural development of a ship, or suggest a programme of research to resolve the question.

35. 'Quantities,' *Philosophical Review* (1969). I should make it clear that nothing in my discussion here of natural things *versus* artifacts is meant to rule out the possibility of borderline cases—think of a wasp's nest or (in another category and relatively undeveloped parts of the world) cheese or bread: and that the discussion is intended to find a distinction with respect to essence between natural kinds and other kinds which will supersede the principle of distinction implicit in the etymology of 'artifact.'

36. See Bernard Williams, 'Are Persons Bodies?' in S. Spicker, ed., *The Philosophy of the Body* (Chicago, 1970); also N. Miri, 'Personal Identity and Memory,' *Mind* (January 1972).

37. As Derek Parfit has in several ways suggested, cp. his 'Personal Identity,' *Philosophical Review*, Vol. LXXX, no. 1 (1971).

38. These psychologically interesting differences between different members of a species will presumably give out well before we reach the oyster, to which Lucian thought it was so comical that Aristotle attributed a 'psychology.'

By this proposal, and reasonably enough, *person* will become fully determinate as a strictly individuative concept only when one is told *what sort of* person (e.g., *man*-person or, if dolphins are persons, *dolphin*-person). It is only in this sort of way, after all, that ordinary very high or schematic genera like *animal* can be said to individuate individuals or give covering concepts for their identities. To espouse this solution would be to take one more step along the same 'essentialist' path as Aristotle. But in itself it does not lead to any particular idolatry of the species. What will receive privileged status is rather the highest genuine sortal concept g_n in any chain of restrictions, $g_1, g_2, \ldots$ which carries with it an autonomous individuative force sufficient to determine, without reference to lower sortals, the coincidence and persistence conditions for any g. I should surmise that g_n may possibly be nothing other than a concept which is ultimate in the sense of *Identity and Spatio-Temporal Continuity*, 2.1. On all these questions cp. Leibniz, *Nouveaux Essais*, 3.3.6 and 3.6.

39. Cp. J. M. Shorter, 'Personal Identity, Personal Relationships, and Criteria,' *Proceedings of the Aristotelian Society* (1970-71).

40. I assume that the functional specification is not trivialized by being continued to a point where it coincides with the full set of attributes which human beings (and. . .?) actually have in virtue of their biologically, etc., given nature. Cp. the penultimate paragraph of VI above. This would immediately concede to me everything I am pleading for—and more.

41. I owe this view of needing to Miss Sira Dermen. It is prefigured in one form in Aristotle at Metaphysics Δ.5. More generally, see C. B. MacPherson in Blackburn, ed., *Social Science and Ideology* (London, 1972) pp. 25 ff.

42. Aeschylus, *Prometheus Vinctus*, lines 440 ff. and 250 ff.

43. P. F. Strawson, 'Freedom and Resentment,' *Proceedings of the British Academy* XLVIII (1962).

44. A responsible review of the situation made in the light of the theory of individuation outlined here could not, by explaining the source of the perplexities they create, evade the problems posed by surgical and mechanical interventions which fall short of imperilling the application of *person* and related concepts. It would have to distinguish between the (implausible) necessary conditions and the (perhaps less implausible) sufficient conditions of personal identity which *C could be used to frame. I only remark that it should take nothing for granted about how well we really understand brain transfers of the kind described by Shoemaker. How do we fit the brain to the physiognomy of the new body which is to receive it? (Cp. Williams, 'Identity and Individuation,' *Proceedings of the Aristotelian Society* [1958-59]). How is the existing character expressed in the new body? We are deceived by the quality of the actors and mimics we see on the stage if with the help of greasepaint and props they have made us think this is as simple as the transposition of music from one instrument to another.

CONDITIONS OF PERSONHOOD

Daniel Dennett

I am a person, and so are you. That much is beyond doubt. I am a human being, and *probably* you are too. If you take offense at the "probably" you stand accused of a sort of racism, for what is important about us is not that we are of the same biological species, but that we are both persons, and I have not cast doubt on that. One's dignity does not depend on one's parentage even to the extent of having been born of woman or born at all. We normally ignore this and treat humanity as the deciding mark of personhood, no doubt because the terms are locally coextensive or almost coextensive. At this time and place human beings are the only persons we recognize, and we recognize almost all human beings as persons, but on the one hand we can easily contemplate the existence of biologically very different persons—inhabiting other planets, perhaps—and on the other hand we recognize conditions that exempt human beings from personhood, or at least some very important elements of personhood. For instance, infant human beings, mentally defective human beings, and human beings declared insane by licensed psychiatrists are denied personhood, or at any rate crucial elements of personhood.

One might well hope that such an important concept, applied and denied so confidently, would have clearly formulatable necessary and sufficient conditions for ascription, but if it does, we have not yet discovered them. In the end there may be none to discover. In the end we may come to realize that the concept of a person is incoherent and obsolete. Skinner, for one, has suggested this, but the doctrine has not caught on, no doubt in part because it is difficult or even impossible to conceive of what it would be like if we abandoned the concept of a person. The idea that we might cease to view others and *ourselves* as persons (if it does not mean merely that we might annihilate ourselves, and hence cease to view anything as anything) is arguably self-contradictory.[1] So quite aside from whatever might be right or wrong in Skinner's grounds for his claim, it is hard to see how it could win out in contest with such an intuitively invulnerable notion. If then the concept of a person is in some way an ineliminable part of our conceptual scheme, it might still be in rather worse shape than we would like. It might turn out, for instance, that the concept of a person is only a free-floating honorific that we are all happy to apply to ourselves, and to others as the spirit moves us, guided by our emotions, aesthetic sensibilities, considerations of policy, and the like —just as those who are *chic* are all and only those who can get themselves considered *chic* by others who consider themselves *chic*. Being a person is certainly *something* like that, and if it were no more, we would have to reconsider if we could the importance with which we now endow the concept.

Supposing there *is* something more to being a person, the searcher for necessary and sufficient conditions may still have difficulties if there is more than one concept of a person, and there are grounds for suspecting this. Roughly, there seem to be two notions intertwined here, which we may call the moral notion and the metaphysical notion. Locke says that "person"

> is a forensic term, appropriating actions and their merit; and so belongs only to intelligent agents, capable of a law, and happiness, and misery. This personality extends itself beyond present existence to what is past, only by consciousness—whereby it becomes concerned and accountable. (*Essays*, Book II, Chap. XXVII)

Does the metaphysical notion—roughly, the notion of an intelligent, conscious, feeling agent—*coincide* with the moral notion—roughly, the notion of an agent who is accountable, who has both rights and responsibilities? Or is it merely that being a person in the metaphysical sense is a necessary but not sufficient condition of being a person in the moral sense? Is being an entity to which states of consciousness or self-consciousness are ascribed *the same* as being an end-in-oneself, or is it merely one precondition? In Rawls's theory of justice, should the derivation from the original position be viewed as a demonstration of how metaphysical persons *can become* moral persons, or should it be viewed as a demonstration of why metaphysical persons *must be* moral persons?[2] In less technical surroundings the distinction stands out as clearly: when we declare a man insane we cease treating him as accountable, and we deny him most rights, but still our interactions with him are virtually indistinguishable from normal personal interactions unless he is very far gone in madness indeed. In one sense of "person," it seems, we continue to treat and view him as a person. I claimed at the outset that it was indubitable that you and I are persons. I could not plausibly hope—let alone aver—that all readers of this essay will be legally sane and morally accountable. What—if anything—was beyond all doubt may only have been that anything properly addressed by the opening sentence's personal pronouns, "you" and "I," was a person in the metaphysical sense. If that was all that was beyond doubt, then the metaphysical notion and the moral notion must be distinct. Still, even if we suppose there are these distinct notions, there seems every reason to believe that metaphysical personhood is a necessary condition of moral personhood.[3]

What I wish to do now is consider six familiar themes, each a claim to identify a necessary condition of personhood, and each, I think, a correct claim on some interpretation. What will be at issue here is first, how (on my interpretation) they are dependent on each other; second, why they are necessary conditions of moral personhood, and third, why it is so hard to say whether they are jointly sufficient conditions for moral personhood. The *first* and most obvious theme is that persons are *rational beings*. It figures, for example, in the ethical theories of Kant and Rawls, and in the "metaphysical" theories of Aristotle and Hintikka.[4] The *second* theme is that persons are beings to which states of consciousness are attributed, or to which psychological or mental or *Intentional predicates*, are ascribed. Thus Strawson identifies the concept of a person as "the concept of a type of entity such that *both* predicates ascribing states of consciousness *and* predicates ascribing corporeal characteristics" are applicable.[5] The *third* theme is that whether something counts as a person depends in some way on an *attitude taken* toward it, a *stance adopted* with respect to it. This theme suggests that it is not the case that once we have established the objective fact that something is a person we treat him or her or it a certain way, but that our treating him or her or it in this certain way is somehow and to some extent constitutive of its being a person. Variations on this theme have been expressed by MacKay, Strawson, Amelie Rorty, Putnam, Sellars, Flew, Thomas Nagel, Dwight Van de Vate, and myself.[6] The *fourth* theme is that the object toward which this personal stance is taken must be capable of *reciprocating* in some way. Very different versions of this are expressed or hinted at by Rawls, MacKay, Strawson, Grice, and others. This reciprocity has sometimes been rather uninformatively expressed by the slogan: to be a person is to treat others as persons, and with this expression has often gone the claim that treating another as a person is treating him morally—perhaps obeying the Golden Rule, but this conflates different sorts of reciprocity. As Nagel says, "extremely hostile behavior toward another is compatible with treating him as a person" (p. 134), and as Van de Vate observes, one of the differences between some forms of manslaughter and murder is that the murderer treats the victim as a person.

The *fifth* theme is that persons must be capable of *verbal communication*. This condition handily excuses nonhuman animals from full personhood and the attendant moral responsibility, and seems at least implicit in all social contract theories of ethics. It is also a theme that has been stressed or presupposed by many writers in philosophy of mind, including myself, where the moral dimension of personhood has not been at issue. The *sixth* theme is that persons are distinguishable from other entities by being *conscious* in some special way: there is a way in which *we* are conscious in which no other species is conscious. Sometimes this is identified as *self*-consciousness of one sort or another. Three philosophers who claim—in very different ways—that a special sort of consciousness is a precondition of being a moral agent are Anscombe, in *Intention*, Sartre, in *The Transcendence of the Ego*, and Harry Frankfurt, in his recent paper, "Freedom of the Will and the Concept of a Person."[7]

I will argue that the order in which I have given these six themes is—with one proviso—the order of their dependence. The proviso is that the first three are mutually interdependent; being rational is being Intentional is being the object of a certain stance. These three together are a necessary but not sufficient condition for exhibiting the form of reciprocity that is in turn a necessary but not sufficient condition for having the capacity for verbal communication, which is the necessary[8] condition for having a special sort of consciousness, which is, as Anscombe and Frankfurt in their different ways claim,[9] a necessary condition of moral personhood.

I have previously exploited the first three themes, rationality, Intentionality and stance, to define not persons, but the much wider class of what I call *Intentional systems*, and since I intend to build on that notion, a brief résumé is in order. An Intentional system is a system whose behavior can be (at least sometimes) explained and predicted by relying on ascriptions to the system of *beliefs* and *desires* (and other Intentionally characterized features —what I will call *Intentions* here, meaning to include hopes, fears, intentions, perceptions, expectations, etc.). There may *in every case* be other ways of predicting and explaining the behavior of an Intentional system—for instance, mechanistic or physical ways— but the Intentional stance may be the handiest or most effective or in any case *a* successful stance to adopt, which suffices for the object to be an Intentional system. So defined, Intentional systems are obviously not all persons. We ascribe beliefs and desires to dogs and fish and thereby predict their behavior, and we can even use the procedure to predict the behavior of some machines. For instance, it is a good, indeed the only good, strategy to adopt against a good chess-playing computer. By *assuming* the computer has certain beliefs (or information) and desires (or preference functions) dealing with the chess game in progress, I can calculate —under auspicious circumstances—the computer's most likely next move, *provided I assume the computer deals rationally with these beliefs and desires*. The computer is an Intentional system in these instances not because it has any particular intrinsic features, and not because it really and truly has beliefs and desires (whatever that would be), but just because it succumbs to a certain *stance* adopted toward it, namely the Intentional stance, the stance that proceeds by ascribing Intentional predicates under the usual constraints to the computer, the stance that proceeds by considering the computer as a rational practical reasoner.

It is important to recognize how bland this definition of *Intentional system* is, and how correspondingly large the class of Intentional systems can be. If, for instance, I predict that a particular plant—say a potted ivy—will grow around a corner and up into the light because it "seeks" the light and "wants" to get out of the shade it now finds itself in, and "expects" or "hopes" there is light around the corner, I have adopted the Intentional stance toward the plant, and lo and behold, within very narrow limits it works. Since it works, some plants are very low-grade Intentional systems.

The actual utility of adopting the Intentional stance toward plants was brought home to me talking with loggers in the Maine woods. These men invariably call a tree not "it" but "he," and will say of a young spruce "he wants to spread his limbs, but don't let him; then he'll have to stretch up to get his light" or "pines don't like to get their feet wet the way cedars do." You can "trick" an apple tree into "thinking it's spring" by building a small fire under its branches in the late fall; it will blossom. This way of talking is not just picturesque and is not really superstitious at all; it is simply an efficient way of making sense of, controlling, predicting, and explaining the behavior of these plants in a way that nicely circumvents one's ignorance of the controlling mechanisms. More sophisticated biologists may choose to speak of information transmission from the tree's periphery to other locations in the tree. This is less picturesque, but still Intentional. Complete abstention from Intentional talk about trees can become almost as heroic, cumbersome, and pointless as the parallel strict behaviorist taboo when speaking of rats and pigeons. And even when Intentional glosses on (e.g.) tree-activities are of vanishingly small heuristic value, it seems to me wiser to grant that such a tree is a very degenerate, uninteresting, negligible Intentional system than to attempt to draw a line above which Intentional interpretations are "objectively true."

It is obvious, then, that being an Intentional system is not sufficient condition for being a person, but is surely a necessary condition. Nothing to which we could not successfully adopt the Intentional stance, with its presupposition of rationality, could count as a person. Can we then define persons as a subclass of Intentional systems? At first glance it might seem profitable to suppose that persons are just that subclass of Intentional systems that *really* have beliefs, desires, and so forth, and are not merely *supposed* to have them for the sake of a short-cut prediction. But efforts to say what counts as really having a belief (so that no dog or tree or computer could qualify) all seem to end by putting conditions on genuine belief that (1) are too strong for our intuitions, and (2) allude to distinct conditions of personhood farther down my list. For instance, one might claim that genuine beliefs are necessarily *verbally expressible* by the believer,[10] or the believer must be *conscious* that he has them, but people seem to have many beliefs that they cannot put into words, and many that they are unaware of having—and in any case I hope to show that the capacity for verbal expression, and the capacity for consciousness, find different *loci* in the set of necessary conditions of personhood.

Better progress can be made, I think, if we turn to our fourth theme, reciprocity, to see what kind of definition it could receive in terms of Intentional systems. The theme suggests that a person must be able to reciprocate the stance, which suggests that an Intentional system that itself adopted the Intentional stance toward other objects would meet the test. Let us define a *second-order Intentional system* as one to which we ascribe not only simple beliefs, desires and other Intentions, but beliefs, desires, and other Intentions *about* beliefs, desires, and other Intentions. An Intentional system S would be a second-order Intentional system if among the ascriptions we make to it are such as *S believes that T desires that p, S hopes that T fears that q*, and reflexive cases like *S believes that S desires that p*. (The importance of the reflexive cases will loom large, not surprisingly, when we turn to those who interpret our sixth condition as *self*-consciousness. It may seem to some that the reflexive cases make all Intentional systems automatically second-order systems, and even n-order systems, on the grounds that believing that p implies believing that you believe that p and so forth, but this is a fundamental mistake; the iteration of beliefs and other Intentions is never redundant, and hence while some iterations are normal [are to be expected] they are never trivial or automatic.)

Now are human beings the only second-order Intentional systems so far as we know? I take this to be an empirical question. We ascribe beliefs and desires to dogs, cats, lions, birds, and dolphins, for example, and thereby often predict their behavior—when all goes well—but it is hard to think of a case where an animal's behavior was so sophisticated that we would need to ascribe second-order Intentions to it in order to predict or explain its behavior. Of course if some version of mechanistic physicalism is true (as I believe), we will never *need* absolutely to ascribe any Intentions to anything, but supposing that for heuristic and pragmatic reasons we were to ascribe Intentions to animals, would we ever feel the pragmatic tug to ascribe second-order Intentions to them? Psychologists have often appealed to a principle known as Lloyd Morgan's Canon of Parsimony, which can be viewed as a special case of Occam's Razor; it is the principle that one should attribute to an organism as little intelligence or consciousness or rationality or mind as will suffice to account for its behavior. This principle can be, and has been, interpreted as demanding nothing short of radical behaviorism[11] but I think this is a mistake, and we can interpret it as the principle requiring us when we adopt the Intentional stance toward a thing to ascribe the simplest, least sophisticated, lowest-order beliefs, desires, and so on, that will account for the behavior. Then we will grant, for instance, that Fido *wants* his supper, and *believes* his master will give him his supper if he begs in front of his master, but we need not ascribe to Fido the further *belief* that his begging induces a *belief* in his master that he, Fido, *wants* his supper. Similarly, my *expectation* when I put a dime in the candy machine does not hinge on a further *belief* that inserting the coin induces the machine to *believe* I *want* some candy. That is, while Fido's begging looks very much like true second-order interacting (with Fido treating his master as an Intentional system), if we suppose that to Fido his master is just a supper machine activated by begging, we will have just as good a predictive ascription, more modest but still, of course, Intentional.

Are dogs, then, or chimps or other "higher" animals, incapable of rising to the level of second-order Intentional systems, and if so why? I used to think the answer was Yes, and I thought the reason was that nonhuman animals lack language, and that language was needed to represent second-order Intentions. In other words, I thought condition four might rest on condition five. I was tempted by the hypothesis that animals cannot, for instance, have second-order beliefs, beliefs about beliefs, for the same reason they cannot have beliefs about Friday, or poetry. Some beliefs can only be acquired, and hence represented, via language.[12] But if it is true that some beliefs cannot be acquired without language, it is false that all second-order beliefs are among them, and it is false that non-humans cannot be second-order Intentional systems. Once I began asking people for examples of non-human second-order Intentional systems, I found some very plausible cases. Consider this from Peter Ashley (in a letter):

> One evening I was sitting in a chair at my home, the *only* chair my dog is allowed to sleep in. The dog was lying in front of me, whimpering. She was getting nowhere in her trying to "convince" me to give up the chair to her. Her next move is the most interesting, nay, the *only* interesting part of the story. She stood up, and went to the front door where I could still easily see her. She scratched the door, giving me the impression that she had given up trying to get the chair and had decided to go out. However as soon as I reached the door to let her out, she ran back across the room and climbed into her chair, the chair she had "forced" me to leave.

Here it seems we must ascribe to the dog the *intention* that her master *believe* she *wants* to go out—not just a second-order, but a third-order Intention. The key to the example, what makes it an example of a higher-order Intentional system at work, is that the belief she intends to induce in her master is false. If we want to discover further examples of animals behaving as second-order Intentional systems it will help to think of cases of deception, where the animal, believing *p*, tries to get another Intentional system to believe *not-p*. Where an animal is trying to induce behavior in another which *true* beliefs about the other's environment would not induce, we cannot "divide through" and get an explanation that cites only first-level Intentions. We can make this point more general before explaining why it is so: where *x* is attempting to induce behavior in *y* which is inappropriate to *y*'s *true* environment and needs but appropriate to *y*'s *perceived* or *believed* environment and needs, we are forced to ascribe second-order Intentions to *x*. Once in this form the point emerges as a familiar one, often exploited by critics of behaviorism: one can be a behaviorist in explaining and controlling the behavior of laboratory animals only so long as he can rely on there being no serious dislocation between the actual environment of the experiment and the environment perceived by the animals. A tactic for embarrassing behaviorists in the laboratory is to set up experiments that deceive the subjects: if the deception succeeds their behavior is predictable

from their false *beliefs* about the environment, not from the actual
environment. Now a first-order Intentional system is a behaviorist; it ascribes no Intentions to anything. So if we are to have good
evidence that some system *S* is *not* a behaviorist—is a second-order
Intentional system—it will only be in those cases where behaviorist
theories are inadequate to the data, only in those cases where
behaviorism would not explain system *S*'s success in manipulating
another system's behavior.

This suggests that Ashley's example is not so convincing after
all, that it can be defeated by supposing his dog is a behaviorist of
sorts. She need not believe that scratching on the door will induce
Ashley to believe she wants to go out; she may simply believe, as a
good behaviorist, that she has conditioned Ashley to go to the
door when she scratches. So she applies the usual stimulus, gets
the usual response, and that's that. Ashley's case succumbs if this
is a *standard* way his dog has of getting the door opened, as it
probably is, for then the more modest hypothesis is that the dog
believes her master is conditioned to go to the door when she
scratches. Had the dog done something *novel* to deceive her
master (like running to the window and looking out, growling sus-
piciously) then we would have to grant that rising from the chair
was no mere conditioned response in Ashley, and could not be
"viewed" as such by his dog, but then, such virtuosity in a dog
would be highly implausible.

Yet what is the difference between the implausible case and the
well-attested cases where a low-nesting bird will feign a broken
wing to lure a predator away from the nest? The effect achieved is
novel, in the sense that the bird in all likelihood has not repeatedly
conditioned the predators in the neighborhood with this stimulus,
so we seem constrained to explain the ploy as a bit of genuine
deception, where the bird *intends* to induce a false *belief* in the
predator. Forced to this interpretation of the behavior, we would
be mightily impressed with the bird's ingenuity were it not for the
fact that we know such behavior is "merely instinctual." But why
does it disparage this trick to call it merely instinctual? To claim it
is instinctual is to claim that all birds of the species do it; they do it
even when circumstances aren't entirely appropriate; they do it
when there are better reasons for staying on the nest; the behavior
pattern is rigid, a tropism of sorts, and presumably the controls
are genetically wired in, not learned or invented.

We must be careful not to carry this disparagement too far; it is not that the bird does this trick "unthinkingly," for while it is no doubt true that she does not in any sense run through an argument or scheme in her head ("Let's see, if I were to flap my wing as if it were broken, the fox would think . . ."), a man might do something of similar subtlety, and of genuine intelligence, novelty, and appropriateness, and not run through the "conscious thoughts" either. *Thinking the thoughts*, however that is characterized, is not what makes truly intelligent behavior intelligent. Anscombe says at one point "If [such an expression of reasoning] were supposed to describe actual mental processes, it would in general be quite absurd. The interest of the account is that it described an order which is there whenever actions are done with intentions."[13] But the "order is there" in the case of the bird as well as the man. That is, when we ask why birds evolved with this tropism we explain it by noting the utility of having a means of *deceiving* predators, or inducing false beliefs in them; what must be explained is the provenance of the bird's second-order Intentions. I would be the last to deny or dismiss the vast difference between instinctual or tropistic behavior and the more versatile, intelligent behavior of humans and others, but what I want to insist on here is that if one is prepared to adopt the Intentional stance without qualms as a tool in predicting and explaining behavior, the bird is as much a second-order Intentional system as any man. Since this is so, we should be particularly suspicious of the argument I was tempted to use, viz., that *representations* of second order Intentions would depend somehow on language.[14] For it is far from clear that all or even any of the beliefs and other Intentions of an Intentional system need be *represented* "within" the system in any way for us to get a purchase on predicting its behavior by *ascribing* such Intentions to it.[15] The situation we elucidate by citing the bird's desire to induce a false belief in the predator seems to have no room or need for a representation of this sophisticated Intention in any entity's "thoughts" or "mind," for neither the bird nor evolutionary history nor Mother Nature need think these thoughts for our explanation to be warranted.

Reciprocity, then, provided we understand by it merely the capacity in Intentional systems to exhibit higher-order Intentions, while it depends on the first three conditions, is independent of the fifth and sixth. Whether this notion does justice to the reciprocity discussed by other writers will begin to come clear only when we see how it meshes with the last two conditions. For the fifth condition, the capacity for verbal communication, we turn to Grice's theory of meaning. Grice attempts to define what he calls non-natural meaning, an utterer's meaning something by uttering something, in terms of the *intentions* of the utterer. His initial definition is as follows:[16]

> "U meant something by uttering x" is true if, for some audience A, U uttered x intending
> (1) A to produce a particular response *r*.
> (2) A to think (recognize) that U intends (1).
> (3) A to fulfill (1) on the basis of his fulfillment of (2).

Notice that intention (2) ascribes to U not only a second- but a third-order Intention: U must *intend* that A *recognize* that U *intends* that A produce *r*. It matters not at all that Grice has been forced by a series of counterexamples to move from this initial definition to much more complicated versions, for they all reproduce the third-order Intention of (2). Two points of great importance to us emerge from Grice's analysis of nonnatural meaning. First, since nonnatural meaning, meaning something by saying something, must be a feature of any true verbal communication, and since it depends on third-order Intentions on the part of the utterer, we have our case that condition five rests on condition four and not vice versa. Second, Grice shows us that mere *second*-order Intentions are not enough to provide genuine reciprocity; for that, *third*-order Intentions are needed. Grice introduces condition (2) in order to exclude such cases as this: I leave the china my daughter has broken lying around for my wife to see. This is not a case of meaning something by doing what I do intending what I intend, for though I am attempting thereby to induce my wife to believe something about our daughter (a second-order Intention on my part), success does not depend on her recognizing this intention of mine, or recognizing my intervention or existence at all. There has been no real *encounter*, to use Erving Goffman's apt term, between us, no *mutual recognition*. There must be an encounter between utterer and audience for utterer to mean anything, but encounters can occur in the absence of non-natural meaning (witness Ashley's dog), and ploys that depend on third-order Intentions need not involve encounters (e.g., *A* can intend that *B* believe that *C* desires that *p*). So third-order Intentions are a necessary but not sufficient condition for encounters which are a necessary but not sufficient condition for instances of nonnatural meaning, that is, instances of verbal communication.

It is no accident that Grice's cases of nonnatural meaning fall into a class whose other members are cases of deception or manipulation. Consider, for instance, Searle's ingenious counterexample to one of Grice's formulations: the American caught behind enemy lines in World War II Italy who attempts to deceive his Italian captors into concluding he is a German officer by saying the one sentence of German he knows: *"Kennst du das Land, wo die Zitronen blühen?"*[17] As Grice points out, these cases share with cases of nonnatural meaning a reliance on or exploitation of the rationality of the victim. In these cases success hinges on inducing the victim to embark on a chain of reasoning to which one contributes premises directly or indirectly. In deception the premises are disbelieved by the supplier; in normal communication they are believed. Communication, in Gricean guise, appears to be a sort of collaborative manipulation of audience by utterer; it depends, not only on the rationality of the audience who must sort out the utterer's intentions, but on the audience's *trust* in the utterer. Communication, as a sort of manipulation, would not work, given the requisite rationality of the audience, unless the audience's trust in the utterer were *well-grounded* or reasonable. Thus the *norm* for utterance is sincerity; were utterances not normally trustworthy, they would fail of their purpose.[18]

Lying, as a form of deception, can only work against a background of truth-telling, but other forms of deception do not depend on the trust of the victim. In these cases success depends on the victim being *quite* smart, but not quite smart enough. Stupid poker players are the bane of clever poker players, for they fail to see the bluffs and ruses being offered them. Such sophisticated deceptions need not depend on direct encounters. There is a book on how to detect fake antiques (which is also, inevitably, a book on how to *make* fake antiques) which offers this sly advice to those who want to fool the "expert" buyer: once you have completed your table or whatever (having utilized all the usual means of simulating age and wear) take a modern electric drill and drill a hole right through the piece in some conspicuous but perplexing place. The would-be buyer will argue: no one would drill such a disfiguring hole without a reason (it can't be supposed to look "authentic" in any way) so it must have served a purpose, which means this table must have been in use in someone's home; since it was in use in someone's home, it was not made expressly for sale in this antique shop...therefore it is authentic. Even if this "conclusion" left room for lingering doubts, the buyer will be so preoccupied dreaming up uses for that hole it will be months before the doubts can surface.

What is important about these cases of deception is the fact that just as in the case of the feigning bird, success does not depend on the victim's *consciously entertaining* these chains of reasoning. It does not matter if the buyer just notices the hole and "gets a hunch" the piece is genuine. He *might* later accept the reasoning offered as his "rationale" for finding the piece genuine, but he might deny it, and in denying it, he might be deceiving himself, even though the *thoughts* never went through his head. The chain of reasoning explains why the hole works as it does (if it does), but as Anscombe says, it need not "describe actual mental processes," if we suppose actual mental processes are conscious processes or events. The same, of course, is true of Gricean communications; neither the utterer nor the audience need consciously entertain the complicated Intentions he outlines, and what is a bit surprising is that no one has ever used this fact as an objection to Grice. Grice's conditions for meaning have been often criticized for falling short of being sufficient, but there seems to be an argument not yet used to show they are not even necessary. Certainly few people ever consciously framed those ingenious intentions before Grice pointed them out, and yet people had been communicating for years. Before Grice, were one asked: "Did you intend your audience to recognize your intention to provoke that response in him?" one would most likely have retorted: "I intended nothing so devious. I simply intended to inform him that I wouldn't be home for supper" (or whatever). So it seems that if these complicated intentions underlay our communicating all along, they must have been unconscious intentions. Indeed, a perfectly natural way of responding to Grice's papers is to remark that *one was not aware* of doing these things when one communicated. Now

Anscombe has held, very powerfully, that such a response establishes that the action under that description was not intentional.[19] Since one is not *aware* of these intentions in speaking, one cannot be speaking *with* these intentions.

Why has no one used this argument against Grice's theory? Because, I submit, it is just too plain that Grice is on to something, that Grice is giving us necessary conditions for nonnatural meaning. His analysis illuminates so many questions. Do we communicate with computers in Fortran? Fortran seems to be a language; it has a grammar, a vocabulary, a semantics. The transactions in Fortran between man and machine are often viewed as cases of *man communicating with machine*, but such transactions are pale copies of human verbal communication precisely because the Gricean conditions for nonnatural meaning have been bypassed. There is no room for them to apply. Achieving one's ends in transmitting a bit of Fortran to the machine does not hinge on getting the machine to recognize one's intentions. This does not mean that all communications with computers in the future will have this shortcoming (or strength, depending on your purposes), but just that we do not now communicate, in the strong (Gricean) sense, with computers.[20]

If we are not about to abandon the Gricean model, yet are aware of no such intentions in our normal conversation, we shall just have to drive these intentions underground, and call them unconscious or preconscious intentions. They are intentions that exhibit "an order which is there" when people communicate, intentions of which we are not normally aware, and intentions which are a precondition of verbal communication.[21]

We have come this far without having to invoke any sort of consciousness at all, so if there is a dependence between consciousness or self-consciousness and our other conditions, it will have to be consciousness depending on the others. But to show this I must first show how the first five conditions by themselves might play a role in ethics, as suggested by Rawls's theory of justice. Central to Rawls's theory is his setting up of an idealized situation, the "original position," inhabited by idealized persons, and deriving from this idealization the first principles of justice that generate and illuminate the rest of his theory. What I am concerned with now is neither the content of these principles nor the validity of their derivation, but the nature of Rawls's tactic. Rawls supposes that a group of idealized persons, defined by him as rational, self-interested entities, make calculations under certain constraints about the likely and possible interactive effects of their individual and antagonistic interests (which will require them to frame higher-order Intentions, for example, beliefs about the desires of others, beliefs about the beliefs of others about their own desires, and so forth). Rawls claims these calculations have an optimal "solution" that it would be reasonable for each self-interested person to adopt as an alternative to a Hobbesian state of nature. The solution is to agree with his fellows to abide by the principles of justice Rawls adumbrates. What sort of a proof of the principles of justice would this be? Adopting these principles of justice can be viewed, Rawls claims, as the solution to the "highest order game" or "bargaining problem." It is analogous to derivations of game theory, and to proofs in Hintikka's epistemic logic,[22] and to a "demonstration" that the chess-playing computer will make a certain move because it is the most rational move given its information about the game. All depend on the assumption of ideally rational calculators and hence their outcomes are intrinsically normative. Thus I see the derivations from Rawls's original position as continuous with the deductions and extrapolations encountered in more simple uses of the Intentional stance to understand and control the behavior of simpler entities. Just as truth and consistency are norms for belief,[23] and sincerity is the norm for utterance, so, if Rawls is right, justice as he defines it is the norm for interpersonal interactions. But then, just as part of our warrant for considering an entity to have any beliefs or other Intentions is our ability to construe the entity as *rational*, so our grounds for considering an entity a person include our ability to view him as abiding by the principles of justice. A way of capturing the peculiar status of the concept of a person as I think it is exploited here would be to say that while Rawls does not at all intend to argue that justice is the inevitable result of *human* interaction, he does argue in effect that it is the inevitable result of *personal* interaction. That is, the concept of a person is itself inescapably normative or idealized; to the extent that justice does not reveal itself in the dealings and interactions of creatures, to that extent they are not persons. And once again we can see that there is "an order which is there" in a just society that is independent of any actual episodes of conscious thought. The existence of just practices and the "acknowledgment" implicit in them does not depend on anyone ever consciously or deliberately going through the calculations of the idealized original position, consciously arriving at the reciprocal agreements, consciously adopting a stance toward others.

> To recognize another as a person one must respond to him and act towards him in certain ways; and these ways are intimately connected with the various prima facie duties. Acknowledging these duties in some degree, and so having the elements of morality, is not a matter of choice or of intuiting moral qualities or a matter of the expression of feelings or attitudes...it is simply the pursuance of one of the forms of conduct in which the recognition of others as persons is manifested.[24]

The importance of Rawls's attempt to derive principles of justice from the "original position" is, of course, that while the outcome is recognizable as a *moral* norm, it is not *derived as* a moral norm. Morality is not presupposed of the parties in the original position. But this means that the derivation of the norm does not in itself give us any answer to the questions of when and why we have the right to hold persons *morally* responsible for deviations from that norm. Here Anscombe provides help and at the same time introduces our sixth condition. *If I am to be held responsible for an action* (a bit of behavior of mine under a particular description), I must have been *aware* of that action under that description.[25] Why? Because only if I was aware of the action can I *say* what I was about, and participate from a privileged position in the question-and-answer game of giving reasons for my actions. (If I am not in a privileged position to answer questions about the reasons for my actions, there is no special reason to ask *me*.) And what is so important about being able to participate in this game is that only those capable of participating in reason-giving can be argued into, or argued out of, courses of action or attitudes, and if one is incapable of "listening to reason" in some matter, one cannot be held responsible for it. The capacities for verbal communication and for awareness of one's actions are thus essential in one who is going to be amenable to argument or persuasion, and such persuasion, such reciprocal adjustment of interests achieved by mutual exploitation of rationality, is a feature of the optimal mode of personal interaction.

This capacity for participation in mutual persuasion provides the foundation for yet another condition of personhood recently exposed by Harry Frankfurt.[26] Frankfurt claims that persons are the subclass of Intentional systems capable of what he calls *second-order volitions*. Now at first this looks just like the class of second-order Intentional systems, but it is not, as we shall see.

> Besides wanting and choosing and being moved *to do* this or that, men may also want to have (or not to have) certain desires and motives. They are capable of wanting to be different, in their preferences and purposes, from what they are.... No animal other than man, however, appears to have the capacity for reflective self-evaluation that is manifested in the formation of second-order desires. (p. 7)

Frankfurt points out that there are cases in which a person might be said to want to have a particular desire even though he would not want that desire to be effective for him, to be "his will." (One might, for instance, want to desire heroin just to know what it felt like to desire heroin, without at all wanting this desire to become one's effective desire.) In more serious cases one wants to have a desire one currently does not have, and wants this desire to become one's will. These cases Frankfurt calls second-order volitions, and it is having these, he claims, that is "essential to being a person" (p. 10). His argument for this claim, which I will not try to do justice to here, proceeds from an analysis of the distinction between having freedom of action and having freedom of the will. One has freedom of the will, on his analysis, only when one can have the will one wants, when one's second-order volitions can be satisfied. Persons do not always have free will, and under some circumstances can be responsible for actions done in the absence of freedom of the will, but a person always must be an "entity for whom the freedom of its will may be a problem" (p. 14)—that is, one capable of framing second-order volitions, satisfiable or not. Frankfurt introduces the marvelous term "wanton" for those "who have first-order desires but...no second-order volitions." (Second-order volitions for Frankfurt are all, of course, *reflexive* second-order desires.) He claims that our intuitions support the opinion that all nonhuman animals, as well as small children and some mentally defective people, are wantons, and I for one can think of no plausible counterexamples. Indeed, it seems a strength of his theory, as he claims, that human beings—the only persons we recognize—are distinguished from animals in this regard. But what should be so special about second-order volitions? Why are they, among higher-order Intentions, the peculiar province of persons? Because, I believe, the "reflective self-evaluation" Frankfurt speaks of is, and must be, genuine self-consciousness, which is achieved only by adopting toward *oneself* the stance not simply of communicator but of Anscombian reason-asker and persuader. As Frankfurt points out, second-order desires are an empty notion unless one can *act* on them, and acting on a second-order desire must be logically distinct from acting on its first-order component. Acting on a second-order desire, doing something to bring it about that one acquires a first-order desire, is acting upon oneself just as one would act upon another person: one *schools* oneself, one offers oneself persuasions, arguments, threats, bribes, in the hopes of inducing oneself to acquire the first-order desire.[27] One's stance toward oneself *and access to oneself* in these cases is essentially the same as one's stance toward and access to another. One must *ask oneself* what one's desires, motives, reasons really are, and only if one can say, can become aware of one's desires, can one be in a position to induce oneself to change.[28] Only here, I think, is it the case that the "order which is there" cannot be there unless it is there in episodes of conscious thought, in a dialogue with oneself.[29]

Now, finally, why are we not in a position to claim that these necessary conditions of moral personhood are also sufficient? Simply because the concept of a person is, I have tried to show, inescapably normative. Human beings or other entities can only aspire to being approximations of the ideal, and there can be no way to set a "passing grade" that is not arbitrary. Were the six conditions (strictly interpreted) considered sufficient they would not ensure that any actual entity was a person, for nothing would ever fulfill them. The moral notion of a person and the metaphysical notion of a person are not separate and distinct concepts but just two different and unstable resting points on the same continuum. This relativity infects the satisfaction of conditions of personhood at every level. There is no objectively satisfiable sufficient condition for an entity's *really* having beliefs, and as we uncover apparent irrationality under an Intentional interpretation of an entity, our grounds for ascribing any beliefs at all wanes, especially when we have (what we always *can* have in principle) a non-Intentional, mechanistic account of the entity. In just the same way our assumption that an entity is a person is shaken precisely in those cases where it matters: when wrong has been done and the question of responsibility arises. For in these cases the grounds for saying that the person is culpable (the evidence that he did wrong, was aware he was doing wrong, and did wrong of his own free will) are in themselves grounds for doubting that it is a person we are dealing with at all. And if it is asked what could *settle* our doubts, the answer is: nothing. When such problems arise we cannot even tell in our own cases if we are persons.

NOTES

1. See my "Mechanism and Responsibility," in T. Honderich, ed., *Essays on Freedom of Action* (London: Routledge & Kegan Paul, 1973).

2. In "Justice as Reciprocity," a revision of "Justice as Fairness" printed in S. Gorovitz, ed., *Utilitarianism* (Indianapolis: Bobbs Merrill, 1971), Rawls allows that the persons in the original position may include "nations, provinces, business firms, churches, teams, and so on. The principles of justice apply to conflicting claims made by persons of all these separate kinds. There is, perhaps, a certain logical priority to the case of human individuals" (p. 245). In *A Theory of Justice* (Cambridge, Mass.: Harvard University Press, 1971), he acknowledges that parties in the original position may include associations and other entities not human individuals (e.g., p. 146), and the apparent interchangeability of "parties in the original position" and "persons in the original position" suggests that Rawls is claiming that for some moral concept of a person, the moral person is *composed* of metaphysical persons who may or may not themselves be moral persons.

3. Setting aside Rawls's possible compound moral persons. For more on compound persons see Amelie Rorty, "Persons, Policies, and Bodies," *International Philosophical Quarterly*, Vol. XIII, no. 1 (March 1973).

4. J. Hintikka, *Knowledge and Belief* (Ithaca: Cornell University Press, 1962).

5. P. F. Strawson, *Individuals* (London: Methuen, 1959), pp. 101-102. It has often been pointed out that Strawson's definition is obviously much too broad, capturing all sentient, active creatures. See, e.g. H. Frankfurt, "Freedom of the will and the concept of a person," *Journal of Philosophy* (January 14, 1971). It can also be argued (and I would argue) that states of consciousness are only a proper subset of psychological or Intentionally characterized states, but I think it is clear that Strawson here means to cast his net wide enough to include psychological states generally.

6. D.M. MacKay, "The use of behavioral language to refer to mechanical processes," *British Journal of Philosophy of Science* (1962), pp. 89-103; P.F. Strawson, "Freedom and resentment," *Proceedings of the British Academy* (1962), reprinted in Strawson, ed., *Studies in the Philosophy of Thought and Action* (Oxford, 1968); A. Rorty, "Slaves and machines," *Analysis* (1962); H. Putnam, "Robots: machines or artificially created life?" *Journal of Philosophy*

(November 12, 1964); W. Sellars, "Fatalism and determinism," in K. Lehrer, ed., *Freedom and Determinism* (New York: Random House, 1966); A. Flew, "A Rational Animal," in J.R. Smythies, ed., *Brain and Mind* (London: Routledge & Kegan Paul, 1968); T. Nagel, "War and Massacre," *Philosophy and Public Affairs* (Winter 1972); D. Van de Vate, "The problem of robot consciousness," *Philosophy and Phenomenological Research* (December 1971); my "Intentional Systems," *Journal of Philosophy* (February 25, 1971).

7. H. Frankfurt, "Freedom of the will and the concept of a person," op. cit.

8. And sufficient, but I will not argue it here. I argue for this in *Content and Consciousness* (London: Routledge & Kegan Paul, 1969), and more recently and explicitly in my "Reply to Arbib and Gunderson," APA Eastern Division Meetings, December 29, 1972.

9. I will not discuss Sartre's claim here.

10. Cf. Bernard Williams, "Deciding to Believe," in H.E. Kiefer and M.K. Munitz, eds., *Language, Belief and Metaphysics* (New York: New York University Press, 1970).

11. E.g., B.F. Skinner, "Behaviorism at Fifty," in T.W. Wann, ed., *Behaviorism and Phenomenology* (Chicago: University of Chicago Press, 1964).

12. For illuminating suggestions on the relation of language to belief and rationality, see Ronald de Sousa, "How to give a piece of your mind; or, a logic of belief and assent," *Review of Metaphysics* (September 1971).

13. G.E.M. Anscombe, *Intention* (Oxford: Blackwell, 1957), p. 80.

14. Cf. Ronald de Sousa, "Self-Deception," *Inquiry*, 13 (1970), esp. p. 317.

15. I argue this in more detail in "Brain Writing and Mind Reading," in K. Gunderson, ed., *Language, Mind, and Knowledge* (Minneapolis: University of Minnesota Press, 1975), and in my "Reply to Arbib and Gunderson."

16. The key papers are "Meaning," *Philosophical Review* (July 1957), and "Utterer's meaning and intentions," *Philosophical Review* (April 1969). His initial formulation, developed in the first paper, is subjected to a series of revisions in the second paper, from which this formulation is drawn (p. 151).

17. John Searle, "What is a Speech Act?" in Max Black, ed., *Philosphy in America* (London: Allen & Unwin, 1965), discussed by Grice in "Utterer's Meaning and Intentions," p. 160.

18. Cf. "Intentional Systems," pp. 102-103.

19. G.E.M. Anscombe, *Intention*, p. 11.

20. It has been pointed out to me by Howard Friedman that many current Fortran compilers which "correct" operator input by inserting "plus" signs and parentheses, etc., to produce well-formed expressions arguably meet Grice's criteria, since within a very limited sphere, they diagnose the "utterer's" intentions and proceed on the basis of this diagnosis. But first it should be noted that the machines to date can diagnose only what might be called the operator's syntactical intentions, and second, these machines do not seem to meet Grice's subsequent and more elaborate definitions, not that I wish to claim that no computer could.

21. In fact, Grice is describing only a small portion of the order which is there as a precondition of normal personal interaction. An analysis of higher order Intentions on a broader front is to be found in the works of Erving Goffman, especially in *The Presentation of Self in Everyday Life* (Garden City: Doubleday, 1959).

22. See Hintikka, *Knowledge and Belief*, p. 38.

23. See Dennett, "Intentional Systems," pp. 102-103.

24. J. Rawls, "Justice as Reciprocity," p. 259.

25. I can be held responsible for events and states of affairs that I was not aware of and ought to have been aware of, but these are not intentional actions. In these cases I am responsible for these further matters in virtue of being responsible for the foreseeable consequences of actions—including acts of omission—that I was aware of.

26. H. Frankfurt, "Freedom of the will and the concept of a person." Frankfurt does not say whether he conceives his condition to be merely a necessary or also a sufficient condition of moral personhood.

27. It has been brought to my attention that dogs at stud will often engage in masturbation, in order, apparently, to *increase their desire* to copulate. What makes these cases negligible is that even supposing the dog can be said to act on a desire to strengthen a desire, the effect is achieved in a non-Intentional ("purely physiological") way; the dog does not appeal to or exploit his own rationality in achieving his end. (As if the only way a person could act on a second-order volition were by taking a pill or standing on his head, etc.).

28. Margaret Gilbert, in "Vices and self-knowledge," *Journal of Philosophy* (August 5, 1971), p. 452, examines the implications of the fact that "when, and only when, one believes that one has a given trait can one decide to change out of it."

29. Marx, in *The German Ideology*, says: "Language, like consciousness, only arises from the need, the necessity, of intercourse with other men. . . . Language is as old as consciousness, language is practical consciousness." And Nietzsche, in *The Joyful Wisdom*, says: "For we could in fact think, feel, will, and recollect, we could likewise 'act' in every sense of the term, and nevertheless nothing of it at all need necessarily 'come into consciousness' (as one says metaphorically; . . . . *What* then is *the purpose* of consciousness generally, when it is in the main *superfluous*?—Now it seems to me, if you will hear my answer and its perhaps extravagant supposition, that the subtlety and strength of consciousness are always in proportion to the *capacity for communication* of a man (or an animal), the capacity for communication in its turn being in proportion to the *necessity for communication*. . . . In short, the development of speech and the development of consciousness (not of reason, but of reason becoming self-conscious) go hand in hand."

VIII

PERSONS, CHARACTER AND MORALITY

Bernard Williams

I

Much of the most interesting recent work in moral philosophy has been of basically Kantian inspiration; Rawls's own work[1] and those to varying degrees influenced by him such as Richards[2] and Nagel[3] are very evidently in the debt of Kant, while it is interesting that a writer such as Fried[4] who gives evident signs of being pulled away from some characteristic features of this way of looking at morality nevertheless, as I shall not later, tends to get pulled back into it. This is not of course a very pure Kantianism, and still less is it an expository or subservient one. It differs from Kant among other things in making no demands on a theory of noumenal freedom, and also, importantly, in admitting considerations of a general empirical character in determining fundamental moral demands, which Kant at least supported himself not to be doing. But allowing for those and many other important differences, the inspiration is there and the similarities both significant and acknowledged. They extend far beyond the evident point that both the extent and the nature of opposition to Utilitarianism resembles Kant's: though it is interesting that in this respect they are more Kantian than a philosophy which bears an obvious but superficial formal resemblance to Kantianism, namely Hare's. Indeed, Hare now supposes that when a substantial moral theory is elicited from his philosophical premises, it turns out to be a straightforward version of Utilitarianism. This is not merely because the universal and prescriptive character of moral judgments lays on the agent, according to Hare, a requirement of hypothetical identification with each person affected by a given decision—so much is a purely

Kantian element. It is rather that each identification is treated just as yielding 'acceptance' or 'rejection' of a certain prescription, and they in turn are construed solely in terms of satisfactions, so that the outputs of the various identifications can, under the usual Utilitarian assumptions, be regarded additively.

Among Kantian elements in these outlooks are, in particular, these: that the moral point of view is basically different from a non-moral, and in particular self-interested, point of view, and by a difference of kind; that the moral point of view is specially characterized by its impartiality and its indifference to any particular relations to particular persons, and that moral thought requires abstraction from particular circumstances and particular characteristics of the parties, including the agent, except in so far as these can be treated as universal features of any morally similar situation; and that the motivations of a moral agent, correspondingly, involve a rational application of impartial principle and are thus different in kind from the sorts of motivations that he might have for treating some particular persons (for instance, though not exclusively, himself) differently because he happened to have some particular interest towards them. Of course, it is not intended that these demands should exclude other and more intimate relations nor prevent someone from acting in ways demanded by and appropriate to them: that is a matter of the relations of the moral point of view to other points of view. But I think it is fair to say that included among the similarities of these views to Kant's is the point that like his they do not make the question of the relations between those points of view at all easy to answer; the deeply disparate character of moral and of non-moral motivation, together with the special dignity or supremacy attached to the moral, make it very difficult to assign to those other relations and motivations the significance or structural importance in life which some of them are capable of possessing.

It is worth remarking that this detachment of moral motivations and the moral point of view from the level of particular relations to particular persons, and more generally from the level of all motivations and perceptions other than those of an impartial character, obtains even when the moral point of view is itself explained in terms of the self-interest under conditions of ignorance of some abstractly conceived contracting parties, as it is by

Rawls, and by Richards, who is particularly concerned with applying directly to the characterization of the moral interest, the structure used by Rawls chiefly to characterize social justice. For while the contracting parties are pictured as making some kind of self-interested or prudential choice of a set of rules, they are entirely abstract persons making this choice in ignorance of their own particular properties, tastes, and so forth; and the self-interested choice of an abstract agent is intended to model precisely the moral choice of a concrete agent, by representing what he would choose granted that he made just the kinds of abstraction from his actual personality, situation and relations which the Kantian picture of moral experience requires.

Some elements in this very general picture serve already to distinguish the outlook in question from Utilitarianism. Choices made in deliberate abstraction from empirical information which actually exists are necessarily from a Utilitarian point of view irrational, and to that extent the formal structure of the outlook, even allowing the admission of *general* empirical information, is counter-Utilitarian. There is a further point of difference with Utilitarianism, which comes out if one starts from the fact that there is one respect at least in which Utilitarianism itself requires a notable abstraction in moral thought, an abstraction which in this respect goes even further than the Kantians': if Kantianism abstracts in moral thought from the identity of person, Utilitarianism strikingly abstracts from their separateness. This is true in more than one way. First, as the Kantian theorists have themselves emphasized, persons lose their separateness as beneficiaries of the Utilitarian provisions, since in the form which maximizes total utility, and even in that which maximizes average utility, there is an agglomeration of satisfactions which is basically indifferent to the separateness of those who have the satisfactions; this is evidently so in the total maximization system, and it is only superficially not so in the average maximization system, where the agglomeration occurs before the division. Richards,[5] following Rawls, has suggested that the device of the ideal observer serves to model the agglomeration of these satisfactions: equivalent to the world could be one person, with an indefinite capacity for happiness and pain. The Kantian view stands opposed to this; the idea of the contractual element, even between these shadowy and abstract participants, is in part to make the point that there are limitations built in at the bottom to permissible trade-offs between the satisfactions of individuals.

A second aspect of the Utilitarian abstraction from separateness involves agency.[6] It turns on the point that the basic bearer of value for Utilitarianism is the *state of affairs*, and hence, when the relevant causal differences have been allowed for, it cannot make any further difference who produces a given state of affairs: if S1 consists of my doing something, together with consequences, and S2 consists of someone else doing something, with consequences, and S2 comes about just in case S1 does not, and S1 is better than S2, then I should bring about S1, however *prima facie* nasty S1 is. Thus, unsurprisingly, the doctrine of negative responsibility has its roots at the foundation of Utilitarianism; and whatever projects, desires, ideals, or whatever I may have as a particular individual, as a Utilitarian agent my action has to be the output of *all* relevant causal items bearing on the situation, including all projects and desires within causal reach, my own and others, As a Utilitarian agent, I am just the representative of the satisfaction system who happens to be near certain causal levers at a certain time. At this level, there is abstraction not merely from the identity of agents, but, once more, from their separateness: for a conceivable extension or restriction of the causal powers of a given agent could always replace the activities of some other agent, so far as Utilitarian outcomes are concerned, and an outcome allocated to two agents as things are could equivalently be the product of one agent, or three, under a conceivable redistribution of causal powers.

In this latter respect also the Kantian outlook can be expected to disagree. For since we are concerned not just with outcomes, but at a basic level with actions and policies, *who* acts in a given situation makes a difference, and in particular *I* have a particular responsibility for *my* actions. Thus in more than one way the Kantian outlook emphasizes something like the separateness of agents, and in that sense makes less of an abstraction than Utilitarianism does (though, as we have seen, there are other respects, with regard to causally relevant empirical facts, in which its abstraction is greater). But now the question arises, of whether the honourable instincts of Kantianism to defend the individuality of

individuals against the agglomerative indifference of Utilitarianism can in fact be effective granted the impoverished and abstract
character of persons as moral agents which the Kantian view seems
to impose. Findlay has said 'the separateness of persons...is...
the basic fact for morals',[7] and Richards hopes to have respected
that fact.[8] Similarly Rawls claims that impartiality does not mean
impersonality.[9] But it is a real question, whether the conception of
the individual provided by the Kantian theories is in fact enough to
yield what is wanted, even by the Kantians; let alone enough for
others who, while equally rejecting Utilitarianism, want to allow
more room than Kantianism can allow for the importance of
individual character and personal relations in moral experience.

II

In this paper I take up, I fear in an obscure, promissory and allu-
sive manner, two aspects of this large subject. They both involve
the idea that an individual person has a set of desires, concerns or,
as I shall often call them, projects, which help to constitute a
character. The first issue concerns the connection between that
fact and the man's having a reason for living at all. I approach this
through a discussion of some recent work by Derek Parfit; though
I touch on a variety of points in this, my overriding aim is to
emphasize the basic importance for our thought of the ordinary
idea of a self or person which undergoes changes of character, as
opposed to an approach which, even if only metaphorically,
would dissolve the person, under changes of character, into a
series of 'selves'.

In this section I am concerned just with the point that each person has a character, not with the point that different people have
different characters. That latter point comes more to the fore on
the second issue, which I take up in part III, and which concerns
personal relations. Both issues suggest that the Kantian view contains an important misrepresentation.

First, then, I should like to comment on some arguments of
Parfit which explore connections between moral issues and a certain view of personal identity: a view which, he thinks mights
offer, among other things, '*some* defence'[10] of the Utilitarian
neglect of the separateness of persons. This view Parfit calls the

'Complex View'. This view takes seriously the idea that relations of psychological connectedness (such as memory and persistence of character and motivation) are what really matter with regard to most questions involving personal identity: the suggestion is that morality should take this seriously as well, as there is more than one way of its doing so. Psychological connectedness (unlike the surface logic of personal identity) admits of degrees. Let us call the relevant properties and relations which admit of degrees, *scalar* items. One of Parfit's aims is to make moral thought reflect more directly the scalar character of the phenomena which underly personal identity. In particular, in those cases in which the scalar relations hold in reduced degree, this fact should receive recognition in moral thought.

Another, and more general, consequence of taking the Complex View is that the matter of personal identity may appear altogether less deep, as Parfit puts it, than if one takes the Simple View, as he calls that alternative view which sees as basically significant the all-or-nothing logic of personal identity. If the matter of personal identity appears less deep, the *separateness* of persons, also, may come to seem less an ultimate and specially significant consideration for morality. The connection between those two thoughts is not direct; but there is more than one indirect connection between them.[11]

So far as the problems of *agency* are concerned, Parfit's treatment is not going to help Utilitarianism. His loosening of identity is diachronic, by reference to the weakening of psychological connectedness over time: where there is such weakening to a sufficient degree, he is prepared to speak of 'successive selves', though this is intended only as a *façon de parler.*[12] But the problems that face Utilitarianism about agency can arise with any agent whose projects stretch over enough time, and are sufficiently grounded in character, to be in any substantial sense *his* projects; and that condition will be satisfied by something that is, for Parfit, even *one* self. Thus there is nothing in this degree of dissolution of the traditional self which can help over agency.

In discussing the issues involved in making moral thought reflect more directly the scalar nature of what underlies personal identity, it is important to keep in mind that the talk of 'past selves', 'future selves' and generally 'several selves' is only a convenient fiction; neglect of this may make the transpositions in moral thought required by the Complex View seem simpler and perhaps more inviting than they are, since they may glide along on what seems to be a mere multiplication, in the case of these new 'selves', of familiar interpersonal relations. We must concentrate on the scalar facts. But many moral notions show a notable resistance to reflecting the scalar: or, rather, to reflecting it in the right way. We may take the case of promising, which Parfit has discussed.[13] Suppose that I promise to A that I will help him in certain ways in three years time. In three years time a person appears, let us say A*, whose memories, character etc., bear some, but a rather low, degree of connectedness to A's. How am I to mirror these scalar facts in my thought about whether, or how, I am to carry out my promise?

Something, first, should be said about the promise itself. *'You'* was the expression it used: 'I will help *you*', and it used that expression in such a way that it covered both the recipient of these words and the potential recipient of the help: this was not a promise that could be carried out (or, more generally, honoured) by helping anyone else, or indeed by doing anything except helping that person I addressed when I said 'you'—thus the situation is not like that with some promises to the dead (those where there is still something one can do about it).[14] If there is to be any action of mine which is to count as honouring that promise, it will have to be action which consists in now helping A*. How am I to mirror, in my action and my thought about it, A*'s scalar relations to A?

There seem to be only three ways in which they could be so mirrored, and none seems satisfactory. First, the action promised might itself have some significant scalar dimension, and it might be suggested that this should vary with my sense of the proximity or remoteness of A* from A. But this will not do: it is clearly a lunatic idea that if I promised to pay A a sum of money, then my obligation is to pay A* some money, but a smaller sum. A more serious suggestion would be that what varies with the degree of connectedness of A* to A is the degree of stringency of the obligation to do what was promised. While less evidently dotty, it is still, on reflection, dotty; thus, to take a perhaps unfair example, it seems hard to believe that if someone had promised to marry A, they would have an obligation to marry A*, only an obligation which came lower down the queue.

What, in contrast, is an entirely familiar sort of thought is, last of all, one that embodies degrees of doubt or obscurity whether a given obligation (of fixed stringency) applies or not. Thus a secret agent might think that he was obliged to kill the man in front of him if and only if that man was Martin Bormann; and be in doubt whether he should kill this man, because he was in doubt whether it was Bormann. (Contrast the two analogously dotty types of solution to this case: that, at any rate, he is obliged to wound him; or, that he is obliged to kill him, but it has a lower priority than it would have otherwise). But this type of thought is familiar at the cost of not really embodying the scalar facts; it is a style of thought appropriate to uncertainty about a matter of all-or-nothing and so embodies in effect what Parfit calls the Simple View, that which does not take seriously the scalar facts to which the Complex View addresses itself.

These considerations do not, of course show that there are no ways of mirroring the Complex View in these areas of moral thought, but they do suggest that the displacements required are fairly radical. It is significant that by far the easiest place in which to find the influence of the scalar considerations is in certain *sentiments*, which themselves have a scalar dimension: here we can see a place where the Complex View and Utilitarianism easily fit together. But the structure of such sentiments is not adequate to produce the structure of all moral thought. The rest of it will have to be more radically adapted, or abandoned, if the Complex View is really to have its effect.

One vitally important item which is in part (though only in part) scalar is a man's concern for (what commonsense would call) his own future. That a man should have some interest now in what he will do or undergo later, requires that he have some desires or projects or concerns now which relate to those doings or happenings later; or, as a special case of that, that some very general desire or project or concern of his now relate to desires or projects which he will have then. The limiting case, at the basic physical level, is that in which he is merely concerned with future pain, and it may be that that concern can properly reach through any degree of psychological discontinuity.[15] But even if so, it is not our present concern, since the mere desire to avoid physical pain is not adequate to constitute a character: we are here concerned with more distinctive and structured patterns of desire and project, and there are possible psychological changes in these which could be predicted for a person and which would put his future after such changes beyond his present interest. Such a future would be, so to speak, over the horizon of his interest, though of course if the future picture could be filled in as a *series* of changes leading from here to there, he might recapture an interest in the outcome.

In this connection, to take the language of 'future selves' at all literally would be deeply misleading: it would be to take the same facts twice over. My concern for my descendants or other relatives may be, as Parfit says, to some degree proportional to their remoteness from me; equally, my concern for other persons in general can vary with the degree to which their character is congenial to my own, their projects sympathetic to my outlook. The two considerations, of proximity and congeniality, evidently interact—ways in which they can reinforce or cancel one another are, for instance, among the commonplaces of dynastic fiction. But the proximity of Parfitian 'later selves' to their ancestry just consists of the relations of their character and interests to my present ones. I cannot first identify, or at least definitely identify, a later self 'descendant', and then consider the relations of his character to mine, since it is just the presence or lack of these relations which in good part determines his proximity and even his existence as a separate self.

Thus if I take steps now to hinder what will or may predictably be my future projects, as in Parfit's Russian nobleman case,[16] it would be a case of double vision to see this as my treating my future self as another person; for, spelled out, that would have to mean, treating my future self as another person *of whose projects I disapprove*; and therein lies the double vision. To insist here that what I would be doing is to hinder *my own* future projects (where it is understood that that is not necessarily a foolish thing to do) is to keep hold on a number of deeply important facts. One is that to contemplate, or expect, or regard as probable, such changes in my own character is different from my relation to them in someone else (still more, of course, from my attitude to the mere *arrival* of someone else with a different character): the question must arise, how prediction is, in my own case, related to acquiescence, and special and obscure issues arise about the range of methods that it could be appropriate or rational for a man to use to prevent or deflect predicted changes in his own character. Thought about those issues must take as basic the *he* for whom these changes would be changes in *his* character.

Relatedly, there is the question of why I should regard my present projects and outlook as having more authority than my future ones. I do *not* mean by that the question, why I should not distribute consideration equally over my whole life: I shall later touch on the point that it is a mistake of Kantians (and perhaps of some kinds of Utilitarians too) to think it *a priori* evident that one rationally should do that. I mean rather the question of how, in the supposed type of example, I evaluate the two successive outlooks; why should I hinder my future projects from the perspective of my present values rather than inhibit my present projects from the perspective of my future values? It is not enough in answer to that to say that evidently present action must flow from present values. If the future prospect were of something now identified as a growth in enlightenment, present action would try to hinder present projects in its interest. For that to be so, there indeed would have to be now some dissatisfaction with one's present values; but that consideration just turns the attention, in the Russian nobleman case, to the corresponding question, of why the young man is so unquestioningly satisfied with his present values. He may have, for instance, a theory of degeneration of the middle-aged; but then he should no doubt reflect that, when middle-aged, he will have a theory of the naiveté of the young.

I am not saying that there are no answers to any of these questions, or that there is no way out of this kind of diachronic relativism. The point is rather this: if indeed it is true that this man will change in these ways, it is only by understanding his present projects *as the projects of one who will so change* that he can understand them even as his present projects; and if he knows that he will so change, then it is only through such an understanding that he could justifiably give his present values enough authority to defeat his future values, as he clear-headedly conceives them to be. For if he clear-headedly knows that his present projects are solely the projects of his youth, how does he know that they are not *merely* that, unless he has some view which makes sense of, among other things, his own future?

There is a lot more to be said about such cases, but I shall not try to say any of it here. My aim is to make once more the point that one cannot even start on the important questions of how this man, so totally identified with his present values, will be related to his future without them, if one does not take as basic the fact that it is his own future that he will be living through without them.

This leads to the question of why we go on at all.

It might be wondered why, unless we believe in a possibly hostile after-life, or else are in a muddle which the Epicureans claimed to expose, we should regard death as an evil.[17] One answer to that is that we desire certain things; if one desires something, then to that extent one has reason to resist the happening of anything which prevents one getting it, and death certainly does that, for a large range of desires. Some desires are admittedly contingent on the prospect of one's being alive; but not all desires can be in that sense conditional. For it is possible to imagine a person rationally contemplating suicide, in the face of some predicted evil; and if he decides to go on in life, then he is propelled forward into it by some desire (however general or inchoate) which cannot operate conditionally on his being alive, since it settles the question of whether he is going to be alive. Such a desire we may call a categorical desire; and most people have many categorical desires, which do not depend on the assumption of their own existence, since they serve to prevent that assumption's being questioned, or to answer the question if it is raised. Thus one's pattern of interests, desires and projects not only provide the reason for an interest in what happens within the horizon of one's future, but also constitute the conditions of there being such a future at all.

Here, once more, to deal in terms of later selves who were like descendants would be to misplace the heart of the problem. Whether to commit suicide, and whether to leave descendants, are two separate decisions: one can produce children before committing suicide. A man might even choose deliberately to do that, for comprehensible sorts of reasons; or again he could be deterred, as by the thought that he would not be there to look after them. Later selves, however, evade all these thoughts by having the strange property that while they come into existence only with the death of their father, the physical death of their father can abort them entirely. The analogy seems unhelpfully strained, when we are forced to the conclusion that the failure of all a man's projects, and his consequent suicide, would take with him all his 'descendants', although they are in any case a kind of descendants who arise only with his ceasing to exist. More than unhelpfully, it runs together what are two quite different questions: whether, my projects having failed, I should cease to exist, and whether I shall have descendants whose projects may be quite different from mine and are in any case largely unknown. The analogy makes every question of the first kind involve a question of the second kind, and thus obscures the peculiar significance of the first question to the theory of the self. If, on the other hand, a man's future self is not another self, but the future of his self, then it is unproblematic why it should be eliminated with the failure of that which might propel him into it. The primacy of one's ordinary self is given, once more, by the thought that it is precisely what will not be in the world if one commits suicide.

The language of 'later selves', too literally taken, could exaggerate in one direction the degree to which a man's relation to some of his own projects resembles his relation to the projects of others. The Kantian emphasis on moral impartiality exaggerates it in quite another, by providing ultimately too slim a sense in which any projects are mine at all. This point once more involves the idea that my present projects are the condition of my existence,[18] in the sense that unless I am propelled forward by the conatus of desire, project and interest, it is unclear why I should go on at all: the world, certainly, as a kingdom of moral agents, has no particular claim on my presence or, indeed, interest in it. (That kingdom, like others, has to respect the natural right to emigration.) Now the categorical desires which propel one on do not have to be even very evident to consciousness, let alone grand or large; one good testimony to one's existence having a point is that the question of its point does not arise, and the propelling concerns may be of a relatively everyday kind such as certainly provide the ground of many sorts of happiness. Equally, while these projects may present *some* conflicts with the demands of morality, as Kantianly conceived, these conflicts may be fairly minor; after all—and I do not want to deny or forget it—these projects, in a normally socialized individual, have in good part been formed within, and formed by, dispositions which constitute a commitment to morality. But, on the other hand, the possibility of radical conflict is also there. A man may have, for a lot of his life or even just for some part of it, a *ground* project or set of projects which are closely related to his existence and which to a significant degree give a meaning to his life.

I do not mean by that they provide him with a life-plan, in Rawls's sense. On the contrary, Rawls's conception, and the conception of practical rationality, shared by Nagel, which goes with it, seems to me rather to imply an external view of one's own life, as something like a given rectangle that has to be optimally filled in.[19] This perspective omits the vital consideration already mentioned, that the continuation and size of this rectangle is up to me; so, slightly less drastically, is the question of how much of it I care to cultivate. The correct perspective on one's life is *from now*. The consequences of that for practical reasoning (particularly with regard to the relevance of proximity or remoteness in time of one's objective), is a large question which cannot be pursued here; here we need only the idea of a man's ground projects providing the motive force which propels him into the future, and gives him (in a sense) a reason for living.

For a project to play this ground role, it does not have to be true that if it were frustrated or in any of various ways he lost it, he would have to commit suicide, nor does he have to think that. Other things, or the mere hope of other things, may keep him going. But he may feel in those circumstances that he might as well have died. Of course, in general a man does not have one separable project which plays this ground role: rather, there is a nexus of projects, related to his conditions of life, and it would be the loss of all or most of them that would remove meaning.

Ground projects do not have to be selfish, in the sense that they are just concerned with things for the agent. Nor do they have to be self-centred, in the sense that the creative projects of a Romantic artist could be considered self-centred (where it has to be *him*, but not *for* him). They may certainly be altruistic, and in a very evident sense moral, projects; thus he may be working for reform, or justice, or general improvement. It is worth noting here that there is no contradiction in the idea of a man's dying for a ground project: quite the reverse, since if death really is necessary for the project, then to live would be to live with it unsatisfied, something which, if it really is his ground project, he has no reason to do.

That a man's projects were altruistic or moral would not make them immune to conflict with impartial morality, any more than the artist's projects are immune. Admittedly *some* conflicts are ruled out by the projects sincerely being *those* projects; thus a man devoted to the cause of curing injustice in a certain place, cannot just insist on his plan for doing that over others, if convinced that theirs will be as effective as his (something it may be hard to convince him of). For if he does insist on that, then we learn that his concern is not merely that injustice be removed, but that *he* remove it—not necessarily a dishonourable concern, but a different one. Thus some conflicts are ruled out by the project being not self-centred. But not all conflicts: thus his selfless concern for justice may do havoc to quite other commitments.

A man who has such a ground project will be required by Utilitarianism to give up what it requires in a given case just if that conflicts with what he is required to do as an impersonal utility-maximizer when all the causally relevant considerations are in. That is a quite absurd requirement.[20] But the Kantian, who can do rather better than that, still cannot do well enough. For impartial morality, if the conflict really does arise, must be required to win; and that cannot necessarily be a reasonable demand on the agent. There can come a point at which it is quite unreasonable for a man to give up, in the name of the impartial good ordering of the world of moral agents, something which is a condition of his having any interest in being around in that world at all. Once one thinks about what is involved in having a character, one can see that the Kantians' omission of character is both a condition of their ultimate insistence on the demands of impartial morality, and also a reason for finding inadequate their account of the individual.

III

All this argument depends on the idea of one man's having a character, in the sense of having projects and categorical desires with which he is identified; nothing has yet been said about different persons having different characters. It is perhaps important, in order to avoid misunderstanding, to make clear a way in which difference of character does *not* come into the previous argument. It does not come in by way of the man's thinking that only if he affirms these projects will they be affirmed, while (by contrast) the aims of Kantian morality can be affirmed by anyone. Though that thought could be present in some cases, it is not the point of the argument. The man is not pictured as thinking that he will have earned his place in the world, if his project is affirmed: that a distinctive contribution to the world will have been made, if his distinctive project is carried forward. The point is that he wants these things, finds his life bound up with them, and that they propel him forward; thus they give him, in a certain sense, a reason for living his life. But that is compatible with these drives, and this life, being much like others'; it gives him, distinctively, a reason for living this life, in the sense that he has no desire to give up and make room for others, but it does not require him to lead a *distinctive* life. While this is so, and the point has some importance, nevertheless the interest and substance of most of the discussion depends on its in fact being the case that people have dissimilar characters and projects; our *general* view of these matters, and the significance given to individuality in our own and others' lives, would certainly change if there were not between persons indefinitely many differences which are important to us. The level of description is of course also vital for determining what is the same or different; a similar description can be given of two people's dispositions, but the concrete detail be perceived very differently— and it is a feature of our experience of persons that we can perceive and be conscious of an indefinitely fine degree of difference in concrete detail (though it is only in certain connections and certain cultures that one spends much time rehearsing it).

One area in which *difference* of character directly plays a role in the concept of moral individuality is that of personal relations, and I shall close with some remarks in this connection. Differences of character give substance to the idea that individuals are not inter-substitutable. As I have just argued, a particular man so long as he is propelled forward does not need to assure himself that he is unlike others, in order not to feel substitutable; but in his personal relations to others the idea of difference can (even if it is not essential) certainly make a contribution, in more than one way(to the thought that his friend cannot just be equivalently replaced by another friend, is added both the thought that he cannot just be replaced himself, and also the thought that he and his friend are different from each other. This last thought is important to us as part (though of course a qualified one) of our view of friendship, a view thus set apart from Aristotle's opinion that a good man's friend was a duplication of himself. This I suspect to have been an Aristotelian, and not generally a Greek, opinion; and it is connected with another feature of his views which seems even stranger to us, at least with regard to any deeply committed friendship, namely that friendship for him has to be minimally *risky*, and one of his problems is indeed to reconcile the role of friendship with his unappetizing ideal of self-sufficiency. Once one agrees that a three-dimensional mirror would not represent the ideal of friendship, one can begin to see both how some degree of difference can play an essential role; and also, how a commitment or involvement with a particular other person might be one of the kinds of project which figured basically in a man's life in the ways already sketched —something which would be mysterious or even sinister on an Aristotelian account.

For Kantians, personal relations at least presuppose moral relations, and some are rather disposed to go further and regard them as a *species* of moral relations, as in the richly moralistic account given by Richards[21] of one of the four main principles of supererogation which would be accepted in 'the Original Position' (that is to say, adopted as a moral limitation):

> a principle of mutual love requiring that people should not show personal affection and love to others on the basis of arbitrary physical characteristics alone, but rather on the basis of traits of personality and character related to acting on moral principles.

This righteous absurdity is no doubt to be traced to a feeling that love, even love based on 'arbitrary physical characteristics', is something which has enough power and even authority to conflict badly with morality unless it can be brought within it from the beginning; and evidently that is a sound feeling, though it is an optimistic Kantian who thinks that much will be done about that by the adoption of this principle in the Original Position. The weaker view, that love and similar relations presuppose moral relations, in the sense that one could love someone only if one also had to them the moral relations one has to all people, is less absurd, but also wrong. It is of course true that loving someone involves some relations of the kind that morality requires or imports more generally, but it does not follow from that that one cannot have them in a particular case unless one has them generally in the way the moral man does; thus a man might be concerned about the interests of this person, and even about carrying out promises he made to this person, while not very concerned about these things with other persons. In general: to the extent (whatever it may be) that loving someone involves showing some of the same concerns in relation to them that the moral man shows, or at least thinks he ought to show, elsewhere, the lover's relations will be examples of moral relations, or at least resemble them; but this does not have to be because they are *applications to this case* of relations which the lover, *qua* moral man, more generally enters into. (That might not be the best description of the situation even if he *is* a moral man who enters into such relations more generally.)

However, once morality is there, and also personal relations to be taken seriously, so is the possibility of conflict. This of course does not mean that if there is some friendship with which his life is much involved, then a man must prefer any possible demand of that over other, impartial, moral demands: that would be absurd, and also a pathological kind of friendship, since both parties exist in the world and it is part of the sense of their friendship that it exists in the world.

But the possibility is there of conflict, not only, in the outcome, with substantial moral claims of others, but also with moral demands on how the outcome is arrived at: the situation may not have been subjected to an impartial process of resolution, and this fact itself may cause unease to the impartial moral consciousness. There is an example of such unease in a passage by Fried. After an illuminating discussion of the question why, if at all, we should give priority of resources to actual and present sufferers over absent or future ones, he writes:[22]

> surely it would be absurd to insist that if a man could, at no risk or cost to himself, save one or two persons in equal peril, and one of those in peril was, say, his wife, he must treat both equally, perhaps by flipping a coin. One answer is that where the potential rescuer occupies no office such as that of captain of a ship, public health official or the like, the occurrence of the accident may itself stand as a sufficient randomizing event to meet the dictates

of fairness, so he may prefer his friend, or loved one. Where the rescuer does
occupy an official position, the argument that he must overlook personal
ties is not unacceptable.

The most striking feature of this passage is the direction in
which Fried implicitly places the onus of proof: the fact that coin-
flipping would be inappropriate raises some question to which an
'answer' is required, while the resolution of the question by the
rescuer's occupying an official position is met with what sounds
like relief (though it remains unclear what that rescuer does when
he 'overlooks personal ties'—does *he* flip a coin?). The thought
here seems to be that is unfair to the second victim that, the first
being the rescuer's wife, they never even get a chance of being
rescued; and the answer (as I read the reference to the 'sufficient
randomizing event') is that at another level it is sufficiently fair—
although in this disaster this rescuer has a special reason for saving
the other person, it might have been another disaster in which
another rescuer had a special reason for saving them. But, apart
from anything else, that 'might have been' is far too slim to sustain a reintroduction of the notion of fairness. The 'random' element in such events, as in certain events of tragedy, should be seen
not so much as affording a justification, in terms of an appropriate application of a lottery, as being a reminder that some situations lie beyond justifications.

But has anything yet shown that? For even if we leave behind
thoughts of higher-order randomization, surely *this* is a justification on behalf of the rescuer, that the person he chose to rescue
was his wife? It depends on how much weight is carried by 'justification': the consideration that it was his wife is certainly, for
instance, an explanation which should silence comment. But
something more ambitious than this is usually intended, essentially
involving the idea that moral principle can legitimate his preference, yielding the conclusion that in situations of this kind it is at
least all right (morally permissible) to save one's wife. (This could
be combined with a variety of higher-order thoughts to give it a
rationale; rule-Utilitarians might favour the idea that in matters of
this kind it is best for each to look after his own, like house insur-
ance.) But this construction provides the agent with one thought
too many: it might have been hoped by some (for instance, by his
wife) that his motivating thought, fully spelled out, would be the

thought that it was his wife, not that it was his wife and that in situations of this kind it is permissible to save one's wife.

Perhaps others will have other feelings about this case. But the point is that somewhere (and if not in this case, where?) one reaches the necessity that such things as deep attachments to other persons will express themselves in the world in ways which cannot at the same time embody the impartial view, and that they also run the risk of offending against it.

They run that risk if they exist at all; yet unless such things exist, there will not be enough substance or conviction in a man's life to compel his allegiance to life itself. Life has to have substance if anything is to have sense, including adherence to the impartial system; but if it has substance, then it cannot grant supreme importance to the impartial system, and that system's hold on it will be, at the limit, insecure.

It follows that moral philosophy's habit, particularly in its Kantian forms, of treating persons in abstraction from character is not so much a legitimate device for dealing with one aspect of thought, but is rather a misrepresentation, since it leaves out what both limits and helps to define that aspect of thought. Nor can it be judged solely as a theoretical device: this is one of the areas in which one's conception of the self, and of oneself, most importantly meet.

NOTES

1. John Rawls, *A Theory of Justice* (Oxford: Oxford University Press, 1972).

2. D. A. J. Richards, *A Theory of Reasons for Action* (Oxford: Oxford University Press, 1971).

3. Thomas Nagel, *The Possibility of Altruism* (Oxford: Oxford University Press, 1970).

4. Charles Fried, *An Anatomy of Values* (Cambridge, Mass.: Harvard University Press, 1970).

5. Richards, op. cit., p. 87 a1; cf. Rawls, op. cit., p. 27; also Nagel, op. cit., p. 134. This is not the only, nor perhaps historically the soundest, interpretation of the device: cf. Derek Parfit, 'Later Selves and Moral Principles', in A. Montefiore, ed., *Philosophy and Personal Relations* (London: Routledge & Kegan Paul, 1973), pp. 149-50 and nn. 30-4.

6. For a more detailed account, see 'A Critique of Utilitarianism', in J. J. C. Smart and B. Williams, *Utilitarianism: For and Against* (Cambridge: Cambridge University Press, 1973).

7. Findlay, *Values and Intentions* (London, 1961), pp. 235-36.

8. Richards, op. cit., p. 87.

9. Rawls, op. cit., p. 190.

10. Parfit, op. cit., p. 160, his emphasis. In what follows and elsewhere in this paper I am grateful to Parfit for valuable criticisms of an earlier draft.

11. Parfit develops one such connection in the matter of distributive justice: pp. 148 ff. In general it can be said that one very natural correlate of being impressed by the separateness of several persons' lives is being impressed by the peculiar unity of one person's life.

12. Ibid., n. 14, pp. 161-62.

13. Ibid., pp. 144 ff.

14. Ibid., p. 144 fin.

15. Cf. 'The Self and the Future', in B. Williams, *Problems of the Self* (Cambridge: Cambridge University Press, 1973).

16. Parfit, op. cit., pp. 145 ff.

17. The argument is developed in more detail in *Problems of the Self*, pp. 82 ff.

18. We can note the consequence that present projects are the condition of future ones. This view stands in opposition to Nagel's: as do the formulations used above, p. 206. But while, as Nagel says, taking a rational interest in preparing for the realization of my later projects does not require that they be my present projects, it seems nevertheless true that it presupposes my having some present projects which directly or indirectly reach out to a time when those later projects will be my projects.

19. It is of course a separate question what the criteria of optimality are, but it is not surprising that a view which presupposes that no risks are taken with the useful area of the rectangle should also favour a very low risk strategy in filling it: cf. Rawls (on prudential rationality in general), op. cit., p. 422: 'we have the guiding principle that a rational individual is always to act so that he need never blame himself no matter how things finally transpire.' Cf. also the passages cited in Rawls's footnote. For more on this and the relations of ground projects to rationality, see 'Moral Luck', in *Proceedings of the Aristotelian Society* supp. vol. 50 (1976).

20. Cf. 'A Critique of Utilitarianism', sections 3-5.

21. Richards, op. cit., p. 94.

22. Fried, op. cit., p. 227.

IX

RATIONAL HOMUNCULI

RONALD DE SOUSA

> My brain I'll prove the female to my soul,
> My soul the father: and these two beget
> A generation of still breeding thoughts
> And these same thoughts people this little world
> In humours like the people of this world:
> For no thought is contented....
> —*Richard II*, V.iv

> All psychological theories seem to imply some
> sort of model man, some notion of what man
> essentially is. Thus psycho-analytic theories
> suggest that man is essentially a battlefield, he
> is a dark cellar in which a maiden aunt and a
> sex-crazed monkey are locked in mortal com-
> bat, the affair being refereed by a rather ner-
> vous bank clerk.
> —D. Bannister in Foss,
> *New Horizons in Psychology*, no. 4, p. 363

Consider propositions forming an inconsistent set. As objects of belief of a single believer, they mark him as inconsistent. When judiciously apportioned among several believers, however, they need not commit any one to inconsistency. This seems too obvious to be said. What is less clear is the bearing of this simple fact on the many theories of human persons that have posited within a single agent a "committee" of quasi-persons. Rational, Desiderative, and Spirited parts; Reason and Pasion; Ego, Id, and Superego: what canons relate the principles of rationality that govern the parts to those that apply to the whole?

To answer this, the strategy may seem simple. First, lay down criteria of rationality for unitary beings. Second, find out whether persons are in fact properly to be thought of as consisting of several such beings. And third, work out the relations between the criteria of rationality that govern unitary beings and those that govern groups of them within one person.

The complication is that these tasks cannot be performed independently. For it is precisely the existence of certain types of conflict, taken to involve irrationality, that is also sometimes interpreted as a sign of multiplicity within a single person. Our criteria of consistency presuppose the unity of the person to whom they apply, but conversely the conception of unity in question becomes a normative one: we praise coherence, integration, unity of purpose.

Nevertheless I shall try to keep these two questions apart: first, what is it that might tempt us to postulate multiplicity in the person? and, second, what bearing do the relevant considerations have on the theory of rationality? I shall argue that in relation to both sorts of question there is a temptation to understand normal persons in terms of a simplified model of rational agent. I shall speak of anything that conforms to such a model as a "homunculus," without further apology for the term. A homunculus in my sense has at least minimal rational structure: what this means, and what other features we might endow it with, will emerge as we go. When a model is too simple for the facts, it should be changed or complicated. But we might also try to assign it to parts instead of the whole of what we want to model. Thus we might view the person as consisting of several simple homunculi. The appeal of this last move lessens as our understanding of persons increases. Yet we shall see that the oversimplified model still prejudices our conception of persons and rationality.

Two more preliminaries. In spite of the fact that the most titillating cases suggesting splits in the person are to be found in abnormal psychology, my discussion is entirely focused on theories that ascribe multiplicity to the normal person. Psychology cannot afford two sets of theories, one for the normal and one for the abnormal. It follows that if my conclusions are correct, they will apply to abnormal psychology. Explicitly, these conclusions imply that schizophrenic "splits" should not be explained in terms of conflict between different agencies at any but the most metaphorical level, and more important that the ideals of psychotherapy should not be unduly influenced by simplified models of rationality. Here it might be useful for me to declare a bias: I hold that the search for principles of rationality throughout the history of philosophy has been under the distorting spell of the notion of an *ideal world;* it has generally been assumed that all goods might exist jointly in such a world and that this ought to be reflected in the coherent integrated structure of the ideally rational man's values and beliefs. As against this view I want to urge that the complexity of our determinations ought to be recognized (without hypostatization), but that value choices among these determinants ought not to be excessively subjected to the Streamlining Instinct of Philosophy.

I

Homunculi in the theory of mind and action

The unity of the person should perhaps simply be grounded on the complex of biological facts that are summarized when we say that each of us has one body: that the same blood flows in the brain and the toes, and whatever else it is about the interdependence and autonomy of parts that differentiates an organism from a mere organization. A story by Arthur Clarke describes the end of human kind by fusion of its members into a larger organism of which they become as cells.[1] This paper should have been prefaced with an analysis of the changes in the individuals and their relations that would justify such a description. But to write it I would have to be a biologist. As I am not, what follows is highly speculative and incomplete, mere epiphenomenopsychobiosophy.

When Dr. Jekyll changes into Mr. Hyde, that is a strange and mysterious thing. Are they two people taking turns in one body? But here is something stranger: Dr. Juggle and Dr. Boggle too, take turns in one body. *But they are as like as identical twins!* You balk: why then say that they have changed into one another? Well, why not: if Dr. Jekyll can change into a man as different as Hyde, surely it must be all the *easier* for Juggle to change into Boggle, who is exactly like him.

We need conflict or strong difference to shake our natural

assumption that to one body there corresponds at most one agent.

Not all distinctions and conflicts between parts of the person, however, will tempt us equally to postulate homunculi. Purely functional ones, for example, seem quite intelligible without the aid of such metaphors. This was the basis of Aristotle's criticism of Plato's divisions of the soul. Aristotle took them to be meant as functional, and rightly pointed out that Plato's scheme involves duplications of calculative functions in the "desiderative" part and conversely:[2] so as a distinction of functions it is not successful. Aristotle's own division has a serial or hierarchic structure: each term (vegetative, nutritive, locomotive, rational) is a necessary condition for the appearance of the next, so that none but the lowest is separable from all the others. This is a truly functional division, which leaves no room for the metaphor of homunculi.

Aristotle's account, unlike Plato's, was not particularly designed to explain inner conflict. And Plato was surely right to look for some explanation of that phenomenon. Nor was his division of the soul absurd, as Aristotle implied, for being partly functional and yet involving duplications of some functions. For a function is frequently carried out by an organ, which may subordinate functions common to several organs. And this may give rise to some form of conflict: the scholar's stomach and his brain, they say, are wont to fight for the blood available after the scholar's dinner. (Some purely mentalistic theories, e.g., of the "the economics of the libido," conform to the same model.) Such conflict is not of the sort that would tempt us to the metaphor of struggling homunculi. What more is required?

Perhaps there is a clue in this: The relation between such organs as the heart or eye to our *self* is characteristically *external*: they are generally not under our voluntary control, and indeed can be made to function in isolation. (Less clearly, some mental contents are sometimes felt to be "external" to our self: obsessive images, or in a different way objectively valid arguments.) Occasionally, however, one feels *identified* with a certain organ (or mental content) so that its autonomy supersedes or is equated with one's own; or else it is felt as a *personal* force, internal, but in conflict with one's self. We say: I *am* my lust. Or: My stomach compels me. My Reason wants me to believe. In such cases what is not the self is up for *endorsement* by the self: but one can endorse as part of oneself only what can be viewed as an *intentional* system.[3] Something is an intentional system, and has what I call "minimal rationality," if its behavior may be thought of as explainable in terms of wants and beliefs. I say "*may* be thought of as explainable" in such terms, because organisms can be considered in this way even though in the present state of our knowledge it is not very natural to do so. And in the present context in which the suitability of various explanatory models is in question, it is not necessary to ask whether in a more metaphysical sense anything *really is* an intentional system.[4]

Putative homunculi, with their wants and beliefs, tend to constitute themselves into the person as a whole: in the most likely cases where we might want to talk about a person divided, it is the conduct of the person as a whole that will show erratic or inconsistent signs. By contrast, conflict at the level of organs manifests itself at the *subpersonal* level: perhaps by some disturbance in the circulation of the blood. Bodily disturbances do not expose a person to the charge of irrationality, unless they are viewed as covert expressions of wants and beliefs.

I have suggested that a homunculus must have a minimal rational structure, and that inner conflict between such structures is a necessary condition for the temptation to split the person. I now want to explain why such splitting is not a profitable move even when these conditions are satisfied. My strategy is this: the extent to which it is useful to posit homunculi seems to be a matter of degree: hence a view would be as good or better that built the degrees not into the evidence for the model or its utility, but *into the model itself*.

This strategy has some essential points in common with Parfit's in "Personal Identity."[5] Parfit argues that the connections between our past and future selves admit of degrees in essential respects, and therefore they neither admit of nor require to be taken as grounding strict relations of identity. This view has an important consequence, which Parfit himself does not draw. Since there are an indefinite number of traits in respect of which we continually change, and an indefinite number in respect of which we stay the same, judgments of identity (or rather, the judgments of *continuity* that supersede them) must be grounded in selections of relevant traits among all possible ones. And the relevant traits are ones that are *important* to the identity of human beings. Our judgments of who people are, and particularly of who they are in relation to who they were, are therefore literally based on value judgments. The view for which I am arguing is—to borrow a term from linguistics—the *synchronic* analogue of Parfit's *diachronic* thesis. It rejects the view, implicit in most of contemporary Decision theory, that the values and preferences of a man at an instant either can or should be capable of being arranged into a single coherent scale determined by the totality of his dispositions to make choices at that instant. One reason for this is that the *importance* of the different factors determining a man's dispositions at an instant cannot be gauged without discovering what role these factors play *over a length of time*: another is that the factors cannot be sorted without evaluative bias. The behaviorism implicit in traditional decision theory may try to do just that: for the value it assigns to any given factor is measured simply by its power over the person in relation to competing factors. But such behaviorism is futile, if only because a man's identity and values are determined as much by his endorsement of some of his determinants as by their mere strength. On the other hand, such endorsement is not free to narrow without limit the field of relevant factors, as Bernard Williams has pointed out in criticism of the Spinozistic conception of freedom as the autonomy of a pure intellect:[6]

> To suppose that [my past, my character, and my desires] are, in the relevant sense, "outside" determinations, is merely to beg the vital questions about the boundaries of the self, and not to prove from premises acceptable to any clearheaded man that the boundaries of the self should be drawn round the intellect.

Questions about the "boundaries of the self" should not be dismissed, as they are by behavioristic theories: but nor should they be answered by reference to theories that draw bounded homunculi *within* the self.

It is now time for me to sketch the alternative model that I favor. Having done so I shall test it against the case of *akrasia*, which provides a classic example of the temptation to split the conflicting self.

Structures involving parts that have minimal rationality are complex, but not necessarily *multiple.* Tinbergen and others[7] have described a complex hierarchical organization of control of behavior which offers a suitable model. Broadly defined tasks are broken down into several levels of subtasks, and at each level the checks and commands are only specific enough to apply to the level immediately below. Controlling mechanisms at each level can be viewed as intentional systems, though not with the same ease. At the highest levels they can be ascribed overall policies shaped in part by information; whereas the lowest levels control specific and mechanical "consummatory acts" consisting in actual muscular motion in response to simple releasing signals. Somewhere along the line, conflict might arise, possibly to be adjudicated in terms of higher level goals. Yet it would be absurd to view this sort of hierarchy of control as consisting of homunculi.

In these terms, a person is a rather messy hierarchy that includes wants and beliefs, and more besides. Component wants and beliefs can be more or less central, and more or less long-lasting. This allows for projects in the hierarchy to be relatively independent of some others; the "center" of the system need not be viewed as a sort of monarch, but as determined in a complex way by the structure of the whole. What counts as central is determined in part by the extent to which a want represents a long-term project of high priority in the hierarchy of wants and projects. A long-term project is not the same as a recurring need. It must be the object of an attitude that gives it a special place and envisages its possibilities for development and change. Thus bodily desires relatively equal in their strength could be ranked for "centrality" on this criterion in an order that would correspond fairly well to the historical frequency with which the distraction they might have caused was thought sinful (the product of a bad will in conflict with the good). On this scale defecation is more peripheral than eating, and eating more than sex. "Possession" is a term that has been used of the lust for power as well as the lust of the flesh, but not of the sin of gluttony nor the virtue of patience. (We do, however, speak of "possession" in connection with the more passionate virtues: For "we can also regard our 'best desires'—whether they are strong or weak—as not fully ours.")[8]

Centrality, however, is not measured by a single standard. Complexity of involvement, long-term importance, and high priority in the immediate future might all be cited, and are not equivalent. Nor is any of them equivalent to strength, as measured by the capacity of a want for "getting its way" in the face of conflict. Any of the simple bodily needs I mentioned as more or less peripheral can become overwhelmingly strong as a result of frustration. It can also, under the same conditions, move to a more central position as its satisfaction comes to require complex and long-term planning and integration with other, formerly more central projects. It is this fluidity, this interpenetration of projects, which makes it implausible to think of them in terms of homunculi. If we are drawn to the homunculi picture, we must I think conceive of them as relatively stable intentional systems.[9] But to accommodate the variety of our strategies, priorities, attitudes, and projects, the boundaries of the homunculi would have to be constantly changing.

I have sketched a model, and adduced some general considerations in its favor. I now want to show how an examination of akrasia leads us to such a model and away from the one I reject. The case is worth going into in some detail. For akrasia has often been taken to provide the strongest motivation for splitting the person into rival agencies, each of which presents us with an intentional structure, possibly adjudicated by a third on some basis other than mere "effective strength."

II

Akrasia: A Case Study

At least three models of akrasia have had currency. I present them in an order intended to let each be encompassed by the next, and I endeavor at each stage to formulate descriptions in terms of homunculi.

1. The most general description is that the akratic does what in the light of his better judgment he *wants less*. This constitutes a paradox for any view which sees *actions*, properly so-called, as determined by wants and beliefs. The defeated want must somehow have been *endorsed* by the person, or the Will, or the Self: yet it has failed of its determining power. This suggests that it must have been defeated in conflict with another *want*. Thus we are invited to construe the case as involving a committee of conflicting

homunculi some of which are more clearly identified with the Self than others. Perhaps two homunculi propose conflicting projects: a third endorses one, yet the second is performed. The problem here is to decide, in terms of the homunculus model, *by whom* the action is performed. Is it by the Endorsing Self? But then he exhibits the problematic split within himself. Or is by the proponent of the inferior desire? In that case akrasia sounds more like a case of compulsion, until the relation between the different homunculi are described more explicitly. We have so far no explanation of the difference between the more privileged and the more successful homunculus.

2. The second way of talking specifies the last point. It views akrasia as essentially involving *second-order* wants. To express it in a way which expands on the first view: it holds that what "endorsement" *consists* in is the existence of a suitable second-order want. Adapting a phrase of Frankfurt's,[10] mere first-order want structures constitute "wanton" homunculi. Unfortunately we now have homunculi with second-order wants that refer, apparently, to the wants of *other* homunculi. If a homunculus has a second-order want, he is by definition no longer "wanton"; but a want is not second-order in the right sense if it refers to some other being's wants. For a person is not subject to criticism on the ground of inconsistency between first-order and second-order beliefs if the first-order beliefs are someone else's!

Still, this may be one of the points on which the homunculus metaphor demands that we introduce criteria of consistency for persons that are formulated in terms of the beliefs or wants of component homunculi but not applicable to the homunculi themselves: the relevant difference being that homunculi are simple while persons are complex. But there is another trouble. The present mode of description rests on the existence of second-order wants. But such wants are essentially unstable: arguments involving them can be carried to the next level up, and then the next, indefinitely high, without major reorganization of the lower levels. It therefore looks as if the essential element of this type of description—the existence of higher level wants—has a sort of wispy and ephemeral quality that is unfavorable to the generation of homunculi. For we have already noted a demand for some degree of stability in our homunculi. Shifting levels, quickly formed and dissolved, are incompatible with this demand. The length of one practical argument falls below any plausible lower limit on the endurance of a homunculus. Moreover insofar as these structures rehearse the wants and beliefs involved at lower levels, the elements of which they are constituted are *common* to what, on a strict application of the criterion of conflict, amount to a great many different homunculi. So one would be only partially distinct from another.

3. On the third view the structures that compete are practical arguments. Davidson has pointed out the curious fact about practical arguments that two of them can have incompatible conclusions while being both valid and sound.[11] As we shall see later, Davidson is too swift in assuming that there is always something logically odd about a pair of contrary "ought-" statements both being true at once. But let us take that for granted for the moment. The solution to this problem is then to regard the conclusions of practical arguments as requiring a rule of detachment. This rule of detachment now plays the role assigned in the previous descriptions to endorsement and second order wants.

Davidson called attention to a parallel between arguments of the following types:

(A) The probability of p on e is very high
  e,
  So (probably) p.

and

(B) I want p,
  q is under the circumstances the best means to p,
  So, I want q.

He has pointed out that in either argument the conclusion should strictly speaking be relativized to the premises, since an incompatible conclusion might be obtainable from another set of equally acceptable premises. We need a special rule, in each case, laying down the conditions under which its conclusion may be detached. The familiar rule for statistical arguments is the rule of "Total Evidence": Infer categorically to the conclusion supported by the *most inclusive available evidence*. Davidson proposes an analogous "Principle of Continence" for practical arguments: "perform the action judged best on the basis of all available relevant reasons" (p. 112).

Before going any further in exploring this proposal, it might be questioned whether it is compatible with the previous descriptions of akrasia. Surely, of a number of arguments available to an agent, the one he *endorses* need not be the most comprehensive one? To endorse any other is perhaps perverse: but then some cases of "*enkrateia*" or strength of will may be as perverse as some cases of akrasia. This possibility, allowed by the earlier account, is excluded by the present one.

Actually I think this objection is mistaken. But to show why may reveal something artificial about the notion of a "most comprehensive argument." If a man is aware of a more comprehensive argument but chooses to endorse a less comprehensive, he thereby shows that in his estimation the additional considerations adduced by the more comprehensive argument are worthless. At best, the two arguments are then for him equally balanced, though one can imagine someone anxious *not* to act upon worthless motives choosing the "less comprehensive" argument for just that reason. There is no general way of assessing the bearing of different considerations. Endorsement itself therefore *constitutes* the endorsed argument as the more comprehensive. And in this way, because of a kind of triviality about the notion of an argument's being more comprehensive, the two notions come to the same thing.

A similar objection might be raised relative to second-order wants: what have they to do with comprehensiveness? The reply is akin to the last. First note that the Principle of Continence is not just another premise. If it is expressed as a premise, it is ineliminably second-order: for it says: "the following considerations and the present consideration are all the relevant ones." And this rule, or second-order premise, determines a second-order *want*. This can be seen in the light of the previous argument: to declare certain considerations relevant and sufficient is in effect to *want* them *to be the decisive ones*.

The account derived from Davidson, then, is not out of line with what seemed plausible in the previous ones. It requires some refinement, however, because the concept of *detachment* is a highly ambiguous one.

The most general ambiguity is this. To every rule of rationality there corresponds some sort of causal principle, which explains why the rule is followed when it is. (There is not necessarily any single explanation of the cases where the rule isn't followed, for many factors can interfere with the "normal" or rational course of events.)[12] This is no less true in the case of statistical arguments than in that of practical ones, but in the former case we are not normally interested in actual behavior. In the latter, on the contrary, it is the discrepancy between the rule of rationality and the causal order that interests us. For that is what an account of akrasia must find a model to explain.

At each of the levels of "detachment" now to be distinguished, this duality of normative and causal principles must be borne in mind.

A (i) In the statistical case, we may first seek a rule for detaching unqualified probability from relative probability. The requirement of Total Evidence is adequate to this: unqualified probability most plausibly measures the most reasonable betting odds for a man to act on a given proposition, and that is given by the probability on the most complete available information: He can do no better short of changing his evidential base.

A refinement of this level would distinguish a stage at which probability on hypothetical evidence is computed (for example, in relation to sample distributions), from a stage at which the evidence is asserted to *exist*. At the first stage, we have "conditional" probability which is contingent on possible evidence; at the second, "relative" probability contingent on actual evidence.[13]

B (i) Corresponding to the detachment of a degree of belief from an objective statistical probability, one might look for a rule to assign to a want a definite strength or rank. A parallel with A (i) might be sought in the distinction between two ways for wants to be conditional: on *contingencies*, (as when I want to be killed swiftly, *if I am to be killed*;) or on *reasons*[14] (I want dry food in that dry food is good for man). At the first stage, the want is relativized to considerations that might possibly bear on the actual case, while at the second stage it is relativized to considerations that have an actual bearing. But beyond this point the cases are disanalogous: for *reasons* are relevant to contingent wants as well as those that are based in fact: it is just that their practical bearing may be different under different circumstances. We do not have here a simple advance from hypothetical to actual grounds.

A (ii) A further detachment rule is required to pass from unqualified probability to *belief*, also unqualified. Not all our propositional attitudes of a cognitive category are subjective probabilities, though some have urged that they should be.[15] Nor is it merely a matter of fact that we sometimes detach a belief from its subjective probability assignment: it is *more rational* to do so in some cases than others. In a lottery, for example, Harman and others have argued that a probability however high is never good enough to justify belief; in other cases we may be content with a relatively low probability, provided the proposition in question also *explains* the evidence that supports it.[16] The principles involved here appear much more complicated than Total Evidence, and of a different sort altogether.

B (ii) In the practical case, on the other hand, the principle that governs the move most closely analogous to the last is the analogue of Total Evidence, the "Principle of Continence." This principle cleaves the want not from its grounds, but from *comparisons*. It is presumably rational sometimes to arrive at wants unqualified by comparatives just as it is sometimes rational to arrive at unqualified beliefs. And in the case of wants the principle would seem to be that the unqualified want must take account of all available considerations. Want what is *best*.

B (iii) We have still not arrived at the point of *action*, which was on Davidson's scheme supposed to be the analogue of belief. A gap remains between the unqualified want and the action, and for this we need a third principle. The principles of rational *reasoning* have done all their work before the actual moment of action. But the best argument, though duly detached by B (ii), may still fail to get plugged into the motor system. This stage of "detachment" has no analogue in the case of beliefs, simply because *action* involves one more step than is needed in the chain of "detachments" and arguments that lead to belief. Note that one might also consider *action* not as an addition to the line of filiation from relative to absolute wants, but as a point where that line joins up with the filiation from probability to belief. The continent man acts on his wants *and beliefs*. *What* he is to do has already been determined at other levels of reasoning both about wants and beliefs: so while the causal factors involved are complex and obscure, the *principle of* rationality is very simple: "Do what you *will*!" Agents sometimes do, and sometimes don't: they are sometimes irrational in being akratic.[17] My reservation about this alternative way of describing things stems from the fact that belief is not *necessary* for rational action: as we have seen (note 15), some have denied that detachment of belief from subjective probability is ever rational, particularly for the purposes of action.

In any case, all variants of this view involve a hierarchy of control. At each level, certain information, or a certain instruction, is the outcome of the processing at the higher level. It is then plugged in, together with the relevant principle for detachment at the next level. In regular cases of rational action, the want detached at the second stage in accordance with the rational rule is plugged into the next: whereas in cases of akrasia it is another want that is plugged in.

Now from this very sketchy model there emerges, I think, no temptation to interpret akrasia as the outcome of a split between homunculi. The reasons are these:

First, as we saw in connection with the more general accounts, the structures of wants-and-beliefs that compete for emergence into action are short-lived and tied to a particular occasion. Akrasia differs in this from cases of long-term and systematic clashes between whole sets of projects in a single person; though repeated instances of akrasia of a fairly constant sort might lead us to view the want-and-belief structures involved as more constant.

Second, even where we are dealing with more constant structures, the projects that enter into conflict may have any number of elements in common: the factual minor premises in two conflicting practical arguments are usually the same, and moreover insofar as one argument rationally dominates another it is, according to Davidson's principle, because it *contains* it and more. The conflicts therefore are not between separate structures, but merely between the conclusions of arguments which have many of the same elements in common. Of course, two persons may have the same beliefs and wants too, and not therefore be any less two people: but in the case of two people we start with the assumption that they are separate and therefore conclude that two similar beliefs in two different intentional projects are numerically distinct. In trying to distinguish homunculi, on the contrary, what is precisely at issue is whether we should take the metaphor of multiplicity seriously. And we are not pressed to do so by finding structures that appear to constitute themselves ephemerally out of elements common to several.

A third related point is this. On the model I have adopted from Davidson, we have a multilevel hierarchy of control in which things can go wrong either within some level or in the transition from one level to another. Intuitively what we wished to think of as a homunculus was a complete project-structure, ready for action. But it is arbitrary to select our candidates for the status of homunculus just at the level of action: for both higher and lower levels have "minimal rationality." The higher levels, that is, are not unstructured for leaving their output "undetached" in some senses: as we have seen, the last level which precedes action itself requires one extra step to *take* action. Aristotle's formula: "The conclusion of a practical syllogism is an action"[18] remains, at some level, correct, provided we modify it slightly to read: "the detachment of the last of a chain of conclusions is an action." And the agency that finally takes action is the person as a whole, not just some part of him. Otherwise, indeed, there would be no problem of akrasia, but only a peculiar problem of social choice and the enforcement of social policy.

III

Rationality

Akrasia is a form of irrationality. It signals a disunity in the self. I have argued that disunity is not multiplicity: but neither should an adequate conception of rationality impose a model of a unitary being with a single integrated set of projects. That a person is not a group of homunculi does not mean that he *ought* to be a *single one.* Hence the somewhat arbitrary air of some of the "Principles of Rationality" that are found in the literature. This last section will consist of some rather partial remarks on this theme.

My argument will follow this somewhat tortuous path. First, I shall summarize well-known considerations that tend to justify certain requirements on consistent belief. This will rule out the option of treating as rational one who believes incompatible propositions by pretending that he can be viewed as a plurality. Second, I shall try on a parallel for consistency of wants, and find that there the case is different: what initially appear to be inconsistencies, on the criteria first applied to belief, are found not to be so when the criteria are suitably refined. So a contrast will be set up between wants and beliefs in this regard. In a final volte-face, I shall cast some fresh doubts on the contrast thus delineated.

From the point of view of an agent, the demand for truth in belief is easily understood. The planning of an action requires an adequate representation of its setting; a policy appropriate to one set of circumstances can be ineffective in others, and the outcome of an action based on false belief can only be *accidentally* successful. But the conditions on rational belief go further than can be deduced from these considerations alone. For it might be held that adequacy is a relative matter: the accuracy, the aspect chosen, and the mode of a representation may vary from case to case. And at least one of these features (accuracy) is such that if one limited one's search for truth in accordance with the needs of particular contexts, we might get contrary beliefs proving "adequate" for different projects. The pains we take to avoid such a situation, for example by specifying the degree of accuracy involved in measurements, spring from an assumption of realism about the objects of belief: the world is as it is, and there are no contradictions in nature. Attempts have been made to chalk this up to conventions of language, but these have proved a failure.[19] That there can be no contradictory truths is a principle to which rational agents are subject, even though it cannot simply be inferred from the conception of "minimal rationality." It follows from this principle that the search for truth has a generality which goes beyond anything that could be deduced from the conditions of rational agency— whether agents are viewed as simple homunculi or complex persons. Nevertheless, conflicts might arise between different principles of rational belief, and so presumably a believer might find himself embodying such a conflict. Under what conditions does such a situation establish that a believer is being irrational?

The rationality of belief can come up for consideration at various levels. I consider only principles of consistency. On the broadly realist view I have mentioned, consistency is the most abstract necessary condition on the success of any belief set: insofar as belief aims at congruence with what is true, inconsistency shows the set as a whole to be unsuccessful since it guarantees that some member of it must be false. Considered from this abstract point of view, inconsistency is always irrational. Yet as James pointed out[20] the goal of belief has two sides, the pursuit of true belief and the avoidance of false belief: these are parts of the main goal, and from the point of view of one engaged in criticizing his beliefs the two parts of the goal may at some time dictate different strategies. And different strategies may involve belief in inconsistent propositions.

One characteristic example of this sort of situation is presented by the "Preface Paradox": If a man writes a book of which he is convinced he *knows* each sentence, he may nevertheless also *know* on general grounds that he has certainly made some mistake somewhere. Yet this means that he cannot rationally conjoin his beliefs.

The answer might seem to lie in giving up the requirement that beliefs be conjunctible.[21] One then effectively places oneself in the position of pretending to be several people. For as I observed at the outset, a set of inconsistent propositions can be believed without any one being inconsistent providing there is more than one person to do the believing. But as we saw the splitting of a person into homunculi has nothing to recommend it. The *candidates* for the status of homunculi are structured *projects*: and although it is true that in some given project the use of a false proposition may do no harm, still this remains a mere *use* of the proposition: it does not constitute belief. Beliefs are ascribed to persons, not to projects. And so far as the *person* is concerned, the rejection of conjunction amounts to an avowal of failure to entertain only true beliefs. Such is the consequence of the unity of the epistemic goal.

I now want to bring out a contrast between the case of beliefs and the case of wants, by looking at a decision problem parallel in crucial respects to the conjunction problem for belief.

First, let me recast the belief problem slightly. In place of the preface paradox consider this simple model situation (a version of the well known "Lottery Paradox"). Three candidates are up for election in the absence of any information about their relative popularity. If my *threshold of belief* (the lowest probability sufficient for belief) is 2/3, I may believe of each one that he will lose, yet disbelieve the conjunction of those beliefs.

Now consider the following analogous problem. Suppose that I must choose between three policies, A, B, and C, and that three different principles of choice or criteria of evaluation assign the following rankings, respectively: A > B > C; B > C > A; C > A > B. If we suppose that we must choose some policy by majority rule (a principle that plays a role analogous to conjunctibility in the previous puzzle), then we have a paradox, for this yields no transitive and coherent preference ranking.[22]

Now here are the parallels and contrasts I wish to bring out:

In both puzzles, the distribution of beliefs and policies over a number of homunculi would avoid the problem for any single homunculus, *but not for the person*—nor, for that matter, for any genuine society of actual persons committed to a single belief or policy.

However, we saw that in the epistemic puzzle the putative unity of the epistemic goal meant that some member of the group (or some belief of the person) was bound to be *wrong* under these circumstances. In the case of wants, on the other hand, the "bind" may be merely practical: it may be due not to irrationality of a person or group, but *to the very nature of the evaluative facts involved*. To support this claim, I have elsewhere defined two concepts applicable to propositional attitudes:[23] their *success*, and their *satisfaction*. To summarize briefly here: I say that a propositional attitude is *satisfied*, *iff* the proposition that constitutes its object is *true*. But I shall say that it is *successful*, *iff* its object has the property specified as the *formal object* of the attitude. The formal object of belief is truth, and so a belief is satisfied *iff* it is successful. The formal object of a want, on the other hand, is goodness (or desirability): thus a want can be *successful* without being *satisfied*.

In terms of these, we can now define further terms applicable to sets of propositional attitudes. I shall say that a set of propositional attitudes is *inconsistent*, *iff* its form guarantees that not all its members are *successful*. But I shall say that it is *incompatible*, *iff* not all its members can be *satisfied* at once. Again, this yields the usual class of inconsistent beliefs, which is the same as the class of incompatible ones. But the classes of inconsistent and incompatible *wants* are *not* identical.[24]

It has often been assumed that the harboring of incompatible wants by a single person was a token of irrationality; and the assumption to support this was that it involved inconsistency. We can now see that even if inconsistency is always irrational, desires differ crucially from beliefs in that *incompatibility* among beliefs is a sufficient condition for inconsistency, but not so among wants. Once again, the assumption that rationality demands the compatibility of desires is perhaps suitable for homunculi: for one could argue that for a given *project* or want-and-belief structure anything that interferes with it or lessens its chances of successful achievement cannot be rationally integrated into the project. To incorporate it would be *self-defeating*, and self-defeat is irrational. But want-and-belief structures or projects cannot be viewed as homunculi: consequently what defeats a project does not defeat a *self*. It cannot therefore be irrational on that account.

My argument has proceeded on the assumption that with respect to the unity of their *goals*, epistemic strategies and other sorts of strategies are radically different. I want to end by casting some doubt on this assumption from both sides.

First, let us suppose that at a very abstract level the principles of epistemic rationality are well ordered. This means that the lowest level principle (consistency) might be satisfied when the higher levels were not, and so on in an orderly way up through a ladder of principles. Then sacrifices of one principle for the sake of another can only arise when we approach the task of discovery and systematization from a position of inconsistency and ignorance; conflict, which would be only apparent, would be settled by appeal to the relevant higher level principle up to the supreme principle: promote the greatest congruence between the truth and our beliefs.

But of course this is misleading in two ways. First, we are *always* in a position of inconsistency and ignorance. Consequently it is always a truth worth remembering (and not to be suppressed out of a fear of acknowledged inconsistency) that we are inconsistent and have false beliefs. Besides, the unity of the supreme principle does not by itself guarantee that all subsidiary principles may be well ordered. For it may not be possible to gauge just exactly what the contribution of a given subsidiary principle may be to the attainment (impossible as it is) of the single end.

But most important, it may simply be a fiction that the end of epistemic endeavor can be represented as unitary. Even the apparent unity in the "match between beliefs and truths" really has two parts, when considered as a goal. And James was right in suggesting that the different parts (the pursuit of true belief, the avoidance of false) might be differently *weighted*. In any case a simple match between truths and beliefs is not the only end of science. Systematic order and explanatory power are independent of simple truth as aims of science, and the strictures of the lottery paradox suggest that they must sometimes be weighted *against* the mere likelihood of truth in the search for knowledge. So there may be *incompatible aims* in the pursuit of knowledge as in other pursuits.

Finally, to blur the contrast from the other side: consider more concretely what is lost by insisting that rational wants must be compatible. In Freudian terms, we may contrast the *"outer"* reality of circumstances in the external world, with the *"inner"* reality of our drives, wants, or fantasies. The process of psychotherapy is sometimes viewed as a sort of stoic enterprise: like Montaigne's "changer plutôt soi que la fortune," it makes a virtue of the compatibility of our desires with each other and the world. But if the talk of an "inner reality" is taken seriously, that is, if we admit the possibility that goodness or worth are objective qualities, not simply reflections of subjective wants, then this stoic aim of therapy prejudices a genuine dilemma: whether and to what extent a rational man ought to sacrifice the *success* of his wants to their *satisfaction*: his inner reality to outer circumstance. If what he desires is unattainable but worthy of being wanted, then to bear with the dissatisfaction is to insist on the importance of the desire's *success*. By the very standards of realism that we *prima facie* assumed must unequivocally govern epistemic consistency, he *has* in one sense got an adequate or congruent picture of reality: namely of what is good. Conversely, to renounce success in one's wants for the sake of satisfaction is to be in that sense less realistic: though "realism" is to be sure the name that such a policy frequently usurps. Few are willing to advocate the nightmare utopias of *Brave New World*, where this sort of "realism" is implemented by securing the mechanical satisfiability of controlled and simplified desires. Yet many appear to think that in the abstract the concept of rationality is committed to it. To think so is to confuse persons with homunculi.

NOTES

1. Arthur Clarke, *Childhood's End* (New York: Ballantine Books, 1963).

2. Aristotle, *De Anima* III 9.

3. In the sense of D. C. Dennett, "Intentional Systems," in *Journal of Philosophy* 68 (1971), 87 ff. I do not argue for this claim here, but am resting some of my remarks on its plausibility. It might be objected that sometimes people identify themselves with machines—in certain psychotic states, they think that they are machines. But it is essential to these identifications that they are psychotic, that they can also be described as cases of loss of self rather than of the endorsement of a particular kind of self.

4. In the sort of way claimed for humans in Charles Taylor's *The Explanation of Behaviour* (London, 1964). Taylor's thesis is that teleological explanations in terms of intentions are indispensable and irreducible. I happily do not need to decide that issue: "a particular thing is an Intentional System only in relation to the strategies of someone who is trying to explain and predict its behavior" (Dennett, op. cit., p. 87).

5. Derek Parfit, "Personal Identity," *Philosophical Review*, 80 (1971), 3 ff.

6. Bernard Williams, *Problems of the Self* (Cambridge, 1973), p. 97.

7. V. N. Tinbergen, *The Study of Instinct* (Oxford, 1951), pp. 102 ff.; A. Kortland, "Aspects and prospects of the concept of instinct (vicissitudes of the hierarchy theory)" in *Archives Néerlandaises de Zoologie* (1956). Cf. also G. A. Miller, E. Galanter, and K. H. Pribram, *Plans and the Structure of Behavior* (New York, 1960).

8. Amélie Oksenberg Rorty, "Persons, Policies, and Bodies," *International Philosophical Quarterly* XIII, 1 (March 1973), 66.

9. This is in part because homunculi are human-*like*, and we cannot think of something human-like that does not have some continuity through time. There may also be a certain underlying materialist bias: we would be more inclined to believe in homunculi if it could be demonstrated that they correspond to some stable physical structures of the brain. Many philosophers have found exciting and suggestive the brainsplitting experiments reported by R. W. Sperry (in *Brain and Conscious Experience*, ed. J. C. Eccles [New York, 1966]), as well as the facts about the apparent evolutionary ages of parts of the brain (P. MacLean, quoted by A. Koestler in *The Ghost in the Machine* [London, 1967], ch. XVI). But just *what* exactly these experiments suggests is not yet very clear.

10. H. Frankfurt, "Freedom of the Will and the Concept of a Person," *Journal of Philosophy* 68 (1971), 11.

11. D. Davidson, "How is Weakness of the Will Possible?," in *Moral Concepts*, ed. J. Feinberg (London, 1969). The following pages draw heavily on Davidson's account. Further page references in the text are to his article.

12. Thus in the case of akrasia as of any other kind of irrationality, the factors that actually explain why it happened must be of a *subrational* kind: Physiological-cybernetic factors must ultimately *explain* the *occurrence* of akrasia. This point has been obscured, and therefore denied, because of the fact that physiological factors contribute nothing to our understanding of the *description* of akrasia.

13. Note that it might also be conditional on evidence which existed, but the status of which *as evidence* was in doubt. An example of Ian Hacking's: I pick up

a newspaper scrap on which there is a weather forecast: if it is today's, it confers very high probability on the statement that it will rain tomorrow; but the date is obliterated and it might be last week's, or last year's.

14. Here I am indebted to Bas van Fraassen.

15. E.g. R. C. Jeffrey, "Dracula meets Wolfman," in *Induction, Acceptance, and Rational Belief*, ed. M. Swain (Dordrecht, 1970). Cf. also "How to Give a Piece of Your Mind," *Review of Metaphysics* 25 (1971), esp. 55.

16. Cf. various papers by G. Harman, especially "Detachment, Probability, and Maximum Likelihood," *Noûs* 1 (1967).

17. It may be argued that this, and this alone, is the locus of akrasia: irrationality not of thought but of *action*. I think this was the burden of a reply to Davidson's paper delivered some years ago by D. G. Brown. It seems to me less important to settle this issue than to see the hierarchy involved in the multiple levels of detachment that lie on the route from thought to action.

18. Aristotle, *De Motu Animalium*, 701a 13 ff.

19. Cf. W. V. O. Quine, "Truth by Convention," in *The Ways of Paradox and Other Essays* (New York, 1966).

20. W. James, "The Will to Believe," in W. Kaufmann, ed., *Religion from Tolstoy to Camus* (New York, 1961). James's two goals are not the only ones possible. In I. Levi's *Gambling with Truth* (New York, 1967), the goals are the avoidance of falsehood and "relief from agnosticism."

21. An expedient suggested by a number of writers, including Fred Schick in "Consistency," *Philosophical Review* 75 (1966), Levi, in *Gambling with Truth*, and H. Darmstadter in "Consistency of Belief, *Journal of Philosophy* 68 (1971).

22. This is a very simple version of the famous "Voting Paradox" generalized by Arrow's General Impossibility Theorem. V. K. Arrow, *Social Choice and Individual Values* (New York, 1963).

23. "The Good and the True," *Mind*, 83 (1974).

24. According to a recent Additional Note on two earlier papers, Bernard Williams now seems to hold a similar view. See *Problems of the Self*, pp. 205-206. Cf. also the excellent discussion of the theory that Persons are Rational Agents ("PRAT"), in Amélie Oksenberg Rorty, "Persons, Policies, and Bodies."

X

IDENTIFICATION AND EXTERNALITY

Harry Frankfurt

I

One of the central and most difficult problems in the theory of action is often formulated in some such way as the following. What account is to be given of the difference between the sort of thing that goes on when a person raises his arm (say, to give a signal) and the sort of thing that happens when a person's arm rises (say, because of a muscular spasm) without his raising it? The question invokes a contrast between events that are actions, in which the higher faculties of human beings come into play, and those movements of a person's body—instances of behavior other than actions, or mere bodily happenings—that he does not himself make. This contrast can evidently be generalized. It is a special case of the contrast between activity and passivity, which is considerably wider in scope.

Actions are instances of activity, though not the only ones even in human life. To drum one's fingers on the table, altogether idly and inattentively, is surely not a case of passivity: the movements in question do not occur without one's making them. Neither is it an instance of action, however, but only of being active. The occurrence in human life of events that are neither actions nor mere happenings is sometimes overlooked, but it should not be surprising.[1] The contrast between activity and passivity is readily discernible at levels of existence where we are disinclined to suppose that there are actions. Thus, a spider is passive with respect to the movements of its legs when its legs move because the spider has received an electric shock. On the other hand the spider is active with respect to the movements of its legs—though it performs no action—when it moves its legs in making its way along the ground.

We should not find it unnatural that we are capable, without lapsing into mere passivity, of behaving as mindlessly as the spider.

It is far from easy to explicate the difference between being active and being passive, and in fact philosophers have for some time generally neglected the task. Aristotle took a step by dividing the events in a thing's history into those whose moving principle is inside the thing and those whose moving principle is outside. This is suggestive: a thing is active with respect to events whose moving principle is inside of it, and passive with respect to events whose moving principle is outside of it. But the internal-external distinction, which appears to underlie that between activity and passivity, is unfortunately no less difficult to understand. Clearly, the terms "inside" and "outside" cannot be taken in their straightforwardly spatial meanings. If a man is carried somewhere by the wind, what moves him is outside his body. If his body or some part of his body is moved by a spasm that occurs in his own muscles, he is equally passive with respect to the event although its moving principle is inside his body. To what, then, is the moving principle in this case pertinently "external"?

I shall not attempt to explore the basis of the distinction between activity and passivity. Instead, I shall consider a further extension of the scope of the distinction with which I began. The contrast between those movements of a person's body that are mere happenings in his history, and those that are his own activities, leads not only away from human life into the lower realms of creation. It also leads, in virtue of its analogues in the psychological domain, into the center of our experience of ourselves.

In our intellectual processes, we may be either active or passive. Turning one's mind in a certain direction, or deliberating systematically about a problem, are activities in which a person himself engages. But to some of the thoughts that occur in our minds, as to some of the events in our bodies, we are mere passive bystanders. Thus there are obsessional thoughts, whose provenances may be obscure and of which we cannot rid ourselves; thoughts that strike us unexpectedly out of the blue; and thoughts that run willy-nilly through our heads.

The thoughts that beset us in these ways do not occur by our own active doing. It is tempting, indeed, to suggest that they are not thoughts that *we think* at all, but rather thoughts that we *find* occurring within us. This would express our sense that, although these thoughts are events in the histories of our own minds, we do not participate actively in their occurrence. The verb "to think" can connote an activity—as in "I am thinking carefully about what you said"—and with regard to this aspect of its meaning we cannot suppose that thoughts are necessarily accompanied by thinking. It is not incoherent, despite the air of paradox, to say that a thought that occurs in my mind may or may not be something that *I think*. This can be understood in much the same way as the less jarring statement that an event occurring in my body may or may not be something that *I do*.

It is the passions, however, that I want particularly to consider. The fact that the very word "passion" conveys passivity presents something of a linguistic obstacle to the comfortable application to the passions of the distinctions with which I have been dealing. It may well be, moreover, that this obstacle is more substantial than a mere etymology. Nonetheless I believe that there is a useful distinction to be made, however awkward its expression, between passions with respect to which we are active and those with respect to which we are passive. Among our passions, as among the movements of our bodies, there are some whose moving principles are within ourselves and others whose moving principles are external to us.

This is apparently denied by Terence Penelhum. According to him, any person who attempts to represent his desires as external to himself is engaged in a "form of moral trickery" involving "gross literal falsehood."[2] He condemns every representation of this kind as evasive and inauthentic, because "it denies that some desire... is part of one's ongoing history when it is" (671). Penelhum acknowledges that when a person has a desire that he would prefer not to have, or when he is moved to act by a desire that he does not want to move him to act, the person may feel that his desire is somehow alien to him. In such cases, admittedly, the person may say that he does not identify himself with the desire. But Penelhum maintains that the desire with which a person does not identify himself is "just as much part of him as that with which he does" (672). His argument for this claim is a simple one: every desire must, after all, belong to *someone*, and a desire with which a person does not identify himself clearly does not belong to anyone else (674).

This way with the matter strikes me as being too hasty. It is not so unequivocally obvious, it seems to me, that a human desire must be the desire of some person. At least, I think we may say that there is an interesting sense, distinct from the sense in which this *is* quite obvious, in which it is not obvious at all. Suppose that one person in a lurching and crowded vehicle is impelled against another, and that the second person asks merely out of curiosity who it was that pushed him; then it would be sensible enough for the first person to say that it was he who did it, and to let the matter go at that, even though the push involved no activity on his part. A human bodily movement, even when it is a mere happening in the history of the person whose body moves, can for certain purposes be identified appropriately as a movement of that person and of no one else. However, we find it useful to reserve a sense in which a movement of this kind is strictly attributable not to the person at all but only to his body. We acknowledge that in this strict sense there is *no person* to whom it can be attributed—no person of whom it is "just as much part of him" as his actions and his activities are. Now why may a desire not, in a similar way, be an event in the history of a person's mind without being that person's desire? Why may not certain mental movements, like certain movements of human bodies, in this sense belong to no one?

We think it correct to attribute to a person, in the strict sense, only some of the events in the history of his body. The others—those with respect to which he is passive—have their moving principles outside him, and we do not identify him with these events. Certain events in the history of a person's mind, likewise, have their moving principles outside of him. He is passive with respect to them, and they are likewise not to be attributed to him. A person is no more to be identified with everything that goes on in his mind, in other words, than he is to be identified with everything that goes on in his body. Of course, every movement of a person's body is an event in his history; in this sense it is his movement, and no one else's. In this same sense, all the events in the history of a person's mind are his too. If this is all that is meant, then it is undeniably true that a passion can no more occur without belonging to someone than a movement of a living human body can occur without being someone's movement. But this is only a gross literal truth, which masks distinctions that are as valuable in the one case as they are in the other.

Penelhum's strictures are too severe. They ignore the fact that there are, in the relation of a person to his passions, problems analogous to the more familiar problems concerning the relation of a person to the movements of his body. To insist unequivocally that every passion must be attributable to someone is thus as gratuitous as it would be to insist that a spasmodic movement of a person's body must be a movement the person makes, unless there is some other person of whom it can be said that *he* makes the movement. There is in fact a legitimate and interesting sense in which a person may experience a passion that is external to him, and that is strictly attributable neither to him nor to anyone else.

Recognizing this need not prevent us from agreeing with Penelhum that such a passion is part of the person's ongoing history. It may be noted, moreover, that declining to attribute to a person certain of the passions he experiences does not commit us to regarding those passions as altogether irrelevant in reaching a fair judgment concerning what we can expect from him. A passion is no less genuine, and its thrust is no less forceful, for being external to the person in whose history it occurs, any more than a bodily movement is less palpable in its occurrence or in its effects for being a movement that is not made by the person in whose body it occurs.

No doubt we would be providing people with opportunities for moral evasion, as Penelhum suggests, if we were to allow that it may be legitimate for someone to disclaim certain of his passions as external. For a person may of course be acting in bad faith when he denies that a passion he finds in himself is unequivocally to be attributed to him. But we routinely make room for similar evasiveness and inauthenticity already, without thinking that it is a mistake for us to do so, in our acceptance of the practice of disclaiming certain bodily movements as external. A person may dishonestly and successfully seek to escape an unfavorable judgment to which he would otherwise be subject, after all, by denying that a certain movement of his body was one that he made, and by professing that the moving principle of the physical event in question was actually quite external to him. Moreover it may be as hope-

lessly difficult to uncover the self-deception or the lie when someone pretends that a movement of his body is one that he did not
make, as it often is to discover a person's insincerity when he
maintains that a passion he experiences is not to be attributed to
him. The ambition to make our tasks as moral judges less difficult
is no more a good reason in the one case than it is in the other,
surely, for ignoring a distinction that corresponds to a significant
difference of fact.

III

We need now to consider which of the passions in a person's history *are* external to him, and to examine the conditions of their
externality. A passion is especially likely to be external when it is
artificially induced by such means as hypnosis or the use of drugs.
In cases of this sort, the passion generally does not arise as a response to a perceived experience. It may well present itself to the
person in whose history it is contrived to occur, accordingly, as
discontinuous with his understanding of his situation and with his
conception of himself. Even so, the person often appears by a kind
of instinct to circumvent these discontinuities with rationalization:
he instantaneously provides the passion with meaning, or somehow construes it as having a natural place in his experience. Then,
despite its origin, the passion becomes attached to a moving principle within the person; and the person is no more a passive by-
stander with respect to it than if it had arisen in more integral
response to his perceptions.

It is not only passions aroused by contrivance, however, that are
external. Consider the following exemplary episode:

> In the course of an animated but amiable enough conversation, a man's
> temper suddenly rushes up in him out of control. Although nothing has hap-
> pened that makes his behavior readily intelligible, he begins to fling dishes,
> books, and crudely abusive language at his companion. Then his tantrum
> subsides, and he says: "I have no idea what triggered that bizarre spasm of
> emotion. The feelings just came over me from out of nowhere, and I couldn't
> help it. I wasn't myself. Please don't hold it against me."

These disclaimers may be, of course, shabbily insincere devices for
obtaining unmerited indulgence. Or they may be nothing more

than emphatic expressions of regret. But it is also possible that they are genuinely descriptive. What the man says may appropriately convey his sense that the rise of passion represented in some way an intrusion upon him, that it violated him, that when he was possessed by the anger he was not in possession of himself. It is in statements like the ones made by the man in this example, and in the sense of oneself that such statements express, that we most vividly encounter the experience of externality.

Which features of episodes like this one are essential conditions or marks of externality, and which are inessential? The answer that comes most readily to mind is that passions are external to us just when we prefer not to have them, or when we prefer not to be moved by them; and that they are internal when, at the time of their occurrence, we welcome or indifferently accept them. On this account a passion is unequivocally ours when it is what we want to feel, or are willing to feel, while a passion whose occurrence in us we disapprove is not strictly ours.

Sometimes, when we disapprove of the course our passions have taken, we say that it does not represent what we "really" feel. We do not intend in this way to deny that the passions in question occur, but to indicate that we regard them as being in some manner incoherent with our preferred conception of ourselves, which we suppose captures what we are more truly than mere undistilled description. People are often inclined, at least until they reach a certain age, to construe what they really are as what they would like to be. They consider their "real" passions to be those by which they would like to be motivated, or with which they would prefer to be identified by those who know them, even though these passions may in fact be dimmer and less influential upon their behavior than others.

This equation of the real with the ideal does play a role in the way some people think about themselves. Nonetheless, the distinction between internal and external passions is not the same as the distinction between what is and what is not "real" in the sense of conforming to a person's ideal image of himself. Surely it is possible for a person to recognize that a certain passion is unequivocally attributable to him, even when he regrets this fact and wishes that the passion did not occur in him or move him at all. Perhaps after long struggle and disillusion with himself, a person may become resigned to being someone of whom he himself does not altogether approve. He no longer supposes that he is capable of bringing the course of his passions into harmony with his ideal concept of himself, and accordingly he ceases to reserve his acceptance of his passions as they are.

It is also not essential to the externality of a passion that it be of irresistible intensity. We are ordinarily led to disclaim a passion only when it happens to be one to which we would have preferred not to be subject, or when it interferes in some important way with the sovereignty of other passions that we regard as more genuinely our own. Considerations of this sort account for our interest in *calling attention to* the externality of certain passions, but they are not conditions of externality itself. There is nothing in the notion of externality that implies irresistibility or, for that matter, any particular level of relative intensity. Thus it is quite intelligible that a person should find in himself a desire with which he does not identify, and yet that he should have no difficulty whatever in preventing that desire from moving him or from usurping his will. In my example, the person regrets his inability to control his anger. This explains his eagerness to dissociate himself publicly from that passion and from the desires to which it led. Neither his inability nor his regret, however, accounts for the fact—if it was a fact— that the anger and the angry desires were not strictly his own.

IV

I have maintained that the question of whether a passion is internal or external to a person is not just a matter of the person's attitude toward the passion. Still, I am reluctant to suggest that the attitudes of a person toward his passions can be dismissed as altogether irrelevant to this question. Suppose someone disclaims a passion that occurs in him on a certain occasion, but we know both that he experiences passions of this sort regularly on such occasions, and that he is quite willing and satisfied to do so. We are unlikely to treat his disclaimer very seriously, in that case, and this response seems reasonable. What is unclear is the basis on which we would rightly be skeptical.

Perhaps we think that whether or not a person is to be identified with a certain passion is, at least sometimes, up to him. Perhaps we have the idea, in other words, that there is something a person can do that makes a passion fully his own, and that there is sometimes nothing to stop him from doing this if he chooses to do it. Then we would find it difficult to understand, when a person contentedly and with predictable regularity experiences a certain passion, that he has not done whatever it takes to identify himself with it. That would explain our skepticism.

The fact that a person disapproves of a passion that occurs in him is not by itself tantamount to the passion's being an external one. For it is possible, as I have already observed, that someone should become resigned to what he judges to be his defects. A person may acknowledge to himself that passions of which he disapproves are undeniably and unequivocally his; and he may then cease to feel, if he ever felt, that these passions are in any way alien or that they intrude upon him. The fact that a person disapproves of a passion is not, accordingly, a sufficient condition of the passion's externality to him. On the other hand, it may be that disapproval is a necessary condition of externality. It is in fact difficult to think of a convincing example in which a person to whom a passion is external nonetheless approves of the occurrence of the passion in him. And the difficulty of finding an example of this kind also tends to support the conjecture that a person's approval of a passion that occurs in his history is a sufficient condition of the passion's being internal to him.

Whatever the truth about these relationships may be, it is important to notice that there is a quite basic error in thinking that the concepts of internality and externality are to be explicated *simply* in terms of a person's attitudes. It is fundamentally misguided to suggest that a passion's externality is entailed by the person's disapproval of it, or that its internality is entailed by his approval. The trouble with this approach to the problem of understanding internality and externality is that it fails to take into account the fact that attitudes toward passions are as susceptible to externality as are passions themselves. Suppose that a person has mixed feelings about one of his passions: he is aware of having an inclination to approve of the passion and also of having an inclination to disapprove of it. Suppose he resolves this conflict by decisively adopting an attitude of disapproval toward the passion. He may find nonetheless that his inclination to approve of the passion persists, though it is now external to him and not properly to be attributed to him as his own.

The fact that a person has a certain attitude toward a passion can be construed as determining either the internality or the externality of the passion, surely, only if the attitude in question is itself genuinely attributable to him. An attitude in virtue of which a passion is internal, or in virtue of which a passion is external, cannot be merely an attitude that a person finds within himself; it must be one with which he is to be identified. But given that the question of attribution arises not only with regard to a person's passions, but also with regard to his attitudes toward his passions, an infinite regress will be generated by any attempt to account for internality or externality in terms of attitudes. For the attitude that is invoked to account for the status of a passion will have to be an internal one; its internality will have to be accounted for by invoking a higher-order attitude—that is, an attitude toward an attitude; the internality of this higher-order attitude will have to be accounted for in terms of an attitude of a still higher order; and so on. This precludes explication of the concepts of internality and externality by appealing merely to the notion of orders of attitudes.

V

I cannot provide a satisfactory account of what it means to characterize a passion as internal or as external. It may be possible for me to clarify these notions a bit further, however, by discussing two sorts of conflict of desire. Suppose that a person wants to go to a concert, and that he also wants to see a film. Imagine further that in the circumstances these desires conflict, so that the person must decide whether he prefers to spend his evening in the one way or in the other. Now it is likely that both the desire to see the film and the desire to go to the concert are equally internal to the person. The situation is simply one in which he wants to do two things and cannot do both of them. He would resolve the problem this conflict presents just by deciding which of the two things in question he prefers to do.

Conflicts of this kind require only that the desires at issue be ordered. Their essential feature is that the conflicting desires belong to the same ordering, though as long as the conflict is unresolved their relative positions in that ordering are unsettled. Membership in the same ordering may be explained as follows.

Suppose the person decides that he actually prefers to see the film, but it turns out that he is unable to obtain a ticket. Then it would be quite natural for him to revert to his second choice and go to the concert. After all, he wants to do that too. His original decision against doing it meant only that satisfying his desire to go to the concert was lower in his ordering than satisfying his desire to see the film.

When a person suffers a conflict of the second kind, his problem is not to assign one desire that he feels to a lower position than another on a single scale. It is to reject one of the desires that he feels altogether. Conflicts between conscious and unconscious desires are typically of this kind, but both of the conflicting desires may well remain conscious. Suppose that a person wants to compliment an acquaintance for some recent achievement, but that he also notices within himself a jealously spiteful desire to injure the man. It may be that, as things turn out, he finds no opportunity to make the friendly remark that he had (we may imagine) decided to make. This would not naturally lead him to see if he can salvage the satisfaction of his other desire. When a person is frustrated in his desire to see a film, he naturally turns to his second choice and goes to a concert. In the present example, however, the alternative of injuring his acquaintance is not second to the person's first choice of paying him a compliment. It is in this sense that the friendly and the jealous desires, unlike those concerning the concert and the film, do not belong to the same ordering.

There is no reason to presume that the person's desire to injure his acquaintance occurs in the first instance as an external desire, and that his desire to compliment the man occurs originally as an internal one. To be sure, it may happen that way. If it does, then the two desires will present themselves from the start as belonging to different orderings; and the person will have no conflict to resolve, though he may have to fight off the influence of the external desire. On the other hand, it may happen that, at an early stage in his confrontation of his feelings, the person finds that the one desire is no less internal to him than the other. In that case, the person himself is in conflict and not merely the desires that are occurring in his mental history. He has the problem of not knowing what he wants to do, in a familiar sense that is quite compatible with his knowing both that he wants to injure his acquaintance and that he wants to pay him a compliment, and the conflict his uncertainty manifests requires resolution.

The person cannot resolve this conflict by deciding that his first choice is to satisfy one of the conflicting desires and that satisfying the other desire is his second choice. The conflict is not one to be resolved by *ordering* the conflicting desires, in other words, but by *rejecting* one of them. In rejecting the desire to injure his acquaintance, presuming that this is what he does, the person withdraws himself from it. He places the rejected desire outside the scope of his preferences, so that it is not a candidate for satisfaction at all. Although he may continue to experience the rejected desire as occurring in his mental history, the person brings it about in this way that its occurrence is an external one. The desire is then no longer to be attributed strictly to him, even though it may well persist or recur as an element of his experience.

In a conflict of the kind, the person's decision to go to the film does not mean that he does not want to go to the concert. It only means that he does not want to go to the concert *as much* as he wants to go to the film. In the second, the person's rejection of the desire to injure his acquaintance does not mean simply that he wants to compliment him *more* than he wants to injure him. It means that he does *not* want to injure him, even though the desire to injure is something that he experiences. It would be a bit misleading to insist that since the desire to compliment prevails over the desire to injure, the situation is merely that the former is stronger than the latter. This wrongly suggests that both desires occupy positions in the same ordering, and that they differ only in strength. There is a better way, I believe, to describe the fact that the desire to compliment prevails over the desire to injure. It is to say that *the person*, who wants to pay his acquaintance a compliment, is stronger than the desire to injure him that he finds within himself.

By deciding that what he wants after all is to compliment his acquaintance, and that his desire to injure the man is finally to be excluded from the order of candidates for satisfaction, the person renders the second desire external to himself and identifies himself with the first. Here it appears to be by making a particular kind of decision that the relation of the person to his passions is established. It may be that a decision of this kind, even when it is not so visible as in the present example, lies behind every instance of the establishment of the internality or externality of passions. Or perhaps it is by referring to something more general, of which decisions are only special cases, that we must seek to understand the phenomena in question. In any event, the nature of decision is very obscure.[3]

VI

The problem of attribution or of externality with regard to bodily movements is to explain what differentiates a movement that a person makes from a mere happening in the history of his body. The corresponding problem with regard to psychic phenomena concerns the nature of identification: what does it mean for a person to be identified with one rather than with another of two passions (or whatever), both of which are in the gross literal sense his? Each of these problems is, in its own realm, both fundamental and frustratingly recalcitrant. I have done little more than to suggest that they are in certain respects analogous. It remains to be seen in what important ways they may differ, and whether it is likely that they are susceptible to analogous solutions.

NOTES

1. One result of overlooking events of this kind is an exaggeration of the peculiarity of what humans do. Another result, related to the first, is the mistaken belief that a twofold division of human events into actions and mere happenings provides a classification that suits the interests of the theory of action.

2. Terence Penelhum, "The Importance of Self-Identity," *Journal of Philosophy* LXVIII (1971), 670. The numbers within parentheses in the remainder of the current paragraph refer to the pages of this essay.

3. Decisions, unlike desires or attitudes, do not seem to be susceptible both to internality and to externality. Invoking them here would appear to avoid, accordingly, the difficulty considered in the preceding section.

XI

SELF-IDENTITY AND SELF-REGARD

TERENCE PENELHUM

In his discussion of personal identity Hume draws a distinction to which his readers have not paid much attention. It is a distinction between "personal identity, as it regards our thought or imagination, and as it regards our passions or the concern we take in ourselves."[1] I want in this paper, to examine this distinction and the use Hume makes of it. Although in doing so, I will be commenting some of the time on questions of Humean exegesis, my main concern is to try to throw some light on the role that the idea of oneself plays in our thinking about some of the areas of the emotional life that Hume considers.

I

Let us first see why Hume introduces this distinction where he does. It appears in the Section "Of Personal Identity" (Section VI of Part IV of Book I of the *Treatise*), and he says he must make it in order to answer a question about self-identity which he says, correctly, will carry his readers "pretty deep." The question he wants to ask is this:

> What then gives us so great a propension to ascribe an identity to these successive perceptions, and to suppose ourselves possest of an invariable and uninterrupted existence thro' the whole course of our lives? (p. 253)

This is a question about the origin of what I shall call the belief in the unity of a person. He raises it after dismissing the view of "some metaphysicians" that each of us is aware of a *self* that has perfect identity and simplicity, and asserting that as far as he and the rest of mankind are concerned, each of us is "nothing but a bundle or collection of different perceptions" in which there is "properly no simplicity...at any one time, nor identity in different." I interpret his answer to it as one that denies that the invariable and uninterrupted existence he refers to is an actual feature of human life, and offers us a psychological account of how we come to suppose that it is. It is this which constitutes his account of "personal identity, as it regards our thought or imagination." The upshot of his account is that the life-history of a person (or mind) is merely a sequence of "different perceptions," which has no "identity in different," but to which such an identity is indeed ascribed by the "thought or imagination" because of various connections and relationships between its successive members.

This is not the question of how one such biography is to be distinguished from other parallel ones—which I will dub the question about Individuation. I do not think Hume ever addresses himself to this question directly. I have argued elsewhere that a case of sorts can be built up, in the terms of Hume's own philosophical system, for denying that this question needs to be raised before the question of Unity can be.[2] I shall not repeat this here.

But whatever the precise dimensions of the problem of the Unity of the person, readers of the *Treatise* have noticed that Hume proceeds in Book II as though the problem is safely behind him. They have sometimes felt that he is not entitled to proceed like this, and that he makes use of the idea of the self in his account of the genesis of some of the passions, and in his description of the mechanism of sympathy, in a way that is inconsistent with what he has said about it in Book I. There is little doubt that at least part of the reason for his introducing the distinction between personal identity as it concerns the thought or imagination, and personal identity as it regards our passions, in the midst of his discussion in Book I, is to forestall this criticism. He would achieve this end by making readers think that the role the idea of the self is said to play in Book II is one it might very well play whether his treatment of it in Book I is correct, or whether it is not: that the two discussions are logically independent.

Of course, if this is what Hume wishes his readers to think, he may be wrong. It might turn out on reflection that the uses he ascribes to the idea of the self in our emotional life, or the uses that the idea of the self actually has in the emotional life, are uses that it could not have unless the analysis in Book I, or some part of it, were false: or that if the analysis of Book I were true, it would expose our uses of the idea of the self in the emotional life to a charge of confusion or irrationality.

Before looking at this possibility, I must put aside another. Hume clearly does not think that the idea of the self that plays a key role in the genesis of some of the passions is the one he ascribes to those metaphysicians that he attacks at the outset of the Section in the first Book. He insists that he at least does not *have* such an idea, because it is not traceable to any impression. Although some commentators seem willing enough to accuse him of the most blatant inconsistency at this point, there seems little need to read him as though he holds that our emotional life depends critically upon an idea that by his own account we do not even have. There may be inconsistency, but it is likely to be at a deeper level than this.

He tells us himself what idea he has in mind when he refers to what he calls the "object" of pride and humility as "self, or that succession of related ideas and impressions, of which we have an intimate memory and consciousness" (p. 277). This adjectival clause is manifestly inserted to make it clear that he is *not* referring to the alleged idea of a metaphysical pure ego, but to that sequence of perceptions for which it was supposed to provide a principle of unity: to what many philosophers have called the empirical self. His use of the idea thus identified makes it clear that he takes it for granted, in Book II, both that the problem of the ascription of Unity to that sequence need not be raised again, and also that we do have at our disposal, and presuppose in our emotional life, some manner of answering the question about Individuation. With regard to the latter question, there are countless places where his description of the arousal of the emotions requires us to be able to distinguish other persons from ourselves, and from one another; and it is certainly a pity that he nevers offers a direct and detailed answer to the question of Individuation in order to help his readers understand how these vital distinctions are available to us. But not offering an answer is not the same as being in no position to offer one; and does not of itself constitute inconsistency, open or concealed.

The case is more complex, however, when we look at his use of the idea of the self in Book II in order to compare it with his views on the question he *does* try to answer in Book I—the problem of the Unity of the person. Suppose it should emerge (as I think it does on the most cursory investigation) that his account of the emotions requires him to ascribe to us not only the use of the distinction between oneself and another, but also the presupposition of the Unity of oneself through time? It would then follow that Hume would be making use in Book II of the belief in something that he described in Book I as a fiction, as something read into a sequence of heterogeneous perceptions that does not contain it. Admittedly he holds that such a fiction is one of which we could not rid ourselves if we tried, but it is a fiction for all that. This is something that he refrains from recalling to us in Book II; for he has a well-known habit of himself adopting in one place those beliefs he has tried to show in other places to be baseless but ineradicable.

Ineradicable or not, the fictional status of the Unity of the self has an intriguing consequence, which is the reason for the exegetical comments in this essay. An emotion that is founded on a fiction is a mistaken or false emotion. Insofar as the ascription of unity to oneself is an inescapable element in the genesis of any of our emotions, then these emotions would seem to be mistaken or false mental states. To decide how far such a sweeping conclusion is justified, we would have to decide whether Hume is right in holding that the unity of the self is a fiction. I cannot undertake this here. I have argued elsewhere that Hume gives no adequate reasons for such a radical doctrine. But he does espouse it; and I think it likely that he introduces the distinction between personal identity as it concerns the thought or imagination, and personal identity as it concerns the passions, in order to prevent any difficult consequence it has from obstructing his account of the passions.

What I wish to do is to see what we can learn from him about the role we give to the idea of the self in our emotional life and in our moral criticisms of it. I wish also to ask what presuppositions have to be made for such roles to be possible. Although Hume's expository separation of the two aspects of personal identity is not enough by itself to clarify these presuppositions, let alone justify them, I shall suggest in conclusion that when the presuppositions are understood, his making the separation in the way that he does is still instructive.

II

I turn first, then, to the functions that Hume says the idea of oneself discharges in the genesis of the passions. It must be remembered here that Hume regards every passion as a unique and simple impression. Any account that he gives of a passion, therefore, cannot be presented as an analysis of it, since what is simple is unanalyzable. It must rather be an account of how such an impression arises and what its results are. An account so circumscribed is bound to be one in which what contemporary philosophers would think of as points of logic appear as psychological accounts of causes and consequences. If we treat them as points of logic (which I shall do) it must be clear that we are not following Hume's own procedure. Hume's psychologism is at all times deliberate, and to translate him into the language of conceptual analysis is to commit an anachronism.[3] So when Hume tells us the role of the idea of the self plays in the passions, he understands this to be a causal role. There are two places where it is prominent: in the genesis of the indirect passions of pride and humility and in the mechanism of sympathy.

The distinction between the direct and the indirect passions is itself a causal distinction. The indirect passions have a more complex origin than the direct ones do. They do not arise merely from "good or evil, pain or pleasure," but also require the "conjunction of other qualities" (pp. 276-277). He lists them as "pride, humility, love, hatred, envy, pity, malice, generosity, with their dependents." He explains their special character another way, by saying that they do not only have a *cause* (an "idea which excites them") but also an *object*, which he describes as "that to which they direct their view, when excited" (p. 278). This looks a quite different way of distinguishing them, but it is not. We can see that it is not when we notice that he tells us that two passions like pride and humility have one and the same object (namely myself), but that the object cannot be "sufficient *alone*" to excite them. So, paradoxically, both the cause and the object are causes of these passions, and neither is sufficient alone. The pattern is roughly this: that some pleasing fact can give me joy, but neither pride nor love; to generate pride or love this pleasing fact (the cause) has to be joined with the idea of myself, in which case it then generates pride, or with the idea of another person, in which case it generates love. If the fact is displeasing, it will give rise to humility if joined with the idea of myself, and hatred if joined with the idea of another. The self or the other person (or, more exactly, the ideas of them) are the objects of these emotions, but it is clear from his account that they are nevertheless to be understood as partial causes of them.

The mechanism of sympathy is one which Hume considers to lead to an imaginative, participatory awareness of the passions of other persons. The process seems to be one in which I first become aware by inference from another person's behavior that he is experiencing a particular passion. The idea of his passion, however, becomes more lively and gives place to an impression: some sort of counterpart in me of the very passion that he has. Hume clearly thinks that we pass from a mere cognizance of his emotional state to a participation in it by some kind of imitation, a transition that his system incorporates as the enlivening of an originally faint perception into a vivid one. What does the enlivening is the idea of the self. It seems to do it through my recognition of the similarity between the other's mental life and my own. Passions are catching; and the idea of the self is one of the vehicles of the emotional infection.

In spite of the great importance that the mechanism of sympathy has in Hume's theory of the passions and in his moral philosophy, I shall not discuss it here any further. To include it would lead to unnecessary prolixity, when there is no question about the status of the idea of the self in the emotional life that arises exclusively in connection with it. For the mechanism of sympathy, as Hume outlines it, to operate, each of us has to be aware that every other person is a person like himself; but the theory does not help us to spell out the nature of that which is thought to be the same in each one.[4] I will confine my examination to the self-regarding indirect passions of pride and humility. My objective in this is not to carry the exegesis of Book II of the *Treatise* into detail, but to discover the role that the idea of oneself actually plays in these emotional states.

Indeed, Hume's theoretical framework forces us to leave him behind if we are to avoid misleading ambiguities. I argued above that his distinction between the cause and the object of the indirect passions, is, in spite of appearances, one which he has to treat as a distinction among the causes of those passions because he thinks all passions are distinct and separate impressions. We may think that the point he makes in this way is really a logical one: that whatever we may feel, it cannot be *called* pride unless something pleasing has come into our purview, and is connected with ourselves, and cannot be *called* humility unless something displeasing has come into our purview and is connected with ourselves. Leaving this aside for the present, it is noticeable that Hume is revealingly ambivalent about the nature of the alleged causal sequence that produces pride and humility. While his arguments' that the cause and the object are each causal conditions of the passion entail that both precede it, when he sets out the sequence most nearly formally, he places the idea of the self, which he has identified as the object, as an idea that comes to the fore *after* the passion of pride or humility has arisen, not before.[6] This is of course suggested by his calling the object "that to which they direct their view, when excited." If they are understood in this way, then pride and humility are passions that make us think about ourselves, not passions that arise in the mind after we do so. Of course, one wants to say, they are both. It is true that I cannot be proud of something unless I presuppose it has some relationship to me; and it is also true that it cannot feed my pride unless it turns my attention *from* itself *to* me. But the trouble is that a linear causal account of the relationship between the self and its qualities and the passions of pride and humility cannot do justice to this. Like all Hume's ambivalences, this one represents his awareness of the complexities of the facts even where his own theories require him to oversimplify them.

For the concepts of pride and humility are not homogeneous. One variation within the concept of pride is reflected in the shift in Hume's causal account of it. I might feel proud of some action or event because of my connection with it, or its with me, on the one hand; or on the other I might be led to reflect on my personal merits by some pleasing fact that I am responsible for. In general terms, I can on the one hand be proud *of* something, because of its actual or supposed connection with myself, or, on the other hand, I can have a general tendency to self-glorification, with its attendant overestimate of those deeds and qualities that would justify it. In the latter case the occasion of my pride may not be that of which I am primarily thinking when I feel it. In the case of humility, the heterogeneity of the phenomena Hume describes is even more obvious, since, as Árdal says,[7] one does not feel humble *of* anything; at the most one feels humble because of it, and the humility one feels is, roughly, a generally low or negative estimate of oneself. What one feels with regard to the fact that occasions humility here is *shame*.

We can distinguish, then, between pride as general self-satisfaction, self-glorification, vanity, or arrogance; and pride as directed to particular facts or events or qualities with which one is connected, which I shall call particular pride. We can also distinguish between humility or general self-deprecation, and *shame*, which is directed to particular facts or events or qualities with which one is connected.[8] Hume's language and his associative theoretical framework, do not encourage a sufficiently clear distinction between these, and different members of each pair seem to be under consideration at different points in his text.[9] I do not wish to suggest that these distinctions are adequate to do justice to the many ambiguities in these complex notions, but they are a sufficient beginning for present purposes.

It is easy to see that they are needed. For one concept in each pair may apply to situations that exclude the other member of the pair. Even though it is true that a proud man (one who has a high estimate of himself) is also someone who is likely to feel proud of facts or events or qualities connected with himself, and to do so quite frequently; and while it is true that a humble man (one who has a low estimate of himself) is someone who is at least readily capable of shame, the connection is not universal. My self-regard can be fed by my shame at particular facts about my actions and circumstances, and can manifest itself in such shame. The man who is too proud to stoop readily to deceit on his tax form or to stay in a cheap hotel is the very man who will be ashamed when he does so. My self-deprecation is not reduced or contradicted by the fact that I am proud of some things that are connected with me. A poor or obscure man who is proud of his children's wealth or success is not necessarily a single step on the road from humility to arrogance when he feels this; indeed, his very humility may be a major source of the pride he feels.

III

I turn first to particular pride, and shame. Here the passion, in a way which is familiar but hard to define, is directed at the phenomenon which occasions the arousal of it. The occasion will be what Hume calls the cause. He holds that the idea of the self is also in some way indispensable to its arousal. Leaving his associationist psychology for the more fashionable idiom of informal logic, I shall try to clarify the role that each plays.

To begin with the occasion, Hume is wrong when he says that the cause of pride has to give me pleasure, and the cause of shame has to give me pain. At least, this is wrong if by "pleasure" we mean "enjoyment." I can certainly be proud of very unenjoyable things, such as paying my tax bill under difficulties, enduring physical pain, or facing danger; I can also be proud of others doing this, if they are connected with me, and my being proud does not entail that I find the contemplation of their doing these things enjoyable. Similarly, I can be ashamed of things that give me enjoyment, such as eating food that my diet forbids, or watching movies of violence.

But although Hume is mistaken if he thinks that what occasions pride is always enjoyable, and what occasions shame is always disagreeable, he is nevertheless close to some important truth when he holds that pleasure and pain are in some manner necessary for pride or shame. In part this just means that being proud and being ashamed are themselves agreeable or disagreeable mental states (as when he tells us that "the sensation of humility is uneasy, as that of pride is agreeable"):[10] a proposition of whose universality I am unsure, but which I have no wish to contest. He is also right in thinking that pleasure and pain, somehow interpreted, play a necessary role in the attitude we take to that which occasions our pride or shame. But this role is not played by enjoyment or dislike. It is played, rather, by our being *pleased* or *displeased*. Those things of which I can be proud but which I do not enjoy are things at which I am still pleased. And those things of which I am ashamed but enjoy, or do not find disagreeable, are still things at which I am displeased. That these are necessary for pride or shame is a logical, and not a psychological, truth.[11] It is not that before I can experience the passion of pride or shame I must first experience the prior passion of pleasure or displeasure, as Hume's account requires: though an insistence on the logical character of the connection does not prohibit such a view either. It is merely that for it to be true that someone is proud or ashamed of something it must be true that that of which he is proud or ashamed is something which pleases or displeases him. He can be pleased or displeased without also being proud or ashamed; but he cannot be proud or ashamed without being pleased or displeased.

What sorts of things can one be pleased or displeased about, and therefore be able to take pride in or feel shame at? In non-Humean language what objects do pleasure and displeasure, and therefore, pride and shame, have? They appear to be ontologically quite heterogeneous: to include physical things, events, abstract objects, facts, qualities, processes, and many more. I can be pleased by my house, my wedding anniversary, the fact that I am a professor, the color of my eyes, the growth of my bank balance, and innumerable other things. If one were to try for ontological economy, and seek to reduce the categories to one, the only plausible candidate here would seem to me to be that of facts. The plausibility of this choice derives from the apparent ease with which one can translate statements about the objects of one's pleasure or displeasure into statements of an overtly factual form. If I am pleased at my dog's new tricks, then I am pleased (at the fact) that he can perform them. If I am ashamed of losing my job, I am ahsamed of the fact that I have lost it. But there are awkward cases, whose significance would be considerable in an ontological debate. If a child is pleased by his new balloon, into what fact or facts is "his new balloon" to be translated? Is it the fact that he *has* a new balloon? Is it the fact that his new balloon has a funny face on it, or is red? No particular choice seems required here, even if the disjunction is finite. Fortunately ontology is not our present concern, and my other arguments will not be affected by the view I express. For presentational economy I would suggest the following: for someone to be pleased or displeased at something, either that at which he is pleased or displeased is a fact, *or* there is some fact, of which he is aware, about that which pleases or displeases him without which it would not do so.

Such a formula covers a multitude of problems. One, which can be left unresolved here, is whether one can think one is pleased or displeased by one fact when one is really pleased or displeased by another: can one, that is, misidentify the object of one's pleasure or displeasure? Another difficulty: what if the fact one is pleased or displeased about is not a fact at all, and one is therefore pleased or displeased mistakenly? Here again I ignore ontological complexities, and state that for someone to be pleased or displeased at something, either that at which he is pleased or displeased is a fact, *actual or supposed*, or there is some fact of which he is aware or thinks he is aware about that which pleases or displeases him without which it would not do so. I can ignore the problem of the ontological standing of supposed facts here, as I have ignored the problem of the ontological standing of actual ones. Perhaps actual and supposed facts can be combined into one class, for example, of propositions, so that one should then ponder *their* ontological standing, but I shall not explore this. (It is worth noting that there is at least one obvious difficulty in the way of suggesting that the category used here should be *beliefs*: even if it is true that I cannot be pleased that my horse has won unless I believe that it has, it is not true that it is my belief that it has won that is what I am pleased about.)[12]

It is very common, though probably not necessary, that the fact which pleases or displeases me is subjected by me to some sort of appraisal, for example, a moral or social or economic one. Such an appraisal would furnish the arguments I might subsequently offer if my pleasure or displeasure (or pride or shame) is criticized. It does not seem impossible, however, to feel pleased or displeased at something *simpliciter*, without having appraisive *reasons*: a result of which is that if our pleasure or displeasure is challenged, the best one can do to defend it is show that the critic's contrary appraisal is unfounded, so that even though I was pleased without reason, there is no reason for me to have felt *displeased*, and vice versa. We have to face the fact that at times we seem to feel pleasure at something that we can see we ought to appraise (and therefore in a sense do appraise) negatively, such as a colleague's discomfiture, and it seems doctrinaire to insist that it *must* look good to us if we do.

So much for what it is that can occasion the pleasure and displeasure. Clearly not every case of these is a case of pride or shame. A necessary condition of one of the latter emotions occurring is the connection of that which arouses them with myself. Hume's insight here seems clearly sound; or at least a logical counterpart to it is. Let us now explore it in some detail.

For the present I will leave aside the question of what *sort* of connection with myself a fact I am proud or ashamed of has to have, and will merely illustrate varying ways in which such a connection may be required for these emotions to be possible. We can readily see that what people take pride or shame in varies widely from person to person and from culture to culture.

Let us imagine the case of a prominent member of a tribe whose wife and immediate family are very fat. Let us suppose further that obesity is highly regarded in that tribe as a sign of wealth and leisure. In that culture, then, being fat is thought pleasing—in contrast with our culture, in which slimness in every social class is the norm, so that obesity is found displeasing. This is not by itself enough to make our citizen proud. For he may not share the preferences of his own tribe and may instead share ours. In that case he cannot be proud of his family's girth, because he is not pleased by it, even though everyone else around him may be.

Even though he cannot feel pride if he does not feel pleasure, he does belong to the select group of those who are *entitled* to do so. If only he *did* feel pleased, he could feel proud. Only he, or other members of the family, or their cook, or their doctor, or their banker (if the tribe has a bank) are in the logical position to be able to feel pride as distinct from mere pleasure (what Hume calls joy) or admiration, or other disinterested emotions; and of course only members of this group can feel shame as distinct from distress or contempt. If the tribe is as sophisticated in its sins as our own society is, and if the family is socially prominent, then it might very well happen that other members of the tribe who could not feel pride or shame might say that they do, in order thereby to imply the connection with the family that such a claim would require.

Even though someone is logically in a position to feel proud or ashamed of something, and does in fact feel pleasure or distress at it, he still may not happen to feel pride or shame at it. He may just happen to be the sort of person whose emotions are too disinterested either by nature or by training. It is not true that pleasure plus connectedness entails pride, or that displeasure plus connectedness entails shame. It is only true that pride entails pleasure plus connectedness, and shame entails displeasure plus connectedness.

There are occasions when the connectedness seems to be the only source of the pleasure or the displeasure. It might be that the fat family's cook takes no pleasure in the fact of fatness *per se*, but is pleased by the family's fatness because, and only because, it is due to their enthusiasm for her cuisine. A philosopher might say that it is *really* their enthusiasm for her cuisine that pleases her in that case, and not the fatness it causes, but while one can say this, we do not always. do so. Their doctor may be displeased by their fatness, not because he is distressed by such things in themselves, but because such things in his patients reflect unhappily on his ability to get them to listen to his instructions on diet. Here it seems that the fact about the family's obesity which accounts for the cook's pleasure and the doctor's displeasure is simply the fact of its connection with themselves. We can put it by saying that the cook is proud of their obesity, but would not be pleased by it if it were not for its connection with her; that the doctor is ashamed of it, but would not be displeased by it but for its connection with him. (I do not think we can say without paradox that the cook is proud but not pleased, or the doctor ashamed but not displeased; the pride entails the pleasure, the shame the displeasure.) In these cases, although the cook and the doctor have to be aware of the obesity of the family, this fact would not, alone, even generate pleasure or distress; it is the fact of its connection with themselves that produces each—though it might not produce either.

To summarize: for me to feel pride or shame, it is logically requisite that that of which I am proud or ashamed pleases me, or displeases me, and is connected with me. Both are logically necessary; neither singly is sufficient; and in some cases their combination may not be sufficient either. Hume seems mistaken in thinking that each must please or displease me independently of its connection with myself, though no doubt this is often the case. And just as I can be pleased, and therefore can be proud, or can be displeased, and therefore can be ashamed, of a supposed fact as well as an actual one, so I can be proud or ashamed in virtue of a supposed connection with myself as well as an actual one. In such cases the pride or shame can be called mistaken.

I turn now to the question of the nature of the actual or supposed connection that is necessary for pride or shame. Here there are competing temptations. On the one hand there is a strong temptation to say that the connection has to be one that established the fact which I am proud or ashamed of is a fact for which I have some responsibility. On the other hand there is a temptation to hold that any sort of connection is capable of generating these emotions. The second view is nearer the truth than the first. It is possible to hold, as a moral conviction, that one *ought* only to be proud or ashamed of that for which one is responsible, but one must not represent this conviction, even if it is true, as a logical truth. It is indeed sometimes true that looser connections that generate pride or shame carry some imputation of responsibility, as in the case of the snob who is proud that a member of his club has been knighted, and feels in his pride that some of the merit that led to the honor has somehow accrued to himself. But however common such suppositions may be, it is not clear that they are present by necessity, even though they might enable us conveniently to classify such forms of pride or shame as false. Indeed, the humble man who is proud of something connected with himself may remain convinced that the connection he has with it is not one that allows him to take any credit for it, and he may even be proud for that very reason.

So far I have written as though the fact that pleases me when I am proud, and the fact of which I am proud, are one and the same, the pride being consequent upon the connection with myself which the fact has. The last question, however, raises the possibility, which is perhaps more in accord with Hume's analysis, that they are not. Perhaps what I am proud of, in each case, is not the fact which pleases me, but the *fact of my connection* with it. Perhaps to say that Jones is proud of his children's achievements is not to say that the fact that they have these achievements makes him proud, but to say that he is proud of the fact that the people who have these achievements are his children. I do not know how to settle such an issue, given that on either reading it is the fact that they are his children that *makes* him proud. There is perhaps no point in deciding it in most cases. (There may be a point in some: the man who is proud of his ancestors' great deeds is probably proud of the fact that the people who did those great deeds are his ancestors, rather than of the deeds they did.) I shall continue for convenience to follow my previous idiom, in which what I am proud or ashamed of is a fact that generates pride because of its connection with myself, rather than the idiom in which what I am proud or ashamed of is the very fact of this connection.

It would seem, then, that pride or shame can be generated by very varied sorts of connections, Men can feel proud or ashamed that they themselves have performed certain actions, have certain qualities, or own certain possessions, and also of the fact that others related to them, acquainted with them, of their nationality, or of their political affiliation, have performed certain actions or have certain qualities or own certain possessions. This variety is a natural source of moral criticism, to which I will now turn.

Criticisms of the emotions of pride or shame can take many forms. They can be thought to be too great for what occasions them; or not great enough. They can be thought to be morally or aesthetically bad emotions in themselves, so that one ought to strive not to feel them even in situations where the necessary conditions of them are present; or one can be thought emotionally deficient for not feeling them when these conditions obtain. They can be criticized as based on a wrong appraisal of the facts that arouse them. They can be thought inappropriate because the connection with oneself that is needed to arouse them is a connection that is judged to be of a sort that ought not to do so. They can be mistaken, or false, because the supposed facts which arouse them are not facts at all. And they can be mistaken or false because the supposed connection with oneself that helps to arouse them does not exist. I shall comment here only upon the last three types of criticism.

(a) The suggestion that a particular connection with oneself ought not to lead to pride or shame, even though it exists, is a familiar source of moral disputes. Disputants here tend to operate with an implied scale on which certain types of emotional response are paired off with facts to which they are thought appropriate, each disputant seeking to persuade others to adopt his own scale. In the present case argument is likely to proceed, at its best, with the parties agreeing that a certain type of connection would justify pride or shame (such as the connection of a parent with his child, or of a teacher with his pupil) and then comparing this agreed type of connection with the controversial one to see whether the latter lacks some crucial feature. It might be argued, for example, that the affluence of my children is something of which I can be proud, but that of my neighbors is not, since the former connection entails a responsibility for that affluence which is absent from the second.

(b) I can go on being pleased at the actual or supposed fact that p only as long as I can go on believing that p. Once the supposition ceases, so does the pleasure at that which is supposed. If pleasure continues, it is necessarily a different one. The same is true of the pride of which pleasure, in this sense, is a condition; and the same reasoning holds for displeasure and the shame that depends upon it. If I am proud because of a false report that my child was top of the class, my pride in his being top necessarily ceases when I find he was not; if I need to go on being proud, then I have to take pride in his being almost top of the class instead. It is easy enough for most of us.

(c) Of greatest importance here is criticism based on the non-existence of the supposed connections with myself. If I cease to believe in these, then here again my pride or shame necessarily ceases also, and if I believe in them when they do not exist, my pride or shame is mistaken or false. This is also a familiar source of moral disputes and of morally reformist arguments. For example, it is possible in some theologies to hold that all genuinely good human deeds are in fact done not by ourselves as we suppose, but through an infusion of divine grace, so that our pride in our achievements is mistaken because they are not really our achievements. More modestly, it is possible to hold that some of the deeds I am ashamed of in my childhood are deeds which, though they were done by me as I suppose, were in some manner not examples of full agency because of my tender years, so that my shame depends upon a mistaken understanding of the connection they have with myself and should cease to exist after therapy. I may be proud of my supposed descent from Sir Francis Drake, only to discover that my great-grandfather took the name of Drake by deed poll. Where a connection is still thought to exist, but merely not to be the one imagined, it is of course quite possible that the pride or shame could continue, with greater, less, or identical intensity. I may, for example, continue to feel pride in my ancestry if I discover that it does derive from Drake, but does so illegitimately.

The questions of error we have just considered take on a particularly intriguing form when we ask if they can be produced by errors about the nature of the very self with which the facts that arouse pride or shame are thought to be connected. The connections, whatever they are, have to be connections with the being feeling the pride or the shame. If these connections logically require a continuity of the self through time that it in fact lacks, then the pride or shame that depends on the positing of these connections is always mistaken. This would not prove the absurd conclusion that such pride and shame never occur; only that they always depend on a false supposition of personal identity.

Read strictly, Hume is committed to this view. The sorts of connections that are required for pride and shame are either the kind that make the occasions of these emotions earlier items in the same personal biography that later includes the emotions themselves, or they are connections that in other ways require the identity of the self at the time of the emotion with the bearer of his name at some earlier stage—such as the connection between the presently proud teacher and the earlier instructor of his now brilliant student. When Hume tells us that personal identity is a fiction he tells us, strictly speaking, that the condition of such connections is never met. Of course we all believe that it is met, since we all share the conventional belief in the Unity of the person; and he tells us in Book I why he thinks we do this. Our error is what makes the self-regarding passions possible, and of course they will reinforce it once it is made. They do not produce it. Hume does not refer to them when he tells us how the error is first entrenched. It comes from the "thought or imagination." But once it is entrenched, the many emotional states it makes possible help to make it even less likely than ever that we will heed the skeptic when he points the error out to us.

The skeptic is in fact wrong, and the conventional ascription of self-identity is not shown to be fictitious by the sorts of consideration Hume advances for this; but this is not the place to argue this. Hume himself talks in Book II as though the problem of the Unity of the person has been solved, and such Unity has been established, not merely as though the fiction of it has been explained. Unless we are prepared to accept the falsity of *all* pride and shame we have to follow him in thinking that the problem has a solution, whatever that solution is.

Whatever it is, we must also follow him in thinking it has to come from the thought or imagination, and not from the passions themselves; for they require it, and so cannot produce it. At least, it cannot come from the consideration of those passions whose freedom from falsity depends on what the answer is. The fact that I feel proud or ashamed of something that I believe I did, and which someone did do, does not show that I did it. The pride or shame does not show its own freedom from falsity; it only guarantees the fact of my belief. And the fact that I feel indifference rather than pride or shame does not show the lack of a connection either. Indifference can also be mistaken: both in the sense that some other attitude may be more appropriate, and in the sense that it may depend on a false belief about what occurred, or about its connection, or lack of connection, with myself.

The appropriateness of the emotion depends on what the facts are and what their connections with the self are believed to be. The correctness or falsity of the emotion depends on the truth or falsity of these beliefs. We cannot justify one emotion, or discredit its alternatives, without independently establishing what the facts are, and what their connections with the self are. For the latter to be possible there have to be independent criteria of personal identity which determine the self's temporal boundaries. Even in the subjectivity of the emotions, this much psychological objectivity is necessary.

Nothing in the above proves that the self's boundaries have to be drawn where we conventionally draw them (wherever this is). It could be that some things that are conventionally classified as part of my past might not have been, or might in the future not be—conventions are not immutable. It might even be that an argument for changing them could be mounted on the very bases I have outlined. It would go somewhat as follows: it is indeed true that I cannot, in logic, be proud or ashamed of what has no connection with me. It is also true that the closer the connection some fact has with me, the more nearly universal is the agreement that it is something that it is morally appropriate, or is reasonable, to be proud or ashamed of. Hence something that, for instance, my immediate ancestor did is something it is more generally agreed I can be proud of, or ashamed of, than is something done by a remote ancestor. Now by convention something done in my youth has a closer connection with me, even in middle age or old age, than something done by even my most recent ancestor; for it was, after all, done by *me*, not by someone else. Hence, pride or shame at it is as appropriate here as it will ever be. But let us now reflect that pride in my past actions can readily lead to moral rigidity and self-righteousness, and shame at my past actions can readily lead to pathological guilt. Both of these are notoriously undesirable. So although the pride or the shame are *prima facie* appropriate, they are not appropriate *all things considered*. A person is best able to make his contribution to a changing society if he is not emotionally burdened by his past. Here then, we have excellent moral grounds for changing the temporal boundaries of the self. If we drew these boundaries more narrowly we could generate a convention in which a middle-aged man's youthful actions were classified roughly as the actions of his immediate ancestor are now classified: as the deeds of an earlier self. This would loosen the conventional connections by making it less appropriate to bé proud or ashamed of those actions: a man would be as free of reflected glory or disgrace from what is now thought of as his own past as he now is free of reflected glory or disgrace from the past doings of his progenitors.

It is tempting to say that this argument is incoherent. For if it is the case that we judge such emotional involvements with past actions as undesirable or inappropriate, and that is the reason for changing the conventions, does it not follow from this that the undesirability of such involvement is discernible on the basis of our *present* conventions? And if someone takes the opposite moral view, and thinks that emotional involvement with such past performances is a good thing, can he not enforce *his* moral preferences on the proposed conventions as well as on the present ones, by insisting that one ought to feel just as proud or ashamed of the doings of an ancestor self who inhabited one's present body as one feels of the recent doings of the present self that inhabit it? Does the proposal not shift the weight of a moral decision onto a conventional one?

I think these criticisms would indeed be sound, but I do not see that they would show the proposed conventional change to be incoherent. They merely show it to be at best morally pointless, and at worst morally undesirable. I shall now, however, change the proposal in order to produce one that is more philosophicaly sophisticated, and more tempting, but which I want to argue *is* incoherent.[13]

We can produce it by making use of some of the arguments that Hume offers in Book I. There Hume does not only say that our conviction of self-identity is erroneous, but gives an account of what generates the supposed error. The causes he lists do not include emotional causes, but we can generate our imaginary proposal if we extend his account to include these. He stresses that the bundle or collection of different perceptions that is a person's life history is one that reveals on examination a large number of inter-relationships between the perceptions within it. It is these inter-relationships that help to disguise the diversity of the contents of the mind from us, and reinforce our belief in its fictional identity. It is their existence to which he draws our attention when he compares the self to a republic or commonwealth. One such interrelationship, on his view, is memory, in which a later perception is a derivative copy of an earlier one. Now it is clear that he might very well say (though in Book I he does not) that some later perceptions are emotional responses to earlier ones. Let us say this for him; and let us now add the suggestion that these relationships are themselves reasons for ascribing identity to the series that includes them. If we think of the relationships as grounds for ascribing identity, it is plausible, though of course not necessary, to add that their absence might be a reason for withholding such an ascription. The analogy with memory is very seductive here, at least for anyone who is prepared to hold that some memory connections with one's own past are necessary and not merely sufficient grounds for calling it one's own. We now have an argument for the view that the emotional concern I show for events in my past is one of the factors that make them a part of it; and that an emotional or emotionless, detachment from it, or in more fashionable parlance an alienation from it, is a ground for not so regarding it. So if I do not feel either proud or ashamed of the deeds of my youth, this is itself a reason for not calling them mine but merely calling them the doings of an ancestral self that used to occupy the body that I now have.

Such a view would have strong appeal to someone who disapproves of emotional absorption in one's past doings. It differs critically from the position I outlined earlier that was also intended to reflect that sort of disapproval. In addition to the major premise that states the undesirability of such absorption, it offers a minor premise to the effect that the later pride and humility help to constitute the identity of the person feeling them with the person who performed those deeds. Consequently the freedom from emotional involvement with one's past that previously appeared as a desirable consequence of the proposed conventional change cannot appear now as a consequence of it at all, but as a condition of the proposed convention having application. So the sense of remoteness and emotional distance that we sometimes experience when we recall our past may be sufficient to constitute a severance from it. And the emotional closeness that pride or shame in it involve may be what keeps it attached to us, like a shell.

There is much in our talk of moral rebirth, conversion, self-estrangement, and even (in its nonphilosophical sense) self-identity, which can, if carelessly interpreted, give such a proposal plausibility. Such talk, however, abounds in metaphor, and to serve its present function, metaphor it must remain. For such language is the language of moral criticism and reformation; and this is a language in which men who vary greatly in their degree and type of emotional concern with their pasts, are judged and compared according to a critic's standards. To apply standards to a group it is requisite that its members be comparable in relevant respects. And men would not be comparable in respect of their estimates and evaluations of their pasts if the nature of those responses themselves determined whether they were their pasts or not. Nor would indifference be an attitude that could be weighed against pride or shame as it has to be if it severed the identity of the agent and they created it. An emotion cannot be well or ill grounded if it creates the grounds on which it is to be judged. It is one thing to say that our concern for our pasts is a burden from which we should be freed, but another thing altogether to say that to eliminate the concern is to eliminate one of its occasions. It is true, of course, that we can be proud or ashamed both of what we regard as part of our own past and of what we regard as connected with ourselves in looser ways. But this does nothing to show that the presence or absence of these emotions, or their strength or weakness, can be a criterion of which type of connection an event or action has.

Perhaps it ought not to be thought important, in judging an emotion, whether what it is a response to is part of the history of the man who has it. This is a moral and not a conceptual thesis. Perhaps it is more important that something leads to certain emotional responses in a man than that it is connected to him by the chain of identity. This too is a moral and not a conceptual thesis. Neither thesis is assisted by the suggestion that the character of the emotional response, or its absence, determines whether it is part of his past or not. On the contrary, both are hindered, for they can only be discussed if there is common agreement on what the criteria are for deciding which things belong to man's past and which do not.

IV

I turn now, more briefly, to the much vaster subject of pride and humility as self-glorification and self-deprecation. These are not naturally spoken of as passions at all, and it is not to Hume that one turns in the first instance for an analysis of them.[14] What follows here will consequently be much more loosely connected with Hume's text than what has gone before.

While particular pride and shame are emotional states of moderate duration, and what one is particularly proud or ashamed of is something connected with oneself, pride and humility are normally of longer duration, and are not episodes in their own right at all. One cannot be suffused with them or overcome by them as one can be with their particular counterparts. One cannot be humble of anything, and the idiom "proud of..." is one whose use indicates particular pride, except in the case of the expression "proud of himself" which may be ambiguous. For to be proud or humble is to estimate oneself very highly or very modestly. It is clear that this estimate has as its object the very subject who makes it, not mere facts connected with him. These facts serve rather as the grounds on which the high or low estimate could be justified. (In this role, incidentally, their ontological heterogeneity, or the appearance of it, vanishes; for things and processes and events only serve in the creation of grounds for anything as constituents of the facts that constitute such grounds.) It is likely that the proud man will feel proud of his own past actions, or his connections, and the humble man feel ashamed of his; but exceptions to this are readily intelligible in specific cases.

The relationship of pride and humility to pleasure and pain is difficult. I have suggested that particular pride and shame entail, if they are not even species of, being pleased and displeased. It is noticeable that there are contexts in which being pleased and displeased are not properly describable as emotional states. Sometimes each seems merely to consist of a favorable or unfavorable appraisal, rather than the emotional condition resulting from it. When the committee says it is pleased to note that the budget is balanced, it is expressing a favorable appraisal of this fact, not recording some emotional state into which its members have been thrown by it. In this context pleasure and displeasure seem to become acts of judgment, not passive emotional conditions that happen to someone. It is in this way that one could say that pleasure and pride, and displeasure and humility, are related: that if I am proud, then I am pleased with myself in that I rate myself favorably, and if I am humble then I am displeased with myself in that I rate myself unfavorably. The pride and the humility are the favorable and unfavorable estimate. The fact that I estimate myself highly causes me to enjoy what I do more, and the fact that I estimate myself poorly causes me to enjoy what I do less, so the proud life is in this distinct sense pleasanter, more enjoyable, than the humble one.

Complexities and ambiguities abound with both notions. Pride is often discussed in theological contexts as though it included all forms of inordinate self-concern or self-absorption, not only those that involve a high estimate of oneself. One very common form of such self-absorption is obsession with one's own inadequacies, so that one can find oneself speaking òf some apparent forms of humility as examples of pride in this sense! It is this very extended understanding of pride as self-centeredness that makes it plausible to argue that concupiscence or sensuality are derivatives of it, in the sense that losing oneself in the concerns of the world and the flesh is a means of hiding one's limitations from one's own sight.[15]

Similarly with humility, though the ambiguities here are less serious. In theological contexts, again, the concept is sometimes widened to cover all cases of the absence of self-absorption, and it is in this wide sense that it is held to be requisite for love or faith.

But since such states are also, in such contexts, said to be the fruits of grace rather than the products of unaided human nature, it is also common to hear that humility in the narrower sense of holding oneself in low esteem, is a necessary concomitant of their appearance. I have to leave these matters aside, and I turn instead to some of the possible criticisms to which pride and humility are subject.

(1) They can be the target of general moral or theological objections. It can be held, for example, that all high estimates of oneself are morally evil, or all low estimates are morally debilitating. Or it can be held that some degree of such estimation is in order, but that marked degrees of the one or the other are never appropriate. Such criticisms, however, are likely to be supported by alleged facts about the nature of human beings which men are said to overlook, for example, that they are finite, or created, or have a will to power which is conventionally suppressed.

(2) There can be specific criticisms of the factual presuppositions of the high or low estimate: that the man's achievements are less than imagined, or his motives mixed, or his motivation not charity but fear. Such criticisms imply that if the facts were as they are imagined by the estimator to be, the pride or the humility would be morally acceptable.

(3) There can be criticisms based on the view that some of the facts that serve to support the pride or humility are not of a kind that should do so—again, this type of argument would take the form, as a rule, of a concentration on the differences between these facts and others that the critic accepts as justifying the high or low appraisal. Here pride because of one's wealth (as opposed to particular pride *in* one's wealth) might be criticized by contrast with pride based on political achievements.

(4) Most importantly for our present purposes, there can be criticisms that concentrate on the relation of the facts that support the estimate to the person who is making it.

These can take three forms: (a) The critic can say that the facts that would justify the high or low appraisal of myself are not facts about *me*—that I did not perform these deeds, but other people, or that the ancestry or association I lay claim to is spurious. (b) He may say that even though the connections with myself are as I believe them to be, they are not the sort of connections with myself that justify my self-estimate: that pride or humility is perhaps justifiable if I have certain achievements or character, but not if based on my ancestor's or fellow members' achievements, even though these may be related to me in the way I say. (c) He may base his attack on an analysis of the self which precludes the identity of the proud or humble man and the bearers of the merits and defects that he claims to be his.

Taken strictly, Hume's analysis of the self in Book I would provide the basis for an attack of the last sort. For if it is correct, the unity ascribed to the person through time is fictitious, and anything done by, or connected with, an earlier stage of a person cannot in consequence, be ascribed to, or said to have the same connection with, a later stage. This would not preclude pride and humility from occurring, but it would make them ineluctably groundless, for they would presuppose that the object of the high or low estimate the subject made incorporated stretches of personal history that it could not incorporate. All other criticisms of pride and humility would be ruled out if this were true, and since Hume recognizes that our self-estimates all proceed as if it were false, he too assumes the truth of his own alleged fiction in his account of pride and humility.

There is an interesting historical contrast to Hume's procedure, one which would have surprised Hume if he had been aware of it, and which has been noticed since. I refer to the doctrines of the Buddha.[16] Buddha is said to have argued that the Hindu view of the self as identical with the cosmic soul is false, somewhat as Hume rejects substantial analyses of the self. And just as Hume infers from the absence of a pure ego that the Unity of the individual which pure ego theories are designed to supply is mythical, so Buddha is said to have gone beyond the denial of the identity of the eternal *atman* to the denial of the conventional belief in the persisting identity of the individual. Such conventional belief is an example of *avidya*, or ignorance, and is a major source of the compulsive craving that is the source of human misery. For only if the self has some degree of permanence does the grasping of things to it hold any intelligible promise of satisfaction. The realization (not of course merely an intellectual matter) that the permanence is not there, that instead there is, as it were, only a hole in the middle, is part of the progress to enlightenment which ultimately releases the soul from craving and the misery attendant upon the service of it. This doctrine parallels strikingly the Augustinian derivation of sensuality from pride as the primal sin.

Hume's response to a similar metaphysical predicament is quite opposite. He finds the supposed falsity of the belief in the unity of the person a source of bewilderment and anxiety, and the only cure for the malaise that a skeptical concentration upon it produces is the careless acceptance of the fiction with which we disguise its falsity from ourselves, and the immersion in the life of passion and social intercourse which the acceptance of this fiction makes possible. Instead of nirvana, there is backgammon. So in Book II, the bewilderments of Book I are left behind them.

If we take the view, as I would, that Hume's perplexity is groundless, and that he has not demonstrated the falsity of our belief in the unity of a person, this does not of itself free us from the need to consider philosophical attempts to question our right to draw the boundaries of the history of individual persons in the ways that we actually draw them, whatever these may be. When this is recognized, we are open once more to the suggestion that our moral and emotional lives would benefit from their being drawn differently. So we can now imagine a parallel to the forms of conceptual revisionism that I imagined earlier when discussing the relationship between particular pride and shame and self-identity. It could be said that our self-estimates might change if they were made in a different context, in which a person was thought to have a past in which those actions or characteristics now included within it were not included, or in which other such actions or characteristics were included which are not included now. I would say here, as before, that a recommendation for conventional change based on this possibility is not incoherent, but is either undesirable or pointless. It could be said, second, that the very presence of such self-estimates now ought to be construed as reasons for including those actions and characteristics offered as grounds for them, and their absence construed as a reason for not including them. I would say here, as before, that such a suggestion makes the character of such judgments one of the conditions of the propriety of their having that character, and thus removes them from the sphere of detached criticism.

In conclusion: Hume may have distinguished between personal

identity as it concerns the thought or imagination, and personal identity as it concerns our passions, merely in order to prevent the skeptical perplexities of Book I from obtruding themselves in Book II. But if we are free of those perplexities we can see that his distinction was a wise one for more than tactical reasons. For whatever the span of the self is taken to be, our emotional life, or that part of it which we have scrutinized here, requires for its logical structure that the span of the self is given. And criticism of the emotional life requires this also. What I take to be myself determines what I can be proud or ashamed of, and not the reverse. The personal identity that concerns the passions has to be one and the same as the personal identity that concerns the thought or imagination. But it is the thought or imagination, and not the passions, that have to determine its boundaries.

NOTES

1. David Hume, "Of Personal Identity," Section VI of Part IV of Book I of *A Treatise of Human Nature.* The quotation appears on p. 253 of the Clarendon Press edition, edited by L. A. Selby-Bigge, reprinted 1968. All references to Hume's texts are to this edition.

2. The issues of interpretation that I pass over here are discussed in a paper "Hume's Theory of the Self Revisited" which is due to appear in a volume of essays on Hume edited by Norman S. Care. References to other interpretations are included there. The fundamental interpretation of the argument of Section VI was originally outlined in my "Hume on Personal Identity," published in the *Philosophical Review*, LXIV (1955), 571-589.

3. There are indeed one or two places in which he explicitly rejects interpretations that would make logical connections out of what he considers to be causal ones. See, for example, his discussion of the relationships between benevolence and love, and anger and hatred, in Section VI of Part II of Book II.

4. Any special problems raised by the doctrine of sympathy are likely to be problems about what I have called the problem of Individuation, which is not my concern here.

5. Hume, pp. 277-278.

6. Ibid., pp. 287-288. "We must suppose, that nature has given to the organs of the human mind, a certain disposition fitted to produce a particular impression or emotion, which we call *pride*: To this emotion she has assigned a certain idea, viz. that of *self*, which it never fails to produce."

7. Páll S. Árdal, *Passion and Value in Hume's Treatise* (Edinburgh: Edinburgh University Press, 1966), 33. I am indebted here to the very helpful discussions in chap. 2 of this work.

8. The distinction corresponds roughly to that Ryle makes in *The Concept of Mind* (London: Hutchinson, 1949), Chapter IV, between motives and agitations.

9. The ambiguity comes out nicely in his remark on p. 297 that "by *pride* I

understand that agreeable impression, which arises in the mind, when the view either of our virtue, beauty, riches or power makes us satisfy'd with ourselves:... by *humility* I mean the opposite impression."

10. Ibid., pp. 288-289.

11. On the distinction between pleasure as enjoyment and pleasure as being pleased, see David Perry, *The Concept of Pleasure* (The Hague: Mouton, 1967), and my essay "Pleasure and Falsity," *American Philosophical Quarterly*, I (1964), 81-91.

12. One can of course be pleased about one's beliefs—I am pleased that I am not a Conservative. But obviously it is the fact that I hold non-Conservative beliefs that pleases me here, not some supposed fact that those non-Conservative beliefs assert.

13. In this connection, see Derek Parfit, "Personal Identity," *Philosophical Review*, LXXX (1971), 3-27. My arguments here run parallel to the criticisms I made of Mr. Parfit's position in "The Importance of Self-Identity," *Journal of Philosophy*, LXVIII (1971), 667-678. (See also Parfit's response, pp. 683-690.) I must emphasize that in the present paper my target is a straw man of my own, and his views are at most suggested to me by Parfit's.

14. There is some temptation to agree with Robert Payne's judgment that "When Hume writes of pride in *A Treatise of Human Nature*, he is like a man scrambling for shell-fish among the rocks" (*Hubris: A Study of Pride* [New York: Harper Torchbooks, 1960], 142). A Humean concern with detail might have saved Payne from going on to say that Hume's "dullness" shows us that "the English *(sic)* have failed to understand pride through most of their history."

15. This very broad extension of the idea of pride is present, for example, in Reinhold Niebuhr, *The Nature and Destiny of Man* (London: Nisbet, 1949), Vol. I, Chaps. VII and VIII.

16. The likeness between the Humean and Buddhist doctrines of the self has certainly been noticed before. It is discussed at length in Nolan Piny Jacobson, *Buddhism: The Religion of Analysis* (London: Allen & Unwin, 1966).

XII

RESPONSIBILITY FOR SELF

CHARLES TAYLOR

What is the notion of responsibility which is bound up with our conception of a person or self? Is there a sense in which the human agent is responsible for himself which is part of our very conception of the self?

This is certainly a commonly held idea, among 'ordinary men' as well as among philosophers. Just to mention two contemporary specimens of the latter breed: H. Frankfurt has made the point (*J. Phil.*, Jan. 1971) that a person is more than just a subject of desires, of choices, even of deliberation; that we attribute to persons the ability to form 'second-order desires': to want to be moved by certain desires, or 'second-order volitions': to want certain first-order desires to be the ones which move them to action.

If we think of what we are as defined by our goals, by what we desire to encompass or maintain, then a person on this view is one who can raise the question: Do I really want to be what I now am? (i.e., have the desires and goals I now have). In other words, beyond the *de facto* characterization of the subject by his goals, desires, and purposes, a person is a subject who can pose the *de jure* question: is this the kind of being I ought to be, or really want to be? There is as Frankfurt puts it a 'capacity for reflective self-evaluation...manifest in the formation of second-order desires' (*J. Phil.*, 7).

Or again, we can invoke Heidegger's famous formula, taken up by Sartre: 'das Seiende, dem es in seinem Sein um dieses selbst geht' (*Sein Und Zeit*, 42). The idea here, at a first approximation, is that the human subject is such that the question arises inescapably, which kind of being he is going to realize. He is not just de facto a certain kind of being, with certain given desires, but it is somehow 'up to' him what kind of being he is going to be.

In both these views we have the notion that human subjects are capable of evaluating what they are, and to the extent that they can shape themselves on this evaluation, are responsible for what they are in a way that other subjects of action and desire (the higher animals for instance) cannot be said to be. It is this kind of evaluation/responsibility which many believe to be essential to our notion of the self.

I

1

What is involved here? Let's look first at evaluation. Of course, in a sense the capacity to evaluate can be ascribed to any subject of desire. My dog 'evaluates' that beefsteak positively. But the kind of evaluation implicit in the above formulations is a reflective kind where we evaluate our desires themselves. It is this plainly which we are tempted to think of as essential to our notion of a self.

But the evaluation of desires or desired consummations can itself be understood in both a weak and a strong sense. To take the weaker sense, an agent could weigh desired actions simply to determine convenience, or how to make different desires compossible—he might resolve to put off eating although hungry, because later he could both eat and swim—or how to get the most over-all satisfaction. But there would not yet be any evaluation in a strong sense where I class desires as being bad or unworthy, or lower; where, in other words, desires are classified in such categories as higher or lower, virtuous or vicious, more or less fulfilling, more or less refined, profound or superficial, noble or base; where they are judged as belonging to qualitatively different modes of life, fragmented or integrated, alienated or free, saintly or merely human, courageous or pusillanimous, and so on.

The difference between a reflection which is couched in qualitative distinctions and one which is not has nothing necessarily to do with calculation. The difference is rather (1) that in the latter reflection for something to be judged good it is sufficient that it be desired, whereas in qualitative reflection there is also a use of 'good' or some other evaluative term for which being desired is not sufficient; indeed some desires or desired consummations can be judged as bad, base, ignoble, trivial, superficial, unworthy, and so on.

It follows from this (2) that when in non-qualitative reflection one desired alternative is set aside, it is only on grounds of its contingent incompatibility with a more desired alternative. But with qualitative reflection this is not necessarily the case. Some desired consummation may be eschewed not because it is incompatible with another, or if because of incompatibility, this will not be contingent. Thus I refrain from committing some cowardly act, although very tempted to do so, but this is not because this act at this moment would make any other desired act impossible, but rather because it is base.

But, of course, there is also a way in which we could characterize this alternative which would bring out incompatibility. If we examine my evaluative vision more closely, we shall see that I value courageous action as part of a mode of life; I aspire to be a certain kind of person. This would be compromised by my giving into this craven impulse. Here there is incompatibility. But this incompatibility is no longer contingent. It is not just a matter of circumstances which makes it impossible to give in to the impulse to flee and still cleave to a courageous, upright mode of life. Such a mode of life *consists* among other things in withstanding such craven impulses.

That there should be incompatibility of a noncontingent kind here is not adventitious, for qualitative reflection deploys a language of evaluative distinctions, in which different desires are described as noble or base, integrating or fragmenting, courageous or cowardly, clairvoyant or blind, and so on. But this means that they are characterized contrastively. Each concept of one of the above pairs can only be understood in relation to the other. No one can have an idea what courage is unless he knows what cowardice is, just as no one can have a notion of 'red', say, without some other colour terms with which it contrasts. And of course with evaluative terms, as with colour terms, the contrast may not just be with one other, but with several. And indeed, refining an evaluative vocabulary by introducing new terms would alter the sense of the existing terms, even as it would with our colour vocabulary.

This means that in qualitative reflection, we can characterize the alternatives contrastively; and indeed, it can be the case that we must do so if we are to express what is really desirable in the favoured alternative. But this is not so with non-qualitative reflection. Of course, in each case we are free to express the alternatives in a number of ways, some of which are and some of which are not contrastive. But if I want to identify the alternatives in terms of their desirability, the characterization ceases to be contrastive. What is going for lunching now is that I'm hungry, and it is unpleasant to wait while one's hungry and a great pleasure to eat. What's going for eating later is that I can swim. But I can identify the pleasures of eating quite independently from those of swimming; indeed, I may have enjoyed eating long before swimming entered my life (and the reverse could conceivably be true, if I spent my childhood eating something revolting like brussel sprouts —although failure to enjoy eating, no matter what one is fed, is probably a psychological impossibility). Not being contrastively described, these two desired consummations are incompatible, where they are, only contingently and circumstantially.

Reciprocally, I can describe the issue of my qualitative reflection non-contrastively. I can say that the choice is between saving my life, or perhaps avoiding pain or embarrassment, on one hand, and upholding my honour on the other. Now certainly I can understand preserving my life, and what is desirable about it, without any acquaintance with honour, and the same goes for avoiding pain and embarrassment. But the reverse is not quite the case. No one could understand 'honour' without some reference to our desire to avoid death, pain, or embarrassment, because one preserves honour among other things by a certain stance towards these. Still saving one's honour is not simply contrastively defined with saving one's life, avoiding pain and so on; there are many cases where one can save one's life without any taint to honour, without the question even arising.

But the case we are imagining is not one of these. Rather we are imagining a situation in which I save my life or avoid pain by some cowardly act. In this situation, the non-contrastive description is a cop-out. I can indeed identify the desirability of the 'lower' alternative in a way which makes no reference to the higher, for here the desirability just is that life is preserved or pain avoided. I am certainly not going to mention that the act is cowardly, for this is not part of what recommends it to me. But things are different when we come to the 'higher' alternative. This is desirable because it is an act of courage, or integrity or honour. And it is an essential part of being courageous that one eschew such craven acts as the 'lower' alternative that here beckons. Someone who doesn't understand this doesn't understand what 'courage' means. The incompatibility here is not contingent.

So in qualitative reflection, where we deploy a language of evaluative distinctions, the rejected desire is not so rejected because of some mere contingent or circumstantial conflict with another goal. Being cowardly doesn't compete with other goods by taking up the time and energy I need to pursue them, and it may not alter my circumstances in such a way as to prevent me pursuing them. The conflict is deeper; it is not contingent.

2

The utilitarian strand in our civilization would induce us to abandon the language of qualitative contrast, and this means, of course, abandon our strong evaluative languages, for their terms are only defined in contrast. And we can be tempted to redefine issues we are reflecting on in this non-qualitative fashion. For instance, let us say that I am addicted to over-eating. Now as I struggle with this addiction, in the reflection in which I determine that moderation or controlling my irritation is better, I can be looking at the alternatives in a language of qualitative contrast. I yearn to be free of this addiction, to be the kind of person whose mere bodily appetites respond to his higher aspirations, and don't carry on remorselessly and irresistibly dragging me to incapacity and degradation.

But then I might be induced to see my problem in a quite different light. I might be induced to see it as a question of quantity of satisfaction. Eating too much cake increases the cholesterol in my blood, makes me fat, ruins my health, prevents me from enjoying all sorts of other desired consummations; so it isn't worth it. Here I have stepped away from the contrastive language of qualitative evaluation. Avoiding high cholesterol content, obesity, ill-health, or being able to climb stairs, and so on, can all be defined quite independently from my eating habits.

This is a conflict of self-interpretations. Which one we adopt will partly shape the meanings things have for us. But the question can arise which is more valid, more faithful to reality. To be in error here is thus not just to make a misdescription, as when I describe a motor vehicle as a car when it is really a truck. We think of misidentification here as in some sense distorting the reality concerned. For the man who is trying to talk me out of seeing my problem as one of dignity versus degradation, I have made a crucial misidentification. But it is not just that I have called a fear of too high cholesterol content by the name 'degradation'; it is rather that infantile fears of punishment or loss or parental love have been irrationally transferred on to obesity, or the pleasures of eating, or something of the sort (to follow a rather vulgar Freudian line). My experience of obesity, eating, and so forth, is shaped by this. But if I can get over this 'hang-up' and see the real nature of the underlying anxiety, I will see that it is largely groundless, that is, I do not really incur the risk of punishment or loss of love; in fact there is a quite other list of things at stake here: ill health, inability to enjoy the outdoor life, early death by heart attack, and so on.

So might go a modern variant of the utilitarian thrust, trying to reduce our qualitative contrasts to some homogeneous medium. In this it would be much more plausible and sophisticated than earlier variants which talked as though it were just a matter of simple misidentification, that what people sought who pined after honour, dignity, integrity, and so on, were simply other pleasurable states to which they gave these high-sounding names.

There are of course ripostes to these attempts to reduce our evaluations to a non-qualitative form. We can entertain the counter-surmise that the rejection of qualitative distinctions is itself an illusion, powered perhaps by an inability to look at one's life in the light of some of these distinctions, a failure of moral nerve, as it were; or else by the draw of a certain objectifying stance towards the world. We might hold that the most hard-bitten utilitarians are themselves moved by qualitative distinctions which remain unadmitted, that they admire the mode of life in which one calculates consciously and clairvoyantly as something higher than the life of self-indulgent illusion, and do not simply elect it as more satisfying.

We can't resolve this issue here. The point of introducing this distinction between qualitative and non-qualitative reflection is to contrast the different kinds of self that each involves. In examining this it will, I think, become overwhelmingly plausible that we are not beings whose only authentic evaluations are non-qualitative as the utilitarian tradition suggests; that if evaluation of desires is essential to our notion of the self, it is strong and not just weak evaluation which is in question.

3

Someone who evaluates non-qualitatively, that is, makes decisions like that of eating now or later, taking a holiday in the north or in the south, might be called a simple weigher of alternatives. And the other, who deploys a language of evaluative contrasts ranging over desires we might call a strong evaluator.

Now we have seen that a simple weigher is already reflective in a minimal sense, that he evaluates courses of action, and sometimes is capable of acting out of that evaluation as against under the impress of immediate desire. And this is a necessary feature of what we call a self or a person. He has reflection, evaluation and will. But in contrast to the strong evaluator he lacks something else which we often speak of with the metaphor of 'depth'.

The strong evaluator envisages his alternatives through a richer language. The desirable is not only defined for him by what he desires, or what he desires plus a calculation of consequences; it is also defined by a qualitative characterization of desires as higher and lower, noble and base, and so on. Where it is not a calculation of consequences, reflection is not just a matter of registering the conclusion that alternative A is more attractive to me, or draws me more than B. Rather the higher desirability of A over B is something I can articulate if I am reflecting a strong evaluator. I have a vocabulary of worth.

Faced with incommensurables, which is our usual predicament, the simple weigher's experiences of the superiority of A over B are inarticulable. The role of reflection is not to make these articulate, but rather to step back from the immediate situation, to calculate consequences, to compensate for the immediate force of one desire which might not be the most advantageous to follow (as when I put off lunch to swim-with-lunch later), to get over hesitation by concentrating on the inarticulate 'feel' of the alternatives.

But the strong evaluator is not similarly inarticulate. There is the beginning of a language in which to express the superiority of one alternative, the language of higher and lower, noble and base, courageous and cowardly, integrated and fragmented, and so on. The strong evaluator can articulate superiority just because he has a language of contrastive characterization. So within an experience of reflective choice between incommensurables, strong evaluation is a condition of articulacy, and to acquire a strongly evaluative language is to become (more) articulate about one's preferences.

The simple weigher's reflection is structured by a number of de facto desires, whereas the strong evaluator ascribes a value to those desires. He characterizes his motivation at greater depth. To characterize one desire or inclination as worthier, or nobler, or more integrated, and so forth, than others is to speak of it in terms of the kind or quality of life which it expresses and sustains. I eschew the cowardly act above because I want to be a courageous and honourable human being. Whereas for the simple weigher what is at stake is the desirability of different consummations, those defined by his de facto desires, for the strong evaluator reflection also examines the different possible modes of life or modes of being of the agent. Motivations or desires don't only count in virtue of the attraction of the consummations but also in virtue of the kind of life and kind of subject that these desires properly belong to.

This is what lies behind our ordinary use of the metaphor of depth applied to people. Someone is shallow in our view when we feel that he is insensitive, unaware, or unconcerned about issues touching the quality of his life which seem to us basic or important. He lives on the surface because he seeks to fulfill desires without being touched by the 'deeper' issues, what these desires express and sustain in the way of modes of life; or his concern with such issues seems to us to touch on trivial or unimportant questions, for example, he is concerned about the glamour of his life, or how it will appear, rather than the (to us) real issues of the quality of life. The complete Utilitarian would be an impossibly shallow character, and we can gauge how much self-declared utilitarians really live their ideology by what importance they attribute to depth.

II

We saw that the strong evaluator reflects in another, deeper sense than the simple weigher, and this because he evaluates in a different way. And after this discussion we can perhaps see why we are tempted to make evaluation, and indeed, strong evaluation, an essential characteristic of a person. For any being who was incapable of evaluating desires (as my dog, e.g., is incapable), or who could only evaluate as a simple weigher, would lack the depth to be a potential interlocutor, a potential partner of human communion, be it as friend, lover, confidant, or whatever. And we cannot see one who could not enter into any of these relations as a normal human subject.

I would like now to turn to examine the notion of responsibility for oneself which goes along with this notion of the agent as a strong evaluator. Naturally we think of the agent as responsible, in part, for what he does; and since he is an evaluator, we think of him as responsible in part for the degree to which he acts in line with his evaluations. But we are also inclined to think of him as responsible in some sense for these evaluations themselves.

This more radical responsibility is even suggested by the word 'evaluation', which belongs to the modern, one might almost say post-Nietzscheian, vocabulary of moral life. For it relates to the verb 'evaluate', and the very term here implies that this is something we do, that our evaluations emerge from our activity of evaluation, and in this sense are our responsibility. This active sense is conveyed in Frankfurt's formulation where he speaks of persons as exhibiting 'reflective self-evaluation that is manifested in the formation of second-order desires'. And when we turn to the quote from Heidegger at the beginning of this paper, the notion of responsibility is strikingly put in the idea that Dasein's being is in question in his being, that the kind of being we are to realize is constantly in question.

How are we to understand this responsibility? An influential strand of thought in the modern world has wanted to understand it in terms of choice. The Nietzschean term 'value', suggested by our 'evaluation', carries this idea that our 'values' are our creations, that they ultimately repose on our espousing them. But to say that they ultimately repose on our espousing them is to say that they issue ultimately from a radical choice, that is, a choice which is not grounded in any reasons. For to the extent that a choice is grounded in reasons, these are simply taken as valid and are not themselves chosen. If our 'values' are to be thought of as chosen, then they must repose finally on a radical choice in the above sense.

This is, of course, the line taken by Sartre in *L'Etre et le Néant*, in which he translates verbatim the quote above from Heidegger and gives it this sense that the fundamental project which defines us reposes on a radical choice. The choice, Sartre puts it with his characteristic flair for striking formulae, is 'absurde, en ce sens qu'il est ce par quoi toutes les raisons viennent à l'étre.'* This idea of radical choice is also defined by an influential Anglo-Saxon school of moral philosophers.

But in fact we cannot understand our responsibility for our evaluations through the notion of radical choice. Not if we are to go on seeing ourselves as strong evaluators, as agents with depth. For a radical choice *between* strong evaluations is quite conceivable, but not a radical choice *of* such evaluations. To see this we might examine a famous Sartrian example, which turns out, I believe, to illustrate the exact opposite of Sartre's thesis, the example in *L'Existentialisme est un Humanisme* of the young man who is torn between remaining with his ailing mother and going off to join the Resistance. Sartre's point is that there is no way of adjudicating between these two strong claims on his moral allegiance through reason or the reliance on some kind of considerations. He has to settle the question, whichever way he goes, by radical choice.

Sartre's portrayal of the dilemma is very powerful here. But what makes it plausible is precisely what undermines his position. We see a grievous moral dilemma because the young man is faced here with two powerful moral *claims*. On one hand his ailing mother who may well die if he leaves her, and die in the most terrible sorrow, not even sure that her son still lives; on the other side the call of his country, conquered and laid waste by the enemy, and not only his country, for this enemy is destroying the very foundation of civilized and ethical relations between men. A cruel

---

L'Etre et le Néant (Paris, 1943), p. 559.

dilemma, indeed. But it is a dilemma only because the claims themselves are not created by radical choice. If they were, the grievous nature of the predicament would dissolve, for that would mean that the young man could do away with the dilemma at any moment by simply declaring one of the rival claims as dead and inoperative. Indeed, if serious moral claims were created by radical choice, the young man could have a grievous dilemma about whether to go and get an ice cream cone, and then again he could decide not to.

It is no argument against the view that evaluations do not repose on radical choice that there are moral dilemmas. Why should it even be surprising that the evaluations we feel called upon to assent to may conflict, even grievously, in some situations? I would argue that the reverse is the case, that moral dilemmas become inconceivable on the theory of radical choice. Now in this hypothetical case the young man has to resolve the matter by radical choice. He just has to plump for the Resistance, or for staying at home with his mother. He has no language in which the superiority of one alternative over the other can be articulated; indeed, he has not even an inchoate sense of the superiority of one over the other, they seem quite incommensurable to him. He just throws himself one way.

This is a perfectly understandable sense of radical choice. But then imagine extending this to all cases of moral action. Let us apply it to the case that I have an ailing mother and no rival obligation, as to the Resistance. Do I stay, or do I go for a holiday on the Riviera? There is no question, I should stay. Of course, I may not stay. In this sense, there is always a 'radical choice' open: whether to do what we ought or not. But the question is whether we can construe the determination of what we ought to do here as issuing from a radical choice. What would this look like? Presumably, we would be faced with the two choices, to stay with my mother or to go south. On the level of radical choice these alternatives have as yet no contrastive characterization, that is, one is not the path of duty, while the other is that of selfish indulgence, or whatever.

This contrastive description will be created by radical choice. So what does this choice consist in? Well, I might ponder the two possibilities, and then I might just find myself doing one rather than another. But this brings us to the limit where choice fades into non-choice. Do I really choose if I just start doing one of the alternatives? And above all this kind of resolution has no place for the judgement 'I owe it to my mother to stay', which is supposed to issue from the choice. What is it to have this judgement issue from radical choice? Not that on pondering the alternatives, the sense grows more and more strongly that this judgement is *right*, for this would not be an account of radical choice, but rather of our coming to see that our obligation lay here. This account would present obligations as issuing not from radical choice but from some kind of vision of our moral predicament. This choice would be grounded. What is it then for radical choice to issue in this judgement? Is it just that I find myself assenting to the judgement, as above I found myself doing one of the two actions? But then what force has 'assenting to the judgement'? I can certainly just find myself saying 'I owe it to my mother', but this is surely not what it is to assent. I can, I suppose, find myself feeling suddenly, 'I owe this to my mother'; but then what grounds are there for thinking of this as a *choice*?

In order for us to speak of choice, we cannot just find ourselves in one of the alternatives. We have in some sense to experience the pull of each and give our assent to one. But what kind of pull do the alternatives have here? What draws me to the Cote d'Azur is perhaps unproblematic enough, but what draws me to stay with my mother cannot be the sense that I owe it to her, for that ex hypothesi has to issue from the choice.

The agent of radical choice has to choose, if he chooses at all, like a simple weigher. And this means that he cannot be properly speaking a strong evaluator. For all his putative strong evaluations issue from simple weighings. The application of a contrastive language which makes a preference articulate reposes on fiat, a choice made between incommensurables. But then the application of the contrastive language would be in an important sense bogus. For by hypothesis the experience on which this application reposed would be more properly characterized by a preference between incommensurables; the fundamental experience which was supposed to justify this language would in fact be that of the simple weigher, not of the strong evaluator. For again by hypothesis, what leads him to call one alternative higher or more worthy is not that in his experience it appears to be so, for then his evaluations would be judgements, not choices; but rather that he is led to plump for one rather than the other after considering the attractiveness of both alternatives.

The paradox of the theory of radical choice is that it seems to make the universal feature of moral experience what we identify as the failing of rationalization, dressing up as a moral choice what is really a de facto preference. In fact, however, proponents of the theory would vigorously contest what I have just said; for they see the ideal agent not as a rationalizer, but as one who is aware of his choices.

Perhaps then it is that in radical choice I don't consult preferences at all. It is not that I try to see which I prefer, and then failing to get a result, I throw myself one way or the other; but rather, this kind of choice is made quite without regard to preferences. But then with regard to what is it made? Here we border on incoherence. A choice made without regard to anything, without the agent feeling any solicitation to one alternative or the other, or in complete disregard of such solicitation, is this still choice? But if this is a choice and not just an inexplicable movement, it must have been accompanied by something like: 'damn it, why should I always choose by the book? I'll take B'; or maybe he just suddenly felt that he really wanted B. In either case his choice clearly relates to his preference, however suddenly arising and from whatever reversal of criteria. But a choice utterly unrelated to the desirability of the alternatives would not be intelligible as a choice.

The theory of radical choice in fact is deeply incoherent, for it wants to maintain both strong evaluation and radical choice. It wants to have strong evaluations and yet deny their status as judgements. In fact it maintains a semblance of plausibility by surreptitiously assuming strong evaluation beyond the reach of radical choice, and that in two ways. First, the real answer to our attempted assimilation of radical moral choice to the mere preference of a simple weigher is that the choices talked about in the theory are about basic and fundamental issues, like the choice of our young man above between his mother and the Resistance. But these issues are basic and fundamental not in virtue of radical choice; their importance is given, or revealed, in an evaluation which is constated not chosen. The real force of the theory of radical choice comes from the sense that there are different moral perspectives, that there is a plurality of moral visions, as we said in the previous section, between which it seems very hard to adjudicate. We can conclude that the only way of deciding between these is by the kind of radical choice that our young man had to take.

And this in turn leads to a second strong evaluation beyond the reach of choice. If this is the predicament of man, then it plainly is a more honest, more clairvoyant, less confused and self-deluding stance, to be aware of this and take the full responsibility for the radical choice. The stance of 'good faith' is higher, and this not in virtue of radical choice, but in virtue of our characterization of the human predicament in which radical choice has such an important place. Granted this is the moral predicament of man, it is more honest, courageous, self-clairvoyant, hence a higher mode of life, to choose in lucidity than it is to hide one's choices behind the supposed structure of things, to flee from one's responsibility at the expense of lying to oneself, of a deep self-duplicity.

When we see what makes the theory of radical choice plausible, we see how strong evaluation is something inescapable in our conception of the agent and his experience; and this because it is bound up with our notion of the self. So that it creeps back in even where it is supposed to have been excluded.

III

What then is the sense we can give to the responsibility of the agent, if we are not to understand it in terms of radical choice? There is in fact another sense in which we are radically responsible. Our evaluations are not chosen. On the contrary they are articulations of our sense of what is worthy, or higher, or more integrated, or more fulfilling, and so forth. But this sense can never be fully or satisfactorily articulated. And moreover it touches on matters where there is so much room for self-deception, for distortion, for blindness and insensitivity, that the question can always arise whether one is sure, and the injunction is always in place to look again.

We touch here on a crucial feature of our evaluations—one which has given some of its plausibility to the theory of radical choice. They are not simply descriptions, if we mean by this characterizations of a fully independent object, that is, an object which is neither altered in what it is, nor in the degree or manner of its evidence to us by the description. In this way my characterization of this table as brown, or this line of mountains as jagged, is a simple description.

Our strong evaluations may be called by contrast articulations, that is, they are attempts to formulate what is initially inchoate, or confused, or badly formulated. But this kind of formulation or re-formulation doesn't leave its object unchanged. To give a certain articulation is to shape our sense of what we desire or what we hold important in a certain way.

Let us take the case above of the man who is fighting obesity and who is talked into seeing it as a merely quantitative question of more satisfaction, rather than as a matter of dignity and degra-dation. As a result of this change, his inner struggle itself becomes transformed, it is now quite a different experience. The opposed motivations—the craving for cream cake and his dissatisfaction with himself at such indulgence—which are the 'objects' under-going redescription here, are not independent in the sense outlined above. When he comes to accept the new interpretation of his desire to control himself, this desire itself has altered. True, it may be said on one level to have the same goal, that he stop eating cream cake, but since it is no longer understood as a seeking for dignity and self-respect it has become quite a different kind of motivation.

Of course, even here we often try to preserve the identity of the objects undergoing redescription—so deeply rooted is the ordinary descriptive model. We might think of the change, say, in terms of some immature sense of shame and degradation being detached from our desire to resist over-indulgence, which has now simply the rational goal of increasing over-all satisfaction. In this way we might maintain the impression that the elements are just re-arranged while remaining the same. But on a closer look we see that on this reading, too, the sense of shame doesn't remain self-identical through the change. It dissipates altogether, or becomes something quite different.

Thus our descriptions of our motivations, and our attempts to formulate what we hold important, are not simple descriptions, in that their objects are not fully independent. And yet they are not simply arbitrary either, such that anything goes. There are more or less adequate, more or less truthful, more self-clairvoyant or self-deluding interpretations. Because of this double fact, because an articulation can be *wrong*, and yet it shapes what it is wrong about, we sometimes see erroneous articulations as involving a distortion of the reality concerned. We don't just speak of error but frequently also of illusion or delusion.

We could put the point this way. Our attempts to formulate what we hold important must, like descriptions, strive to be faithful to something. But what they strive to be faithful to is not an independent object with a fixed degree and manner of evidence, but rather a largely inarticulated sense of what is of decisive importance. An articulation of this 'object' tends to make it something different from what it was before. And by the same token a new articulation doesn't leave its 'object' evident or obscure to us in the same manner or degree as before. In the act of shaping it, it makes it accessible and/or inaccessible in new ways. Because articulations partly shape their objects in these two ways, they are intrinsically open to challenge in a way that simple descriptions are not. Evaluation is such that there is always room for re-evaluation. But our evaluations are the more open to challenge precisely in virtue of the very character of depth which we see in the self. For it is precisely the deepest evaluations which are least clear, least articulated, most easily subject to illusion and distortion. It is those which are closest to what I am as a subject, in the sense that shorn of them I would break down as a person, which are among the hardest for me to be clear about.

The question can always be posed: ought I to re-evaluate my most basic evaluations? Have I really understood what is essential to my identity? Have I truly determined what I sense to be the highest mode of life? This kind of re-evaluation will be radical, not in the sense of radical choice, however, that we choose without criteria, but rather in the sense that our looking again can be so undertaken that in principle no formulations are considered unrevisable.

What is of fundamental importance for us will already have an articulation, some notion of a certain mode of life as higher than others, or the belief that some cause is the worthiest that can be served; or the sense that belonging to this community is essential to my identity. A radical re-evaluation will call these formulations into question. But a re-evaluation of this kind, once embarked on, is of a peculiar sort. It is unlike a less than radical evaluation which is carried on within the terms of some fundamental evaluation, when I ask myself whether it would be honest to take advantage of this income-tax loophole, or smuggle something through customs. These latter can be carried on in a language which is out of dispute. In answering the questions just mentioned the term 'honest' is taken as beyond challenge. But in radical re-evaluations the most basic terms, those in which other evaluations are carried on, are precisely what is in question. It is just because all formulations are potentially under suspicion of distorting their objects that we have to see them all as revisable, that we are forced back, as it were, to the inarticulate limit from which they originate.

How then can such re-evaluations be carried on? There is certainly no metalanguage available in which I can assess rival self-interpretations. If there were, this would not be a radical re-evaluation. On the contrary the re-evaluation is carried on in the formulae available, but with a stance of attention, as it were, to what these formulae are meant to articulate and with a readiness to receive any gestalt shift in our view of the situation, any quite innovative set of categories in which to see our predicament, that might come our way in inspiration.

Anyone who has struggled with a philosophical problem knows what this kind of enquiry is like. In philosophy typically we start off with a question, which we know to be badly formed at the outset. We hope that in struggling with it, we shall find that its terms are transformed, so that in the end we will answer a question which we couldn't properly conceive at the beginning. We are striving for conceptual innovation which will allow us to illuminate some matter, say an area of human experience, which would otherwise remain dark and confused. The alternative is to stick to certain fixed terms (are these propositions synthetic or analytic, is this a psychological question or a philosophical question, is this view monist or dualist?).

The same contrast can exist in our evaluations. We can attempt a radical re-evaluation, in which case we may hope that our terms will be transformed in the course of it; or we may stick to certain favoured terms, insist that all evaluations can be made in their ambit, and refuse any radical questioning. To take an extreme case, someone can adopt the utilitarian criterion and then claim to settle all further issues about action by some calculation.

The point has been made again and again by non-naturalists, existentialists and others that those who take this kind of line are ducking a major question, should I really decide on the utilitarian principle? But this doesn't mean that the alternative to this stance is a radical choice. Rather it is to look again at our most fundamental formulations, and at what they were meant to articulate, in a stance of openness, where we are ready to accept any categorical change, however radical, which might emerge. Of course we will actually start thinking of particular cases, e.g., where our present evaluations recommend things which worry us, and try to puzzle further. In doing this we will be like the philosopher with his initially ill-formed question. But we may get through to something deeper.

In fact this stance of openness is very difficult. It may take discipline and time. It is difficult because this form of evaluation is deep in a sense, and total in a sense that the other less than radical ones are not. If I am questioning whether smuggling a radio into the country is honest, or I am judging everything by the utilitarian criterion, then I have a yardstick, a definite yardstick. But if I go to the radical questioning, then it is not exactly that I have no yardstick, in the sense that anything goes, but rather that what takes the place of the yardstick is my deepest unstructured sense of what is important, which is as yet inchoate and which I am trying to bring to definition. I am trying to see reality afresh and form more adequate categories to describe it. To do this I am trying to open myself, use all of my deepest, unstructured sense of things in order to come to a new clarity.

Now this engages me at a depth that using a fixed yardstick does not. I am in a sense questioning the inchoate sense that led me to use the yardstick. And at the same time it engages my whole self in a way that judging by a yardstick does not. This is what makes it uncommonly difficult to reflect on our fundamental evaluations. It is much easier to take up the formulations that come most readily to hand, generally those which are going the rounds of our milieu or society, and live within them without too much probing. The obstacles in the way of going deeper are legion. There is not only the difficulty of such concentration, and the pain of uncertainty, but also all the distortions and repressions which make us want to turn away from this examination; and which make us resist change even when we do re-examine ourselves. Some of our evaluations may in fact become fixed and compulsive, so that we cannot help feeling guilty about X, or despising people like Y, even though we judge with the greatest degree of openness and depth at our command that X is perfectly all right, and that Y is a very admirable person. This casts light on another aspect of the term 'deep', as applied to people. We consider people deep to the extent, inter alia, that they are capable of this kind of radical self-reflection.

This radical evaluation is a deep reflection, and a self-reflection in a special sense: it is a reflection about the self, its most fundamental issues, and a reflection which engages the self most wholly and deeply. Because it engages the whole self without a fixed yardstick it can be called a personal reflection (the parallel to Polanyi's notion of personal knowledge is intended here); and what emerges from it is a self-resolution in a strong sense, for in this reflection the self is in question; what is at stake is the definition of those inchoate evaluations which are sensed to be essential to our identity.

Because this self-resolution is something we do, when we do it, we can be called responsible for ourselves; and because it is within limits always up to us to do it, even when we don't—indeed, the nature of our deepest evaluations constantly raises the question whether we have them right—we can be called responsible in another sense for ourselves whether we undertake this radical evaluation or not. This is perhaps Heidegger's notion in *Sein und Zeit* quoted above that human beings are such that their being is in question in their being, that is, their fundamental evaluations are by the very nature of this kind of subject always in question.

And it is this kind of responsibility for oneself, I would maintain, not that of radical choice, but the responsibility for radical evaluation implicit in the nature of a strong evaluator, which is essential to our notion of a person.

A LITERARY POSTSCRIPT: CHARACTERS, PERSONS, SELVES, INDIVIDUALS

AMELIE OKSENBERG RORTY

The concept of a person is not a concept that stands still, hospitably awaiting an analysis of its necessary and sufficient conditions. Our vocabulary for describing persons, their powers, limitations, and alliances is a very rich one. By attending to the nuances of that vocabulary we can preserve the distinctions that are often lost in the excess of zeal that is philosophic lust in action: abducting a concept from its natural home, finding conditions that explain the possibility of any concept in that area, and then legislating that the general conditions be treated as the core essential analysis of each of the variants. Such legislation—enshrining general and necessary preconditions as essential paradigms—is tantamount to arbitrary rule. We have not furnished an argument that socially defined entities such as nations, families, and persons, varying culturally and historically in their extensions and the criteria for their differentiation, have a place in a tidy taxonomic tree, neatly defined by genera, species, and varieties. Nor could such a proof be constructed, because there is not one to be had. Because the definitions of such entities change historically, forced by changes in social conditions and in answer to one another's weighty inconsistencies, there are layers and accretions of usages that can neither be forced into a taxonomy nor be safely amputated.

"Heroes," "characters," "protagonists," "actors," "agents," "persons," "souls," "selves," "figures," "individuals" are all distinguishable. Each inhabits a different space in fiction and in

society. Some current controversies about criteria for personal
identity, for characterizing and reidentifying human individuals,
are impasses because the parties in the dispute have each selected
distinct strands in a concept that has undergone dramatic historical changes; each has tried to make his strand serve as the central
continuous thread. But criteria for reidentifying characters are different from those for reidentifying figures, and both differ from
the criteria that identify selves or individuals. The concept of a
person is but one in the area for which it has been used as a general
class name. There is good reason for this; but we cannot understand that reason until we trace the historical sequence. The explanation of the recent concentration on the criteria for personal
identity, rather than character identity or individual identity, is not
that it is logically prior to the other concepts in that area, but that
it affords a certain perspective on human agency. Before we can
see what has seemed central about personal identity, we must trace
the history of the notion.

Characters are delineated; their traits are sketched; they are not
presumed to be strictly unified. They appear in novels by Dickens,
not those by Kafka. Figures appear in cautionary tales, exemplary
novels and hagiography. They present narratives of types of lives
to be imitated. Selves are possessors of their properties. Individuals are centers of integrity; their rights are inalienable. Presences
are descendants of souls; they are evoked rather than represented,
to be found in novels by Dostoyevsky, not those by Jane Austen.

The effects of each of these on us and our political uses of their
various structures differ radically. Indeed, we are different entities
as we conceive ourselves enlightened by these various views. Our
powers of actions are different, our relations to one another, our
properties and proprieties, our characteristic successes and defeats, our conceptions of society's proper strictures and freedoms
will vary with our conceptions of ourselves as characters, persons,
selves, individuals.

I want to give a skeleton outline of some of the intellectual,
emotional, and social spaces in which each of these move and have
their being, to depict their structures, their tonalities and functions. I shall perforce use the expressions "person" and "individual" neutrally, to designate the entire class of expressions that
refer to the entities we have invented ourselves to be, but I shall

argue that this usage does not reflect the ontological or the logical priority of those concepts.

CHARACTERS

In beginning with characters, we have already leaped some distance into the story: the Greek concept of character has itself already tamed, socialized, naturalized heroes and protagonists. The fate of heroes is their parentage. To be the child of Athene or of the house of Atreus fixes the major events of one's life, determine one's tasks, and even one's capacities to meet them. Yet at the same time the hero is known by his deeds: setting himself superhuman tasks, providing himself worthy of divine regard, his achievements are in the end acts of heroism rather than heroic performances. What was originally a performance of great deeds becomes courage and endurance in the face of fate and chance; what was originally a test of prowess became fortitude in the recognition of finitude. As the hero's distance from the gods increases, his heroism comes to be exemplified in his character rather than in sheer glory of his action.

Between the hero and the character stands the protagonist: the one who, through successful and bold combat, reveals his true nature, in ancient terms, his lineage. Such protagonists were often foundlings, whose *agones* with forces that might be thought beyond one of such birth revealed their true powers and thus their parentage. But this subtle shift emphasizes the powers of the protagonist, powers revealed in his *agones*; and it is now these powers that determine who he really is.

Oedipus begins as an epic hero, as the king; but he undergoes a new as well as old *agon*, and so ends by depicting the drama of one who has achieved character. He revealed himself to be not only the king but kingly. He transcended—and fulfilled—his fatal lineage. In comparison to heroes, characters are set in *bas relief*; they *are* their individual powers and dispositions. That their stories are set by oracles and inheritance is less important to their identification than the traits manifest in the ways they fulfill prophecy and work through their inheritance. Both strands are still present, but the order of significance is reversed, the brocade turned inside out.

The characters of speech and writing are the sketches and lines of which language is composed, the elementary signs from which complex structures of meaning are constructed. There is all the comfort and sanity of closure: finite rules of combination and transformation make language, narrative, and social life possible. The qualities of characters are the predictable and reliable manifestations of their dispositions: and it is by these dispositions that they are identified. The elements of character tend to become stoic rather than elemental forces. Theophrastus' characters remain fixed; they are not transformed by the unfolding of events. On the contrary, their dispositional characteristics allow them to be used to develop a narrative or to stabilize the structure of a society. Characters are, by nature, defined and delineated. If they change, it is because it is in their character to do so under specific circumstances. Their natures form their responses to experiences, rather than being formed by them.

In its origins, the psychological theory of character derives traits and temperaments, dispositionally analyzed, from the balance of elements constituting an individual. The psychology of character rests in physiology. Since the elements out of which characters are composed are repeatable and their configurations can be reproduced, a society of characters is in principle a society of repeatable and indeed replaceable individuals. In a world of characters, the criteria of identification are not designed to isolate unique individuals; the criteria of reidentification are not criteria of individuation. What is of interest is the configuration of reliable traits, the range of habits and dispositions, the structure of their interaction under various sorts of circumstance and stress, as they age. The physical constitutions of misers or people with choleric or sanguine temperaments will set the ways in which they develop habits under various sorts of social conditions; within limits, it is their character that determines their responses to social and environmental conditions, rather than these conditions determining their character.

In the theory of character there is no mind-body problem: without reducing either to the other, physical and psychological traits are fused as different aspects of a single organism. Mind is the organization of the living body, whose "parts" are identifiable through their functional activity. What cannot see is not really an eye but only the sort of flesh that normally is eye-flesh. Soul is not a separate substance lodged in the body; it is the living principle, the organic force of some sorts of substances.

Nor do characters have identity crises: they are not presumed to be strictly unified. Dispositional traits form an interlocking pattern, at best mutually supportive but sometimes tensed and conflicted. There is no presumption of a core that owns these dispositions. Some characters are sparsely defined and tightly organized; others flow in complex systems reaching diagonally out of an imaginary frame, with little need for harmony among the main lines of their development. Disharmony among characteristics bodes trouble: it is likely to lead to failure in action, but not to a crisis of identity. Because characters are defined by their characteristics rather than by the ultimate principles that guide their choices, form their souls, they need not in normal circumstances force or even face the question of which of their dispositions is dominant. Of course a character may find himself in tragic circumstances with his dispositions in destructive conflict. When this happens in such a way that no resolution is available, a character can indeed be torn. Sometimes the dispositions he reveals when he is sundered reveal his grandeur; but these resplendent dispositions are no more the core of a unique individuality than are the dispositions that conflicted with one another. The character is the entire configuration, without the traits seen as layers with a core holding them together.

To know what sort of character a person is, is to know what sort of life is best suited to bring out his potentialities and functions. Theories of the moral education of characters have strong political consequences. Not all characters are suited to the same sorts of lives: there is no ideal type for them all, even when, according to some social needs or social theories, they are hierarchically arranged. If one tries to force the life of a bargainer on the character of a philosopher, one is likely to encounter trouble, sorrow, and the sort of evil that comes from mismatching life and temperament. Characters formed within one society and living in circumstances where their dispositions are no longer needed—characters in time of great social change—are likely to be tragic. Their virtues lie useless or even foiled; they are no longer recognized for what they *are*; their motives and actions are misunderstood. (The magnanimous man in a petty bourgeois society is seen as a vain fool;

the energetic and industrious man in a society that prizes elegance above energy is seen as a bustling boor; the meditative person in an expansive society is seen as melancholic. Such subtle versions of the theory of character as Aristotle's emphasize the duality of habits, showing how habits that can be exercised for good are the very same habits that can effect harm. Only the empowered are capable of either vice or virtue. Two individuals of the same character will fare differently in different polities, not because their characters will change through their experiences (though different aspects will become dominant or recessive) but simply because a good fit of character and society can conduce to well-being and happiness, while a bad fit produces misery and rejection. Both generate characteristic flowering or decay. Societies at war give courageous characters a large scope, good latitudes for power and action; the same character will lie fallow and unused, restless in societies that prize aesthetic or religious contemplation. A courageous man will find his character exercised and his life fulfilled in the former society, but is likely to be regarded and so become a factious and angry man in the latter.

In fiction, characters are dear to us because they are predictable, because they entitle us to the superiority of gods who can lovingly forsee and thus more readily forgive what is fixed. "To be a character" is to maintain a few qualities, nourish them to excess until they dominate and dictate all others. A character is delineated and thus generally delimited. To "have character" is to have reliable qualities, to hold tightly to them through the temptations to swerve and change. A person of character is neither bribed nor corrupted; he stands fast, is steadfast. Of course there are, at all times and places, social and political pressures on people to think of themselves as characters, people of character, whose public performances are reliable. Before the contrast of "inner" and "outer" comes into play, characters are seen externally, their choices and decisions flow predictably from their constitutions and temperaments. There is not a moment when the inner voice speaks while the outer body is silent. Politically, characters are stable, their roles and even their occupations follow from their natures, *are* their natures.

Because characters are public persons, even their private lives can have universal form, general significance. The dramatic character, writ large, can represent for everyman what only later came to be thought of as the inner life of some; it can portray the myth, the conflicts, reversals and discoveries of each person, each *polis*.

FIGURES

Figures are defined by their place in an unfolding drama; they are not assigned roles because of their traits, but rather have the traits of their prototypes in myth or sacred script. Figures are characters writ large, become figureheads; they stand at the prow leading the traveler, directing the ship.

Biblical and sacred literature provide the figures of the stories of Adam and Christ, the stories of fall and redemption; the Homeric poems also present their cast. In more recent literature, Charles Williams and C. S. Lewis are, rather self-consciously, trying to revive not only a type of literature but an interpretation of human agency. Like some of Faulkner's people, they present us with figures in modern dress.

Sometimes figures are identified by their occupations. Smithies, for instance, are figures of Hephaestus: a smithy is generally a strong, dark, silent man with a limp, betrayed by his wife, vengeful, moved by inarticulate and smoldering passions. Most figures are not, however, identified by their occupations nor by their social roles. Both their roles and their traits emerge from their place in an ancient narrative. The narration, the plot, comes first: it requires a hero, a betrayer, a lover, a messenger, a confidant. Juliet's nurse is the descendant of Phaedra's nurse and of the maids-confidant in Roman comedy. Of course the figures in Christian dramas—the pilgrim, the tempter, the savior, the innocent—are derived from the biblical stories.

Though figures become allegorical, they were, in their earliest appearances, far from being abstractions. They were fully embodied. Endowed with apparently accidental physical characterizations—Hephaestus' limp, the Nurses warts and stoutness, the scholar's long red nose—they became vivid, experienced. But far from being individuating, these traits run true to type, even in their concreteness and specificity. These details are not of course meant to represent versimilitude; rarely is the whole picture presented. Rather, one or two physical details are focused upon, to make a presence salient. Vividness is often taken to be a mark of the real; but it may do so because it is an intensification of the act of attention, rather than a representation of what is visualized. What captures us defines the real for us.

When Miranda is represented as the ingenue figure she is, her experiences will be given order and shaped by her figurative type. An ingenue is someone who finds the marvelous, the novel in each experience. A confidante is someone whose daily experiences crystallize, shaped by the confidences of the day. She may have gone to buy fish, but what *really* happened was the sharing of confidences.

A figure is neither formed by nor owns experiences: his figurative identity shapes the significances and order of the events in his life. Figures of course become exemplary. In late literary traditions, they are used in the genre of the cautionary tale; like the saints, they present lives to be imitated. Based in fact, they are of course idealizations: that is precisely their function. Plutarch's *Lives* straddles genres: written to depict heroic characters, they were read as presenting inspirational models to be imitated, to guide lives and choices. The stories, the discoveries and reversals, the recognition that lives can be narratively and formally isomorphic sets the condition for the possibility of imitation. Autobiographies of revolutionary heroes, the diaries of Che Guevara or letters from Debray, present the same type and have the same function: they are hagiography.

Individuals who regard themselves as figures watch the unfolding of their lives following the patterns of their archtypes. Rather than making their choices following their characteristic dispositions, they regard these dispositions as ordered by an ancestral type. They are Mary or Martha, Peter or Paul. Interpreting their lives by their models, they form the narratives of their lives and make their choices according to the pattern, even sometimes to the point of accentuating some of their physical characteristics, so that they dominate over others.

In contrast with the wholly external perspective on characters, the concept of a figure introduces the germ of what will become a distinction between the inner and the outer person. An individual's perspective on his model, his idealized real figure, is originally externally presented, but it becomes internalized, becomes the internal model of self-representation. Of course in earlier forms, an individual does not choose his figurative type: he is an instance of that type and must discover rather than choose his true identity. But later individuals are thought of as deciding on their figurative identity; with this shift from discovery to choice, we come to the concept of person.

PERSONS

Our idea of persons derives from two sources: one from the theater, the *dramatis personae* of the stage; the other has its origins in law. An actor dons masks, literally *per sonae,* that through which the sound comes, the many roles he acts. A person's roles and his place in the narrative devolve from the choices that place him in a structural system, related to others. The person thus comes to stand behind his roles, to select them and to be judged by his choices and his capacities to act out his personae in a total structure that is the unfolding of his drama.

The idea of a person is the idea of a unified center of choice and action, the unit of legal and theological responsibility. Having chosen, a person acts, and so is actionable, liable. It is in the idea of action that the legal and the theatrical sources of the concept of person come together. Only when a legal system has abandoned clan or family responsibility, and individuals are seen as primary agents, does the class of persons coincide with the class of biological individual human beings. In principle, and often in law, they need not. The class of persons may include what would, in other contexts, be institutions or corporations. Or an individual human being may be regarded as a host of personae, each of which is a distinct and unified agent, a locus of responsibility for a range of choices and actions.

If judgment summarizes a life, as it does in the Christian drama, then that life must have a unified location. Since they choose from their natures or are chosen by their stories, neither characters nor figures need be equipped with a will, not to mention a free will. Of course they can fail to do what they intend, and can intend to do less than they could perform. But the actions of characters and figures do not emerge from the exercise of a single faculty or power: there is no need for a single source of responsibility. But once there is the idea of judgment, especially if it is eternal judgment with heaven and hell and the whole person languishing there even if it is only a crucial part that has ailed or failed, then all that is various and loosely structured in the practice of assigning responsibility to diffuse character traits must be brought together and centered in a unified system, if not actually a unity. It is then that persons are required to unify the capacity for choice with the capacities for action.

Characters can be arranged along a continuum of powers and gifts, but personhood is an all-or-none attribution. One is either legally empowered or one isn't; one is either liable or not. Degrees of excusability can be granted only after liability is accepted. The Christian theological conception of judgment is obviously rooted in a legal context, one that, in its Roman origins, did not treat every human being as a person. As neither women nor slaves could originate suits, others had to act on their behalf. But of course when women and slaves are not legal persons, they are not persons either. Whatever rights and liabilities they had, were theirs by virtue of their being sentient, or by virtue of being members of a family. In fusing the legal and dramatic concepts of person, Christianity made every human being with a will, qualify as a person, in order to make them all equally qualified to receive divine judgment. With this introduction of a conception of unitary and equal persons, Christianity at one stroke changed both the rule of law and the idea of persons.

Interest in the dispositional traits of characters is primarily social and practical; it is concerned with the allocation of responsibilities. Interest in persons is moral and legal, arising from problems in locating liability. This shift in the conception of agency carries a shift in the focal interest of moral education. In the eyes of God, persons are all alike; there is one ideal type by which all are judged. Of course any complex society must have a variety of roles to be filled: there must be the lives of the bakers and diggers, as well as that of the king. Their virtues and defects in these occupations, like their virtues and defects as sons and husbands, turn out to be incidental to their following the moral law. It is the formation of intention rather than the habits of action which are crucial to the moral education of a person. This separation marks the beginning of the separation of morality from practical life, duty from prudence. When the obligations entailed by social roles are distinct from moral obligations, a person's moral essence becomes completely internal and private. No longer is the internal model derived from the external type: the external type becomes judged by the internal motive.

Personal integrity or disintegration will of course be manifest in the tonality of actions and habits; nevertheless, it is the intentions, the capacities for choice rather than the total configuration of traits which defines the person. Here the stage is set for identity crises, for wondering who one *really* is, behind the multifold variety of actions and roles. And the search for that core person is not a matter of curiosity: it is a search for the principles by which choices are to be made.

When the paradigms of persons are actors who choose their roles, a person is a player and worldliness consists of his ability to enact, with grace and aplomb, a great variety of roles. But when the paradigms for persons come from law rather than the theater, ownership becomes the mask of worldliness. The measure and scope of a person, his powers, lie in his ability to transform the lives of those around him. Initially, the powers of persons lay in their rights to sacred and ritual agency; these were tantamount to their political rights as well. But when property determines the right and power of agency and choice, persons become transformed into selves.

The two strands that were fused in the concept of person diverge again: when we focus on persons as sources of decisions, the ultimate locus of responsibility, the unity of thought and action, we come to think of them as souls and minds. When we think of them as possessors of rights and powers, we come to think of them as selves. It is not until each of these has been transformed into the concept of individuality that the two strands are woven together again.

SOUL AND MIND

Because persons are primarily agents of principle, their integrity requires freedom; because they are judged liable, their powers must be autonomous. But when this criterion for personhood is carried to its logical extreme, the scope of agency moves inward, away from social dramas, to the choices of the soul, or to the operations of the mind. What, after all, is it that is ultimately responsible, but only the will? It is the will that chooses motives, that accepts or rejects desires, principles. To the extent that such activities of the soul or the mind must remain autonomous, unconditioned, free, they are in principle indifferent not only to social class but to physical presence. To find the primary, uncaused cause of action—where that action is to be judged eternally liable —is to look for a simplicity and unity that is its own agency. The shadow of disembodiment that was implicit in the idea of a legal person moves forward, stands stage center: we have a person who is a pure *res cogitans* (or, in the religious versions, one that can survive death).

And it is here, of course, that the mind/body problems loom large, and that problems of individuation are seen as presenting moral and theological difficulties. For the theory of character, there is no expectation of individuation, no need for it. Nor did legal and dramatic persons need to be unique. But souls that are equal in the eyes of God, souls that can be disembodied, souls whose social history is detachable from their nature, have serious problems about choice. Without individual histories, they nevertheless condemn or save themselves. From character as structured dispositions, we come to soul as pure agency, unfathomable, inexpressible.

The Enlightenment version of this view gladly accepted the consequence of minimal individuation. It was an elegant way of assuring universality of rational discourse, even though the investigation began with a private act of introspective, reflective meditation. Mind became the clearest best self: the touchstone to the real, its reflections, the strongest certainties.

SELVES

A person's place in society determines the range of his property and his rights in disposing of it; his status is determined not by his capacity to appropriate roles but by the roles that are considered appropriate to him. When a society has changed so that individuals acquire their rights by virtue of their powers, rather than having their powers defined by their rights, the concept of person has been transformed to a concept of self. At first, the primary real possession is that of land, and a person of substance is one of the landed gentry. But when a man's industry determines whether he is landed, the story of men's lives are told by their achievements rather than by their descent. The story of fulfilled ambition is shaped by an individual's capacity to amass goods, by the extent of his properties. The quality of an individual self is determined by his qualities: they are his capital, to invest well or foolishly.

Once an individual's properties and qualities are his possessions, rather than his essence, the problem of alienation can arise. The crises of personal identity center on the discovery of principles that essentially guide choices; the crises of self-identity center on the alienation of properties. Judgments of persons are moral; judgments of souls are theological; judgments of selves are economic and political. Societies of persons are constructed to assure the rights of choice and action; they emerge from a contract of agents; societies of selves are also formed to protect and guarantee the rights of their members. But when the members of a society achieve their rights by virtue of their possessions, the protection of rights requires the protection of property, even though in principle everyone is equally entitled to the fruits of his labors and protection under law.

Jane Austen describes a world of persons on the verge of becoming a world of selves. Her favored characters have a finely attuned sense of propriety, of their proper place. There are of course coarse and vulgar gentry; but an elevated sense of propriety, a sense of the niceties of what is due to each person arises initially from property. To be sure some people of great refinement live in genteel poverty. This marks the transition. Such people are the real gentry: gentry has become gentility. Delicate sensibility is allied with good sense in the avoidance of pretense. In the novel of sensibility we have the seeds of the novel of insight and consciousness; its full growth requires the conception of individuality.

The world that Trollope describes is one that has become a world of selves, many of whom are nostalgic for the world of persons. The property required for stature is no longer land, but an

assured income. Rights and the ground of rights become transformed into obligations: an individual is entitled to what is owed
to him. Individuals who claim obligations by virtue of their sta-
tion, rather than by virtue of their qualities appear inflated and
hollow; the old order is presented as comic.

The concerns of selves are their interests; their obligations are
the duties with which they are taxed or charged. The grammar and
the semantics of selfhood reveal the possessive forms. Whatever
will come to be regarded as crucial property, or the means to it,
will be regarded as the focus of rights; the alienation of property
becomes an attack on the integrity if not actually the preservation
of the self.

Metaphysical and epistemological analyses of the self make the
conscious possession of experiences the final criterion of identity.
The continuity of the self is established by memory; disputes about
the validity of memory reports will hang on whether the claimant
had as *hers*, the original experience. Puzzles about identity will be
described as puzzles about whether it is possible to transfer, or to
alienate memory (that is, the retention of one's own experience)
without destroying the self. In pathological terms, it is alienists
who are charged with the therapy of those who suffer the loss of
their identities because they have misplaced or lost their ultimate
possession: their memories, whose just assessment is a guide to
appropriate responses to experiences.

Societies of selves are liable to rapid social and economic
change; they are expansive with the ideology if not the actuality of
mobility. Although selves become ranked in a hierarchical order
by their power and success, the older conception of the equality of
persons remains latently present in the notion that everyone is
equally entitled to make the most of himself. The conflict that is
latent in this view, between the equal rights of persons and the
unequal distribution of property (and therefore, in practice, of
rights as well) by achieving selves, becomes more manifest as an
expanding society tends to polarize goods, even while improving
the general condition.

Metaphysically and epistemologically, the concept of the self
also comes into stress. There is difficulty in describing the core
possessor, the owner of experiences who is not herself any set of
them. One can speak of characters as sets of traits without looking

for a center; but it is more difficult to think of bundles of properties without an owner, especially when the older idea of the person as an agent and decision-maker is still implicit. It is presumed that the self as an owner is also endowed with capacities to choose and to act. It is in the search for a concept that will fuse the notion of inalienable properties and principles of rational choice that the concept of self is transformed into the concept of an individual.

INDIVIDUALS

From the tensions in the definition of the alienable properties of selves, and from the corruptions in societies of selves—the divergence of practice from ideological commitments—comes the invention of individuality. It begins with conscience and ends with consciousness.

Unlike characters and figures, individuals actively resist typing: they represent the universal mind of rational beings, or the unique private voice. Individuals are indivisible *entities*: initially, they are defined against existing and presumably corrupt societies. Invented as a preserve of integrity, an autonomous *ens*, an individual transcends and resists what is binding and oppressive in society and does so from an original natural position. Although in its inception, individuality revives the idea of person, the rights of persons are formulated *in* society, while the rights of individuals are demanded *of* society. The contrast between the inner and outer person becomes the contrast between the individual and the social mask, between nature and culture.

A society of individuals is quite different from one composed of selves. Individuals contract to assure the basic rights to the development of moral and intellectual gifts, as well as legal protection of self and property. Because a society of individuals is composed of indivisible autonomous units, from whose natures—their minds and conscience—come the principles of justice, their rights are not property; they cannot be exchanged, bartered. Their rights and their qualities are their very essence, inalienable. Society's attempt to assure the development of persons comes to be seen as a possible source of corruption as well. Rousseau describes the dangerous duality of the powers of society: in the dialectic between

individuality and community, there is the difficult balance between fulfillment and invasion. Society is at once the benefit and
the misery of individuals who remain rudely unformed in nature,
but become denaturalized in highly developed society. Rousseau-
ean individuals implicitly give society far more power than the
minimal contractual base granted by a Hobbesian person, because
they add the right to the pursuit of happiness to the political rights
of the protection of life and property.

There were, of course, earlier reforming theories: the moral
authority that Luther located in an individual's relation to God
only later came to rest in natural law. But that reformer's stance,
the clear eye of the autonomy of conscience, universalises at the
same time that it forms an entity. Initially, there was no opposition between the individual and the universal: indeed the individual was the universal's ally against the social. It was through the
individual that the universal could be voiced. Individuality, in that
sense, has nothing to do with individuation and everything to do
with integrity. Here we have the accounts of individuality given to
us by Luther and Kant.

But once political and cultural reforms are effected, and the
opposition between natural right and social malformation is
blurred, once the society composed of autonomous individuals is
formed, the individual can no longer define himself *against* a
society that purports to be ruled by his voice, each legislating for
all. What was only implicit in the idea of autonomy and self-
formulation becomes dominant, and the quest for uniqueness
begins its way toward frenzy. Initially, one's rightful and natural
place is the particular stance one has on the world, the way in
which social and historical forces exemplify themselves through
the pinpoint of consciousness which is one's perspective, one's
own vision. It is then that being an individual requires having a
room of one's own, not because it is one's possession, but because
only there, in solitude, away from the pressure of others, can one
develop the features and styles that differentiate one's own being
from others. Integrity comes to be associated with difference; this
idea, always implicit in individuality, of preserving one's right
against the encroachment of others within one's own society,
emerges as dominant. From having been the source of moral
insight, the individual shifts to being the self-reliant pioneer, an

isolated being hewing out his place in the world, forming the perspective that is an individual's vision of the world. Conscientious consciousness is then the transparent eye that illuminates the substance of social life.

Insight, which was always the primary agency of individuality, becomes clarity of sight: we have Henry James and Virginia Woolf. At first the passion for clarity dominates, and the eye's self-forming action is so wholly absorbed in what it sees that it is all but unaware of seeing. But the pressure of differentiation in consciousness leads to that reflection on inwardness that leads the individual to a unique mode of sensibility. What is seen drops out and the passion for being the seer, eventually the passion for being *this* seer takes over. But when we have a sensibility in quest of a rightful definition, a character whose scope of action is simply to establish the uniqueness of its own perception, when the point of consciousness becomes a light rather than a power, then action is no longer agency, and the order of perceptions becomes arbitrary. From James, we move to Sartre, and from Woolf to Beckett. There is nothing to be alienated; everything could have been otherwise—and remained the same. Such wholly unique individuals become obsessed with the horrors of choice: they come to see themselves as the inventors of their own principles, inventors without purpose, direction, or form. Because they are defined by their freedom, they no longer choose from their natures but choose their identities. But since such choice is itself ungrounded, they are simply the act of choosing; their attempt to submerge themselves in their choices is a necessary act of bad faith.

The rugged indomitable survivors of hardships, the upright representative of social equality against the viciousness of social selves, the members of the Kingdom of Ends, Daniel Boone and Thoreau, figures of moral endurance, have become Molloy and Malone, monologues describing the wintry ending, the fading of the northern light.

The comic and grotesque forms establish the right to uniqueness down to the swirl of the last flourish of a thumbprint. This is the antithesis of figure: the zaniness of an individual soldier in the midst of an insane war: Yossarian in the army or Lucky Jim in academia. The body returns, insistent in its demands, language goes mad.

The comic forms, stretching as always they do towards sanity, cannot reach far enough. In the swirl of achieving individuality, the styles of speech flow loose, fall apart. Experiments with modes of type on a printed page are the representations of differentiated character. At its best, the insanity leads to Universal History again, and the voices of *Finnegans Wake*, each with its own pattern of breathing, blend into history. But it is a history whose forms are so large in scope, aeons and mountain ranges just nearby specks, that the mind swirls, and dies of richness just as surely as it did of wintry cold.

PRESENCES

And all along this while there has been The Russian Novel. Novels of a person tell a tale of development, of discovered responsibility, fulfilled or failed. A person's life has a form: it is continuous and unified. Myshkin or Alyosha are not persons: they are presences, the return of the unchartable soul. A Myshkin does not possess his experiences; but he does not choose his principles either. The details of their lives, the content of their experiences could have been quite different, and yet Myshkin or Alyosha would have been the same. They are a mode of attending, being present to their experiences, without dominating or controlling them. This is the antithesis of Sartrean consciousness-as-non-being-trying-to-objectify-itself. It is precisely the absence of willfulness, or choice of roles, of grace or enactment, swirl of action that make an Alyosha present, with immense gravity and density, to his experiences. We can try to give character sketches of them, but we must fail; we can try to project their lives into the future, but they are presence to whom anything can happen. Transparent to their experiences, never holding themselves back, their lives are nevertheless not revealed on any surface. Their powers are always magnetic, always at service, but never centered. Though they are questers, there is nothing incomplete about them. Though others respond strongly to the quality of their presence, to something of the mood they induce, they are not agents. One rarely knows their occupations; whatever it is, it doesn't form them. Their psychological and physical characteristics are incidental to them. Though generally tortured, they are innocent and invulnerable though they may commit crimes of unspeakable horror. The figure of such presences is the Christian, the holy innocent.

Understanding other conceptions of persons puts one on the way of being them; but understanding presences—if indeed there is understanding of them to be had—does not put one any closer to being one. It cannot be achieved by imitation, willing, practice, or a good education. It is a mode of identity invented precisely to go beyond achievement and willfulness. Dostoyevsky paradigmatically, but occasionally Hardy and (usually unsuccessfully) Lawrence present presences as endowments of grace received beyond striving.

AND WHAT IS LEFT?

What, one might well ask, is the point of this fast trip through history with a slanted *camera obscura*, catching persons in transforming attitudes? The distinctions that I have drawn are forced; most philosophers and novelists blend the notions that I have distinguished. One would hardly find a pure case: Locke tries to fuse the concept of self with that of individual; Kant borrows from everywhere. And of course as the inheritance becomes more complex, it becomes more difficult to separate the various layers, even in a purely analytic way. All of the concepts of identity that I have so briefly sketched remain as undercurrents in our lives, provide the norms by which we judge ourselves and others. Implicitly, they form our conceptions of the principles that ought to guide our choices. Our philosophical intuitions—the intuitions that guide our analyses of criteria for personal identity—have been formed by all these notions: they are the archeological layers on which our practices rest. As is obvious, they are latently in conflict; if we try to be all of them, conceiving of each as having the final obligation over us, we shall indeed be torn.

And society imposes conflicting roles on us as well. We are provided with paradigmatic figures, and at the same time exhorted to be individuals, as if these were in fact easily reconcilable; we intend to become unified persons and also achieved selves, as if these were easily harmonized. And our literature is a hodgepodge of nostalgia as well: much science fiction is an attempt to revive the early idea of individuality, to see figures of stature, half-earthlings of the future, present a vivid ingenuity that will magically return to us our heroic Promethean selves. We have the nostalgia for Soul; and the depiction of figural identities and ironies of figural identities.

We have our sentimental returns to each of these views as well as our strategies of irony against each. Our literary moves play them off against one another in elaborate shifting patterns. Internally, we play ourselves off against one another in these patterns, sensing ourselves torn because we believe persons ought to be unified.

The concept of *person* now emerges as dominant in philosophic analysis and in social life—with the concept of individuality receding—precisely because these aspects of our history are in conflict, and because when we are torn, we cast about for that concept of identity that shores and anchors principles of choice. And it has always been the concept of a person that has unified action, that was concerned with choice.

Philosophers would very properly ask whether there is not, in all these various strands of agency and identity that I have so crudely sketched, one underlying notion, one that makes the transformation be the transformation of *one* concept? After all, it might be said that this is a history *of* the concept of person, with implicit guidelines for inclusion and exclusion. We have left out toads and toadstools, have followed the main pull of *a* history.

In a full treatment of this history, we would have discussed the links that connect one moment in the history to another, and have shown how the remnants of the earlier views remain latently present in later versions, sometimes in disguise and sometimes as providing tensed balances to a dominant theme. The important and interesting point is that the details of the transition and of the functions of the archeological traces are always different. Sometimes it is the development of an implicit contradiction that forward the story—from self to individual; sometimes it is the force of political circumstance—the invasion of a foreign power; sometimes it is the wild invention of a novel, growing its hairshirt in private, caught and carried. There are indeed connecting links. But they are not an underlying substance. The connective and recessive tissue always have their own characters. It is always possible to distinguish the nostalgia for a form from its first appearance, the sentimental from the naive; but the distinction is not always drawn in the same place.

Perhaps one might look for a mock-Hegelian form that characterized all these shifts, the pattern of a dialectic. But Hegel knew that such a form is a mere abstraction; properly speaking the concept is not the form of the dialectic but its whole history, no more, no less. So indeed, there is sense to the objection: there is a concept of a person—there is our present concept of persons, and this (better and more fully told) is its history. So understanding "the" concept of a person is understanding history, just as understanding any particular individual is understanding *his* history.

If the objection demands that we provide an account of the internal unity of this history, of the preoccupations that any theory of persons must satisfy, an account of why the concept changed in the way it did, then it is indeed to the *regional* concept of a person that we turn. The concept of a person was, after all, invented to do just that: when we look for a *unity* of roles, or a single source of change, it is the concept of a person we want. But it would be a mistake to suppose that having analyzed the concept of *person*, we have uncovered the concept from which the others—character, self, individual—could in any sense be derived or unfolded. We have found the concept in that area which required a construction, a location for the unity of principles of choice and the principles of action. Naturally enough, if we try to fuse this concept with those that were constructed to provide continuity of genetic lineage, or to give an account of the patterning of character traits, we shall find just the sorts of puzzles that crop up whenever we have cross-classifications. This should cause no surprise; what *is* puzzling is that it should be supposed that conceptual analysis could, by itself, restructure and reform these notions so that we could simply discover the "logical" relations among these concepts.

We should use the concept of a person just where it belongs, the area for locating the unity of choice, realizing that we have other preoccupations besides the unification of consciousness in memory or in the principles of choice. For instance, we might do well to focus on the analysis of the development of character traits, to inquire into the ways various traits support different conceptions of responsibility. In doing that, we move away from the agonies of self-definition, of strong personal identification, and turn to thinking about the sorts of traits of imagination and sociability that might be socially and politically beneficial. For this we would do well to concentrate less on persons and more on characters.

The theory of character has other important uses for us. Of all the concepts of persons, it is the one in which psychological and physiological traits are most closely linked. It is around the primacy of psychological and physiological continuity as criteria for personal identity that many controversies center. But more significantly, the outrageously skimpy and forced history of the concept of person that I have sketched is willful and incomplete because in the rush of telling the story, I have disconnected the concept of person from the concept of a human being, a certain sort of organism, not all of whose motives and needs are defined by its conception of itself. Though the concept of a person is, in the larger sense, given by its history, it nevertheless is also closely interwoven with a nonhistorical concept, one that gives it its natural and biological base. The theory of character is a natural context for the investigation of the connection between the biological base of the concept of persons and its historical transformations.

The issue of whether the class of persons exactly coincides with the class of biologically defined human beings—whether corporations, Venusians, mongolian idiots, and fetuses are persons—is in part a conceptual question. It is a question about whether the relevant base for the classification of persons requires attention to whether things *look* like "us," whether they are made out of *stuff* like "ours," or whether it is enough that they *function* as we take "ourselves" to function. If Venusians and robots come to be thought of as persons, at least part of the argument that will establish them will be that they function as we do: that while they are not the *same* organisms that we are, they are in the appropriate sense the same *type* of organism or entity. Does an entity have to be an organism to be a person? When is a well-organized, self-sustaining entity an organism?

Of course there may be a time when Venusians and robots are called persons by science fiction writers and philosophers and by no one else. The question of the personhood of Venusians and robots becomes serious when we actually start raising questions about their legal rights and obligations. It is a very complex matter: if Venusians and robots come increasingly to be treated as persons are now treated, their inclusion in the class will come to modify our conceptions and treatment of human organisms. Treating ourselves as of the same *type* as Venusians will gradually and subtly come to affect leading questions and presuppositions about the nature of an organism. But there is no point speculating about what we *shall* say in transitional periods, and certainly none in legislating in advance what we shall decide. Whether we shall, when the time comes, classify Venusians as persons will certainly depend on what they are like, on whether we like them, and on our political and social preoccupations when the issue becomes a live one.

Humans are just the sorts of organisms that interpret and modify their agency through their conceptions of themselves. This is a complicated biological fact about us. Whether there are other sorts of entities that do this is in part but not wholly an empirical question. The fullest analysis of the concept of person would investigate the biologically adaptive functions of the various cultural grafts: the obsessions with unification and choice, salvation and simplicity, isolated integrity and achievement. From this larger perspective, we might be able to see how the cultural history of the various versions of the concept of a person has been modified by and has in turn modified its biological base.

BIBLIOGRAPHY

This bibliography was compiled in 1971 by George Graham, John Perry, Sydney Shoemaker, and Amélie Rorty. Though some classical work has been included, there has been no attempt to cover the full history of the subject. Nor have we tried to include comprehensive bibliographies of related subjects: analyses of the psychodynamics of the ego; discussions of artificial intelligence and simulation of thinking, remembering and decision-making; debates about mind-body identity. For a bibliography on ego psychology, see David Schechter, "Identification and Individuation," *Journal of American Psychoanalytic Association*, 16 (1968); for a bibliography on minds and machines, see Alan Anderson, ed. *Minds and Machines*. Englewood Cliffs, N.J.: Prentice-Hall, 1964; for a bibliography on the mind-body problem, see David Rosenthal, ed. *Materialism and the Mind-Body Problem*. Englewood Cliffs, N.J.: Prentice-Hall, 1971.

Articles marked by an asterisk have been reprinted in full or in part in John Perry, ed., *Personal Identity*. Berkeley, Los Angeles, London: University of California Press, 1975.

Alexander, S. "The Self as Subject and Person." *Proceedings of the Aristotelian Society*, 11 (1910-1911).

Allison, Henry E. "Locke's Theory of Personal Identity: A Re-examination." *Journal of the History of Ideas*, 27 (1966), 41-58.

Allport, G. *The Person in Psychology*. Boston: Beacon Press, 1968.

Anscombe, G. E. M. "The Principle of Individuation." *Proceedings of the Aristotelian Society*, supp. vol. 27 (1953), 83-96.

———, and Geach, Peter. *Three Philosophers*. Ithaca: Cornell University Press, 1961. See Anscombe's article on Aristotle, pp. 7 ff.

Armstrong, D. M. "Absolute and Relative Motion," *Mind* (1963).

Ayer, A. J. *The Foundations of Empirical Knowledge*. New York: Macmillan, 1940.

———. "Individuals," *Mind* (1952).

———. *Language Truth and Logic*. New York: Dover, 1946. Chap. 7, "The Self and the Common World."

———. *Philosophical Essays*. New York: Dover, 1963, Chap. 2, "The Identity of Indiscernibles." Originally in *Proceedings of the XIth International Congress of Philosophy*, vol. 1 (1953).

———. *The Problem of Knowledge*. Harmondsworth: Penguin Books, 1956. Chap. 5, "Myself and Others."

———. "The Concept of a Person." *The Concept of a Person*. London: Macmillan, 1963. Pp. 82-128.

Behmann, Heinrick. "Three Paradoxical Aspects of Identity," *Ratio* (1963).

Beloff, John. *The Existence of Mind*. New York: Citadel Press, 1962. Chap. 2.

Bennett, Jonathan. "The Simplicity of the Soul," *Journal of Philosophy*, LXIV, 20 (October 26, 1967), 648-660.

Black, Max. "The Identity of Indiscernibles," *Mind* (1952). Reprinted in *Problems of Analysis*. London: Routledge & Kegan Paul, 1954.

Blake, R.M. "The Identity of Indiscernibles and the Principle of Individuation," *Philosophical Review* (1927), pp. 45-57.

Bogen, J. "Identity and Origin," *Analysis* (1965-1966).

Bosanquet, Bernard. "The Philosophical Importance of a True Theory of Identity." *Essays and Addresses*. London, 1891.

Bradley, F.H. *The Principles of Logic*. 2d ed. Vol. 1. Oxford: Oxford University Press, 1922. V, VI, sects. 4 and 5.

———. *Appearance and Reality*. Oxford: Oxford University Press, 1930. VIII, IX, X, XXII, XXIII, XXIV, Appendix C.

Bradley, M.C. "Critical Notice" of Wiggins' *Identity and Spatio-Temporal Continuity*. *Australian Journal of Philosophy* (May 1969).

Brentano, Franz. *Psychology vom empirischen Standpunkt*. Edited by Oskar Kraus. 3d ed. Leipzig, 1925.

Broad, C.D. *The Mind and Its Place in Nature*. London, 1925. Chap. XIII, "The Unity of the Mind."

———. "McTaggart's Principle of the Dissimilarity of the Diverse." *Proceedings of the Aristotelian Society* (1931-1932).

———. *Examination of McTaggart's Philosophy*. Vol. II, pt. I. Cambridge: Cambridge University Press, 1938.

Brody, Baruch. "Is There a Philosophical Problem About the Identity of Substances?" *Philosophia*, 1, 1-2 (January 1971), 43-59.

———. "Locke On the Identity of Persons," *American Philosophical Quarterly*. 9. 4 (October 1972), 327-334.

Butchvarov, P. "The Self and Perceptions: A Study in Human Philosophy," *Philosophical Quarterly* (1959).

Butler, Joseph (Bishop). "Of Personal Identity." *The Works of Bishop Butler*. Edited by J.H. Bernard. Vol. II. London, 1900. Also in *Body, Mind and Death*. Edited by A. Flew. New York: Macmillan, 1964.*

Campbell, C.A. "On Selfhood and Godhood," Lecture VI. London, 1957.

Cartwright, Helen. "Heraclitus and the Bathwater," *Philosophical Review* (1965).

Chandler, Hugh. "Wiggins on Identity," *Analysis* (April 1969).

———. "Shoemaker's Arguments Against Locke," *Philosophical Quarterly*, vol. 19, no. 76 (July 1969).

Chappell, Vere. "Sameness and Change," *Philosophical Review* (1960).

Chisholm, Roderick. "Identity Through Possible Worlds, Some Questions," *Nous* (March 1967).

———. "The Loose and Popular and the Strict and Philosophical Senses of Identity" and "Reply," *Perception and Personal Identity*. Edited by Norman S. Care and Robert H. Grimm. Cleveland: Case Western Reserve Press, 1969. Pp. 82-139.

———. "Identity Through Time." *Language, Belief, and Metaphysics*. Edited by Howard E. Kiefer and Milton K. Munitz. Albany: State University of New York Press, 1970. Pp. 163-182.

———. "Problems of Identity (especially 'Identity and Persistence')." *Identity and Individuation*. Edited by Milton K. Munitz. New York: New York University Press, 1971. Pp. 3-30.

Coburn, Robert C. "Bodily Continuity and Personal Identity." *Analysis*, vol. 20, no. 5 (April 1960).

Cook, John W. "Wittgenstein on Privacy," *Philosophical Review*, LXXIV (July 1965), 281-314.

Cowley, Fraser. "The Identity of a Person and His Body," *Journal of Philosophy*, Vol. LXVIII, no. 20 (October 21, 1971).

Daniels, Charles B. "Personal Identity," *American Philosophical Quarterly*, vol. 6, no. 3 (July 1969).

Donellan, K. "Proper Names and Identifying Descriptions." *Semantics of Natural Language*. Edited by G. Harman and D. Davidson. Dordrecht: Reidel, 1972. Pp. 356-379.

Edwards, Jonathan. "The Great Christian Doctrine of Original Sin Defended." Part IV, chap. 3, in *The Works of President Edwards*. 8 vols. Worcester, Mass., 1808.

Emmet, D. *Rules, Roles and Relations*. New York: Macmillan, 1966.

Erikson, Erik H. *Identity: Youth and Crisis*. New York: W.W. Norton, 1968.

Ettinger, R.C.W. *The Prospect of Immortality*. New York: Macfadden, 1966. Chap. VIII.

Feigl, Herbert. "The 'Mental' and the 'Physical'." *Minnesota Studies in the Philosophy of Science*. Edited by H. Feigl, M. Scriven, and G. Maxwell. Minneapolis: University of Minnesota Press, 1958.

Feldman, Fred. "Geach and Relative Identity," *Review of Metaphysics*, Vol. XXII, no. 3 (March 1969).

———. "A Rejoinder," *Review of Metaphysics*, Vol. XXII, no. 3 (March 1969).

Flew, Antony. "Locke and the Problem of Personal Identity," *Philosophy* (1951).

———. " 'The Soul' of Mr. A.M. Quinton," *Journal of Philosophy* (1963).

———. ed. *Body, Mind and Death*. New York: Macmillan, 1964.

Fortes, Myer. "Totem and Taboo," *Proceedings of the Royal Anthropological Institute* (1966).

Frankfurt, Harry. "Freedom of the Will and the Concept of a Person," *Journal of Philosophy*, 68 (January 14, 1971), 5-20.

Frege, G. "Uber Sinn und Bedeutung." Translated by Max Black as "On Sense and Reference." In P. Geach and Max Black, *Translations from the Philosophical Writings of Gottlob Frege*. 2d ed. Oxford: Basil Blackwell, 1960.

———. *Grundlagen der Arithmetic*. Translated by J.L. Austin as *The Foundations of Arithmetic*. 2d ed. New York: Harper Torchbooks, 1960.

———. *Grundgesetze der Arithmetic*. Translated in part by Montgomery Furth as *The Basic Laws of Arithmetic*. Berkeley and Los Angeles: University of California Press, 1964.

Freud, Anna. *Ego and the Mechanisms of Defense*. New York, 1946.

Frondizi, R. *The Nature of the Self*. New Haven: Yale University Press, 1953.

Gale, Richard M. "A Note on Personal Identity and Bodily Continuity," *Analysis*, XXIX, 6, 132 (June 1969), 193-195.

Gallie, Ian. "Is The Self a Substance?" *Mind* (1936).

Geach, P.T. *Mental Acts*. New York: Humanities Press, 1957.

———. "On Beliefs about Oneself," *Analysis* (1957-1958).

———. *Reference and Generality*. Ithaca: Cornell University Press, 1962. esp. sec. 31.

———. "Identity," *Review of Metaphysics*, XXI, 1 (September 1967), 3-12.

———. "A Reply," *Review of Metaphysics* (March 1969).

———. *God and Soul*. London: Routledge & Kegan Paul, 1969. Chaps. 1, 2, and 3.

———. *Logic Matters*. Ithaca: Cornell University Press, 1972.

Geach, P.T., and Anscombe, G.E.M. *Three Philosophers*. Ithaca: Cornell University Press, 1961.

Geertz, Clifford. *Person, Time and Conduct in Bali*. Southeast Asia Studies no. 14. New Haven: Yale University Press, 1966.

Gert, Bernard. "Personal Identity and the Body," *Dialogue* (1971).

Goffman, E. *The Presentation of Self in Everyday Life*. Garden City, N.Y.: Doubleday, 1959.

Gordon, C., and Gergen, K., eds. *The Self in Social Interaction*. Vols. 1 and 2. New York: John Wiley, 1968.

Greenwood, Terence. "Personal Identity and Memory," *Philosophical Quarterly* (October 1967).

Grice, H.P. "Personal Identity," *Mind*, 50, 200 (October 1941), 330-350.*

Hampshire, Stuart. *Thought and Action*. Chatto & Windus, 1959. Chap. I.

Hartmann, H. *Ego Psychology and the Problem of Adaptation*. New York: International Universities Press, 1958.

Hegel, G.W.F. *Encyclopedia of Philosophy*. Translated by G.E. Mueller. New York, 1959. Sects. 53-75.

Heraclitus. Fragments in Kirk, C.S., and Raven, J.E. *The Presocratic Philosophers*. Cambridge: Cambridge University Press, 1957.

Hildegard, E. "Human Motives and the Concept of Self." *Personality*. Edited by R.S. Lazarus and E. Opton, Jr. Harmondsworth and Baltimore: Penguin Books, 1967. Pp. 255-258.

Hintikka, Jaakko. "Individuals, Possible Worlds, and Epistemic Logic," *Nous* (March 1967).

Hobbes, T. *De Corpore*. II. 11. (Page 136 of the Molesworth edition.)

Hospers, John. *Introduction to Philosophical Analysis*. Englewood Cliffs, N.J.: Prentice-Hall, 1967. "Personal Identity," pp. 410-415.

Hume, D. *A Treatise of Human Nature*. Book I, Part IV, sects. 1, 5, 6, esp. sect. 6, "Of Personal Identity."*

Ishiguro, Hide. "A Person's Future and the Mind-Body Problem." *Linguistic Analysis and Phenomenology*. Edited by W. Mays and S. Brown. London: Macmillan, 1972.

James, William. *The Principles of Psychology*. New York: Dover Press, 1950. Especially Ch. X, "The Consciousness of Self."

Johnson, W.E. *Logic*. Part I, Ch. XII, "The Relation of Identity," and Part III, Ch. VII, "The Continuant." Cambridge: 1921 and 1924.

Jones, J.R. "The Self in Sensory Cognition." *Mind*. (1949).

Jones, J.R., and Miles, T.R. "Self-Knowledge," Symposium in *Proceedings of the Aristotelian Society*, supp. vol. (1956).

Jones, O.R. "Identity and Countability," *Analysis* (1963-1964).

Kant, Immanuel. *Critique of Pure Reason*. Especially the Transcendental Deduction (chap. 2 of Book I of the Transcendental Analytic), the First and Second Analogies (in sect. 3 of chap. 2 of Book II of the Transcendental Analytic), and the Paralogisms of Pure Reason (chap. 1 of Book II of the Transcendental Dialectic).

Kenny, Anthony. "Criterion." *Encyclopedia of Philosophy*. Edited by Paul Edwards. New York: Macmillan, 1967. 2: 258-261.

Kripke, Saul. "Identity and Necessity." in *Identity and Individuation*. Edited by M. Munitz. New York: New York University Press, 1971.

———. "Naming and Necessity." *Semantics of Natural Languages*. Edited by G. Harman and D. Davidson. Dordrecht: Reidel, 1972.

Laing, R.D. *Self and Others*. New York: Pantheon Books, 1969.

Lazarus, R.S., and Opton, E.M., ed. *Personality*. Harmondsworth and Baltimore: Penguin Books, 1967.

Leibniz, G.W. *New Essays Concerning Human Understanding*. Translated by Langley. La Salle, Ill.: Open Court, 1949. Especially Book II, chap. XXVII.

———. *Discourse on Metaphysics*. Especially XXXIV.

———. *Mondalogy*. 9, 10, 14, 22, 47, 62, 71.

———. *The Leibniz-Clarke Correspondence*. Edited by H.G. Alexander. Manchester: Manchester University Press, 1956.

Levy-Bruhl, L. *The "Soul" of the Primitive*. London: Allen & Unwin, 1965. Pp. 86-95.

Lewis, David K. "Counterpart Theory and Quantified Modal Logic," *Journal of Philosophy* (March 7, 1968).

———. "Counterparts of Persons and their Bodies," *Journal of Philosophy*, 68 (1971), 203-211.

Lewis, H.D. *The Elusive Mind*. London: Allen & Unwin, 1969.

Lewy, C. "Equivalence and Identity," *Mind*, vol. 55 (1946).

Linsky, L. "Hesperus and Phosphorus," *Philosophical Review*, vol. 68 (1959).

———. "Substitutivity and Descriptions," *Journal of Philosophy*, Vol. LXIII (November 10, 1966).

Locke, J. *An Essay Concerning Human Understanding*. Book II, chap. XXVII, "Of Ideas of Identity and Diversity."*

Mace, C.A. "Self-Identity," *Proceedings of the Aristotelian Society*, supp. vol. (1939).

Mackintosh, J. "Personal Identity and Memory." *The Business of Reason*. London: Routledge & Kegan Paul.

McTaggart, J.M. *The Nature of Existence*. Vol. II. Cambridge: Cambridge University Press, 1927.

Martin, C.B. "Identity and Exact Similarity," *Analysis* (1957-1958).

———. *Religious Belief*. Ithaca: Cornell University Press, 1959. Chap. 6.

Mead, G.H. *Mind, Self and Society*. Chicago: University of Chicago Press, 1934. Especially pp. 144-145, 149-152.

Menne, Albert. "Identity, Equality, Similarity," *Ratio*, 4 (1962), 50.

Meyers, G.E., *Self*. New York, 1969.

Middleton, John, ed. *Magic, Witchcraft and Curing*. New York: Doubleday, 1967.

Mill, James. *A System of Logic*. London, 1843, Chap. 1, p. 201.

———. *An Examination of Sir William Hamilton's Philosophy*. London, 1872. Chap. XII.

———. *Analysis of the Phenomena of the Human Mind*. Vol. II. London, 1878.

Minkus, P.A. *Philosophy of the Person*. Oxford: Basil Blackwell, 1960.

Miri, Mrinal. "Memory and Personal Identity," *Mind*, LXXXII, 325 (January 1973), 1-21.

Muehlmann, Robert. "Russell and Wittgenstein on Identity," *Philosophical*

Quarterly (July 1969).

Munitz, M.K., ed. *Identity and Individuation*. New York: New York University Press, 1971.

Nagel, Thomas. "Brain Bisection and Unity of Consciousness," *Synthese* (May 1971).*

Nelson, Jack. "Logically Necessary and Sufficient Conditions for Identity Through Time," *American Philosophical Quarterly* (April 1972).

Nerlich, G.C. "Sameness, Difference and Continuity," *Analysis* (1957-1958).

———. "On Evidence for Identity," *Australasian Journal of Philosophy* (1957-1958).

———. " 'Continuity' Continued," *Analysis* (1960-1961).

Odegard, Douglas. "Personal and Bodily Identity," *Philosophical Quarterly* (January 1969).

———. "Identity Through Time," *American Philosophical Quarterly* (January 1972).

Palma, A.B. "Memory and Personal Identity," *Australasian Journal of Philosophy*, 42.1 (May 1964), 53-68.

Parfit, Derek. "Personal Identity," *Philosophical Review*, LXXX, I (January 1971), 3-27.*

———. "On 'The Importance of Self-Identity.' " *Journal of Philosophy*, LXVIII, 20 (October 21, 1971), 683-690.

Paton, H.J. "Self Identity." *In Defense of Reason*. London: Hutchinsons, 1951. Pp. 99-116.

Pears, D.F. "Critical Study of *Strawson* (Part I)," *Philosophical Quarterly* (1961).

———. "Hume on Personal Identity." *David Hume: A Symposium*. Edited by D.F. Pears. London: Macmillan, 1963.

Penelhum, Terence. "Hume on Personal Identity," *Philosophical Review* (1955).

———. "On Analysis Problem #11," *Analysis* (1957).

———. "Personal Identity, Memory, and Survival," *Journal of Philosophy* (1959).

———. "Personal Identity." *Encyclopedia of Philosophy*. Edited by Paul Edwards. New York: Macmillan, 1967. 6:95-106.

———. *Survival and Disembodied Existence*. London: Routledge and Kegan Paul; New York: Humanities Press, 1970.

———. "The Importance of Self-Identity," *Journal of Philosophy*, LXVIII, 20 (October 21, 1971), 667-677.

Perry, John. "Identity." Ph.D. dissertation, Cornell University, 1968.

———. "The Same F," *Philosophical Review* (1970).

———. "Can the Self Divide?" *Journal of Philosophy*, LXIX, 16 (September 7, 1972), 463-488.

———. "Personal Identity, Memory, and the Problem of Circularity."*

———. "Review of Bernard Williams *Problems of the Self*," *Journal of Philosophy*, forthcoming.

———, ed. *Personal Identity* (Berkeley, Los Angeles, London: University of California Press, 1975).

Pike, Nelson. "Hume's Bundle of Theory of the Self," *American Philosophical Quarterly* (1957).

Plantinga, Alvin. "Things and Persons," *Review of Metaphysics* (1960-1961).

Popper, Karl R. "The Principle of Individuation," *Proceedings of the Aristotelian Society*, supp. vol. 27 (1953), pp. 97-120.

Prior, A.N. "Report on Analysis Problem #11," *Analysis* (1957).
———. "Opposite Number," *Review of Metaphysics* (1957-1958).
———. "Time, Existence, and Identity," *Proceedings of the Aristotelian Society* (1966).
Puccetti, Roland. "Brain Transplantation and Personal Identity," *Analysis*, XXIX.3 (January 1969), New Series, 65-77.
———. *Persons.* New York, 1969.
———. "Remembering the Past of Another," *Canadian Journal of Philosophy*, II, 4 (June 1973), 523-532.
———. "Multiple Identity," *The Personalist*, LIV, 3 (Summer 1973), 203-215.
Purtill, R.L. "About Identity Through Possible Worlds," *Nous* (February 1968).
Quine, W.V.O. "Reply to Professor Marcus," *Synthese*, Vol. XIII (1961).
———. "Identity, Ostension, and Hypostasis." *From a Logical Point of View.* New York: Harper & Row, 1963. Pp. 65-79.
———. "Review of Geach's *Reference and Generality*," *Philosophical Review* (January 1964).
———. *Word and Object.* Cambridge, Mass.: M.I.T. Press, 1969. p. 171 passim.
———. "Review of *Identity and Individuation*," ed. M.K. Munitz, *Journal of Philosophy*, LXIX. 16 (September 7, 1972), 488-497.
Quinton, Anthony. "The Soul," *Journal of Philosophy*, LIX, 15 (July 19, 1962), 393-409.*
———. "Two Conceptions of Personality," *Revue Internationale de Philosophie*, 22d year (1958), pp. 387-402.
———. *The Nature of Things.* London: Routledge & Kegan Paul, 1973. Part I.
Ralls, Anthony. "The Ascription of Personal Responsibility and Identity," *Australian Journal of Philosophy* (1963).
Read, Kenneth. "Morality and the Concept of the Person among the Gahuku-Gama." Reprinted in J. Middleton, *Myth and Cosmos.* New York: Doubleday, 1967.
Reichenbach, Hans. *The Direction of Time.* Edited by Maria Reichenbach. Berkeley and Los Angeles: University of California Press, 1956. Chap. II, esp. sect. 5.
Reid, Thomas. *Essays on the Intellectual Powers of Man.* Essay III, chaps. 4 and 6. Edinburgh, 1785. As edited by A.D. Woozley. London: Macmillan, 1941.*
Rescher, N. "Identity, Substitution and Modality," *Review of Metaphysics*, vol. 14 (1961).
Rorty, Amélie Oksenberg, "Persons, Policies, and Bodies," *International Philosophical Quarterly*, XIII, no. 1 (March 1973), 63-80.
———. "The Transformations of Persons," *Philosophy*, 48, 185 (July 1973), 261-275.
Ruddock, R. *Six Approaches to the Person.* London: Routledge & Kegan Paul, 1972.
Russell, Bertrand. "The Philosophy of Logical Atomism," *The Monist* (1918). Reprinted in *Logic and Knowledge.* Edited by R.C. Marsh. London: Allen & Unwin, 1956.
Sanford, David. "Locke, Leibniz and Wiggins on Being in the Same Place at the Same Time," *Philosophical Review* (January 1970).
Sartre, J.-P., *The Transcendence of the Ego.* New York: Noonday Press, 1957.
Schechter, D. "Identification and Individuation," *Journal of American Psychoanalytic Association*, 16 (1968), 48-80.
Schutz, A. *Collected Papers.* The Hague: Nijhoff, 1962. Pp. 16-18, 221-222.

Schwayder, D. "=." *Mind* (1956).

Sellars, Wilfred. "Metaphysics and the Concept of a Person." *The Logical Way of Doing Things*. Edited by K. Lambert. New Haven: Yale University Press, 1969.

Shoemaker, Sydney. "Personal Identity and Memory," *Journal of Philosophy*, 56 (1959), 868-882.*

——. *Self-Knowledge and Self-Identity*. Ithaca: Cornell University Press, 1963.

——. "On Knowing Who One Is," *Common Factor*, 4 (Autumn 1966), 49-56.

——. "Comments." *Perception and Personal Identity*. Edited by Norman S. Care and Robert H. Grimm. Cleveland: Case Western Reserve Press, 1969.

——. "Persons and Their Pasts," *American Philosophical Quarterly* (October 1970).

——. "Wiggins on Identity." *Identity and Individuation*. Edited by Milton K. Munitz. New York: New York University Press, 1971. Pp. 103-107. Reprinted from *Philosophical Review* (October 1970).

Shorter, J.M. "More About Bodily Continuity and Personal Identity," *Analysis* (1962).

——. "Personal Identity, Relationships, and Criteria," *Proceedings of the Aristotelian Society* (1970-1971), pp. 165-186.

Sperry, R.W. "The Great Cerebral Commissure," *Scientific American*, 210 (1964), 42-52.

——. "Hemisphere Deconnection and Unity in Conscious Awareness," *American Psychologist*, vol. 23, no. 10 (October 1968).

Spinoza, B. *Ethics*. Book 1, sects. 3, 5, 6, 8, 13.

Strawson, P.F. *Individuals*. Garden City, N.Y.: Anchor Books, 1963. Chap. 3, "Persons," pp. 81-113. Also Chaps. 1 and 2.

——. *The Bounds of Sense*. London: Methuen, 1966. "Soul," pp. 163-174.

——. "Self, Mind, and Body," *Common Factor*, 4 (Autumn 1966), 5-13.

——. "Chisholm on Identity Through Time." *Language, Belief, and Metaphysics*. Edited by H.E. Kiefer and M.K. Munitz. Albany: State University of New York Press, 1970. Pp. 183-186.

Stroll, Avrum. "Identity." *The Encyclopedia of Philosophy*. Edited by Paul Edwards. New York: Macmillan, 1967.

Swinburne, Richard. *Space and Time*. London: Macmillan, 1968. Chap. 1.

Taylor, Richard. "Spatial and Temporal Analogies and the Concept of Identity," *Journal of Philosophy* (1955). Reprinted in *Problems of Space and Time*. Edited by J.J.C. Smart. London: Macmillan, 1964.

——. "De Anima," *American Philosophical Quarterly*, vol. 10, no. 1 (January 1973).

Thomson, J. Jarvis. "Time, Space and Objects," *Mind* (1965).

Van der Vate, Dwight. "The Problem of Robot Consciousness," *Philosophy and Phenomenological Research* (December 1971).

Wallace, Kyle, "Shoemaker on Personal Identity," *Personalist*, 54 (Winter 1973), 71-74.

Webb, C.W. "Antinomy of Individuals," *Journal of Philosophy*, vol. 55 (1958).

Wheatly, Jon. "Like," *Proceedings of the Aristotelian Society* (1961-1962).

Wiener, Norbert. *The Human Use of Human Beings*. New York: Avon Books, 1971. Chap. V, pp. 129-141.

Wiggins, D. "Identity-Statements," *Analytical Philosophy*. Edited by R.J. Butler. 2d series. Oxford: Basil Blackwell, 1965.

――――. "The Identification of Things and Places," *Proceedings of the Aristotelian Society*, supp. vol. (1963).

――――. "On Being in the Same Place at the Same Time," *Philosophical Review* (January 1968).

――――. "Reply to Mr. Chandler," *Analysis* (April 1969).

――――. *Identity and Spatio-Temporal Continuity*. Oxford: Basil Blackwell, 1971.

Will, F.L. "Internal Relations and The Principle of Identity," *Philosophical Review*, 49 (1940), 497.

Williams, Bernard. "Personal Identity and Individuation," *Proceedings of the Aristotelian Society* (1956-1957).

――――. "Bodily Continuity and Personal Identity," *Analysis* (1960).

――――. "Mr. Strawson on Individuals," *Philosophy* (1961).

――――. "Imagination and the Self," *Proceedings of the British Academy* (1966). Reprinted in *Studies in Thought and Action*. Edited by P.F. Strawson, Oxford: Oxford University Press, 1968.

――――. "The Self and the Future," *Philosophical Review*, LXXIX, 2 (April 1970, 161-180.*

――――. "Are Persons Bodies?" *The Philosophy of the Body*. Edited by S. Spicker. Chicago: University of Chicago Press, 1970.

――――. *Problems of the Self*. Cambridge: Cambridge University Press, 1973.

Wilson, N.L. "Space, Time and Individuals, *Journal of Philosophy* (1955).

――――. "Identity, Substitution and Modality," *Review of Metaphysics*, vol. 14 (1961).

Wittgenstein, Ludwig. *The Blue and Brown Books*. Oxford: Basil Blackwell, 1958.

――――. *Philosophical Investigations*. Translated by G.E.M. Anscombe. New York: Macmillan, 1965. Section 404 passim.

Wollheim, R. "The Mind and the Mind's Image of Itself," *International Journal of Psycho-Analysis*, 50 (1969), 209-220.

Woods, M.J. "The Identification of Things and Places." *Proceedings of the Aristotelian Society*, supp. vol. (1963).

――――. "Identity and Individuation." *Analytical Philosophy*. Edited by R.J. Butler. 2d series. Oxford: Basil Blackwell, 1965.

Wright, J.N. "Self-Identity," *Proceedings of the Aristotelian Society*, supp. vol. (1939).